THE
CALIFORNIA
HERITAGE
COOKBOOK

THE CALIFORNIA HERITAGE COOKBOOK

THE JUNIOR LEAGUE OF PASADENA

DOUBLEDAY

NEW YORK LONDON TORONTO SYDNEY AUCKLAND

The purpose of the Junior League is exclusively educational and charitable and is to promote voluntarism; to develop the potential of its members for voluntary participation in community affairs; and to demonstrate the effectiveness of trained volunteers.

The profit realized by the Junior League of Pasadena, Inc., from the sale of *The California Heritage Cookbook* will be used for projects which we sponsor in the community, and it is to this community program that we dedicate our book.

PUBLISHED BY DOUBLEDAY
a division of Bantam Doubleday Dell Publishing Group, Inc.
666 Fifth Avenue, New York, New York 10103

DOUBLEDAY and the portrayal of an anchor with a dolphin are trademarks of Doubleday, a division of Bantam Doubleday Dell Publishing Group, Inc.

Library of Congress Cataloging in Publication Data
The California heritage cookbook.
    Includes index.
    1. Cookery, American—California.
TX715.C1515   641.5′9794   75-42495
ISBN: 0-385-41677-6

CONTENTS

THE
CALIFORNIA
HERITAGE
COOKBOOK

CHAPTER I

THE MONTEREY PENINSULA

HORS D'OEUVRES, APPETIZERS, & SOUPS

GREBES and cormorants and golden eyes patrol the coastal waters of Monterey County, undisturbed by the swooping and diving gulls who pursue a more erratic course. On the surface of the water, dozens of scoters bob about, looking as artificial as carelessly constructed decoys. On the shore, wrens and robins, blue jays and woodpeckers, search for food. At a sea lion crèche nearby, females keep vigil over their baby pups paddling and scuffling in the shallow water. In the forest's mottled shade, a spotted fawn rests hidden among the ferns. Gray squirrels scamper and chatter and scold, oblivious to the dangers from hawks, dogs, and passing automobiles. Sea otters and black-clad skin divers swim in the kelp beds while a golfer waits at the tee for several deer to wander off the fairway. And always the famous Monterey cypresses with their twisted shapes and gnarled trunks stand gracefully against the skyline.

People who live in Carmel, Pebble Beach, Big Sur, or anywhere else on the Monterey Peninsula enjoy the advantages of an ever cool climate, the daily view of verdant headlands, the foaming surf, the trees full of monarch butterflies, fields of California poppies, lupin, and lilac, and the secret forest's glades brimming with wild iris. They also live with certain inconveniences—the lack of electricity in winter storms, the loss of privacy due to the steady flow of tourists, the possibility of being stranded on washed-out roads during heavy rains, and the daily bother of picking up mail at the post office or trying to find a parking place. But those who live in this area like its somewhat isolated country flavor and want others to see and appreciate its charm. There is an aura of civility and welcome that no doubt had its precedence in the famed hospitality of the early Spanish settlers.

The town of Monterey has retained its Spanish flavor more perhaps than any other California town. Some of the old adobes are preserved simply as monuments to the past, but the great majority of them remain the homes they were originally built to be. Others, including one that in early days had a dance hall on the second floor, are now office buildings, and still others have become clubhouses. Few have been extensively remodeled. The buildings were strong when they were built, requiring only ordinary repairs and maintenance to keep them useful.

Because Monterey is a seaport and the home of a fishing fleet, there is a fisherman's wharf, and it, too, is very functional. It attracts tourists, of course, and perhaps would be less well groomed if it did not; but its open-air fish markets are patronized almost entirely by careful local housewives who enjoy freshly caught bass, bay shrimps, and abalone.

Along with many excellent restaurants and numerous gourmet shops, this area can also boast of Monterey Jack cheese. A mild, creamy cheese, with its own subtle flavor, it was originated on the old Molera Ranch in 1892. It was first made in a simple keg with a heavy board pressed down across the top by a jack. The name, Monterey Jack, has lasted through the years, and this delicious cheese has always enjoyed great popularity.

The Spanish explorer Juan Rodríguez Cabrillo, in 1542, was the first to make mention of this area. Sailing north along the California coast, his expedition arrived in the latitude where Monterey was supposed to be. Here, on November 11, just off the headland later called Point Pinos, a severe storm struck and Cabrillo's ships were driven six leagues out to sea. When the gale had subsided, they continued north as far as Fort Ross, but in doing so they never saw the great Bay of Monterey. The storm had driven them too far away.

In 1595 Sebastián Rodríguez Cermeño, Manila galleon commander, was commissioned to search the shores of California for a safe harbor where the valuable Manila galleon could take refuge following its exhausting six-month return trip from Manila to Spain. A port was needed for repairs that offered some degree of safety from marauding pirates and also one that had fresh water and food. Cermeño's ship finally reached Drake's Bay, where it was pounded to pieces in a storm. Constructing a small open boat from the wreckage, Cermeño and his men headed for Mexico. In his official report, Cermeño noted many points along the California coast, including the future site of Monterey. It was the more lyrical Sebastián Vizcaíno who chose the permanent name. Vizcaíno had accompanied Cermeño on the earlier expedition, but in 1602 he returned in command of his own ship and anchored in the bay. Enchanted by the beauties of the land, he expounded in his report on all that met his delighted gaze. Being a practical man, too, he noted the abundance of towering pines and evergreen oaks. So completely enraptured was Vizcaíno that he referred to the bay, which is actually a coastal indentation twenty miles wide, as a "harbor." This term proved very confusing to later explorers.

Taking possession of the land in the name of the King of Spain, Vizcaíno called it Monterey in honor of the Conde de Monterrey, the viceroy of New Spain. The ceremony was held under a spreading oak tree near the shore. He also named a small nearby river, Río Carmelo, in honor of the Carmelite friars who were part of the ship's company. Thus was Monterey found, claimed, named—and abandoned.

There is no record of any white men visiting Monterey during the next 167 years. Then, in the summer of 1769, the first planned expedition for settlement of Alta California left Mexico for San Diego. In command of this group was Don Gaspar de Portolá, soldier-governor of Baja California. Also on the expedition was the dedicated Franciscan priest Junípero Serra.

Reaching San Diego, Portolá established the first presidio in California, which he named El Presidio Real de Monterey. At the same time Father Serra founded the first mission, San Diego de Alcala.

From San Diego Portolá took a small group north to search for Monterey. His orders were specific: He was to locate the "magnificent harbor" Vizcaíno had described and establish a second presidio. The expedition passed Monterey and traveled north till they reached the southern extreme of today's Golden Gate harbor at San Francisco. Realizing they had gone too far, they turned south and wearily retraced their steps back to San Diego.

After several months' rest, Portolá again started north, this time accompanied by Father Serra. Realizing that the wide bay they had passed on their first expedition must be the site of Monterey, they hastened their steps. On June 3, 1770, the little troupe arrived and founded the second royal presidio; Father Serra said mass under the same oak tree where Vizcaíno had claimed this land for Spain. The mission was named San Carlos Borromeo and thus became the second in a long chain of California missions. Soon thereafter, the mission was moved a short distance south of Monterey, where it became Serra's headquarters as Father President of the mission chain.

The Vizcaíno-Serra oak died in 1905, but a portion of this revered tree is preserved behind Monterey's oldest building, the Royal Presidio Chapel on Church Street. Over the hill to the south, in the San Carlos Mission church, is the tomb of Father Serra. He is buried under the church floor just in front of the chancel in the mission some say was always dearest to his heart.

The beginnings of Monterey were humble, as were all presidios, missions, and later pueblos—a rough stockade, a roof of tules or boughs, walls daubed with mud. In the case of Monterey, it achieved an early distinction. Only seven years after its founding, it was made the capital of Alta California.

Monterey also became a base for further exploration. Within a few years, groups of priests and soldiers starting from Monterey had founded missions at Santa Clara and San Antonio de Padua, and a mission and presidio at San Francisco.

During the first forty years of its existence, Monterey consisted solely of the Presidio with all the inhabitants living within its walls. Shedlike structures with dirt floors and roofs of tules backed up to the inside of the Presidio walls and formed homes for the settlers. Outside the walls were pastures, soldiers' barracks, corrals, and gardens. The whole Presidio enclosure, which also included a governor's house and tiny chapel, measured a mere 300 yards by 258 yards. Living conditions were primitive, but the Presidio gave a semblance of protection against wild animals and unfriendly Indians.

Olive trees and vineyards flourished here. In the warm inland valley now known as the Salinas Valley, most of the vegetables native to Spain could be grown. One of the vegetables that the Spanish brought to California was the artichoke. Popular in the countries bordering the Mediterranean Sea, the artichoke probably originated in Turkey. Perhaps as early as the fifteenth century, it was introduced into the agriculture of Spain, France, and Italy. Even though the town of Castroville, just north of Monterey, now produces enough artichokes each year to provide one for every man, woman, and child in the United States, many people have never tasted one. Those who enjoy them prepare them in many delicious ways— simply boiled and served with mayonnaise, or perhaps cold, stuffed with the tiny bay shrimp for which Monterey is famous.

The harbor became a fairly busy place in the early years because of the presence of the sea otter. The kelp beds off the shores of Monterey abounded with these valuable little animals. The skins of the sea otter were the incentive that brought Russian hunters from Alaska as far south as Santa Barbara. This frightened Spain into colonizing Alta California. One skin traded in Canton could bring $100. Spain promoted the sea otter trade to the point that between 1786 and 1790 almost ten thousand skins, with a value of about $3,000,000, were traded to China. In the early 1800s the Americans entered the sea otter trade, forming the Russian-American Fur Company of Alaska, and in the next twenty years these animals became almost extinct.

By the end of the eighteenth century, the day of the explorer and settler in Alta California was drawing to a close. El Camino Real (the Royal Highway) now stretched from San Diego to San Francisco. There were already eighteen missions founded along this road. Four presidios were built to secure the missions at San Diego, Monterey, Santa Barbara, and San Francisco. The missions were thriving and were, for the most part, successful.

In 1822 Mexico achieved its independence from Spain, and in 1825 the legislative assembly met at Monterey to swear allegiance to the new Republic of Mexico. José María Echeandía was the first Mexican governor. He was thirty-seven years of age, a native of Mexico City. A man with sound views and good intentions, Echeandía proved to be a poor administrator. He recalled the Territorial Deputation, a form of legislature set up during the Spanish rule, and then he ordered a new election. The Deputation consisted of five electors, one from each presidio and one from Los Angeles. New laws were established, such as granting citizenship to the Indians and allowing them to seek their own living away from the mission. This plan was not very successful, as the Indians had grown to depend on the missions for their existence.

During this time of new independence, Monterey thrived as a seaport. Lucrative duties were collected from all foreign ships. Smuggling was also a popular pastime. More foreign settlers came on ships from England and France. New

England whalers also favored Monterey's hospitality and stopped often to repair and resupply their ships.

In 1833 the Secularization Act was passed. With one stroke of the pen the California missions lost most of their valuable land holdings and became mere parish churches. These lands, now freed for private ownership, could be obtained as land grants from the governor, and a land-hungry people moved quickly to avail themselves of these ranchos. From 1833 to 1846, the governor awarded approximately 750 grants of land to a class rapidly emerging as the famed Spanish dons. So dawned the era of large feudal estates, of splendid leisure, of color, and of romance.

By 1840 it became apparent that Mexico, a financially impoverished country, could no longer support nor assist California in any way. The presidios were in ruins, while soldiers and officials were no longer being paid. The local governments of the tiny pueblos stumbled on as best they could. The government of California was slowly but surely creaking to a halt. Mexico City was far away and incapable of offering the strong arm that was needed. The United States had desires to purchase Alta California, as did England and France. Californians, feeling deserted by an economically impoverished Mexico, desired a strong government to take over.

On July 7, 1846, with rising hostilities between Mexico and the United States, and with the independent action of the Bear Flag Revolt in Sonoma, Commodore John Sloat was sent to Monterey. As commander of the United States forces in the Pacific, he sailed into Monterey Bay and landed 250 marines. They hesitantly took possession of the town and raised the American flag over the Monterey Custom House. A week later, Commodore Robert Stockton replaced Sloat, and events took another turn. Stockton was a young, vigorous leader, often called "Gassy Bob" behind his back. He admired the spirit of the Bear Flaggers and officially enlisted these volunteers into the navy. He took full responsibility for Sloat's action but was determined to push the conquest south to Los Angeles and claim all of Alta California for the United States. Thus California became part of the United States, and three years later, with the discovery of gold, the state capital was moved to Sacramento.

Although there are many interesting old buildings in Monterey, one in particular deserves mention. Amid adobes and other Monterey-style houses with flower-filled patios stands Colton Hall. This souvenir of New England might have been transported directly from New Bedford or Salem, Massachusetts, yet it blends harmoniously with its surroundings. The Reverend Walter Colton, chaplain of the United States frigate *Congress* and later alcalde (mayor) of Monterey, built Colton Hall in 1846. For years, it was the most useful building in town, serving as schoolhouse, courthouse, public assembly hall, constitutional hall, and place of worship.

Monterey County has been, over the years, the site of many creative endeavors. Frank Lloyd Wright designed interesting and unusual houses there. One of the most famous is shaped somewhat like an elegant cabin cruiser, its prow extending into the surf. The artist colony at Carmel is well known, and the annual Carmel Bach Festival has drawn visitors from many states and countries. Craftsmen and skilled artisans find the atmosphere conducive to their pursuits, and so do writers. Robert Louis Stevenson came to Monterey in 1879 to be with his true love, Fanny Osbourne, who was ill. Penniless, Stevenson traveled from Scotland as a steerage passenger and crossed the American continent on an immigrant train. His experiences of this arduous trip are described in *The Amateur Emigrant* and *Across the Plains*.

John Steinbeck also wrote here. He was born nearby in Salinas and worked as a ranch hand, in a fish hatchery, and as a chemist in a sugar beet factory before beginning his writing career. He started as a newspaperman, and later began writing novels, most of which are set in California. Two of his most famous are *East of Eden*, based on his grandparents' experiences as farmers in the Salinas Valley, and *Cannery Row*, which made the wharf district of Monterey world-famous.

Monterey's interesting inhabitants, its eccentricities and inconveniences—wild boars, narrow streets, foggy, damp weather during much of the year—give it a piquancy that keeps it from being too perfect. The development of the peninsula has been wisely planned and overseen. The trees that Vizcaíno admired are still standing. The otters, once close to extinction, have returned. There are few billboards or neon signs. Here, perhaps more than anywhere in California, the cadence of life is slower, and old-fashioned amenities prevail.

CRUDITÉS WITH SPINACH DIP

SERVES 6–8

must be prepared 24 hours in advance

1 package frozen chopped spinach or 2 cups finely chopped fresh spinach
1 cup sour cream
¼ cup mayonnaise
¼ cup minced fresh parsley
¼ cup minced scallions (whites only)
½ teaspoon Beau Monde seasoning
½ teaspoon dried dill weed
Salt and pepper to taste
Endive, cucumber, zucchini, carrots, celery, radishes, cauliflower, snow peas
1 small head red cabbage

Cook frozen spinach according to package directions. (If using fresh spinach, cook in a 2-quart saucepan and drain thoroughly in a strainer.) In a bowl mix together the sour cream, mayonnaise, parsley, scallions, and spices. Add the spinach and stir thoroughly. Taste for seasoning. Cover and refrigerate overnight or longer. Serve with chilled fresh vegetables such as endive leaves, peeled fingers of cucumber, zucchini, carrots, or celery; also radishes and cauliflowerettes and other raw vegetables in lettuce cups. Place the spinach dip in the center of a hollowed-out small cabbage head.

CALIFORNIA JALAPEÑO MOLD

SERVES 6–8

1 envelope unflavored gelatin
1 cup cold water
1 cup sour cream
¼ cup mayonnaise
¼ teaspoon salt
8 ounces Cheddar cheese, shredded
2 tablespoons finely chopped green pepper
2 tablespoons finely chopped pimiento
1–2 tablespoons minced onion
4 ounces green chiles, finely chopped
1 teaspoon Worcestershire sauce
Parsley sprigs
1 red pepper, seeded and cut in thin rings
Crackers or toast rounds

Sprinkle gelatin over cold water in a small saucepan. Stir constantly over low heat until dissolved, 3–4 minutes. In a mixing bowl combine sour cream and mayonnaise and gradually add gelatin. Mix until well blended. Stir in the salt, cheese, green pepper, pimiento, onion, chiles, and Worcestershire, mixing well. Chill until slightly thickened, about 20–30 minutes, then stir and refrigerate for 4 hours or until firm. Unmold onto a serving platter and garnish with parsley and red pepper rings. Serve with crackers or toast rounds.

NOTE: This tastes better if it stands overnight.

GUACAMOLE

2 avocados, very ripe
3 tablespoons fresh lemon juice
2–3 tablespoons finely minced
 onion
1 tomato, peeled and finely
 chopped
3–4 dashes Tabasco sauce,
 depending on taste
¼ teaspoon salt
Sour cream
Scallions, including tops,
 finely minced
Fresh coarsely ground pepper
Sliced ripe olives
Tortilla chips, crackers

Peel the avocados and mash until fairly smooth, reserving the seeds. Add the lemon juice and blend well. Add the onion, tomato, Tabasco, and salt and mix well, using a fork. Cover and chill in the refrigerator until ready to serve. To prevent discoloration, place the avocado seeds in the guacamole until serving time. The guacamole may be served in a bowl garnished with a dollop of sour cream, scallions, peppers, and olives. Salted tortilla chips or other types of chips or crackers may be used for dipping the guacamole.

NOTE: Guacamole may be stored in the freezer by placing the prepared mixture in an airtight container. Cover the guacamole with a ⅛-inch layer of freshly squeezed lemon juice. Place a layer of transparent wrap over the container and cover with a tight-fitting top.

PICKLED SHRIMP

24 medium-sized raw green
 shrimp
1 cup dry white wine
2 bay leaves
1 cup olive oil
2 small onions, finely chopped
¼ cup fresh lemon juice
1 teaspoon dried tarragon or
 1 tablespoon chopped fresh
 tarragon
Dash Tabasco sauce
1 teaspoon Worcestershire
 sauce
½ teaspoon salt
Dash fresh coarsely ground
 pepper
Lettuce leaves
2 tablespoons chopped fresh
 parsley

In a heavy 10–12-inch skillet cook the shrimp in the wine with the bay leaves until pink, about 10 minutes. Drain the shrimp. Peel and devein them. Mix all the remaining ingredients except the lettuce and parsley in a large bowl. Stir to blend thoroughly. Add the shrimp to the marinade and stir well to coat the shrimp evenly. Cover and chill at least 2 hours. Stir once or twice during this time. Drain most of the marinade from the shrimp and serve on a lettuce-lined serving plate sprinkled with chopped parsley.

CALIFORNIA CHICKEN LIVERS

2 pounds chicken livers
½ cup soy sauce
¼ cup dry sherry
1 tablespoon sugar
1 teaspoon onion powder
1 teaspoon finely minced
  orange peel
½ teaspoon curry powder
1½ pounds sliced bacon,
  uncooked
Watercress

Cut each chicken liver in half and place in a small bowl with a tight-fitting lid. In another small bowl combine the soy sauce, sherry, sugar, onion powder, orange peel, and curry powder and blend the mixture completely. Pour the marinade over the chicken livers, coating carefully. Cover tightly and marinate in the refrigerator for 24 hours.

When ready to serve, cut each strip of bacon in half crosswise and roll a strip of bacon around each chicken liver half. Secure the bacon with a round toothpick (flat toothpicks burn in the broiler) and place on a rack in a preheated broiler, about 4 inches from the flame. Broil for 5 minutes on each side until the bacon is crisp. Serve on a warm plate garnished with watercress.

CHEESE LOG

SERVES 10–12

½ pound Cheddar cheese,
  grated
3 ounces cream cheese,
  softened
1 tablespoon butter, softened
2 teaspoons chopped fresh
  parsley
1 tablespoon grated onion
½ teaspoon salt
1 teaspoon Worcestershire
  sauce
Dash Tabasco sauce
½ cup chopped pistachio nuts
1 parsley sprig
Assorted crackers

BLUE CHEESE FROSTING
2 ounces blue cheese (or
  Roquefort)
3 ounces cream cheese
2 tablespoons heavy cream
Dash Tabasco sauce

To prepare the log, in the large bowl of your electric mixer beat together until well blended (it will be quite soft) the Cheddar, 3 ounces cream cheese, butter, parsley, onion, salt, Worcestershire, and dash Tabasco. Place mixture on a large sheet of waxed paper and roll to form a log approximately 8 inches long and 2 inches in diameter. Close the ends of the waxed paper. Place in the freezer for 30 minutes.

To prepare frosting, beat together in a small bowl the blue cheese, 3 ounces cream cheese, heavy cream, and Tabasco until light and fluffy. Remove the cheese log from the freezer (it should be *stone-hard*). Coat evenly with the Blue Cheese Frosting. Place in the freezer for 5 minutes. Remove and roll the log in the pistachio nuts, making sure to cover all sides and ends evenly. Roll in plastic wrap and refrigerate for at least 4 hours. Place on a serving plate with a sprig of parsley for color. Serve with assorted crackers.

NOTE: Decorated with a fresh sprig of holly, this is very colorful during the holiday season.

MARINATED BABY ARTICHOKES

12 fresh baby artichokes
¼ cup wine vinegar
¼ cup salad oil
1 teaspoon dried oregano
1 tablespoon chopped fresh
  parsley
1 teaspoon salt
⅛ teaspoon fresh coarsely
  ground pepper
1 or 2 cloves garlic
Watercress or parsley sprigs

In a 3-quart saucepan cook the artichokes in water to cover until tender, about 15–20 minutes. Drain the artichokes. Cut the artichokes in half and remove the choke and the tough outer leaves. Place the artichokes in a large bowl. In a small bowl combine the vinegar, oil, oregano, parsley, salt, and pepper. Pour the mixture over the artichokes. Split the garlic cloves and spear with toothpicks. Add the cloves to the marinade. Cover the marinade and refrigerate overnight or longer, turning occasionally to marinate evenly. When ready to serve, remove the garlic and drain the artichokes. Place a toothpick in the middle of each artichoke and arrange on a serving plate garnished with watercress or parsley.

NOTE: This is an excellent addition to an antipasto tray.

BACLAZANA

1 cup chopped onion
1 large eggplant, peeled and
  cut into ½-inch cubes
  (about 4 cups)
2 large green peppers, seeded
  and chopped
2½ cups chopped fresh
  tomatoes, peeled and
  seeded
½ cup chopped celery
½ cup olive oil
¼ cup California dry white
  wine
1 teaspoon sugar
1 teaspoon Worcestershire
  sauce
Salt and pepper to taste
2 tablespoons capers
Pumpernickel, rye, or French
  bread

In a large bowl place the onion, eggplant, green pepper, tomato, and celery and mix well. Heat the oil in a 10–12-inch heavy skillet and add the vegetables. Cook over low heat, stirring frequently, for 30 minutes. Add the white wine, sugar, Worcestershire, and salt and pepper to taste. Continue cooking for 15 minutes longer. Add the capers and check the seasoning. Cook an additional 15 minutes. Cool and chill the mixture in the refrigerator for at least 2 hours. When ready to serve, place in a serving crock surrounded by pumpernickel, rye, or French bread, sliced, for spreading.

NOTE: This makes an excellent addition to an antipasto tray. It is also excellent when heated and served with a lamb dinner.

MARINATED BRUSSELS SPROUTS

SERVES 6–8

1½ pounds brussels sprouts
1½ teaspoons finely minced
  onion
1 cup tomato sauce
1 clove garlic, crushed
1 teaspoon sugar
Pinch cayenne pepper
1½ teaspoons olive oil
2½ tablespoons dill vinegar
1 large bay leaf

Wash the brussels sprouts, trim the base, and remove any discolored outer leaves. Pierce the base of each sprout with a small knife so that they will cook evenly. Bring 1½ quarts of water to boiling in a 3-quart saucepan. Add the sprouts, remove from heat, and allow to cool. Using a quart jar or similar-size container with tight-fitting lid, combine the remaining ingredients. Add the brussels sprouts and invert the covered container completely, covering with the marinade. Refrigerate the marinated sprouts for 24 hours. Remove the bay leaf from the marinade before serving.

NOTE: This is an excellent addition to an antipasto tray.

BASQUE PICKLED BEANS

SERVES 8

1 pound small white beans
½ cup finely minced onion
2 cloves garlic, crushed
¼ cup finely chopped fresh
  parsley
¾ cup red wine vinegar
1¼ cups salad oil
1 teaspoon salt
½ teaspoon fresh coarsely
  ground pepper
¼ teaspoon dried oregano,
  crushed

In a 3–4 quart covered saucepan, soak the beans overnight in about 8 cups of cold water. After soaking, drain and return the beans to the saucepan with 2½ quarts fresh water. Cook until tender, about 1½ hours. Rinse the beans well with cool water and drain. While the beans are cooking, make a marinade by mixing the rest of the ingredients together in a small bowl. Pour the marinade over the warm beans. Stir well, cover, and chill at least 6 hours.

NOTE: This is an excellent addition to an antipasto tray.

HONEYDEW AND ROQUEFORT CHEESE

SERVES 6–8

1 honeydew melon
3–4 tablespoons fresh lime
  juice
8 ounces Roquefort cheese,
  softened to room temperature

Cut the honeydew melon in half lengthwise. Seed and peel the melon. Cut into ½-inch-wide slices. Place on a flat plate and sprinkle with lime juice. Cover and chill the melon in the refrigerator. In a medium bowl beat the Roquefort cheese.

1 cup heavy cream
Mint leaves

In another bowl whip the cream until it forms soft peaks. Add the whipped cream to the cheese, beating them together. Arrange 3 slices of melon on each salad plate. Top with about ¼ cup of the cheese mixture. Chill for at least 30 minutes. Serve garnished with mint leaves as a first course.

SHRIMP BUTTER

SERVES 10–12

8 ounces cooked shrimp, chopped
8 ounces cream cheese, softened
¼ cup butter, softened
2 tablespoons minced scallions (whites only)
4 tablespoons lemon juice
¼ teaspoon dried dill weed
2–4 drops Tabasco sauce
¼ teaspoon salt
Bread, thinly sliced

In a mixing bowl mix together all ingredients except the bread. Stir well to blend thoroughly. Spoon into a decorative serving crock. Cover and refrigerate for 24 hours. Serve with thinly sliced white or rye bread.

WALNUT DUXELLES

SERVES 8–10

4 tablespoons butter
4 cups chopped fresh mushrooms
½ cup chopped scallions (whites only)
¼ teaspoon dried thyme
1 teaspoon salt
⅓ cup sherry
8 ounces cream cheese, softened
1 cup finely chopped walnuts, toasted
¼ cup chopped fresh parsley
Dash Tabasco sauce
¼ cup finely chopped fresh chives
Crackers

In a heavy 10–12-inch skillet melt the butter over moderate heat. Add the mushrooms, scallions, and thyme. Cook, stirring, until scallions are transparent, about 5–8 minutes. Add the salt and sherry and cook until the liquid is almost evaporated. Remove from heat and cool. Mix the softened cream cheese and the mushroom mixture in a large bowl. Stir and blend thoroughly. Stir in the walnuts, parsley, and Tabasco. Put into a serving dish or crock. Chill, covered, for at least 2 hours. Sprinkle the top with chives. Serve with crackers.

MEDITERRANEAN LOAF

1 loaf sourdough bread,
   unsliced
5 medium tomatoes, peeled,
   seeded, and finely chopped
4 scallions, whites only,
   thinly sliced
½ cup chopped ripe olives
½ cup olives with pimiento
   center, chopped
4 tablespoons chopped fresh
   parsley
4 tablespoons freshly grated
   Parmesan cheese
¼ teaspoon dried thyme
½ teaspoon dried oregano
3 tablespoons olive oil
3 tablespoons California dry
   white wine
Salt and pepper to taste

Cut off the ends from the bread. Using a long-handled kitchen fork, scoop out enough bread dough to make a long hollow tube with a ½-inch crust, reserving the bread crumbs. In a large mixing bowl combine the bread crumbs with the tomatoes, scallions, olives, parsley, cheese, thyme, and oregano. Gently but thoroughly mix. Add the olive oil, white wine, and salt and pepper. Thoroughly mix again. Holding one end of the tube of sourdough bread closed with the palm of your hand, stuff the hollow bread with the tomato mixture, being sure to pack firmly. Wrap the stuffed loaf with aluminum foil and chill for 24 hours.

When ready to serve, cut carefully with a very sharp knife into ½-inch slices. Serve as an appetizer on a chilled small plate with fork and knife. May also be used on a picnic accompanied by wine, fruit, and cheese.

CAVIAR MOLD

1 tablespoon gelatin
¼ cup water
1 cup sour cream
2 tablespoons mayonnaise
2 tablespoons fresh lemon
   juice
2 teaspoons grated onion
¼ teaspoon sugar
Dash Tabasco sauce,
4 ounces caviar, lumpfish, or
   whitefish
Salt and white pepper to taste
2 tablespoons sour cream
Parsley sprigs
Toast rounds or crackers

Dissolve the gelatin in the water. In a 1–2-quart heavy saucepan heat the sour cream over low heat. Add the softened gelatin, stirring constantly until the gelatin melts, 1–2 minutes. Remove from the heat and add the mayonnaise, lemon juice, onion, sugar, and Tabasco, blending well. Place the caviar in a strainer and carefully run cold water over it to rinse out the juice. Thoroughly shake the strainer to remove all the excess water. Reserving 1 tablespoon of the caviar, add the rest to the sour cream mixture, stirring gently. Taste for salt and pepper. Pour into an oiled 2-cup mold and chill until firm, about 3–4 hours.

Unmold on a serving plate. Place about 6 dollops of sour cream on top of the mold, and on top of each dollop divide the reserved caviar. Surround with parsley sprigs and serve with toast rounds or unsalted crackers.

HOT EGGPLANT CAVIAR

1 large eggplant
4 tablespoons olive oil
1 clove garlic, crushed
⅓ cup finely chopped onion
⅓ cup seeded and finely
  chopped green pepper
2 cups finely chopped Italian
  plum tomatoes
2 teaspoons capers
1 tablespoon fresh lemon juice
⅛ teaspoon Tabasco sauce
1 teaspoon salt
⅛ teaspoon pepper
3 tablespoons garlic wine
  vinegar
1 teaspoon dried basil
Melba toast rounds
⅓ cup freshly grated Parmesan
  cheese

Place unpeeled eggplant in a shallow pan in a preheated 350° oven and bake for 1 hour. Remove from oven and cool. Heat olive oil in a 10–12-inch skillet over medium heat and add the garlic, onion, and green pepper. Cook until the onion is tender, about 5 minutes, stirring frequently. Cut the eggplant lengthwise and scoop out the flesh, discarding the skin. If there are any large pieces of eggplant, mash them with a potato ricer or cut them into small pieces with a sharp knife. Stir the eggplant into the onion mixture and add the tomatoes, capers, lemon juice, Tabasco, salt, pepper, vinegar, and basil. Simmer over low heat uncovered for 20 minutes. Remove from the heat and chill in the refrigerator a minimum of 2 hours.

To serve, spread a heaping teaspoon of eggplant caviar on each melba toast round, sprinkle with the cheese and place under a preheated broiler until bubbly, about 2–3 minutes. Serve at once.

GREEK ARTICHOKES

3 medium boiling potatoes
3 medium onions
3 medium carrots
1 clove garlic, crushed
¼ cup olive oil
12 artichoke bottoms, in
  bite-sized pieces
1 teaspoon dried dill weed
½ teaspoon salt or to taste
¼ teaspoon pepper or to taste
2 tablespoons fresh lemon
  juice
½ cup ripe olives

Peel potatoes and onions and cut into large bite-sized pieces. Peel the carrots and cut into 1½-inch lengths, splitting the thick top ends lengthwise. Cook the potatoes, onions, carrots, and garlic in the olive oil in a medium-sized saucepan over low heat. Cook until the vegetables are tender, without being browned, about 15–20 minutes. Prepare the artichoke bottoms according to directions for Boiled Fresh Artichokes (*see Index*). Add the artichoke bottoms to the saucepan and cook until barely tender, about 2–3 minutes. Add the dill weed, salt, pepper, lemon juice, and olives. Serve at room temperature.

NOTE: This is an excellent addition to an antipasto tray.

STEAK TARTARE

SERVES 8

1¼ pounds round steak or lean
  sirloin
½ cup grated onion
1 egg, beaten
1 teaspoon salt
¼ teaspoon pepper
1 tablespoon Worcestershire
  sauce
½ teaspoon garlic salt
3 tablespoons capers
Dash Tabasco sauce
½ teaspoon seasoned salt
¼ cup minced fresh parsley
Crackers

Have the butcher put the meat through the grinder twice. Place the ground meat in a medium-sized bowl and add the onion, egg, salt, pepper, Worcestershire, garlic salt, 2 tablespoons of the capers, and Tabasco. Mix the ingredients well but very gently with the hands. Mold the steak tartare on a serving plate. Cover and refrigerate 2–6 hours.

Just prior to serving the steak tartare, sprinkle with seasoned salt and minced parsley. Serve garnished with the remaining capers and surrounded by crackers.

SPINACH-WRAPPED CHICKEN WITH ORIENTAL DIP

SERVES 6–8
MAKES 50 TO 60 PIECES

2 whole chicken breasts
1¾ cups chicken broth
¼ cup soy sauce
1 tablespoon Worcestershire
  sauce
1 pound fresh spinach
Lettuce leaves

ORIENTAL DIP
1 cup sour cream
2 teaspoons toasted sesame
  seeds
½ teaspoon ground ginger
4 teaspoons soy sauce
2 teaspoons Worcestershire
  sauce

In a 3-quart saucepan simmer the chicken breasts in the chicken broth, ¼ cup soy sauce, and 1 table-spoon Worcestershire until tender, about 15–20 minutes. Remove the chicken breasts from the broth and cool. Thoroughly wash and remove stems from the spinach leaves, reserve smaller leaves for another use, and pour 2–3 quarts of boiling water over them. Completely drain and set the spinach aside to cool. When breasts are cool, discard the bones and skin. Cut the meat into 1-inch cubes.

To assemble, place a chicken cube at the stem end of a spinach leaf. Roll over once, fold leaf in on both sides, and continue rolling around the chicken piece. Secure the end of the leaf with a toothpick and chill in the refrigerator. Cover a serving plate with lettuce leaves. Place Oriental Dip in a small bowl in the center and surround it with the spinach-wrapped chicken pieces.

To prepare dip, in a small serving bowl combine the sour cream, sesame seeds, ground ginger, 4 teaspoons soy sauce, and 2 teaspoons Worcester-shire. Stir gently to combine the ingredients. Chill for 4 hours in the refrigerator.

CHINESE MEATBALLS

6 6½-ounce cans water chestnuts
3 bunches scallions
5 pounds finely ground lean
   pork (use pork butt)
¼ cup soy sauce
6 eggs, slightly beaten
1 tablespoon salt
Pepper to taste
½ teaspoon dried rosemary,
   crushed
2½ cups fine dry bread crumbs
1 cup cornstarch
Oil

GINGER SOY GLAZE
1 cup vinegar
2 cups pineapple juice
¾ cup sugar
2 cups beef consommé
2 tablespoons soy sauce
3 tablespoons grated fresh
   ginger root
½ cup cornstarch
1 cup cold water

Drain and chop the water chestnuts. Chop the scallions, including the tops. In a large bowl mix the scallions with the meat. Add the ¼ cup soy sauce, eggs, salt, pepper, rosemary, and bread crumbs. Mix thoroughly by hand and chill. When ready to use, form the meat mixture into small meatballs, about 1 tablespoon each, and roll in cornstarch. In a heavy 10–12-inch skillet sauté the meatballs in 1 inch of oil, until well browned. Serve the meatballs hot in a chafing dish. Add just enough sauce to form a glaze and coat the meatballs evenly. Serve with toothpicks.

To prepare glaze, in a 3-quart saucepan heat the vinegar, pineapple juice, sugar, consommé, 2 tablespoons soy sauce, and ginger. Gradually stir in the cornstarch, which has been mixed with the water. Continue to cook, stirring, until clear and thickened.

CEVICHE

1 pound fillet of sole or any
   boneless whitefish, chopped
8 tablespoons fresh lime juice
1 large tomato
1 large avocado
8–10 scallions, including tops,
   finely sliced
1 teaspoon ground coriander
1 teaspoon salt
Dash pepper
1 head lettuce
Crackers

Chop the fish into ½-inch cubes with a sharp knife. Place fish in a 2½–3-quart glass or porcelain bowl, cover with the lime juice, and refrigerate at least 4 hours to "cook" fish. The fish should lose its translucent appearance. About 1 hour before serving, peel and chop the tomato, removing the seeds. In a medium-sized mixing bowl mash the avocado with a fork. Add the chopped tomato, the scallions, coriander, salt, and pepper. Drain the fish thoroughly and add to the avocado mixture. Refrigerate until ready to serve. May be served as an appetizer on a bed of lettuce leaves with crackers or as a salad on lettuce leaves on individual plates.

NOTE: The fish must be very fresh.

SALMON CEVICHE

3 pounds salmon fillets
1 medium onion, finely minced
3 cloves garlic, crushed
5 tablespoons fresh lemon juice
4 tablespoons fresh lime juice
1 tablespoon Dijon mustard
4 tablespoons chopped fresh
    parsley
2 tablespoons chopped fresh
    dill or 2 teaspoons dried dill
    weed
3 tablespoons cognac
1 teaspoon salt or to taste
1 teaspoon freshly ground
    pepper
Lettuce leaves
Parsley or watercress sprigs
Toast points, buttered

Remove the skin and every bone from the salmon with pincers. Chop the salmon into $\frac{1}{4}$-inch pieces with a very sharp knife. In a large mixing bowl mix well the onion, garlic, lemon and lime juices, mustard, the chopped parsley, dill, cognac, salt, and pepper. Add the salmon, stir well, and refrigerate for at least 2 hours. Before serving, taste for additional seasoning. Serve on a lettuce-lined chilled platter garnished with fresh parsley or sprigs of fresh watercress and surround with buttered toast points.

NOTE: The fish must be very fresh.

BLEU CHEESE MOLD

2 $10\frac{1}{2}$-ounce cans consommé
2 tablespoons unflavored
    gelatin
6 tablespoons cold water
4 tablespoons sherry
9 ounces cream cheese, at room
    temperature
3 ounces bleu cheese, at
    room temperature
1 tablespoon Worcestershire
    sauce
Parsley sprigs
Assorted crackers

In a medium-sized saucepan heat the consommé over medium heat for 5–7 minutes. Dissolve the gelatin in cold water in a small bowl and then add to the hot consommé. Blend well and add 2 tablespoons of the sherry. Stir until well blended and set aside to cool. When completely cool, pour a 1-inch layer of gelatin into a lightly buttered 9-inch ring mold. Reserve the rest of the gelatin, keeping in a warm place to prevent its jelling. Place the ring mold in the refrigerator for 30 minutes or until set. Meanwhile, mix the cream cheese, bleu cheese, Worcestershire, and remaining sherry with a fork in a small mixing bowl. When the mold is set, gently spoon the cheese mixture evenly over the gelatin in the ring mold, completely covering it. Pour the reserved gelatin over the mold, spreading it evenly. Refrigerate until ready to serve.

To serve, unmold the gelatin onto a chilled serving plate, garnish with parsley sprigs, and serve with assorted crackers.

CRAB WON TON

8 ounces cream cheese

7–8 ounces crab meat

2 tablespoons soft bread crumbs

½ teaspoon sesame seeds

½ teaspoon monosodium
  glutamate

Peanut oil

24 ounces won ton dough,
  defrosted

Remove the cream cheese from the refrigerator and allow it to come to room temperature. In the meantime, flake the crab with a fork and place it in a tea towel, wringing it well to remove as much moisture as possible. In a medium-sized mixing bowl blend the cream cheese, crab meat, bread crumbs, sesame seeds, monosodium glutamate, and 2–3 drops of peanut oil. Blend this mixture well and set aside. Remove 1 sheet of won ton dough from the package and cover the rest with a damp tea towel to keep from drying out. Place slightly less than 1 teaspoon of the crab filling in the center of the won ton square. Fold the square in half, matching opposite corners. Then fold one of the sides into the center, moistening the dough with a little bit of water to seal the fold. Fold in the other side of the dough to the center, again moistening the flap with a little bit of water to seal. Set this packet aside and proceed to make the rest of the packets of dough. Cover well and refrigerate until ready to serve. Heat 1 inch of peanut oil in a large heavy skillet to 370°. Carefully place the won ton squares in the hot oil, keeping them from touching each other. Deep-fry for 3 minutes or until lightly browned and puffed, turning over halfway through the cooking. Serve immediately with Chinese Hot Mustard.

CHINESE HOT MUSTARD
MAKES ½ CUP

¼ cup dry mustard

¼ cup water

To prepare mustard, in a small bowl blend mustard and water. Cover with a saucer or plate and leave at room temperature for 1 hour. Serve in a small dish with Crab Won Ton.

NOTE: These won ton pastries can be quickly fried, for about 1½ minutes, again turning halfway through the cooking, and frozen immediately. They will keep indefinitely in a freezer if they are sealed airtight. When ready to serve, proceed as above.

CALIFORNIA PÂTÉ MAISON

2 tablespoons butter

1 large onion, finely minced

1 cup cognac

¾ pound ground lean pork

½ pound ground veal

½ pound ground calf liver or chicken livers

2 or 3 eggs, beaten

2 teaspoons salt

⅛ teaspoon pepper

⅛ teaspoon ground allspice

½ teaspoon dried thyme

1 clove garlic, crushed

2 canned truffles, chopped

½ cup chopped pistachio nuts (optional)

½ pound fresh pork fat, very thinly sliced

1 bay leaf

Parsley sprigs

Toast triangles

In a small skillet over moderate heat melt the butter and sauté the onion for 5 minutes, stirring occasionally. Using a slotted spoon, remove the onion to a large mixing bowl, reserving the butter in the skillet. Pour the cognac into the skillet and boil it down over high heat to ¼ cup. Add the ground meats, eggs, salt, pepper, allspice, thyme, garlic, truffles, pistachio nuts, and cognac to the onions in the mixing bowl and mix together until thoroughly blended and light in texture. Do not add the pork fat or the bay leaf at this time.

Pâtés should be seasoned perfectly when served. To determine whether or not the flavor is just what you desire, sauté a tablespoon of the mixture in a little butter and taste it. If necessary, mix in additional seasonings.

Line the bottom and sides of a 4 × 9-inch loaf pan with the pork fat. Spoon the pâté mixture in, tamping down to fill the corners, lay the bay leaf on top, and cover the pan tightly with a piece of foil.

Place the loaf pan inside another pan which has been filled with hot water. Bake in a preheated 350° oven for 1 hour and 40 minutes. The pâté should shrink from the sides of the pan and be surrounded with a clear yellow liquid when done. Remove the pan from the water and set out to cool, placing a weight (such as a 5-pound sack of sugar) on top of the pâté, so that the pâté will be solidly packed with no air holes. Cool pâté for several hours, then chill overnight with weight still on top of the loaf pan.

To serve, remove the weight and the bay leaf and unmold onto a serving platter which is garnished with parsley sprigs. Slice thinly and serve with small toast triangles. Surrounding layer of fat may be left on or removed, as desired.

DOLMA

30–35 grape leaves, preserved
  in brine, bottled or canned
3 large onions, finely chopped
1 cup olive oil
1 cup long-grain rice
1 cup chopped fresh dill or
  1–2 tablespoons dried dill
  weed
½ cup chopped fresh parsley
1 bunch scallions, including
  tops, chopped
1½ cups water
3 tablespoons pine nuts
4 tablespoons fresh lemon
  juice
1 teaspoon salt
¼ teaspoon pepper
Lemon wedges
1 pint unflavored yogurt

Preserved grape leaves are generally found in gourmet food stores or markets that carry imported foods. Gently separate the leaves and blanch them a few at a time in boiling water. Spread the individual leaves on paper towels to drain.

To prepare stuffing, in a heavy 10–12 inch skillet sauté the onion in ½ cup olive oil over low heat for 3–5 minutes, until golden, stirring frequently. Add rice, mix well, and sauté for 10 minutes, stirring occasionally. To the skillet add the dill, parsley, scallions, ½ cup of the water, pine nuts, 2 tablespoons of the lemon juice, salt, and pepper. Cook the mixture about 10 minutes until all the liquid is absorbed, stirring occasionally. Remove the pan from the heat and cool.

Place the grape leaves on a board, shiny sides down, and put 1 teaspoon of rice mixture in the center of each leaf. Fold the sides of the leaves to the center, then roll them up tightly, starting from the stem end. Arrange the dolma in layers in a 4–5-quart saucepan. Mix together 1 cup water, ½ cup olive oil, and 2 tablespoons lemon juice. Pour over the rolls. Place a small platter or a couple of old plates on top of the rolls to prevent the rolls from unwrapping during the cooking. Bring the mixture to a boil over high heat, turn the heat to low, and simmer for 30 minutes or until the liquid is absorbed. Cool, leaving the platter covering the rolls. Chill at least 3–4 hours. Serve on a large serving dish surrounded by lemon wedges with a small bowl of yogurt in the center.

NOTE: This can be made several days ahead and stored covered in the refrigerator.

CHEESE-STUFFED MUSHROOMS

SERVES 10–12

40 medium-sized fresh mushrooms, stems removed
¼ cup butter
8 ounces cream cheese, softened
¾ cup freshly grated Parmesan cheese
5 tablespoons milk
½ teaspoon garlic powder
2 tablespoons finely chopped fresh chives

Wash the mushrooms and dry completely. Melt the butter in a small saucepan and dip each mushroom in it, coating all sides and the cavity well. Place the buttered caps on a cookie sheet and set aside.

In a medium-sized mixing bowl blend the cream cheese, Parmesan cheese, milk, garlic powder, and chives thoroughly. Place a generous teaspoonful of this mixture in each mushroom cap, letting it mound instead of tamping it down. Bake in a preheated 350° oven for 15 minutes or until nicely browned. Serve at once.

NOTE: The mushrooms may be prepared ahead and frozen. To serve, bake the mushrooms while still frozen, they become mushy when thawed. Add about 5 minutes to the baking time.

COGNAC MUSHROOMS

SERVES 6–8

1 pound fresh medium mushrooms
5 tablespoons butter
1 tablespoon finely grated onion
4 ounces pâté
3 ounces cream cheese
1 tablespoon cognac
1 teaspoon monosodium glutamate
Salt and freshly ground pepper to taste
Parsley sprigs or watercress

Thoroughly wash the mushrooms, pat dry, and remove the stems. Chop the stems finely and set aside. Melt 2½ tablespoons butter in a 10–12-inch skillet and sauté the mushroom caps over medium heat until brown, about 5–6 minutes. Remove the browned mushroom caps to a plate. Add to the skillet the remaining 2½ tablespoons butter, the onion, and chopped mushroom stems. Sauté until brown, about 3–4 minutes. Remove the skillet from the heat and add the pâté and cream cheese to the warm mushroom mixture. Add the cognac, monosodium glutamate, salt, and pepper and blend the ingredients thoroughly. Fill the mushroom caps with the mixture. If desired, the filled mushroom caps may be refrigerated overnight. Place the filled mushroom caps on a broiler pan and broil, 8 inches from the flame, just long enough to heat, being careful not to overcook. Serve on a platter garnished with parsley sprigs or watercress.

SPINACH-FILLED MUSHROOMS

3 pounds fresh spinach, washed
  and stems removed, or
  2 10-ounce packages frozen
  spinach
36 fresh large mushrooms
1¼ cups butter
3 cloves garlic, crushed
3 onions, finely chopped
½ cup fine bread crumbs
2 teaspoons salt
¼ teaspoon pepper
¼ teaspoon dry mustard
½ teaspoon ground nutmeg
5 tablespoons freshly grated
  Parmesan cheese

In a medium-sized saucepan cook the spinach in ½ cup unsalted water for 5–7 minutes over moderate heat or until thoroughly wilted. (If using frozen spinach, cook according to package directions.) Drain the spinach thoroughly, squeezing out as much water as possible. Purée the spinach in an electric blender for 2 minutes at medium speed and set aside. Wipe the mushrooms with a damp towel and remove the stems. Chop the stems finely and set them aside. Melt the butter in a 10–12-inch skillet, add the garlic, and cook the mixture for 1 minute over moderate heat. Dip the mushroom caps in the melted butter, coating them well on all sides, and place them, cavity side up, on a cookie sheet. Reheat the remaining butter and sauté the chopped onions and mushroom stems for 5–8 minutes or until very soft. Add to the skillet the puréed spinach, bread crumbs, salt, pepper, mustard, and nutmeg and mix well. Fill the mushroom caps with the mixture, mounding it high. Sprinkle the mushroom caps with grated cheese.

Bake mushrooms in a preheated 375° oven for 15 minutes, watching them carefully to prevent scorching. Cool slightly. Serve on a platter garnished with parsley sprigs or watercress. These would also be an excellent first course with 4–5 per person.

PARSLEY AND ONION ROUNDS

1 loaf thin-sliced bread,
  cut in 2-inch rounds
¼ pound butter, softened
1 red sweet onion, finely
  chopped
1 cup mayonnaise, preferably
  homemade (*see Index*)
2 cups chopped fresh parsley
Parsley sprigs

Assemble bread rounds. Spread half with soft butter. Place ½ teaspoon red onion on these and place the unspread rounds on top of the onion, making a sandwich. Roll sides of sandwiches in mayonnaise and then in the chopped parsley. Refrigerate for 1 hour. Serve on a chilled serving platter surrounded by parsley sprigs.

SPECIAL CHEESE ROUNDS

SERVES 8   MAKES ABOUT 60 ROUNDS

1 cup grated extra-sharp
   Cheddar cheese
½ cup freshly grated mozzarella
   cheese
¼ cup freshly grated Parmesan
   cheese
⅛ teaspoon Beau Monde
   seasoning
⅛ teaspoon garlic powder
4 scallions, including some of
   the tops, diced
½ cup mayonnaise, preferably
   homemade (*see Index*)
1 loaf sourdough bread,
   thinly sliced and cut in half

In a medium-sized bowl mix the Cheddar, mozzarella, Parmesan, Beau Monde, garlic powder, and scallions. Add the mayonnaise and increase as necessary to achieve a spreadable consistency. Spread the cheese mixture on the sourdough slices. Cut into smaller pieces if desired and put on a cookie sheet or broiler pan. Place in a preheated broiler and broil until bubbly, about 2–3 minutes, and serve at once on a heated plate.

SESAME CHEESE PUFFS

SERVES 10–12

1¾ cups flour
1 teaspoon garlic salt
½ cup butter
½ cup sour cream
1 cup grated Cheddar cheese
2–3 tablespoons sesame seeds

Sift the flour and garlic salt into a medium-sized bowl. Use a pastry blender to blend in the butter until the mixture is crumbly. Lightly stir in the sour cream with a fork just until the pastry holds together and cleanly leaves the sides of the bowl. Add the cheese and mix well. Wrap the pastry in plastic wrap and chill in the refrigerator at least 4 hours, preferably overnight.

On a lightly floured pastry cloth or board, roll out the pastry to a thickness of ¼ inch. Cut the pastry into 1¼-inch rounds or use a fancy cutter to obtain desired shapes. Place the cut rounds on an ungreased cookie sheet. Brush the cut rounds with a pastry brush dipped in water. Sprinkle with the sesame seeds. Bake in a preheated 400° oven for 14 minutes until puffed and golden. Remove from the cookie sheet and serve at once.

NOTE: If they are to be served later, cool on wire racks and reheat in the oven for a minute or two just before serving. The cheese puffs may be stored for several days in an airtight container.

CHEESE PUFFS

¼ pound butter
¾ pound Cheddar cheese, grated
1 teaspoon Worcestershire sauce
3 tablespoons grated onion
Dash cayenne pepper
2 eggs
1 loaf sourdough French bread, crusts removed, cut into 1-inch cubes

In the top of a large double boiler, over simmering water, melt the butter and cheese together, stirring with a wire whisk. Blend in the Worcestershire, onion, and cayenne. With an electric beater, thoroughly beat in the eggs. Turn the heat off. Carefully dip each bread cube into the cheese mixture and turn to coat thoroughly. Shake off all excess cheese mixture and place the cubes on a cookie sheet and freeze. After the cubes are frozen, store airtight in a plastic bag in the freezer until ready to use. These will keep frozen for months.

Place the frozen cubes on a cookie sheet and bake in a preheated 350° oven for 10–12 minutes. Serve at once.

FETA CHEESE TARTS

1 cup light cream
1 pound feta cheese, shredded
3 eggs
1 teaspoon cornstarch
½ teaspoon dried thyme
1 clove garlic, crushed
Pepper to taste
1 3-ounce package cream cheese, softened
½ cup butter, softened
1 cup flour, sifted
6 ripe olives, sliced

To prepare filling, combine the cream, feta cheese, and eggs in the container of an electric blender. Blend at medium speed for 2 minutes or until thoroughly mixed. Add the cornstarch, thyme, garlic, and pepper to the mixture and blend for 45 more seconds. Set aside.

To prepare tarts, blend the cream cheese and butter in a mixing bowl. Cut in the flour with a fork. Chill the dough 1 hour. Using 1½-inch tart pans, evenly press 2 teaspoons of the dough into each tin. Prick the sides and bottoms of the dough with a fork. Bake in a preheated 350° oven for 7–8 minutes before filling the tart shells.

To assemble, pour 1–2 tablespoons of the cheese filling mixture into each prepared tart shell. Top each tart with a slice of olive. Place on cookie sheets and bake for 30–35 minutes. Serve the cheese tarts immediately.

PHYLLO DOUGH HORS D'OEUVRES

Phyllo dough is a very thin, paperlike dough that is most often sold in Greek or Armenian markets. It is usually packaged by the pound and consists of approximately 15–20 sheets of dough, 18 inches by 16 inches. The dough freezes very well and will also keep for some time in the refrigerator if left in the original wrappings.

After you have prepared one of the following filling recipes, remove the dough from the refrigerator and allow it to come to room temperature, still fully wrapped. Meanwhile, melt ½ cup butter in a small saucepan over low heat and set aside. Then unwrap the dough, and working fairly quickly, cut the dough lengthwise into 8 strips (these strips should be about 2 × 18 inches). Keeping 1 stack of dough out to work with, wrap the remaining strips airtight and replace them in the refrigerator to keep from drying out. Keep a damp towel over the strips you are working with, removing 1 at a time to fill.

Place 1 teaspoon of one of the following fillings at the bottom end of one of the strips. Fold the corner over to form a triangle. Continue folding the pastry in triangles (much as you would fold a flag) down the full length of the strip, to make 1 multilayered triangle. Prepare the remaining strips in the same way, covering each triangle with a damp towel as it is completed to keep it from drying out. Brush each triangle liberally on all sides with the melted butter, using the butter to seal any loose ends of dough. The triangles can then be cooked immediately, or refrigerated, tightly covered, to keep them from drying out, and cooked the next day, or they can be frozen in an airtight container and kept indefinitely.

Place the filled triangles on a cookie sheet, ½ inch apart. Bake in a preheated 375° oven for 20 minutes or until slightly crisp and lightly browned. Serve at once.

CHEESE PHYLLO

MAKES 100 PIECES

1 pound Monterey Jack cheese, grated
½ pound sharp Cheddar cheese, grated
1 cup chopped fresh parsley
2 eggs, beaten
½ teaspoon pepper
1 teaspoon onion salt

In a medium-sized mixing bowl mix all ingredients. Stir to blend thoroughly. Follow the above directions to make phyllo pastries.

CHICKEN PHYLLO

2 tablespoons butter
¼ cup finely minced onion
¼ cup finely minced fresh
  mushrooms
2 cups finely minced cooked
  chicken
2 tablespoons finely chopped
  fresh parsley
1 teaspoon crumbled dried
  tarragon
½ teaspoon salt or to taste
¼ teaspoon pepper or to taste
1 egg, beaten
¾ cup grated Gruyère cheese

Melt the butter in a 10–12 inch skillet and sauté the onion and mushrooms over moderate heat, stirring frequently, for 7–10 minutes or until the moisture has evaporated. Then in a large mixing bowl combine the mushroom mixture with the remaining ingredients. Blend thoroughly. Follow the above directions to make phyllo pastries.

CRAB PHYLLO

¾ cup Besciamella (*see Index*)
2 cups shredded cooked crab
1 tablespoon fresh lemon juice
3 teaspoons minced fresh chives
1 teaspoon salt
¼ teaspoon cayenne pepper or
  to taste

In a medium-sized mixing bowl combine all ingredients. Stir to blend thoroughly. Follow the above directions to make phyllo pastries.

MUSHROOM PHYLLO

1 pound fresh mushrooms
3 tablespoons butter
1 tablespoon oil
2 large leeks, whites only,
  finely chopped
¼ cup fresh finely chopped
  chives
½ cup sour cream
1 tablespoon dried dill weed
½ teaspoon salt or to taste
¼ teaspoon pepper or to taste

Wipe mushrooms clean and mince them very finely, including the stems. Squeeze all the moisture out of the mushrooms by squeezing a handful at a time in a tea towel. Melt the butter and heat the oil in a 10–12-inch skillet. Sauté the mushrooms, leeks, and chives over moderate heat until all the moisture has evaporated, about 10 minutes, stirring frequently. Set aside to cool. Add the sour cream, dill weed, salt, and pepper, stirring to blend thoroughly. Follow the above directions to make phyllo pastries.

TERRACE SCALLOPS

MAKES 24 PIECES

¾ pound bay scallops
½ pound uncooked sliced, bacon
2 eggs, beaten
¼ cup milk
Salt and pepper to taste
⅓ cup sesame seeds, toasted
Lime wedges

Clean and dry the scallops. Cut the bacon strips in half. In a small mixing bowl combine the eggs, milk, salt, and pepper. Dip the scallops in the egg mixture and roll in the sesame seeds. Wrap each scallop in a piece of bacon and secure with a round toothpick. Place the scallops on a wire rack in a baking pan and place under a preheated broiler, about 4–5 inches from the heat. Turn once after about 2 minutes and broil the other side for 2 more minutes, watching closely to prevent the scallops from burning. Serve at once with fresh lime wedges.

NOTE: These may be prepared 4 hours ahead and kept in the refrigerator until time to cook. If they have been refrigerated, allow 2–3 more minutes of broiling time.

ARTICHOKE SQUARES

SERVES 10–12

3 6-ounce jars marinated
    artichoke hearts in oil
1 clove garlic, crushed
½ cup chopped onion
4 eggs
¼ cup Seasoned Bread
    Crumbs II (*see Index*)
½ pound sharp Cheddar cheese,
    grated
2 tablespoons minced fresh
    parsley
¼ teaspoon salt
⅛ teaspoon dried oregano
⅛ teaspoon pepper
⅛ teaspoon Tabasco sauce
Watercress or parsley sprigs

Drain the oil from 1 jar of the artichoke hearts into a 12-inch skillet and, using moderate heat, gently heat the oil. Sauté the garlic and onion in the oil for 5 minutes and set aside. Drain and discard the oil from the remaining artichoke hearts. Chop the hearts finely and set aside.

In a medium-sized bowl beat the eggs until foamy and blend in the bread crumbs, cheese, parsley, oregano, salt, pepper, and Tabasco. Add the finely chopped artichoke hearts to the egg mixture and stir gently to blend. Add the onion and garlic. Again mix well and spoon into a greased 9 × 9-inch pan. Bake in a preheated 325° oven for 30 minutes. Cool well before cutting into 2-inch squares.

Before serving, place in a 325° oven for 10–12 minutes, then place on a warm serving plate garnished with watercress or parsley sprigs.

SHRIMP PARISIENNE

SERVES 6–8

¼ teaspoon salt
2 teaspoons fresh lemon juice
1 clove garlic, crushed
¼ teaspoon pepper
2 teaspoons mayonnaise,
    preferably homemade
    (*see Index*)
1 pound medium-sized shrimp,
    cleaned and cooked
¾ cup Seasoned Bread Crumbs I
    (*see Index*)
1 teaspoon dried oregano
1 teaspoon dried basil
1 tablespoon chopped fresh
    parsley
¼ cup melted butter
2 tablespoons olive oil
Parsley sprigs

Combine the salt, lemon juice, garlic, pepper, and mayonnaise in a medium-sized bowl with tight-fitting cover. Add the shrimp and marinate covered for at least 12 hours.

Mix together the bread crumbs, oregano, basil, and parsley. Coat the shrimp with the crumb mixture and place in an ovenproof 9 × 12-inch baking dish. Combine the butter and olive oil and dribble over the shrimp.

When ready to serve, place in a preheated 400° oven for 15 minutes. Serve immediately on a heated serving plate surrounded with parsley and accompanied by toothpicks for individual servings.

SHRIMP MOUSSE

SERVES 15–20

1 10¾-ounce can condensed
    tomato soup
8 ounces cream cheese
2 envelopes unflavored gelatin
¼ cup cold water
1 pound cooked bay shrimp,
    minced
¼ cup grated onion
1 cup finely chopped celery
1 cup mayonnaise, preferably
    homemade (*see Index*)
1 teaspoon fresh lemon juice
Pinch salt
Parsley sprigs
Watercress
Lemon slices
Assorted crackers

Heat the tomato soup and cream cheese in a double boiler over simmering water. Gently stir the mixture with a wire whisk to blend. In a small bowl dissolve the gelatin with the water. When the hot mixture is completely blended, add the dissolved gelatin, stirring to blend. Cool the mixture to room temperature, as the mixture must be cooled to prevent the mousse from having a fishy taste. When completely cool, add the shrimp, onion, celery, mayonnaise, lemon juice, and salt. Blend the mixture thoroughly and pour into a 5-cup decorative mold. Chill in the refrigerator for 4 hours. When ready to serve, unmold on chilled serving plate, surround with parsley, watercress, and lemon slices for garnish. A separate plate or basket should be filled with an assortment of crackers for spreading.

NOTE: If desired, the mousse may also be used as a small luncheon salad to serve 8.

MANDARIN CHICKEN WINGS

SERVES 10–12

24 chicken wings
1 cup cornstarch
2 eggs, beaten
½ teaspoon salt
½ teaspoon monosodium
  glutamate
Dash garlic salt
¼ cup milk
4 cups cooking oil

Cut the chicken wings at the joint with a sharp knife. (If extra large wings are used, both pieces may be used.) Discard the wing tips. Scrape and push the meat to one end of the bone so that each piece resembles a small drumstick. Refrigerate covered until ready to use.

In a large mixing bowl combine the cornstarch, eggs, salt, monosodium glutamate, garlic salt, and milk. Use a wire whisk to blend completely. Dip each chicken drumstick into the batter, coating completely. Heat the cooking oil in a heavy 12–14-inch skillet (the oil should be at a depth of 1 inch) over moderate heat, until sizzling but not smoking. Cook the batter-coated pieces, a few at a time, over moderate heat 5–6 minutes, turning often, until lightly browned. Remove from fat and set aside to drain on paper towels.

Dip each fried chicken piece in Peking Sauce, and place in a single layer in a shallow baking pan. Pour the remaining sauce over the chicken wings and bake in a preheated 350° oven for 30 minutes or until the sauce is absorbed. Baste and turn the chicken wings frequently. Serve warm or cold.

PEKING SAUCE
1 cup sugar
¼ cup water
½ cup Japanese vinegar
1 teaspoon soy sauce
1 tablespoon catsup

To prepare sauce, in a small saucepan combine the sugar, water, Japanese vinegar, soy sauce, and catsup. Blend and place over medium heat, stirring constantly until the sugar is dissolved, 7–10 minutes. Remove from the heat.

NOTE: This is an excellent appetizer for a Chinese dinner. The chicken wings may be frozen after they are deep-fried. Dip the frozen wings in the sauce and bake according to directions.

HERB TOAST

SERVES 8–10

¼ pound butter, softened to
  room temperature
¼ teaspoon dried oregano
¼ teaspoon dried rosemary
¼ teaspoon dried thyme
2 tablespoons finely minced
  fresh parsley

In a small bowl cream the butter and add the herbs and parsley. When well blended, spread on individual slices of bread, from which the crusts have been trimmed. If desired, cut into diagonal pieces, thin strips, or fancy shapes with a cutter. Place the slices of bread on an ungreased cookie sheet and bake in a preheated 250° oven for

1 loaf white bread, thinly
    sliced
Parsley or watercress sprigs

1 hour. The toast should be nicely browned before removing from the oven. Serve on a serving platter garnished with watercress or parsley sprigs.

NOTE: This toast is a nice accompaniment to soup or a crisp green salad.

SALMON CREPES WITH DILL   SERVES 6–12   MAKES 12 CREPES

¾ cup flour
1 cup milk
2 eggs
¼ cup water
½ teaspoon salt
2 tablespoons butter, melted
    and cooled
1½ tablespoons dried dill weed
1 cup sour cream
8 ounces smoked salmon,
    sliced
Dill Mustard Sauce (*below*)
Parsley sprigs

In a blender mix the flour, milk, 2 eggs, water, and ½ teaspoon salt for 30 seconds. After scraping the sides of the blender well, add butter and blend for 5 seconds more. Transfer batter to a medium-sized bowl and refrigerate for 2 hours. Remove and add 1½ tablespoons dill weed to the batter before making the crepes. Use approximately 1 ounce of batter for each individual crepe. Proceed to make the crepes in accustomed manner.

Spread each cooked crepe with a thin layer of sour cream. On the bottom half of the crepe place a small slice of smoked salmon, dividing it evenly among the crepes. Spread the salmon with 1½ teaspoons of Dill Mustard Sauce. Fold the crepe in half and then in half again, forming a triangle, and set in rows in a shallow 10 × 13-inch ovenproof casserole. Heat in a preheated 350° oven for 10–15 minutes or until warm. Serve at once on a warm plate garnished with parsley sprigs. An excellent first course.

DILL MUSTARD SAUCE
2 egg yolks
1 tablespoon dry mustard
1 teaspoon Dijon mustard
½ teaspoon sugar
¼ teaspoon salt
1 cup olive and corn oil mixed
    together
2 tablespoons tarragon
    vinegar
1 tablespoon dried dill weed

To prepare sauce, in a medium bowl beat the egg yolks and add dry mustard, Dijon mustard, sugar, and ¼ teaspoon salt, beating in well. Beat in the cup of mixed oil, drop by drop (as for mayonnaise). Continue beating until sauce is thick enough. Beat in tarragon vinegar and 1 tablespoon dill weed. Set aside, cover, and chill in refrigerator. Makes about 1½ cups.

NOTE: The crepes may be made up to 2 hours ahead, covered, and refrigerated. In this case remove from the refrigerator ½ hour before cooking and cook an extra 5–10 minutes.

CHICKEN LIVER PÂTÉ

SERVES 15–20

1 cup walnuts, finely chopped
½ pound chicken livers
2 tablespoons minced onion
3 tablespoons butter
½ teaspoon curry powder
¼ teaspoon paprika
½ teaspoon salt
½ teaspoon pepper
¼ cup chicken broth
16 ounces cream cheese,
   softened
Buffet rye bread

Lightly toast the walnuts under the broiler for about 3–5 minutes and set aside. In a 10-inch skillet sauté the chicken livers and onion in the butter for 5 minutes over moderate heat. Add curry powder, paprika, salt, pepper, and chicken broth. Cool slightly. Place this mixture in a blender and mix for 30 seconds or until smooth. Beat the softened cream cheese in a large bowl and combine with the chicken liver mixture. Stir in the walnuts. Chill in the refrigerator for 5–6 hours to blend flavors. Spoon into a chilled serving crock. Serve with buffet rye bread.

MINIATURE PIZZAS

SERVES 15–20

1 pound ground pork sausage
18 ounces tomato paste
3 teaspoons Worcestershire
   sauce
⅓ cup finely minced onion
⅛ teaspoon Tabasco sauce
Salt and freshly ground pepper
   to taste
1 loaf miniature rye bread,
   sliced
10–12 ounces sharp Cheddar
   cheese, grated
½ pound fresh mushrooms,
   cooked and sliced

In a medium-sized bowl place the sausage meat, tomato paste, Worcestershire, onion, Tabasco, salt, and pepper. Mix well, using both hands, to completely blend the ingredients. At this point the mixture may be refrigerated for 4–6 hours.

When ready to serve, spread the meat mixture on individual slices of rye bread. Sprinkle the grated cheese on top and garnish with slices of mushroom. Place the completed pizzas on a cookie sheet and bake in a preheated 350° oven for 15 minutes. Serve piping hot on a heated serving platter.

TOSTADILLAS

MAKES 96 PIECES

12 corn tortillas
4 cups salad oil
2–3 tablespoons salt

With a sharp knife cut each tortilla into 8 wedge-shaped pieces. In a 10–12-inch skillet heat oil over medium heat to 375°. When the oil is heated thoroughly, add the tortilla pieces one by one until the bottom of the skillet is covered, but the chips are not overlapping. Turn the tortilla pieces as they cook and remove when golden brown and crisp, about 1–2 minutes. Drain tortilla pieces on absorbent paper towels. Salt immediately while the chips are still hot with oil. Fill the skillet again with uncooked strips and proceed until all of the tortilla pieces are cooked.

NOTE: Tostadillas are excellent as a snack or served with Guacamole or California Chile (*See Index*).

PUMPERNICKEL TOAST

MAKES 30–40 PIECES

1 loaf unsliced pumpernickel bread
¼ pound butter
1–2 cloves garlic, crushed
½ cup freshly grated Parmesan cheese

Freeze the loaf of unsliced pumpernickel bread. While still frozen, slice paper-thin with a sharp knife. Arrange the bread slices in a single layer on an ungreased cookie sheet.

In a 1–1½-quart saucepan melt the butter over low heat. Add the garlic and cheese and stir for a few seconds to blend well.

With a pastry brush, spread 1 side of the bread with the butter mixture. Bake in a preheated 350° oven until crisp, about 15–20 minutes. Bread will curl slightly at the edges. Cool and store in an airtight container until ready to use.

NOTE: This toast is an interesting appetizer and is also delicious when served with soups or salads.

BRIE WAFERS

MAKES ABOUT 60 WAFERS

¼ pound butter
½ pound Brie cheese
1 cup flour
½ teaspoon cayenne pepper
¼ teaspoon seasoned salt
½ cup (approximately) sesame seeds

Place the butter and cheese in a medium-sized bowl and let stand until they have softened to room temperature. Add the flour, cayenne pepper, and seasoned salt and beat well. Divide the mixture in half and place one portion on waxed paper. Form the mixture into a long round roll and wrap the waxed paper around the roll. Follow the same procedure for the other half. Refrigerate for at least 12 hours.

Slice the chilled rolls into thin wafers, about ¼-inch thick. Sprinkle with the sesame seeds. Place on a cookie sheet and bake in a preheated 400° oven for about 8 minutes. Cool and store in a tightly covered container.

CURRIED CAULIFLOWER

SERVES 6–8

1 medium-sized cauliflower
1 teaspoon salt
2 cups mayonnaise, preferably
    homemade (*see Index*)
2 teaspoons curry powder
1 teaspoon garlic powder
1 tablespoon grated onion
Assorted crackers

Leaving the cauliflower whole, trim and clean and place in a large saucepan. Add enough cold water to cover the cauliflower. Add the salt to the water and bring the water to a boil over high heat. Cover the pan, reduce the heat to moderate, and cook the cauliflower for 20 minutes or until a fork will pierce the stem easily. Drain well and let cool. In a medium-sized mixing bowl combine the mayonnaise, curry powder, garlic powder, and onion, mixing well. Ice the cauliflower with this mixture as you would ice a cake. Cover and place in the refrigerator for 24 hours. Serve on a plate with a small knife and surrounded with assorted crisp crackers. Spread the cauliflower with some of the sauce onto crackers.

CHILE CON QUESO

SERVES 6–8

¾ pound Monterey Jack cheese,
    shredded
2 tablespoons cornstarch
¼ teaspoon garlic powder
6 slices bacon, minced
½ cup chopped scallions,
    including tops
2 medium tomatoes, chopped
4 ounces green chiles, diced
½ cup California dry white
    wine
Tortilla chips

In a small bowl toss the cheese lightly with the cornstarch and garlic powder. Set aside. Place the minced bacon in a 12-inch skillet and fry until crisp. Drain the bacon pieces on a paper towel. Stir the scallions into the bacon fat in the skillet. Add the tomatoes and chiles and gently stir the ingredients. Add the wine to the skillet and heat until the mixture comes to the boiling point. Lower the heat and gradually stir in the cheese, using a fork to blend. Do not allow the hot mixture to boil. When all the ingredients are thoroughly blended, place in a chafing dish, keeping the chafing dish temperature low enough to prevent the cheese mixture from boiling or burning. Serve the Chile con Queso as a dip with tortilla chips.

CALIFORNIA QUESADILLAS

SERVES 8–10

12 flour tortillas
¼ pound butter
2–3 tablespoons salt
1 cup grated Monterey Jack
  cheese
1 cup grated mozzarella cheese
1 15-ounce jar sweet cherry
  peppers, seeded and chopped

Spread tortillas with softened butter on both sides. Place on a clean counter top and salt individual tortillas on one side. Every 30 minutes, turn the tortillas over and salt the upturned side, rubbing a little more butter into the tortilla at the same time. Continue turning, buttering, and salting every 30 minutes for 3 hours. When ready to serve, spread the cheeses and sweet cherry peppers on top of each of the butter-covered tortillas, making an open-faced sandwich. Place on an ungreased cookie sheet and broil for about 5–6 minutes. Broiler should be 4–5 inches from the tortillas. Remove from oven, cut into pie-shaped wedges, and serve at once.

NOTE: This is an excellent appetizer for a Mexican dinner.

BAH WONG'S TERIYAKI STRIPS

SERVES 8–10

½ cup sugar
1 cup soy sauce
1 clove garlic, crushed
½-inch piece of fresh ginger,
  peeled and crushed
¼ cup sherry
2 tablespoons finely minced
  onion
2 pounds top sirloin steaks,
  very thinly sliced
2 cups pineapple chunks,
  drained

In a small saucepan combine the sugar, soy sauce, garlic, ginger, sherry, and onion. Bring to a boil over moderate heat. Remove from the heat and strain the liquid into a medium-sized bowl. Place the thinly sliced sirloin pieces and pineapple chunks into the marinade. Stir well to cover the meat thoroughly. Marinate for approximately 30 minutes, but no longer. Thread 1 or 2 meat pieces, alternating with the pineapple chunks, onto bamboo skewers. Cover and refrigerate if necessary, up to 2 hours. When ready to serve, have guests barbecue the strips over hot coals in a miniature hibachi for 2–3 minutes, depending on preference, turning frequently to prevent burning.

NOTE: The meat will be easier to slice if it is frozen first. Allow the meat to thaw before placing in the marinade.

HOT CRAB MEAT COCKTAIL

SERVES 30

24 ounces cream cheese,
  softened to room temperature
½ cup mayonnaise, preferably
  homemade (*see Index*)
⅔ cup California dry white wine
¼ teaspoon garlic salt
2 teaspoons prepared mustard
2 teaspoons confectioners'
  sugar
1 teaspoon onion juice
Dash seasoned salt
1¼ pounds fresh crab meat
Assorted crackers or toasted
  rounds of rye bread

Place the cream cheese, mayonnaise, and wine in a blender and blend for 45 seconds at medium speed. Add the garlic salt, mustard, sugar, onion juice, and seasoned salt to the blended ingredients and blend for an additional 45 seconds. Place the blended ingredients in a double boiler and heat over simmering water, stirring occasionally. Gently add the crab meat to the ingredients in the double boiler. When the ingredients are heated thoroughly, place in a chafing dish and serve immediately with an assortment of crackers or toasted rye bread rounds.

CHEESE CHILE APPETIZER

SERVES 8–10

½ cup butter
10 eggs
½ cup flour
1 teaspoon baking powder
Dash salt
8 ounces green chiles, chopped
1 pint cottage cheese, small
  curd
1 pound Monterey Jack cheese,
  grated

Melt the butter over low heat in a 13 × 9 × 2-inch pan. In a large bowl lightly beat the eggs. Add the flour, baking powder, and salt and blend until well mixed. Add the melted butter from the baking pan, the chiles, cottage cheese, and jack cheese. Mix until just blended. Pour the cheese mixture into the pan in which the butter was melted. Bake for 15 minutes in a preheated 400° oven, reduce the temperature to 350°, and bake for 45–55 minutes longer or until firm in the center. Cool slightly and cut into bite-sized squares. Serve warm on a heated platter.

JOSEPHINAS

SERVES 10–12

4 ounces green chiles, diced
¼ pound butter, softened to
  room temperature
1 cup mayonnaise, preferably
  homemade (*see Index*)
½ pound Monterey Jack cheese,
  grated
2 loaves French bread, small
  diameter
Parsley sprigs

In a medium-sized bowl mix the chiles, butter, mayonnaise, and cheese until well blended. Slice the French bread into thin slices and spread amply with the cheese mixture, making sure to completely cover the bread. Place the bread slices on an ungreased cookie sheet in a preheated broiler and broil about 5–10 minutes until the spread is bubbly. Serve on a large serving plate garnished with parsley sprigs.

CHICKEN BROTH

5 pounds stewing chicken
Chicken parts (1 of each),
   such as feet, backs, necks,
   giblets (optional)
3 quarts cold water
2 leeks
1 bay leaf
2 tablespoons chopped
   fresh parsley
2 stalks celery, including leaves,
   cut in 1-inch pieces
1 teaspoon dried thyme
2 whole cloves
1 medium carrot, sliced
1 large onion, quartered
6 peppercorns, slightly crushed
2 teaspoons salt

Place the chicken and the parts in an 8-quart kettle and add the cold water. Bring the mixture to a boil over medium heat. Skim the scum from the surface with a spoon. Add the remaining ingredients, cover the kettle loosely, and reduce the heat to simmer. Simmer the mixture for 2½–3 hours. Remove all the chicken pieces with a slotted spoon and discard. Strain the broth through a fine sieve or a piece of cheesecloth. Refrigerate the broth overnight or until cool. Remove the hardened fat from the surface. The broth may then be refrigerated for an indefinite length of time but must be brought to a boil every 3–4 days to keep it from spoiling. The broth may also be bottled immediately and frozen indefinitely.

CHILLED AVOCADO SOUP

3 ripe avocados, mashed
4 cups chicken broth
¼ cup fresh lemon juice
¼ teaspoon salt
¼ teaspoon white pepper
½ teaspoon minced onion
   (optional)
⅛ teaspoon cayenne pepper
2–3 tablespoons white dry
   sherry, or as needed
1 cup sour cream
8 slices bacon, cooked and
   crumbled
½ cup minced fresh chives

Mix avocados, chicken broth, lemon juice, salt, white pepper, onion, pepper, and sherry in a blender. Blend the mixture at low speed until smooth. Add the sour cream, ¼ cup at a time, until well blended. Chill for at least 2 hours. Serve in chilled soup cups garnished with bacon and chives.

NOTE: The onion taste gets stronger with time. The recipe must be made in a blender in 2 batches, as the entire recipe is too large to fill a blender container.

COLD CUCUMBER SOUP

SERVES 8

4 large cucumbers
4 scallions, whites only, sliced
2 tablespoons butter
1 tablespoon salad oil
2 tablespoons flour
2½ cups chicken broth
¼ cup milk
1½ tablespoons fresh lemon
  juice, strained
2 teaspoons dried dill weed
¼ teaspoon salt or to taste
¼ teaspoon white pepper
2 cups sour cream
¼ cup chopped fresh mint

Peel, seed, and slice the cucumbers. In a heavy 10–12-inch skillet sauté the cucumbers and scallions in the heated butter and oil for about 10 minutes, stirring occasionally. Stir in the flour and cook slowly for 3–4 minutes, stirring frequently. In a 1–2-quart saucepan heat the chicken broth and milk and stir this slowly into the cucumber mixture. Add the strained lemon juice, dill weed, salt, and pepper. Simmer gently, stirring, for about 10 minutes, until thickened. Put in blender (it will take 2 batches) until smooth. Put the soup into a large mixing bowl. Cool completely. Add sour cream, taste for seasoning, cover, and refrigerate for at least 6 hours. Serve in chilled soup bowls garnished with chopped fresh mint.

COLD TOMATO SOUP

SERVES 8

2½ pounds ripe tomatoes
1 cup sliced yellow onion
2 tablespoons butter
2 tablespoons oil
2 small cloves garlic, crushed
½ cup chopped celery
½ cup chopped scallions
  (whites only)
1½ teaspoons sugar
3 tablespoons flour
½ teaspoon dried basil
½ teaspoon salt
Freshly ground pepper to
  taste
3¾ cups chicken broth
¼ cup minced fresh parsley

Peel, remove the seeds from, and slice the tomatoes. Set aside. In a heavy Dutch oven sauté the onion in butter and oil over low-moderate heat until golden, about 8–10 minutes. Add the tomatoes, garlic, celery, and scallions. Sauté for another 10 minutes, stirring occasionally. Stir in the sugar, flour, basil, salt, and pepper and cook for another 4–5 minutes. Add the broth and simmer for 20 minutes, stirring occasionally. Cool and purée in a blender. Chill at least 4 hours or overnight. Serve in chilled soup bowls garnished with minced parsley.

COLD GREEN BEAN SOUP

6 cups chicken broth
1 teaspoon dried rosemary
4 cups green beans, washed, trimmed, and chopped into 2-inch pieces
1 onion, quartered
6 lettuce leaves
1 tablespoon salt
3 tablespoons fresh lemon juice
½ cup sour cream

In a large saucepan bring 4 cups of the chicken broth and the rosemary to a boil. Add the green beans and boil for 4 minutes. Remove the saucepan from the heat, drain the chicken broth, and discard—or reserve for other cooking uses. Place the green beans in cold water to stop the cooking process.

Place 2 cups of the green beans into a blender and add 1 cup chicken broth, ½ the onion, and 3 lettuce leaves. Blend until the mixture is smooth and then pour the mixture into a large container. Repeat the procedure with the remaining 2 cups green beans, 1 cup chicken broth, ½ the onion, and 3 lettuce leaves. After puréeing until smooth pour the mixture into the container holding the other half of the puréed soup. Add the salt and lemon juice and stir the soup. Chill at least 4–6 hours. The recipe may be made 24 hours in advance. Serve in chilled soup cups, each garnished with a dollop of sour cream.

COLD GREEN PEA SOUP

2 cups dry green split peas
2 quarts chicken broth
2 stalks celery, coarsely chopped
1 cup coarsely chopped onion
1 carrot, coarsely chopped
⅛ teaspoon ground nutmeg
1 bay leaf
1¼ cup coarsely chopped fresh mint
1 teaspoon salt
Pinch white pepper
½–1 cup chilled light cream

Wash the peas thoroughly and discard any that are discolored. Bring the chicken broth to a boil in a 4-quart pan. Slowly drop the peas into the saucepan, keeping the broth boiling. Add the onion, celery, carrot, nutmeg, bay leaf, and 1 cup of the mint. Reduce the heat and simmer the stock, partially covered, for 1–1½ hours. Remove the bay leaf and discard. Purée the soup completely in a blender at medium speed. Mixture will have to be puréed in 2 batches. When completely puréed, add salt and pepper. Stir in the cream, thinning the soup as desired. Refrigerate the soup for at least 4 hours. Serve in chilled soup cups garnished with the remaining ¼ cup mint.

COLD ZUCCHINI SOUP

SERVES 6–8

1¼ pounds zucchini, unskinned
1 onion, finely minced
4 tablespoons butter
3½ cups chicken stock or broth
Salt to taste
Dash nutmeg
½ cup half-and-half
Skin of 1 zucchini, grated

Wash and thinly slice the zucchini. In a 12-inch skillet over moderate heat sauté the zucchini and onion in butter until soft, about 5 minutes. Stir frequently. Add the chicken stock and salt. Reduce the heat slightly and cook for 15 minutes, until the vegetables are tender. Add nutmeg. Combine the half-and-half with ⅓ of the vegetables in a blender and blend for 1–2 minutes or until smooth. Add the rest of the vegetables and blend again. Cool the soup thoroughly. Cover. Chill in the refrigerator for 4–6 hours. Serve cold, garnished with a sprinkle of grated zucchini skin.

JELLIED MUSHROOM SOUP

SERVES 4–6

4 cups chicken broth
1 pound fresh mushrooms, stemmed and chopped
2 tablespoons gelatin
¼ cup cold water
2 tablespoons sherry
½ teaspoon salt
Dash freshly ground pepper
1 lemon, thinly sliced
½ cup sour cream
Chopped scallions

Simmer the broth and mushrooms together in a 3-quart saucepan for 30 minutes. Dissolve the gelatin in the water. Stir the dissolved gelatin into the hot soup. Add the sherry, salt, and pepper to the hot mixture. Cool and chill the soup in the refrigerator for about 4 hours. Serve in chilled soup cups garnished with a thin slice of lemon, a dollop of sour cream, and chopped scallions.

CALIFORNIA CONSOMMÉ

SERVES 6–8

8 cups chicken broth
2 avocados, peeled and thinly sliced
2 lemons, thinly sliced
8 tablespoons sherry
½ cup chopped fresh parsley

Heat the chicken broth to near boiling in a medium-sized saucepan. Place the thin slices of avocado (about ¼ of an avocado per person) and 2–3 lemon slices in the bottom of each soup bowl. Ladle the hot chicken broth over the avocados and lemons. Add 1 tablespoon of sherry to each serving and sprinkle parsley on the top.

NOTE: This is a very light, especially attractive first-course soup that won't detract from the rest of the meal.

SENEGALESE SOUP

5 cups chicken broth
4 egg yolks
2 cups heavy cream
2 teaspoons curry powder
Dash cayenne pepper
¼ teaspoon lemon juice
Salt
1 cup finely chopped cooked
   chicken breast
3–4 tablespoons minced fresh
   parsley

Heat the chicken broth in the top of a double boiler to the scalding point. Mix the egg yolks, cream, curry powder, cayenne, and lemon juice in a medium-sized bowl. Stir ½ cup of the hot broth into the egg yolk mixture and pour the mixture slowly into the hot broth. Cook, stirring constantly, over simmering water until the soup thickens slightly. Taste; add up to 1 teaspoon salt if necessary. Remove the double boiler from the heat; cool. Refrigerate 3–4 hours. When ready to serve, stir in the chicken. Serve in chilled soup cups garnished with fresh parsley. May be made 24 hours ahead.

CRAB BISQUE

7 tablespoons butter
6 tablespoons chopped onion
4 tablespoons minced celery
2 tablespoons minced shallot
5 tablespoons flour
3 cups light cream
2 cups chicken stock
½ cup dry white wine or
   vermouth
½ teaspoon white pepper
1½ teaspoons salt
3 drops Tabasco sauce
1 pound crab meat, minced
   (shrimp or lobster may be
   substituted)
½ cup brandy
Paprika
½ cup minced chives

In a heavy 5-quart saucepan with a cover, melt 5 tablespoons of the butter and sauté the onion, celery, and shallot for 5 minutes over moderate heat. Sprinkle the flour over the vegetables and cook and stir for another 3 minutes. Gradually add the cream, chicken stock, and wine and stir the bisque until it is smooth and slightly thickened. Season with salt, pepper, and Tabasco sauce. Reduce heat to simmer.

In a medium-sized skillet melt 2 tablespoons butter, add the crab, and cook rapidly over medium-high heat until it is warmed through, about 5 minutes. In a small pan heat the brandy until very warm to the touch and pour it over the crab in the skillet. Ignite the brandy and continue cooking the crab over moderate heat until the fire burns out. Combine the crab and its juices with the cream sauce. Cover the saucepan and simmer the bisque for 10 minutes. Purée the soup in an electric blender on low speed for 3–4 minutes or until smooth. Ladle the soup into individual soup bowls and garnish each serving with a sprinkle of paprika and 1 tablespoon of the minced chives. Both are a very pleasing contrast to the white soup.

LEMON SOUP

6 cups chicken stock
1 teaspoon minced fresh
  parsley
½ teaspoon dried or 1 teaspoon
  chopped fresh herbs—any
  or all of the following:
  chervil, tarragon, chives
1½ teaspoons grated lemon rind
4 eggs
6 tablespoons fresh lemon juice
1½ teaspoons brandy
4–8 tablespoons cooked rice
  or other small pasta
Salt to taste
¼ cup minced fresh mint

In a 6–8 quart Dutch oven bring the stock, parsley, herbs, and lemon rind to a boil over high heat. Reduce the heat, cover, and simmer the soup for 15 minutes. Remove the pan from the heat.

Meanwhile, in a large mixing bowl beat together the eggs, lemon juice, and brandy. Slowly pour in several cups of the stock mixture, stirring constantly (the broth is added to the egg mixture very slowly to keep the eggs from curdling). Return this mixture very slowly to the remaining stock mixture, off of the heat, still stirring constantly. Add the cooked rice or pasta, place the pot over low heat, and stir constantly for 3–5 minutes or until the soup thickens enough to lightly coat the back of the spoon (like a thin pudding). Do not let the soup come to a boil or the eggs will curdle. Add salt and serve at once, making sure that there is rice or pasta in each serving. Garnish with freshly minced mint leaves. The soup may also be made ahead and reheated over very low heat, again taking care not to let it boil.

WHITE GAZPACHO

3 medium cucumbers
1 clove garlic
3 cups chicken broth
2 cups sour cream
1 cup yogurt
3 tablespoons white vinegar
2 teaspoons salt
2 teaspoons pepper
4 medium tomatoes, peeled
  and chopped
½ cup chopped scallions,
  including tops
½ cup chopped fresh parsley
¼ cup toasted almonds or
  sunflower seeds

Peel and dice the cucumbers. Place in a blender with the garlic and a small amount of the chicken broth. Purée the mixture. Add the remaining broth and thoroughly blend the ingredients. Mix the sour cream and yogurt in a medium-sized bowl and thin with about ⅓ of the cucumber mixture. Add the remaining cucumber mixture to the bowl. Season with the vinegar, salt, and pepper. Chill for 6–8 hours. Serve in large chilled bowls surrounded by the tomatoes, scallions, parsley, and almonds or sunflower seeds in smaller bowls.

CHINESE CUCUMBER SOUP

1 tablespoon dry sherry
2 tablespoons soy sauce
1 tablespoon cornstarch
½ pound lean pork, finely
 shredded
2 tablespoons oil
6 cups chicken broth
2 scallions, including tops, sliced
1 medium cucumber, peeled
 and diced
½ teaspoon monosodium
 glutamate
1½ teaspoons salt
¼ teaspoon white pepper
1 egg

In a small mixing bowl combine the sherry, soy sauce, and cornstarch. Mix thoroughly and add the pork, stirring well to coat the meat evenly. In a 6–8-quart Dutch oven heat the oil over moderate heat and quickly brown the pork mixture, about 5–7 minutes. Add the chicken broth, reduce the heat, and simmer for 10–12 minutes. Add the scallions, cucumber, monosodium glutamate, salt, and pepper. Taste for seasoning and correct if necessary. Simmer the soup for 5 minutes more, raise the heat, and bring the soup to a fast boil.

Meanwhile, in a small mixing bowl beat the egg well and set aside. Remove the soup pot from the heat and add the egg, stirring constantly. The egg will turn into cooked shreds. Ladle into soup bowls and serve immediately.

NOTE: This is an excellent first course for a Chinese dinner.

CHEESE SOUP

6 tablespoons butter
¾ cup finely minced onion
¾ cup peeled and finely minced
 carrot
½ cup finely minced celery
4 tablespoons flour
½ teaspoon salt
⅛ teaspoon white pepper
½ teaspoon paprika
Pinch cayenne pepper
4½ cups chicken broth
1 cup heavy cream
2 tablespoons dry sherry
3 cups sharp Cheddar cheese,
 grated and packed firmly
 when measured
¼ cup chopped fresh parsley or
 minced fresh dill weed

In a 3–4-quart saucepan over moderate heat melt the butter and sauté the onion, carrot, and celery for 8–10 minutes, stirring often. Sprinkle in the flour and all the seasonings, blending well. Gradually add the chicken broth, stirring constantly, until the broth has thickened and is smooth. Reduce the heat to simmer and add the cream, sherry, and grated cheese. Stir constantly until the cheese has melted. Correct the seasonings if necessary. Serve at once garnished with parsley or dill as a nice contrast in color.

CRAB VICHYSSOISE

1 cup sliced leeks (whites only)
1 onion, diced
½ cup chopped fresh parsley
3 tablespoons butter
1½ pounds potatoes, peeled
  and cubed
2 cups chicken broth
1 bay leaf
Dash monosodium glutamate
½ teaspoon salt or to taste
¼ teaspoon white pepper or to
  taste
2 cups flaked crab meat
2 cups light cream
Chopped chives

In a 3–4-quart saucepan cook the leeks, onion, and parsley in butter over moderate heat for 5 minutes or until tender, stirring frequently. Add the potatoes, broth, bay leaf, and monosodium glutamate and simmer uncovered over low heat until the potatoes are tender, approximately 30–40 minutes. Press soup and the vegetables through sieve or purée in a blender for 1–2 minutes until smooth. Add salt and pepper and taste for seasoning. Place the soup in a 3-quart bowl and cool thoroughly. Carefully remove any shell or cartilage from the crab meat. Gently stir the crab and cream into the soup. Cover and chill thoroughly in the refrigerator for 4–6 hours. Serve in chilled soup bowls garnished with chives.

HAM AND CHEESE CHOWDER

2 medium potatoes, pared and
  diced in ½-inch cubes
3 tablespoons butter
1 cup finely chopped onion
3 tablespoons flour
⅛ teaspoon pepper
3 cups milk
1½ cups chopped cooked ham
1½ cups grated Cheddar cheese
½ cup Croutons I (*see Index*) or
  chopped fresh parsley

Bring ½ cup water to a boil in a small saucepan and add the cubed potatoes. Reduce heat and simmer the potatoes until tender, about 10 minutes. Drain the potatoes, reserving the liquid.

Melt the butter in a large saucepan. Add the onion and cook over moderate heat for 5–7 minutes or until the onion is tender but not browned. Blend in the flour and cook, stirring, for 2 minutes. Add the pepper.

Add enough water to the reserved liquid from the potatoes to make 1 cup. Add both the potato water and the milk to the onion mixture. Bring to a boil over high heat, stirring constantly. Reduce the heat to simmer and add the cooked potatoes, chopped ham, and grated cheese. Stir until the cheese melts, approximately 5 minutes. Serve in deep soup bowls and garnish each serving with croutons or parsley.

NOTE: This hearty soup, served with a salad and freshly baked rolls, would make a complete meal.

SPLIT PEA WITH HAM SOUP

2 cups split peas
¼ cup olive oil
½ cup grated carrots
1 cup finely chopped onion
1 clove garlic, minced
½ cup diced celery
¼ cup fresh minced parsley
2½ teaspoons salt
½ teaspoon freshly ground
    pepper
Pinch dried basil
1 bay leaf
1 cup milk
1 cup minced cooked ham

Wash the split peas and soak them for 1 hour in warm water. Drain the water from the peas. Bring 2½ quarts of water to a boil in an 8-quart kettle and add the split peas. Simmer over low heat for 2½ hours, stirring occasionally. Heat the olive oil in a large skillet and sauté the carrots, onion, garlic, and celery for 10 minutes over moderate heat. Add the vegetable mixture to the split peas along with the parsley, salt, pepper, basil, and bay leaf. Simmer the mixture over low heat for 30 minutes longer, stirring occasionally.

Remove the bay leaf and discard it. Purée the soup for 2–3 minutes in an electric blender. Return the mixture to the kettle, stir in the milk and ham, and gently reheat 10–15 minutes before serving.

NOTE: Served with bread fresh from the oven, this would be a very hearty meal.

GAZPACHO

8 large tomatoes, peeled
2 medium green peppers
1 bunch scallions, including
    tops
1 medium red onion
2 large cucumbers, peeled
2 tablespoons monosodium
    glutamate
4–5 large cloves garlic, crushed
¼ cup plus 1 tablespoon olive
    or salad oil
2 tablespoons salt
6 tablespoons wine or cider
    vinegar
3 large slices French bread,
    crumbled
1 teaspoon white pepper
¼ teaspoon paprika
2 cups tomato juice
4 cups water, or as needed

Mince all the vegetables into small pieces. Sprinkle the minced vegetables with the monosodium glutamate. The mixture may be held in the refrigerator at this point for 24 hours. Combine the garlic, olive or salad oil, salt, wine or cider vinegar, crumbled French bread, white pepper, and paprika in a deep bowl. Stir these ingredients. Add the minced vegetables to the sauce. Combine the tomato juice and water in a small bowl. Mix the tomato juice and water and pour over the sauce and minced vegetables. Refrigerate. (Once the tomato juice has been added, serve within 4–6 hours.) Serve in chilled soup cups or tall chilled glasses.

BEEF BROTH OR STOCK

5 pounds beef shin or soup
 meat with bones
1–2 pounds marrow bones,
 cracked
3 quarts cold water
2 stalks celery, including
 leaves, diced
2 onions, quartered
2 carrots, sliced
1 turnip, peeled and
 quartered
1 or 2 leeks
2 cloves garlic, peeled
8 peppercorns, slightly crushed
¼ teaspoon dried thyme
1 bay leaf
2 whole cloves
1 tablespoon chopped fresh
 parsley
1 tablespoon salt

Preheat oven to 450°.

Remove any meat from the shin bones and cut into 1-inch cubes. Crack the bones with a hammer or have the butcher cut them into 2–3-inch lengths. Place the bones and meat in a shallow pan in the preheated oven. Roast for 30 minutes. Turn all the pieces and roast for 30 minutes more or until all the pieces are well browned. Browning the meat first gives the stock a rich brown color. Place all the meat and bones in an 8-quart kettle and add the water. Bring to a boil over medium heat, occasionally skimming off the fat that forms. Add the remaining ingredients and cover the kettle loosely, adding more water if necessary to cover the ingredients. Reduce the heat and simmer the mixture for 2½–3 hours, occasionally skimming the fat from the surface. Remove the bones and meat with a slotted spoon and discard them. Strain the rest of the broth through a fine sieve or cheesecloth. Refrigerate the broth overnight or until cool, and then remove the hardened fat from the surface. The broth may then be refrigerated for an indefinite length of time, but it must be brought to a boil every 3–4 days to keep it from spoiling. The broth may also be bottled immediately and frozen indefinitely.

FRESH TOMATO DILL SOUP

2 tablespoons salad oil
1 large onion, thinly sliced
3 pounds tomatoes, peeled,
 seeded, cored, and sliced
3 tablespoons tomato paste
1¾ teaspoons dried dill weed
3½ cups beef broth
4 teaspoons sugar
¾ teaspoon salt

Heat the salad oil over moderate heat in a heavy 5-quart kettle with a cover. Add the sliced onion and cook 5–7 minutes or until it is limp but not brown. Stir in the tomatoes, tomato paste, and dill weed. Bring to the boiling point over moderate heat, stirring often to break up the tomatoes. Reduce heat, cover the kettle, and simmer the mixture for 15 minutes. Purée the soup in small portions in an electric blender until smooth,

¼ teaspoon pepper
1 tablespoon dry white wine
Dash Tabasco sauce
Croutons I (*see Index*)

2–3 minutes. This much may be done early in the day and held in the refrigerator.

To serve, combine the tomato mixture with the beef broth, sugar, salt, pepper, white wine, and Tabasco in the kettle. Bring the soup to simmering and serve hot. Garnish with freshly toasted croutons.

MINESTRONE

SERVES 8–10

1 cup dried split peas
1 cup dried lima beans
1 cup barley
12 cups beef stock
2–3 cloves garlic, crushed
6 tomatoes, peeled and chopped
½ cup chopped fresh parsley
2 tablespoons tomato paste
8 strips bacon or ½ pound salt
   pork, diced
3 onions, chopped
1 cup chopped celery,
   including leaves
1 leek, white part only, minced
1 tablespoon dried basil
1 tablespoon salt
¼ teaspoon pepper
2 zucchini, sliced
2 carrots, sliced
3 stalks celery, sliced
⅓ bunch spinach, chopped
1 cup red wine
⅔ cup small macaroni or
   broken spaghetti
½ head cabbage, shredded
½ pound Parmesan cheese,
   freshly grated

Place the split peas and the lima beans in a large kettle and cover with water to soak overnight. The next day pour off the water, reserving the dried beans. Place the beans in an 8-quart Dutch oven and add the barley, beef stock, garlic, tomatoes, parsley, and tomato paste. Set aside.

In a small skillet fry the bacon or salt pork until crisp. Remove the bacon from the skillet with a slotted spoon and set aside on paper toweling to drain, reserving the bacon fat. Break the bacon into bite-sized pieces. In the same skillet, using the reserved bacon fat, sauté the onion, celery, and leek over low to moderate heat for 5–7 minutes or until limp.

Remove the vegetables from the skillet with a slotted spoon, drain well, and add to the Dutch oven containing the beans. Add the bacon to this pot, as well as the basil, salt, and pepper. Cover the pot, set over low heat, and simmer for 1–2 hours. Add the zucchini, carrots, celery, and spinach to the soup and continue simmering for an additional 45 minutes. Add the wine, pasta, and shredded cabbage and let the minestrone simmer for 3–5 more hours. This much can be done ahead of time.

When ready to serve the soup, bring back to serving temperature over moderate heat, ladle into large soup bowls, and garnish each serving with the cheese.

EGGPLANT SUPPER SOUP

2 tablespoons olive oil
2 tablespoons butter
1 medium onion, chopped
1 pound ground beef
1 medium eggplant, peeled and diced
1 clove garlic, crushed
1 cup chopped carrot
1 cup diced celery
6–8 tomatoes, peeled and diced
3½ cups beef broth
¼ teaspoon ground nutmeg
1 teaspoon sugar
1 teaspoon salt
¼ teaspoon pepper
¼ cup barley or macaroni
2 tablespoons minced fresh parsley
2 cups grated sharp Cheddar cheese

Melt the oil and butter in a 6–8-quart Dutch oven, add the onions, and sauté them for 5–7 minutes or until lightly browned. Add the meat and cook, stirring to break up with a fork, until the meat is browned, 8–10 minutes. Drain excess fat from the pan. Add the eggplant, garlic, carrot, celery, tomatoes, broth, nutmeg, sugar, salt, and pepper. Cover, reduce the heat, and simmer the soup 45 minutes. Add the barley and parsley and simmer 10 minutes more or until the barley is cooked. Ladle the soup into large soup bowls, cover the top with the grated cheese, and serve piping hot with a green salad and freshly baked biscuits.

MUSHROOM SOUP

¼ cup butter
1 pound fresh mushrooms, sliced
3 tablespoons fresh lemon juice
8 teaspoons powdered beef stock base
2½ cups boiling water
1½ cups sour cream
¾ cup chopped fresh parsley

Melt the butter over low heat in a 2-quart saucepan. Add the sliced mushrooms and lemon juice and sauté for 8–10 minutes or until tender, stirring frequently (the juice the mushrooms exude during this time will enhance the flavor of the soup).

In a separate bowl combine the beef stock base and water and mix well. Add the liquid to the mushrooms, mixing well to blend. Remove the pan from the heat and let cool about 10 minutes. Slowly blend in the sour cream, stirring to mix thoroughly. This much can be done 2–3 days in advance and the soup may then be held in the refrigerator, tightly covered.

Shortly before serving the soup, return the pan to low heat, stirring until hot enough to serve.

Do not let the soup come to the boil or the sour cream will separate. Fold the parsley into the soup and ladle into small soup bowls.

NOTE: This is a very tasty soup, an excellent first course if served in small portions. As a main course, this amount would serve 4.

GERMAN OXTAIL SOUP

SERVES 6–8

1 pound oxtails
6 tablespoons butter
½ cup diced carrots
½ cup peeled and diced potatoes
½ cup peeled and diced turnip
¼ cup diced celery
2 quarts water
½ pound fresh mushrooms, sliced
1 bay leaf
⅛ teaspoon dried thyme
4–5 whole peppercorns
½ cup pearl barley
1 small onion, minced
3 tablespoons flour
Dash paprika
Salt and pepper to taste

Have the butcher cut the oxtails into 2-inch lengths. Melt 3 tablespoons butter over moderate heat in an 8-quart kettle. Add the oxtails, carrots, potatoes, turnips, and celery. Cook, stirring occasionally, until the oxtails are browned, about 15–20 minutes. Add the water, mushrooms, bay leaf, thyme, and peppercorns. Cover, bring to a boil over high heat, reduce the heat, and simmer the soup for 2 hours. Remove the oxtail pieces, trim off the meat, discard the bones, and return the meat to the soup kettle. Add the barley and cook covered 45 minutes more or until the barley is tender.

In a small skillet melt 3 tablespoons butter and cook the onion over moderate heat 5–7 minutes or until golden. Blend in the flour, cook, and stir until lightly browned, 3–5 minutes. Blend a small amount of the soup into the flour mixture, stir to blend well, and add to the soup. Cook, stir to blend well, and bring to a boil over high heat. Remove from the heat, stir in the paprika, salt, and pepper. Correct the seasonings if necessary and serve in large heated soup bowls.

NOTE: This is a very rich vegetable soup to be served with a light green salad and a dry red wine.

WINTER VEGETABLE BEEF SOUP

SERVES 6–8

2 tablespoons butter

3 onions, finely chopped

1½ pounds lean ground beef
   or lean stewing beef

1 clove garlic crushed

3 cups beef stock

2 (1-pound-12-ounce) cans
   Italian-style tomatoes

1 cup peeled and diced
   potatoes

1 cup diced celery

1 cup peeled and diced carrots

1 cup green beans, cut in
   1-inch lengths

1½ cups dry red wine

½ teaspoon dried basil

2 tablespoons fresh chopped
   parsley

¼ teaspoon dried thyme

2 teaspoons salt

¼ teaspoon pepper

In an 8-quart kettle melt the butter and cook the onions over moderate heat until they are tender and golden, about 5–7 minutes. Stir in the ground beef, separating the meat with a fork, add garlic and cook, over moderate heat, until the meat has browned. Add the remaining ingredients. Bring the soup to a boil over high heat, reduce the heat, and simmer the soup covered for 1½ hours.

NOTE: This hearty soup freezes nicely. It is better if it is made a day or two before it is served. This soup stretches easily to feed extra guests. Add carrots, potatoes, or other vegetables to the soup kettle, cover with additional stock, and simmer until the vegetables are tender.

ITALIAN SAUSAGE SOUP

SERVES 8–12

1½ pounds Italian sausage, medium spice, cut in ¼-inch slices

2 cloves garlic, minced

2 onions, chopped

2 pounds tomatoes, peeled and
   cored

1½ cups dry red wine

5 cups beef stock

½ teaspoon dried basil

¼ teaspoon dried oregano

3 tablespoons chopped fresh
   parsley

1 medium green pepper,
   seeded and chopped

2 medium zucchini, sliced
   ¼-inch thick

In a 5-quart Dutch oven cook the sausage over medium heat until lightly browned, 7–10 minutes. Remove the sausage with a slotted spoon to a plate. Drain all but 3 tablespoons of the fat from the kettle. Add the garlic and the onions to the same kettle and sauté for 2–3 minutes or until transparent. Add the slightly cooked sausage and cook another 2–3 minutes, stirring constantly. Add the tomatoes, stirring to break them apart. Add the wine, stock, basil, and oregano and simmer uncovered for 30 minutes. (At this point, you may refrigerate the soup.) Skim the excess fat from the top of the soup. Reheat the soup before proceeding, if necessary. Add the parsley, green pepper, zucchini, and noodles. Simmer covered for 25 minutes or until the noodles are al

2 cups bow-tie noodles
Salt and pepper to taste
½ cup freshly grated
   Parmesan cheese

dente. Serve in deep soup bowls, passing the Parmesan in a separate bowl.

ITALIAN VEGETABLE CHOWDER

SERVES 6–8

½ pound zucchini, halved
   lengthwise and thinly sliced
2 onions, halved and thinly
   sliced
2 cups tomatoes, peeled,
   seeded, and drained (about
   4 medium tomatoes)
1 pound canned garbanzo
   beans, drained
4 tablespoons butter
2 cups dry white wine
2 teaspoons minced garlic
5 tablespoons finely chopped
   fresh parsley
1 teaspoon dried basil
1 bay leaf
¼ teaspoon sage
2 teaspoons salt
¼ teaspoon pepper or to taste
1 cup grated Monterey Jack
   cheese, firmly packed
1 cup freshly grated Romano
   cheese
1 cup heavy cream
1½ cups milk

In a heavy 4–5-quart casserole place the zucchini, onions, tomatoes, beans, butter, wine, garlic, 3 tablespoons parsley, herbs, salt, and pepper. Stir well to mix together thoroughly. Cover the casserole and bake in a preheated 400° oven for 30 minutes. Remove from the oven and stir well to mix all the ingredients. Replace the cover and return to the oven for another 30 minutes. Remove from the oven and thoroughly stir in the cheeses, cream, and milk. Reduce oven heat to 350° and return the casserole, covered, for 20 minutes. Remove from the oven and stir the soup well. The cheese does not melt completely. Serve at once with remaining parsley sprinkled on the top. This recipe makes about 2 quarts of a rich, hearty dinner soup.

FRENCH ONION SOUP

3 pounds beef knuckles, cracked

2 onions, quartered

2 carrots, cut in chunks

2 stalks celery, including leaves

4 quarts water

1 leek, including top, chopped

3 whole cloves

3 bay leaves

3 teaspoons salt

1 tablespoon oil

12 tablespoons butter

4 or 5 onions, thinly sliced,
to make 6–7 cups

¼ teaspoon sugar

3 tablespoons flour

¾ cup dry white wine or
vermouth

8–10 slices French bread, cut
¾ inch thick

1½ cups grated Swiss cheese

½ cup freshly grated Parmesan
cheese

4 tablespoons cognac or other
brandy

Salt and pepper to taste

In a large roasting pan place the beef bones, the quartered onions (not the sliced), carrots, and celery. Place the pan in a preheated 450° oven for 30–40 minutes or until the meat is browned. Turn the meat and vegetables occasionally to brown evenly. Remove the bones and vegetables to an 8-quart Dutch oven or soup pot. Drain the fat from the roasting pan. Add 1 cup water and, over a burner on low heat, stir and scrape up all of the browning juices. Pour over the bones and the vegetables in the soup pot and add cold water to cover (4 quarts). Add the leek, cloves, bay leaves, and 2 teaspoons of the salt. Cover, bring to a boil over high heat, reduce the heat, and simmer the stock for 4–5 hours. Strain the liquid through a fine sieve or a piece of cheesecloth, discard the bones and vegetables, and return the broth to the kettle. Reduce the heat to a very low simmer.

Place the oil and 4 tablespoons of the butter in a heavy 4–5-quart saucepan. Add the sliced onions to the saucepan. Cook slowly over moderate heat, covered, for 15 minutes. Uncover and add the remaining 1 teaspoon salt and the sugar. Continue to cook uncovered for 30–40 minutes, stirring frequently, until the onions are an even golden brown. Sprinkle in the flour and simmer, stirring, for 3 minutes. Add the wine and stir until smooth. Add the onion mixture to the simmering soup stock, and simmer partially covered for 30–40 minutes.

Lightly butter the French bread on both sides and arrange the slices in a single layer on a cookie sheet. Place the cookie sheet in a preheated 325° oven for 15–20 minutes or until the bread is lightly browned. Turn the pieces and brown them lightly on the other side, another 15–20 minutes. Set aside to cool.

Before serving the soup, using a small bowl, mix the grated Swiss and the grated Parmesan together and set aside. Add the cognac and salt and pepper to the soup, stirring to mix well. Ladle the soup into crockery bowls, place a slice of toast on top of the soup, and sprinkle the toast with 2–3 tablespoons of the cheese mixture. Place the soup bowls directly under the broiler of the oven until the cheese melts and is bubbly. Serve immediately.

LAMB BONE BEAN SOUP

SERVES 8–10

¾ cup large white northern
  beans
¾ cup kidney beans
Leftover lamb roast bones or
  2 pounds lamb shanks
2 yellow onions, finely sliced
3 leeks, whites only, sliced
1 turnip, peeled and finely
  diced
½ cup shredded cabbage
3 large tomatoes, peeled, cored,
  and quartered
½ cup chopped red pepper
½ cup chopped green pepper
6 fresh mushrooms, sliced
6 cloves garlic, crushed
2 bay leaves
2 tablespoons chopped celery
  leaves
1 teaspoon summer savory
1 teaspoon salt
⅛ teaspoon pepper
1 cup red wine
8–10 cups water
2 tablespoons chopped fresh
  parsley
½ cup freshly grated Parmesan
  cheese

Place the white northern beans and the kidney beans in a large kettle and cover with water. Let the beans soak overnight. The next day, drain off the water and proceed as below.

Place the lamb bones, beans, vegetables, garlic, bay leaves, celery leaves, savory, salt, pepper, and wine in an 8-quart kettle with a cover. Add the water and bring to a boil over moderate heat. Skim the fat from the top of the soup with a spoon. Cover the kettle, reduce the heat, and simmer gently for 4–6 hours, occasionally skimming the fat that continues to form. Add more water to prevent scorching if the mixture becomes too thick. To serve, remove the lamb bones and the bay leaves with a slotted spoon and discard. Taste the soup and correct the seasoning if necessary. Ladle the soup into large heated soup bowls and garnish each serving with some of the parsley and the cheese.

ALBONDIGAS SOUP

1½ pounds ground beef
1 cup fresh bread crumbs
1 egg, beaten
3 tablespoons chopped fresh
  parsley
6 cloves garlic
3 tablespoons minced fresh
  mint
3 teaspoons salt
½ cup flour
4–6 tablespoons olive oil
1 medium green pepper,
  seeded and diced
3 medium onions, diced
1 quart hot water
1½ cups red wine
2 No. 2½ cans tomatoes
1 tablespoon vinegar
1 tablespoon sugar
1 teaspoon dried oregano

In a large bowl combine the meat, broken into bits with a fork, bread crumbs, egg, parsley, 3 crushed cloves garlic, mint leaves, and 1½ teaspoons salt. Mix thoroughly with a fork or your hands. Form the meat mixture into balls about 2 inches in diameter. Roll each ball lightly in the flour and brown in the olive oil, in a large Dutch oven, over moderate heat, for about 7 minutes. Remove the meatballs and set aside.

Sauté the pepper, onions, and 3 crushed cloves garlic over moderate heat for 5–7 minutes in the drippings remaining in the Dutch oven. Add 1½ teaspoons salt and all the other ingredients and cook the soup over moderate heat for 20–30 minutes. Add the meatballs, cover the skillet, and simmer the soup for 1½ hours.

CREAM OF SPINACH SOUP

2 pounds fresh spinach,
  stemmed
3 tablespoons butter
2 tablespoons grated onion
3 tablespoons flour
2½ cups milk, scalded
½ teaspoon salt
⅛ teaspoon pepper
⅛ teaspoon ground nutmeg
Pinch cayenne pepper
2 egg yolks
¾ cup heavy cream
1 tablespoon finely chopped
  fresh parsley
1 tablespoon sweet butter

Wash the spinach thoroughly, drain, and place in a 3-4-quart saucepan without any extra water. Cook the spinach over low heat, covered, for 5 minutes. Turn the leaves over, again cover the pan, and cook the spinach for an additional 3–5 minutes or until wilted. Pour the spinach and its liquid into a blender container and blend, on low speed, for 5–10 seconds. Drain the spinach through a sieve, reserving the liquid. Melt the 3 tablespoons of butter in the same saucepan that was used to cook the spinach, add the onion, and sauté over low heat until the onion colors slightly, about 3 minutes, stirring frequently. Sprinkle the flour over the onions, blend well, and cook for 2–3 minutes. Add the scalded milk, blending thoroughly, and continue stirring until slightly thickened. Strain the soup through a fine sieve into a medium saucepan. Add the reserved spinach and liquid (add water if necessary to make ¼ cup) and add the salt, pepper, nutmeg, and cayenne. Simmer the soup over low heat, 2–3 minutes, stirring occasionally. Beat the egg yolks with the cream in a small bowl and add very slowly to the soup, stirring constantly to keep the egg from curdling. Stir in the parsley and sweet butter, stirring until the butter melts, and serve at once.

CIOPPINO (San Francisco Fish Stew) SERVES 6

¼ cup olive oil
2 tablespoons butter
2 onions, finely chopped
2 cloves garlic, finely chopped
20 fresh medium mushrooms
1 1-pound-12-ounce can
   Italian plum tomatoes with
   basil seasoning
1 6-ounce can tomato paste
½ cup chopped and seeded
   green pepper
1 teaspoon dried basil
½ teaspoon dried oregano
½ cup fresh lemon juice
2 cups dry red wine
1½–2 pounds fresh fish such
   as sea bass, red snapper, or
   halibut steak
½ pound scallops
24 raw shrimp, shelled and
   deveined
1 Dungeness crab, cracked
12 clams

In a 6-8–quart soup pot or Dutch oven heat the oil and butter over low-moderate heat. Add the onions and garlic and sauté for about 5 minutes or until tender, stirring frequently. Add the mushrooms and sauté for 4–5 more minutes. Add the tomatoes, tomato paste, green pepper, basil, oregano, lemon juice, and wine, stirring well to blend. Bring to a boil, reduce the heat, cover, and simmer at least 1 hour. Taste for seasoning and add more lemon juice if necessary. The tomato sauce can be prepared early in the day and reheated, as a longer simmering will produce a richer sauce.

About 25 minutes before serving, add the fish. Cook the stew for 20 minutes or until the fish flakes easily with a fork. Add the scallops, shrimp, and crab, still in its shell, and finally the clams. Stir all the shellfish in gently. Cover and simmer until the clams open, 5–10 minutes.

NOTE: This is delicious served with garlic bread and a dry red wine.

1 pound each halibut, red
   snapper, and scallops or
   3 pounds any whitefish in
   combination
12 tablespoons butter
1 pound small fresh mushrooms
4 tablespoons fresh lemon juice
2–3 cups fish stock or hot water
12 shallots, chopped
6 tablespoons cognac
2 cups chablis
2 small cloves garlic, crushed
¾ cup plus 2–3 tablespoons
   finely chopped fresh parsley
2 teaspoons salt
24 small white onions, peeled
4 tablespoons flour
4 egg yolks
⅔ cup light cream

Wash and dry the fish and cut into 1½-inch chunks. Place 4 tablespoons of the butter in a 10–12-inch heavy skillet. Sauté the halibut and snapper over moderate heat until lightly browned, about 5–7 minutes, stirring often. Reserve the scallops, which will be added later. Place 2 tablespoons butter in a 3–4-quart saucepan, add the mushrooms and lemon juice, and pour in enough hot fish stock to barely cover the mushrooms. Bring to a simmer over moderate heat and cook for 5 minutes. Stir in the browned halibut and red snapper and the shallots and set aside. Place 2 tablespoons butter in the skillet in which the fish was cooked and brown the scallops lightly over moderate heat for 3–5 minutes. Add the cognac, warm slightly, and ignite. Tilt the skillet to evenly spread the cognac. When the flame dies down, add the chablis. Stir and scrape in all the particles from the bottom of the pan. Add the scallop-wine mixture to the saucepan containing the other fish and the mushrooms. Stir in the garlic, ¾ cup parsley, and salt. Cover and cook over moderate heat for 5 minutes. Reduce heat and simmer for 10 more minutes.

Using a slotted spoon, transfer the mixture to a shallow 2–3-quart casserole. Cover with foil and keep warm. Add the peeled onions to the stock, cover, and cook for 20 minutes over moderate heat or until onions are soft. Transfer onions to the casserole. Make a *beurre manie* by blending the flour with the remaining 4 tablespoons butter in a small cup until it becomes a paste. Add to the stock in the saucepan a little at a time, stirring constantly with a whisk. Bring the stock to a boil and boil slowly for 5 minutes. Remove from heat. Place the egg yolks in a small bowl and beat them with the cream. Pour about ½ cup of the hot stock into the egg yolk mixture, beating constantly. Then slowly pour this back into the stock, beating constantly to keep the eggs from curdling. Return the sauce to the heat for a minute. Adjust the seasoning, adding salt and pepper if necessary.

Pour the sauce over the fish and mushrooms and serve at once, garnished with remaining chopped parsley.

NOTE: This fish is delicious accompanied by rice pilaf and a crisp green salad.

FISH CHOWDER

SERVES 8–10

2½–3 pounds whitefish (cod, halibut)

Bouquet garni: 4 sprigs parsley, ¼ teaspoon dried thyme, 2 bay leaves, 1 teaspoon salt, and 6 peppercorns

10 tablespoons butter

1 cup chopped onion

3 cups peeled and diced potatoes

¼ cup chopped celery

¼ cup chopped carrot

5 tablespoons flour

1 cup heavy cream

1½ cups whole milk

Salt and pepper to taste

⅓–½ cup dry sherry

4 tablespoons chopped fresh parsley

Paprika

Clean the fish and rinse well. Place the fish in a 4–5-quart soup kettle. Cover with cold water (5–6 cups), add the bouquet garni (tied in a piece of cheesecloth), and bring the soup to a boil over high heat. Reduce the heat and simmer the chowder for 45 minutes, covered. Strain the mixture through a colander into a 2–3-quart saucepan and reserve the fish stock. Carefully separate the fish meat from the bones and set the meat aside. Discard the bones and the bouquet garni. Melt 5 tablespoons of the butter in a 4–5-quart Dutch oven. Add the onions and sauté over low heat for 5 minutes. Add the potatoes, celery, and carrots and sauté for 10 more minutes, stirring occasionally. Cover and cook, still over low heat, for 20 more minutes, stirring occasionally. Add the rest of the butter, then add the flour and sauté another 4–5 minutes, stirring to blend well.

Heat the cream and the milk in a small saucepan and add to the sautéed vegetables. Stir and cook over low heat until thickened. Taste for seasoning adding salt and pepper if necessary. Heat the fish stock and add to the vegetable-cream mixture. Stir over low heat until the mixture is thickened and well blended, 10–15 minutes. Cover and simmer an additional 20 minutes over low heat or until the potatoes are tender. Add the sherry and chopped parsley. Gently stir in the fish meat. Taste for seasoning and correct if necessary. Serve at once in large soup bowls and sprinkle with paprika for a dash of color.

FISHERMAN'S WHARF BOUILLABAISSE   SERVES 6–8

3 tablespoons olive oil
3 onions, sliced
3 cloves garlic, crushed
1 leek, including top, sliced
4½ cups beef broth
1 teaspoon salt
¼ teaspoon black pepper
¼ teaspoon cayenne pepper
½ teaspoon (or less) saffron
1 bay leaf, crumbled
¾ teaspoon dried basil
¾ teaspoon dried marjoram
1 pound raw shrimp
1 pound haddock
8–12 small lobster tails in their shells
12–18 clams, scrubbed and fresh with shells
4 medium baking potatoes, peeled and cut in 1-inch chunks
⅓ cup dry red wine
¼ cup chopped fresh parsley
1 tomato, peeled and chopped

In an 8-quart Dutch oven heat the olive oil over moderate heat and add the onions, garlic, and leek. Sauté, stirring frequently, for 10 minutes or until limp but not browned. Add the broth, salt, pepper, cayenne, saffron, bay leaf, basil, and marjoram. Blend well. Cover the pot and cook over moderate heat 15–20 minutes or until lightly boiling.

Meanwhile, shell and devein the shrimp. Remove any bones from the haddock. Add the shrimp, haddock, lobster tails, clams, and potatoes to the stew. Stir lightly, replace the cover, and reduce the heat. Simmer for 20 minutes. Test to see if the potatoes are cooked. If not, simmer the soup for 5–10 more minutes. Add the wine, parsley, and tomato and heat for a few more minutes. Ladle the bouillabaisse into large soup bowls, serve a hearty red wine, a green salad, and piping hot French bread.

CHAPTER II

SAN JOAQUIN VALLEY

VEGETABLES, SALADS, & DRESSINGS

THE fragrance of a billion orange blossoms, the warm sweet-sour smell of silage, and the attenuated odor of petroleum distillate characterize the diversity of the produce of San Joaquin Valley. The eye wanders over the fields of baled barley straw and the white-painted trunks of plum trees, while up the road a slow-moving tractor pulls a disk harrow. There are roadside fruit stands with tables piled high with baskets of juicy plums and nectarines. In the distance, rolling, oak-studded foothills stretch upward toward the mountains. Along the valley's eastern side are the Sierra Nevadas, and on its western rim lie the Coast Ranges.

The arable portion of this valley is approximately three hundred miles long and fifty to one hundred miles wide, representing more total acreage than Switzerland, Lichtenstein, and Luxemburg combined. Town names such as Ceres, Orange Cove, Lemon Cove, Sultans, and Raisin hint at the variety of crops grown, yet give no sight nor taste nor smell. There is an unbelievable lushness in a thousand acres of green cotton. Even on the hottest days it seems cooler beside a field of green alfalfa. It is a peaceful, productive valley now, but it hasn't always been so.

The first white man known to have entered San Joaquin Valley was Pedro Fages, twice governor of California. He was chasing bandits. He chased them all the way from San Diego—over the mountains, through the Imperial Valley, through the Cajon Pass, and eventually into the San Joaquin Valley. Fages explored the valley's rivers, streams, and lakes. We don't know whether or not he ever caught the anonymous bandits, but we do know that he found vast amounts of good soil around these lakes. His discovery never benefited the Spanish, however; Indians of the Shoshonean, Chumash, and Yurok tribes already lived in the valley, and in the early 1770s, the Spanish were unable to contemplate settling any lands save the coastal areas. By the early nineteenth century, several exploration parties had visited the lands east of the Coast Range, but apparently no one stayed. Governor José Joaquin Arrillaga hoped to found an inland chain of missions but was unable to obtain money or soldiers to carry out the project.

A trail of sorts led from San Pedro in the south to East Oakland in the north. It was called the Los Angeles Trail or El Camino Viejo (the old road). By 1832 the northern end of this trail connected to the southern terminus of the Oregon Trail, which ended at French Camp south of Stockton. Around 1813 Gabriel Morago, a Spanish explorer whose father had been part of the Anza expedition to northern California, led forty-six successful expeditions against the Indians. It was he who named the San Joaquin River in honor of St. Joachim, the father of the Virgin Mary. Within a few years, the whole valley came to be called the San Joaquin Valley.

Thirteen years later in 1826, Jedediah Smith became the first American to explore the San Joaquin Valley. He followed the old Mojave Trail across the San Bernardino Mountains and turned north into the San Joaquin Valley, trapping around the Kings River and possibly even as far north as the Stanislaus River. His exploitations in the

Far West lasted five more years until he was felled on the Sante Fe Trail by a Commanche arrow.

Another foreigner who visited the valley was Pierre Lebec. He was a French voyageur who was reportedly in the valley to make arrangements for the arrival of Napoleon after his planned escape from Elba. Lebec was killed in a fight with a bear, and a town near the site of his death still carries his name.

A German founded the city of Stockton at the headwaters of the San Joaquin River. In 1841 Charles Weber settled there. Four years later, he fought with General Stockton's army against Mexico. Weber returned to his home when gold was discovered and founded a mining and trading company near Hangtown. He named both his company and the city that emerged for his friend General Stockton. Stockton soon became the gateway to the Mother Lode country, important to both freight and passenger travel because of its situation on the river. After the railroad through the valley was completed, Stockton became the site of mills and warehouses to facilitate the movement of produce from the San Joaquin Valley to the rest of the world.

The largest Mexican land grant in the San Joaquin Valley was Rancho El Tejon. In 1843 nearly 100,000 acres were granted to José Antonio Aguirre, a Spanish Basque, and Ignacio del Valle. Of Señor Aguirre's adobe no trace remains, but Bakersfield to the north has a sizable Basque population even today. Edward Beale, who subsequently bought the ranch, had earlier explored with Kit Carson. In addition to having been surveyor-general for California and Nevada, superintendent of Indian Affairs for the two states (and a very fair one),

and the man who carried gold to the East after the first strike, he was also the first man known to have proved that camels can swim. After the Civil War, Beale brought a camel caravan to the Southwest, believing that camels would be useful for desert transportation. Reportedly his caravan reached a deep river that could be crossed only by swimming the camels. The rest is history. Camels, perhaps because of their interesting personalities, did not become popular. Rumors of wild camels sighted in the desert—putative descendants of Beale's caravan—persist but are discounted. Rancho El Tejon is still there, though increased in size to over 250,000 acres.

Other visitors to the San Joaquin Valley during the middle years of the nineteenth century include an Audubon expedition and Joaquin Murietta, a bandit by trade. The former slept in trees for fear of grizzly bears; the latter was shot down by lawmen while still in his early twenties. The grizzly bear became extinct in California many years ago, but Joaquin Murietta, if legends are to be believed, continued his daring exploits long after the date of his actual demise.

During this period the Overland Stage Company had a route through the valley, carrying mail and passengers from Missouri to Los Angeles and San Francisco. It was a journey of 2,700 miles and took nearly a month. There were many Indian raids and massacres of white settlers in the 1850s, and in 1854 Fort Tejon was established at Rancho El Tejon to accommodate troops brought in to deal with the problem.

During the next decade Colonel Thomas Baker came to the valley with his family, built an adobe house, and began raising corn and alfalfa on what is now the site of Bakersfield's Civic Center. Soon after, other farmers established themselves in the area. A lively market for grain encouraged the newcomers to plant large crops of wheat and barley instead of using their land for ranching. Bakersfield, in those days, typified the wild west. Houses were crude, furniture was mostly homemade, and there were lots of shootings. Malaria was common and was treated with whiskey and quinine. Perhaps fever and whiskey were responsible for some of the violence, but gangs of outlaws were prevalent, too.

In 1869 the completed Transcontinental Railroad gave better access to the valley, but when the Pacific Central completed its railroad up the center of the valley three years later, the economic future of the area was more or less secured. Thousands of Chinese built the railroads, using picks and shovels and sometimes their bare hands. When the job was finished, many of the survivors of this work force returned to San Francisco or even to China, but enough unemployed Chinese remained to undertake a massive reclamation project on the delta lands at the confluence of the Sacramento and San Joaquin rivers. The land reclaimed was excellent farm land. At one time 90 per cent of the canned asparagus eaten anywhere in the world came from there.

Before farming took hold in the San Joaquin Valley, there had been a brief but intensive flurry of gold mining, especially near the town of Havilah in Kern County. When the gold ran out,

Havilah became a ghost town and Bakersfield became the county seat of Kern County. In 1899 Bakersfield's prominence was augmented by a rich oil strike just to the north. Today, Bakersfield's economic base is so broad that there is little danger of Havilah's fate befalling it.

As more water has become available to the southern part of the valley, and as improved methods of processing and shipping perishable foods have come into use, the San Joaquin Valley has become increasingly important to the rest of the United States and to the world. Grapes, grain, oranges, alfalfa, plums, lettuce, figs, onions, potatoes, sugar beets, and peaches—most of us have eaten produce from this abundant source. Nearly all the raisins eaten in the United States come from Fresno. Many of the olives come from Lindsay. In addition, cotton and oil are abundant in the San Joaquin Valley. Mettler Station, Wheeler Ridge, Oildale, Ford City, Taft, Delano, and Buttonwillow are just a few of the typical, colorful towns. John Steinbeck made Weed Patch world-famous, but most of the names of towns in the Central Valley are unknown except locally.

In the early morning, when knee-high ground fog billows across the fields, vague figures may be seen gathering lettuce and beets and strawberries. The car radio brings you "The Morning Farm Reporter" courtesy of Mac's Crop Dusting Service. In this day of mechanization, the way of life in the San Joaquin Valley is unfamiliar to most of us, but of vast necessity to us all.

BOILED FRESH ARTICHOKES

6 large artichokes, about
   12-14 ounces each
1 lemon, cut
3 tablespoons salt

With a very sharp knife trim the bases of the artichokes flat and flush. Snap off the small bottom leaves and any bruised outer leaves. Lay each artichoke on its side and with a sharp knife cut an inch or so off the top cone of the leaves. With scissors trim ¼ inch off the points of the rest of the leaves. Immediately rub all the cut edges with the cut lemon to prevent discoloring. In a large enamel kettle or soup pot over high heat bring 6 quarts water and the salt to a bubbling boil. Drop the artichokes carefully into the water and return the water to a boil. Reduce the heat to medium and boil briskly, uncovered, turning the artichokes occasionally. It will take about 30–40 minutes to cook the artichokes to the perfect stage. They are done when the bases are tender and can be pierced easily with the tip of a sharp knife. Remove the artichokes from the kettle with tongs and drain carefully upside down in a colander. Serve the artichokes hot with melted butter or hollandaise sauce. Artichokes may also be chilled and served cold with Vinaigrette Dressing or mayonaise (*see Index*).

NOTE: Artichokes need plenty of water—a quart each—and the water has to be kept at a bubbling boil for the artichokes to retain their fresh flavor.

To dechoke an artichoke, spread the top of the artichoke apart and pull out the light-colored inside leaves. This will reveal the hairy choke beneath. Scrape the choke out with a small spoon to expose the heart. Dechoking may be done before or after cooking, but it is much easier after they are cooked.

To prepare an artichoke bottom, cook the whole artichoke according to the initial directions above, but reduce the cooking time 5–10 minutes so that the bottoms remain firm. After the artichokes are cooked, carefully remove the leaves and choke, trimming the bottom carefully with a sharp knife so that it is smooth and even. Immediately squeeze fresh lemon juice on all sides to prevent the artichoke from darkening. Keep the bottoms in the lemon juice until ready to use. The leaves may then be scraped and used in a soup or eaten as desired.

ASPARAGUS WITH ORANGE BUTTER SAUCE

SERVES 4–6

1½ pounds fresh asparagus
¼ teaspoon salt
¼ teaspoon pepper or to taste
2 medium oranges
⅓ cup butter, melted and
　clarified
¼ cup orange juice
2 tablespoons grated orange
　rind

Wash the asparagus well, cut off 3 inches of the rough stalk ends, and peel the lower parts of the stalks. Lay the asparagus in a 12–14-inch skillet and place the skillet over moderate-high heat. Pour 1 quart boiling water over the asparagus, making sure the water completely covers the stalks. Add salt and cook the asparagus uncovered for 8 minutes. While the asparagus is cooking, prepare the orange butter sauce.

Peel 1 orange, removing all the pith, and slice it into 12 very thin round slices. Set aside for garnish. Extract the juice from the other orange and strain the juice through a fine sieve. Measure out ¼ cup juice. Grate the rind and set aside. In a small saucepan combine the clarified butter, the ¼ cup orange juice, and the grated rind. Set the pan over moderate-high heat and reduce the mixture until slightly thickened, about 6 minutes.

When the asparagus is just tender, remove the stalks carefully from the water with tongs and place them on a heated serving platter. Cover with the hot orange sauce, garnish with orange slices, and serve at once.

BROCCOLI IN WINE

SERVES 6

3 pounds broccoli
½ teaspoon salt
2 teaspoons butter
2 teaspoons olive oil
2 cloves garlic, finely chopped
2 tablespoons grated orange
　rind
¼ cup fresh orange juice
½ cup dry white wine

Wash the broccoli and trim at least 3 inches from the heavy stalks. Split the larger stalks lengthwise so all are of uniform thickness. Cook broccoli in 2 quarts boiling water, with the salt, approximately 8 minutes. While the broccoli is cooking, prepare the wine sauce. In a large heavy Dutch oven over moderate heat melt the butter and olive oil. Add the garlic and sauté for 3–4 minutes, stirring frequently. Add the orange rind, orange juice, and wine to the Dutch oven. Reduce the orange mixture over high heat until thick and syrupy, about 6–8 minutes, stirring often. Drain the broccoli and place in the Dutch oven with the orange mixture and toss gently until broccoli is coated with the glaze. Serve at once.

STIR-FRIED BROCCOLI

SERVES 6

2 pounds fresh broccoli
2 tablespoons vegetable oil
1 teaspoon salt
½ teaspoon sugar
3 tablespoons chicken stock
1 teaspoon cornstarch

Wash the broccoli thoroughly and using a sharp knife, cut the broccoli flowerettes from their stems in fairly large clusters. Place the flowerettes in a medium-sized bowl and set aside. Peel the stems by cutting about ⅛ inch into the stringy skin and stripping it down as if you were peeling an onion. Slice the stalks diagonally into 1-inch pieces, discarding the woody ends. Place pieces of stalk in a separate bowl and set aside.

Set a 12-inch wok or 10-inch skillet over medium heat for 30 seconds. Pour in the oil, swirl it about in the pan, and heat for another 30 seconds, lowering the heat to moderate if the oil begins to smoke. Drop the broccoli stalks in the hot oil and stir-fry for about 1 minute to coat the vegetable pieces thoroughly with oil. Add the broccoli flowerettes and stir-fry for 1 more minute. Sprinkle the broccoli with the salt, sugar, and 2 tablespoons of the chicken stock, stirring for a few seconds to blend. Cover the pan and cook over moderate heat for 2–3 minutes. The broccoli should be tender but still crisp.

In a small mixing bowl blend the remaining 1 tablespoon chicken stock with the cornstarch, stirring to form a smooth paste. Pour this mixture into the skillet. Stir for a few seconds until the broccoli is coated with a light, clear glaze. Transfer to a heated platter and serve at once.

NOTE: This is an excellent accompaniment to a Chinese meal.

BRUSSELS SPROUTS IN CREAM

SERVES 6

5 pounds brussels sprouts
Salt
1½ cups heavy cream
3½ teaspoons curry powder
   or more to taste
¼ teaspoon pepper or to taste

Carefully trim and wash the sprouts, removing all the withered or yellowed leaves. Put the sprouts in a 4-quart pan, add 2 or more quarts of water (enough to cover the sprouts), cover, and bring to a boil over moderate heat. When the water comes to the boil, transfer the sprouts to another

4-quart pan which contains 2 more quarts of boiling water to which ½ teaspoon salt has been added. Let the sprouts return to a boil and cook for 20 minutes uncovered. This process improves the flavor of the sprouts. Drain thoroughly and chop finely. Place them in a smaller saucepan with the cream and curry powder. Season with salt and pepper. Heat over moderate heat, stirring constantly, for a few minutes or until the sprouts have absorbed most of the cream. Serve at once.

BACON AND ONION GREEN BEANS   SERVES 6

1½ pounds fresh green beans
½ teaspoon salt
6 slices bacon, diced
¼ cup chopped onion
¼ cup cider vinegar
2 tablespoons sugar

Wash the beans thoroughly, snip off the ends, and remove any strings. In a 3–4-quart saucepan over high heat bring 2 quarts water with the salt to a full boil, add the beans, reduce the heat to moderate, and boil them uncovered for 10–12 minutes or until they are just tender. Do not overcook. Immediately drain the beans in a colander.

While the beans are boiling, prepare the bacon and onion sauce. In a 10–12-inch skillet over moderately high heat sauté the bacon bits until crisp. Remove the bacon with a slotted spoon and set aside. Add the chopped onion to the skillet and sauté until limp, approximately 3–4 minutes. Drain all the fat except for 2 tablespoons. Reduce the heat to low and to the onion add the vinegar, sugar, and bacon bits. Stir to incorporate all the loose particles at the bottom of the pan. Bring the heat to high and boil the mixture 1 minute.

Place the hot drained beans in the large kettle. Pour the bacon-onion mixture over the hot beans and toss lightly to coat the beans evenly. Serve at once in a heated serving dish.

NOTE: The beans may be left whole for preparation as in the above recipe or they may be Frenched or cut diagonally.

FRESH CORN, TOMATO, ZUCCHINI POT

SERVES 6

4 ears fresh corn
5 medium fresh tomatoes,
   unpeeled
6 or 7 small zucchini
2 medium onions
2 cloves garlic, minced
Salt and pepper to taste
Lemon pepper (optional)
   to taste
½ cup butter

Using a very sharp knife, cut the corn from the cob into a large earthenware casserole. Wash the tomatoes and zucchini and pat dry. Slice the core ends from the tomatoes and discard, then slice the tomatoes into ¼-inch slices. Trim ¼ inch off each end of the zucchini and discard, then slice the zucchini lengthwise into 4 pieces. Add the tomatoes and zucchini to the casserole as well as the onions, which have been sliced into thin rings and separated. Add the garlic, salt, pepper, and lemon pepper and mix the vegetables together carefully. Dot with butter, cover, and bake in a preheated 325° oven for 45 minutes. Add no extra liquid.

NOTE: This combination of vegetables is especially nice when served with barbecued turkey or Barbecued Butterfly Leg of Lamb (*see Index*.)

MEXICAN CORN PUDDING

SERVES 6

2 eggs, slightly beaten
1¼ cups milk
2½ cups raw corn, scraped
   off the cob
1 cup chopped tomatoes,
   peeled and seeded
1 small onion, finely chopped
1 green pepper, seeded and
   chopped
4 ounces pimiento, chopped
   (optional)
½ cup pitted ripe olives
   (optional)
1 teaspoon salt
¼ teaspoon pepper
¼ teaspoon paprika
¼ teaspoon chili powder
1 cup yellow corn meal
½ cup plus 1 teaspoon butter

In a large mixing bowl combine all ingredients except corn meal and butter. Mix slightly. Add the corn meal and stir with a large spoon until well mixed.

In a small saucepan melt the ½ cup butter over low heat and pour into the corn meal mixture. Grease a 2-quart casserole with 1 teaspoon butter. Add the corn pudding and bake in a preheated 325° oven for 1 hour or until firm.

CAULIFLOWER WITH ALMOND SAUCE

1 large cauliflower (about 3
   pounds)
1 teaspoon salt
6 tablespoons butter
½ cup slivered almonds
¾ cup Seasoned Bread Crumbs I
   (*see Index*)
⅛ teaspoon paprika
Parsley sprigs

Wash the cauliflower head thoroughly, removing any excess outer leaves or thick stalk. Place 1 quart cold water and ½ teaspoon of the salt in a 3-quart saucepan. Place the cauliflower in the saucepan head down and allow it to sit at least 30 minutes. Remove the cauliflower and place in a colander to drain thoroughly.

Bring 3 quarts water to a boil. Add ½ teaspoon salt and the cauliflower, right side up, making sure the water covers the entire head. Cook gently, uncovered, over medium heat 20–30 minutes or until just tender when pierced with a fork. Be careful not to overcook, as the cauliflower should stay in one whole piece and not fall apart. While the cauliflower is cooking, place 2 tablespoons butter in an 8–10-inch skillet and brown the slivered almonds over low heat for about 3 minutes. When brown, remove the almonds from the skillet, using a slotted spoon, and place them on a paper towel. In the same skillet add 4 tablespoons butter and brown the bread crumbs for 3 minutes over medium heat, stirring often to prevent excess browning. Reduce heat to low and add the almonds and paprika.

Drain the cauliflower and place on a heated serving platter. Quickly pour the bread crumb mixture over the cauliflower head. Garnish with a few sprigs of fresh parsley and serve at once.

RED CABBAGE

¼ cup butter
2 tablespoons sugar
½ teaspoon salt
2 tablespoons cider vinegar
2 tablespoons water
1 head red cabbage (2½
   pounds), shredded
½ cup currant jelly
Pinch ground cloves (optional)

In a 6-quart kettle or Dutch oven melt the butter over low heat and to it add the sugar, salt, vinegar, and water. Add the cabbage to the kettle, cover, and simmer over low heat for 1 hour or more.

Just before serving, add the currant jelly and the cloves, if desired. Serve piping hot as an accompaniment to a pork roast or pork chops.

FRESH PEAS WITH LETTUCE AND ONIONS SERVES 4–6

1 head Boston lettuce
½ cup water
1½ tablespoons sugar
¼ teaspoon salt
⅛ teaspoon pepper
6 tablespoons butter
3 pounds fresh peas, shelled
    and washed (reserve 4 pods)
12 small white onions, boiled
    for 5 minutes and peeled
8 parsley sprigs
2 fresh mint sprigs

Carefully wash the lettuce and remove the outer leaves. Cut the head in quarters and tie each quarter securely with white string to prevent the leaves from falling apart. Set aside.

Bring the ½ cup to a boil over medium-high heat in a 3-quart saucepan. Add the sugar, salt, pepper, and 4 tablespoons of the butter to the boiling water. Stir in the peas and onions. Tuck the parsley, mint, and 4 pods in the vegetables. Carefully lay the quartered, tied lettuce sections over the peas and baste all the vegetables with any excess liquid. Return the peas to a boil over high heat and cook for 3–4 minutes. Reduce the heat to low and cover the saucepan with a soup plate into which you pour a little water. This will keep the steam in the saucepan. Simmer the peas slowly for 20–30 minutes or until they are tender. Remove the pan from the heat and carefully remove the lettuce quarters. Immediately discard the parsley, mint, and pods. Add 2 tablespoons butter to the peas and toss quickly and gently. Place the peas and onions piping hot onto a heated serving dish. Carefully untie the lettuce quarters and place the leaves around the peas. Serve at once.

FRENCH CARROTS WITH CELERY SERVES 4–6

½ pound bacon, diced
3 cups peeled and diced
    young carrots
2 cups diced celery
1 cup chopped onion
2 tablespoons flour
½ teaspoon salt
1 bay leaf
¼ teaspoon pepper

In a heavy 10–12-inch skillet over moderate heat fry the bacon until crisp, remove from the pan with a slotted spoon, and drain well on paper toweling. Place the carrots, celery, and onion in the hot bacon drippings and toss lightly over moderate heat until all the fat is absorbed. Sprinkle the flour and salt over the vegetables, mixing in well for a few seconds. Remove the skillet from the heat and stir the bacon bits, bay leaf, and pepper into the vegetable mixture.

Place all the vegetables and the seasonings in a heavy 2-quart casserole and almost cover the vegetables with boiling water (the amount of water will depend on the depth of the pan). Place the pot, covered, in a preheated 400° oven and bake the vegetables for 1½ hours. Remove and discard the bay leaf before serving.

BROCCOLI RING WITH MUSHROOMS
SERVES 6–8

2 pounds fresh broccoli
4 tablespoons butter
2 tablespoons flour
1 cup light cream
4 egg yolks, beaten
¼ teaspoon salt
¼ teaspoon pepper
1 pound fresh mushrooms, trimmed and halved
2 tablespoons fresh lemon juice
4 egg whites
1 hard-boiled egg, grated

Wash broccoli, trim off outer leaves and ends of stems and discard, and cut broccoli into 1-inch pieces. Place in a 5–6-quart kettle with water to cover, 2–3 quarts, and bring to a boil over high heat. Reduce the heat and simmer covered for 10–15 minutes or until easily pierced with a fork. Place the stalks in a colander to drain and when cool, chop broccoli until quite well mashed. Using the same kettle, melt 2 tablespoons butter, remove from the heat, and add the flour. Blend well, return to moderate heat, and stir constantly for 2–3 minutes. Still over moderate heat, slowly pour in the cream, beating constantly. Cook until thick, 5–7 minutes, remove from heat, and add the beaten egg yolks. Blend well, add the broccoli, and season with salt and pepper, correcting seasoning if necessary.

Sauté the mushrooms in a small skillet in the remaining 2 tablespoons butter. Add a dash of salt and pepper and after 2–3 minutes of cooking, add the lemon juice. Set aside to be reheated later. (All of the above can be done in the morning.)

Beat the egg whites, with a pinch of salt, until very stiff and gently fold them into the broccoli mixture. Pour into a buttered, lightly floured 8-cup ring mold. Place in a pan of boiling water and bake in a preheated 350° oven for 30–35 minutes. If necessary, reheat the mushrooms at this time. To serve, unmold the ring onto a heated serving platter, fill the center with the mushrooms, and sprinkle grated egg over the broccoli.

POTATOES, ONIONS, AND MUSHROOMS

5 pounds boiling potatoes
¼ cup butter
1 pound fresh mushrooms,
  sliced
1 cup flour
1 quart milk
1 cup heavy cream
1½ ounces consommé or beef
  broth
1 pound sharp Cheddar cheese,
  grated
1 tablespoon Worcestershire
  sauce
½ teaspoon salt or to taste
½ teaspoon pepper or to taste
1 pound small boiling onions,
  cooked 10–12 minutes and
  peeled
¼ cup grated Cheddar cheese
  or ¼ cup chopped fresh
  parsley

Cook potatoes in jackets 20 minutes or until they can be pierced with a fork. Peel the potatoes and cut them into ½-inch slices. Heat the butter in a 12–14-inch skillet over medium-high heat. Sauté mushrooms until browned, 3–5 minutes. Stir in the flour; add milk, cream, and consommé. Stir the mix until smooth and slightly thickened, 10 minutes. Add the cheese, Worcestershire, salt, and pepper. Stir the sauce until smooth and thickened over moderate heat, approximately 4–6 minutes. Remove the skillet from heat and add the potatoes and the onions. Mix all together carefully.

Spoon the mixture into a *shallow* 4-quart casserole. Bake in a preheated 350° oven for 1 hour or until golden brown and bubbly. Sprinkle with grated cheese or with chopped parsley during the last 5 minutes of cooking. This may be prepared 24 hours in advance and held in the refrigerator until 1 hour before baking.

NOTE: This recipe is a good accompaniment to beef or lamb.

SPINACH-STUFFED ONIONS

8 large Spanish onions
3 bunches fresh spinach,
  washed and stemmed
½ teaspoon salt
¼ teaspoon pepper
¼ teaspoon ground nutmeg
1 tablespoon fresh lemon juice
2 tablespoons freshly grated
  Parmesan cheese
2 tablespoons butter
2 tablespoons flour
¼ cup sour cream
2 eggs, beaten

Peel the onions and place them in boiling water to cover, using a 4-quart kettle. Reduce the heat to medium and cook the onions for 15 minutes. Remove the onions from the kettle and drain well in a colander. Cool and hollow out the centers, leaving approximately a ⅓-inch-thick shell. Reserve the centers of the onion for another use. In a 3–4-quart saucepan with a cover, cook the spinach leaves over low heat, adding no water except for that clinging to the leaves from the washing. Cook covered for 4–5 minutes or until limp. In a colander squeeze all the water from the spinach and chop it finely. Place the chopped spinach in a medium-sized mixing bowl and add the salt, pepper, nutmeg, lemon juice, and cheese.

Place the butter in a heavy 8–10-inch skillet over low heat. As the butter melts, slowly add the flour, stirring constantly to make a roux, about 2–3 minutes. Allow the roux to cool for a few minutes and then blend in the sour cream and beaten eggs. Add the sour cream mixture to the chopped spinach and mix thoroughly.

Fill the onion cups with the combined spinach mixture and place the cups in a shallow baking pan. Bake uncovered in a preheated 375° oven for 20 minutes. Serve at once.

FRESH TOMATO SOUFFLÉ SERVES 6

3 tablespoons butter or margarine
6 large tomatoes, peeled and coarsely chopped
3 tablespoons tomato paste
¼ teaspoon salt
2 teaspoons sugar
¼ teaspoon dried basil
1 tablespoon minced fresh chives
2 tablespoons minced onion
3 tablespoons flour
1 cup milk, scalded
3 tablespoons freshly grated Parmesan cheese
5 eggs, separated

Melt 1 tablespoon of the butter in an 8–10-inch skillet and add the tomatoes. Cook over medium heat, stirring occasionally, until the mixture is thick and the liquid is absorbed, approximately 10–15 minutes. To this add the tomato paste, salt, sugar, basil, chives, and onion, stirring well to blend. Bring to a boil, reduce heat, and simmer for 5 minutes. In a small saucepan over medium-low heat melt the remaining butter and blend in the flour, stirring until bubbly, about 1 minute. Add the hot milk and cook 3–4 minutes longer or until very thick, stirring constantly. Add the cream sauce and the cheese to the tomato mixture and blend well. Set aside to cool, 5–10 minutes.

In a small mixing bowl beat the egg yolks with a wire wisk and slowly add to the cooled tomato mixture, blending well. Beat the egg whites in a large mixing bowl until stiff but not dry. Lightly but thoroughly fold into the tomato mixture. Pour into a lightly buttered 2-quart soufflé dish and bake in a preheated 350° oven for 40 minutes or until puffed and golden. Serve at once.

ZUCCHINI SOUFFLÉ

SERVES 6

5–6 medium zucchini (about
    2 pounds)
¾ teaspoon salt
2 slices white bread
1 cup milk
1 onion, finely chopped
1 clove garlic, minced
2 tablespoons butter
2 tablespoons vegetable oil
4 eggs
½ cup freshly grated Parmesan
    cheese
¼ teaspoon white pepper

Wash the zucchini and cut into ¼-inch slices. Place the zucchini slices in a 3-quart saucepan and add 1 cup water and ¼ teaspoon salt. Bring to a boil over high heat, reduce the heat, and simmer covered for 10–12 minutes or until the zucchini is fork-tender. Place in a colander and drain well.

Meanwhile, in a small bowl soak the bread, which has been torn into bite-sized pieces, in the milk. In an 8–10-inch skillet sauté the onion and the garlic in the butter and oil over low heat until soft, 3–4 minutes, stirring frequently. Prepare a 1½-quart soufflé dish by generoulsy buttering the inside.

Return the drained zucchini to a saucepan and mash it thoroughly with a fork. Add the soaked bread, squeezing out the excess milk. Mix into the zucchini thoroughly.

In a small mixing bowl beat the eggs until they are light and frothy. Add the eggs, sautéed onion, and garlic to the zucchini mixture. Gently fold in the cheese, ½ teaspoon salt, and pepper. Pour into the buttered soufflé dish and bake in a preheated 375° oven for 50 minutes or until firm in the center. Serve at once.

NOTE: This soufflé is a delightful accompaniment to baked chicken or leg of lamb.

CORN SOUFFLÉ

SERVES 4

3 ears fresh corn (or enough
    for 2 cups kernels)
1½ cups milk
2½ tablespoons flour, sifted
3 tablespoons butter
3 eggs, separated
¼ teaspoon salt or to taste

Remove the husks from the ears of corn and boil the ears in salted water for 20 minutes. Remove the ears from the hot water and drain them thoroughly in a colander. Score each row of kernels with a sharp knife and then scrape the kernels off the corn. In a 1½–2-quart saucepan mix 3 tablespoons cold milk with the flour, away

¼ teaspoon white pepper or to
taste
2 tablespoons heavy cream

from the flame. Heat the remainder of the milk in a small saucepan, bringing the milk to the boiling point over moderate heat. Remove from the heat and pour the hot milk into the flour mixture. Add the butter, corn, and beaten egg yolks. Stir vigorously over moderate heat for 3–4 minutes without letting the mixture boil. Season with the salt and pepper and remove from heat.

Beat the egg whites until stiff and fold them, along with the heavy cream, into the yolk-flour mixture. Butter a 1½-quart soufflé dish and pour in the mixture. Bake in a preheated 400° oven for 25 minutes or until firm in the center.

CHILE CHEESE TOMATOES

SERVES 6–8

3 large or 4 medium tomatoes,
firm and ripe
1 cup sour cream
½ teaspoon salt
¼ teaspoon pepper
1 teaspoon sugar
1 tablespoon flour
2 tablespoons finely chopped
scallions, including tops
2 tablespoons chopped green
chiles
1 cup grated sharp Cheddar
cheese
½ cup grated Monterey Jack
cheese

Cut the tomatoes in half and hollow them out. Save the pulp for another use. Drain the tomatoes upside down on paper towels for about 10 minutes while the filling is being prepared.

In a small mixing bowl combine the sour cream with the salt, pepper, sugar, flour, scallions, and chiles, stirring until well blended. Arrange the drained tomato halves right side up in a broiler-proof pan. Spoon the sour cream mixture evenly into the tomato cavities, mounding it evenly over the tops.

Using another small bowl, mix the grated cheeses together and set aside. Place the tomatoes in the broiler and broil about 4 inches from the heat until bubbly, approximately 3–5 minutes, watching closely to keep from burning. When the tomatoes are done, remove from the broiler, sprinkle the cheeses evenly over the tomato tops, and return to the broiler until the cheese is melted and golden, 2–3 minutes.

NOTE: These tomatoes add color to any meal and are an especially nice vegetable with baked ham, prime rib, or flank steak.

CREAMED SPINACH WITH CHARD

2½ pounds fresh spinach,
    thoroughly washed
1 bunch Swiss chard (12–14
    leaves), washed
4 tablespoons butter
3 tablespoons flour
1¼ cups milk
⅛ teaspoon ground nutmeg
½ teaspoon salt
¼ teaspoon pepper
⅓ cup madeira

Remove and discard the stems from the spinach and chard. Chop the leaves coarsely. Cook the spinach and chard over medium heat in a 6–8-quart saucepan, stirring constantly until the leaves are wilted. Do not add water; the leaves contain enough natural water so that they will wilt in about 5 minutes. Continue to cook over low heat, stirring, for 3–5 additional minutes. Cover and cook for 2–3 more minutes, stirring occasionally. Take ½ the spinach mixture at a time and purée it in a blender at low speed for approximately 30 seconds. Purée the other ½ of the spinach mixture and set aside. Melt the butter in a 10–12-inch skillet over low heat. Add the flour and cook, stirring, for 2–3 minutes. Heat the milk in a small saucepan to just below scalding. Add the hot milk to the flour mixture, stirring constantly. Cook until smooth and thickened, approximately 7–10 minutes. Add the seasonings and madeira. Simmer gently for 10 more minutes. Fold in the spinach and chard. Stir, heat to bubbling, and serve.

NOTE: This vegetable is a delicious accompaniment to roast meats, especially lamb.

GLAZED WHITE ONIONS

⅔ cup chicken stock
2 tablespoons butter
¼ teaspoon salt or to taste
¼ teaspoon pepper or to taste
1 bay leaf
16–24 white onions, 1 inch
    in diameter, peeled
1 sprig parsley

In a heavy 8–10-inch skillet bring the chicken stock, butter, salt, pepper, and bay leaf to a boil over high heat. Carefully drop in the onions, reduce the heat, cover, and simmer very slowly for 25–30 minutes or until the onions are tender. Be sure to turn the onions occasionally with a spoon to glaze them evenly. After 30 minutes, the braising liquid should have reduced to a syrupy glaze. If not, remove the onions with a slotted spoon, set aside and keep warm, and boil the liquid down. Gently roll the onions in the pan to moisten them with glaze. Serve in a heated vegetable dish with a touch of parsley in the center.

ZUCCHINI AND SPINACH FRITTATA

8 zucchini, unpeeled and thinly
  sliced
4 tablespoons butter
1 onion, thinly sliced
¾ pound fresh mushrooms,
  thinly sliced
3 cups finely chopped fresh
  spinach
4 eggs
1½ cups light cream
¼ teaspoon salt
¼ teaspoon pepper
½ teaspoon dried thyme
½ teaspoon dried basil
½ cup freshly grated Parmesan
  cheese

In a 10–12-inch skillet sauté the zucchini in 2 tablespoons of the butter over high heat for 15 minutes or until transparent. Remove the zucchini from the skillet with a slotted spoon and place it in the bottom of a shallow 1½–2-quart casserole dish (a quiche pan is excellent).

Add 1 more tablespoon of the butter to the same skillet and sauté the onion over high heat for 5 minutes. Layer the onion on top of the zucchini.

Add the rest of the butter to the skillet and sauté the mushrooms over moderate heat for 3 minutes. Add the spinach and sauté for 3 minutes more, stirring constantly. Place the mixture on top of the zucchini-onion mixture in an even layer.

In a medium-sized mixing bowl beat the eggs thoroughly with a wire whisk, adding the light cream gradually. Quickly mix in the salt, pepper, and herbs. Pour this mixture over the vegetables. Sprinkle generously with the cheese and bake in a preheated 375° oven for 25–30 minutes. Serve very hot, cut in wedges.

NOTE: The vegetables can be sautéed and layered several hours before serving. The eggs, cream, and seasonings can be prepared up to 30 minutes before baking.

ZUCCHINI FRITTATA

2 cups thinly sliced zucchini
1 clove garlic, crushed
4 scallions, including tops,
  sliced
3 tablespoons chopped fresh
  parsley
2–3 tablespoons butter
8 eggs, beaten
¾ cup freshly grated Parmesan
  cheese
¼ teaspoon salt or to taste
¼ teaspoon pepper

In a 10–12-inch skillet sauté the zucchini, garlic, scallions, and parsley in the butter over moderate heat. Stir the vegetables lightly for 3–5 minutes. Remove the skillet from the heat and add to it the eggs, cheese, salt, and pepper. Pour the mixture into a greased 9-inch-square pan. Bake in a preheated 350° oven for 20–25 minutes or until a silver knife inserted in the center comes out clean. Slice in squares and serve at once.

CHAMPIGNONS AU GRATIN

1 clove garlic, minced
1 onion, grated
2 tablespoons chopped fresh
   parsley
⅛ teaspoon dried basil
1 teaspoon salt
¼ teaspoon pepper
⅓ cup salad oil
2 tablespoons wine vinegar
1½ pounds fresh mushrooms,
   trimmed and sliced
¼ pound butter
½ cup fresh bread crumbs
¼ cup freshly grated Parmesan
   cheese

Combine the garlic, onion, parsley, basil, salt, pepper, oil, and vinegar in a large mixing bowl. There will be very little liquid. Add the mushrooms and marinate for 3 hours, stirring frequently.

Melt ½ the butter in a heavy 10–12-inch skillet. Remove the mushrooms from the marinade with a slotted spoon and place in the skillet. Cook the mushrooms over high heat for 1 minute, stirring frequently.

Butter a shallow 1-quart baking dish and place the mushrooms in it. Sprinkle with the bread crumbs and cheese. Dot with the remaining butter. The recipe can be prepared ahead to this point and held in the refrigerator for at least 6 hours.

Place under a preheated broiler, 6–8 inches from the heat, for 3–5 minutes, to brown before serving. Watch carefully to prevent burning.

NOTE: These mushrooms are a tasty complement to all grilled meats. They should be served very hot but should not be overcooked, as they are best when plump and moist.

STUFFED SUMMER SQUASH

8 summer or pattypan squash
6 slices bacon
1 small onion, chopped
1 pint sour cream
½ cup grated Cheddar cheese
½ teaspoon salt
½ teaspoon dried marjoram
1 cup chablis

Stem and hollow out the center of the squash, using a paring knife to make a circle and a grapefruit spoon to carefully remove the seeds and the pulp. Reserve the pulp. Be careful not to cut through the sides or bottom of the squash. Chop the pulp and set aside. Cook bacon in a heavy 8–10-inch skillet until crisp. Remove the bacon, drain on a paper towel, and crumble into pieces. Sauté the squash pulp and onion in the bacon drippings for 3–5 minutes over medium-high heat or until limp, stirring often. Remove the skillet from the heat and allow the onion mixture to cool in the skillet for about 10 minutes.

Add the sour cream, grated cheese, and crumbled bacon to the skillet. Stir to blend thoroughly. Stuff this combination into the hollowed-out squash. Pour the chablis into a 9 × 9-inch baking dish. Place the stuffed squash carefully into the dish, cover with a top or foil, and bake in a preheated 325° oven for 45 minutes.

MORE THAN MUSHROOMS

SERVES 6–8

1½-pounds fresh mushrooms, sliced

4 tablespoons butter

½ cup chopped scallions, including tops

½ cup finely chopped celery

½ cup seeded and finely chopped green pepper

2 tablespoons chopped fresh parsley

¼ teaspoon salt

¼ teaspoon pepper

¼ teaspoon monosodium glutamate

½ cup mayonnaise, preferably homemade (*see Index*)

6–8 slices white bread

3 eggs

3 cups milk

¼ cup freshly grated Parmesan cheese

In a 10–12-inch skillet sauté the mushrooms in the butter for 5 minutes over moderately high heat. Add the vegetables, parsley, salt, pepper, and monosodium glutamate and sauté for 3 more minutes. Remove from heat, add mayonnaise, stirring to blend well, and set aside. Remove the crusts from the bread and cut the slices into quarters. Put ½ the bread in a layer in the bottom of a liberally greased 2½-quart casserole dish. Spoon the mushroom mixture over the bread and cover with the remaining bread. Beat the eggs and milk together in a small mixing bowl until frothy. Pour over the bread-mushroom mixture in the casserole and refrigerate for 1–3 hours.

Bake uncovered in a preheated 350° oven for 45 minutes. Sprinkle with the Parmesan and bake 10 minutes longer. Serve at once accompanied by a crisp green salad.

TOMATO PUDDING

SERVES 6

¼ teaspoon salt
2½ cups tomato purée
1¼ cups brown sugar, packed
¼ cup boiling water
¾ cup butter
3 cups 1-inch cubes sourdough
   bread

In a medium-sized saucepan combine the salt, tomato purée, brown sugar, and boiling water. Place the pan over moderate heat and bring the ingredients to a boil. Let boil for 5 minutes, stirring occasionally. Meanwhile, melt the butter in a small saucepan and keep both the tomato mixture and the butter warm while proceeding with the recipe.

Place the bread cubes in a buttered 9-inch-square pan and pour the *hot* melted butter over them, distributing it very evenly. Pour the *hot* tomato mixture evenly over the buttered bread cubes. Place the pudding in a preheated 375° oven and bake for 45 minutes.

NOTE: This pudding may be prepared 1 hour ahead of time and allowed to sit at room temperature. It is a delicious accompaniment to ham and adds a definite sweet-sour taste to any meal.

NEW POTATOES IN SAVORY SAUCE

SERVES 4

8 small new potatoes
   (approximately 2 pounds)
¼ cup butter
1 tablespoon olive oil
Rind of 1 lemon, grated
¼ cup chopped fresh parsley
2 tablespoons chopped fresh
   chives
⅛ teaspoon ground nutmeg
¼ teaspoon flour
¼ teaspoon salt or to taste
¼ teaspoon pepper or to taste
3 tablespoons fresh lemon
   juice

Wash the potatoes with jackets on and place in a 4-quart saucepan. Cover the potatoes with water and bring to a boil over medium heat. Let boil for 15–20 minutes or until fork-tender. Drain well and peel the potatoes while they are piping hot. Set aside in an attractive serving dish and keep warm.

In a small saucepan melt the butter and oil over low heat. Stir in all the remaining ingredients except the lemon juice. Heat the mixture slowly, stirring constantly, but do not bring it to a boil. It will thicken slightly. Just before serving, stir the lemon juice into the butter mixture and pour the combination over the warm potatoes. Toss the potatoes gently to coat each evenly. Serve at once.

NOTE: These potatoes are a nice addition to broiled fish or baked ham.

ZUCCHINI PANCAKES

6 medium zucchini, grated
3 eggs, beaten
4 tablespoons flour
4 tablespoons freshly grated
    Parmesan cheese
½ teaspoon minced fresh
    parsley
1 clove garlic, crushed
½ teaspoon salt
¼ teaspoon pepper
2 tablespoons oil

In a large mixing bowl combine the grated zucchini with all the other ingredients except the oil. Stir to thoroughly blend. Using your hands, form the mixture into patties 3–4 inches in diameter.

Heat the oil over high heat in a 12-inch skillet. Cook the zucchini pancakes for 3 minutes per side. Remove the pancakes from the skillet with a spatula and drain on paper towels. Cover with another towel to keep warm while cooking the remainder of the pancakes.

NOTE: These pancakes have a definite oriental taste and go nicely with barbecued lamb or any grilled meat.

TOMATO PIE

SERVES 6–8

1 9-inch pie crust
2–3 medium tomatoes, cored,
    peeled, and thickly sliced
½ teaspoon salt
¼ teaspoon pepper
¼ teaspoon dried basil
¼ cup chopped fresh chives
¼ cup mayonnaise, preferably
    homemade (*see Index*)
1 cup shredded sharp Cheddar
    cheese

Preheat oven to 425°. Follow the recipe for Basic Pie Crust (*see Index*), but bake the crust for only 5 minutes. Remove from oven. Reduce oven heat to 400°. Line the pie crust with the tomatoes, covering the bottom completely. Sprinkle the tomato slices with the salt, pepper, basil, and chives.

In a small mixing bowl thoroughly combine the mayonnaise and cheese. Carefully spread the mayonnaise mixture very evenly over the tomato slices, making sure to seal the edges of the pie crust completely. Bake the tomato pie for 35 minutes. Serve at once while still hot and bubbling.

NOTE: This is a nice entree for a spring luncheon or an accompaniment for any grilled meat. The recipe may be prepared using 6 tart shells approximately 2 inches in diameter instead of the 9-inch pie shell. Divide the ingredients among the shells and bake for 20–25 minutes at 400°.

CHERRY TOMATOES

4 tablespoons butter
2 shallots, finely chopped
4 scallions, including some of
   the tops, finely chopped
2 tablespoons finely chopped
   fresh parsley
1 teaspoon dried dill weed
½ teaspoon salt
3 cups cherry tomatoes

Melt the butter over low heat in a heavy 12–14-inch skillet. Add the shallots, scallions, parsley, dill weed, and salt and sauté 4–5 minutes over low heat until tender. Add the cherry tomatoes, stirring gently, and cook for 5–7 minutes or until a few of the tomato skins burst. The tomatoes should be well coated with the butter-vegetable mixture. Serve at once.

NOTE: These tomatoes are especially festive at Christmas or Thanksgiving when served in the center of Broccoli Ring with Mushrooms (*see Index*). The cherry tomatoes would take the place of the mushrooms.

BAKED CHEESE-STUFFED TOMATOES

8 medium tomatoes
2 cups grated Swiss cheese
⅓ cup light cream
2 egg yolks, slightly beaten
2 tablespoons grated onion
½ teaspoon dried marjoram
1 teaspoon dry mustard
1½ teaspoons salt
⅓ cup Seasoned Bread Crumbs I
   (*see Index*)
2 tablespoons melted butter

Peel the tomatoes and carefully core and scoop out the pulp, leaving the shells intact. Chop the pulp coarsely, discarding the seeds, and combine the pulp with all the other ingredients except the bread crumbs and butter. Spoon the cheese mixture into the tomato shells. Toss the bread crumbs with the butter and sprinkle over the cheese mixture. Arrange the tomatoes in a greased 12 × 8-inch shallow baking dish. Bake in a preheated 350° oven for 20–25 minutes. Serve at once.

NOTE: The tomatoes may be prepared early in the day and held in the refrigerator for up to 6 hours before baking. This is a colorful side dish for barbecued lamb or beef.

FRESH SPINACH SALAD

1 bunch fresh spinach
5 slices bacon
⅔ cup oil
¼ cup garlic wine vinegar

Wash well and thoroughly dry the spinach. Tear the leaves into bite-sized pieces and refrigerate. In a heavy skillet fry the bacon until crisp. Drain on paper towels and crumble.

2 tablespoons white wine
2 tablespoons soy sauce
1 teaspoon sugar
1 teaspoon dry mustard
½ teaspoon curry powder
½ teaspoon salt
½ teaspoon seasoned pepper
2 hard-boiled eggs, chopped

Shake the oil, vinegar, wine, soy sauce, sugar, dry mustard, curry powder, salt, and seasoned pepper in a 1-pint jar until well blended.

Pour the dressing over the spinach and toss well to coat the leaves. Sprinkle the crumbled bacon and chopped egg over the spinach. Serve at once.

PALACE COURT SALAD   SERVES 6

1¼ cups plus 3 tablespoons mayonnaise, preferably homemade (*see Index*)
¼ cup chili sauce
1½ tablespoons snipped fresh chives
2 tablespoons chopped fresh parsley
1¼ teaspoons dried tarragon
¾ teaspoon salt
¼ teaspoon pepper
6 fresh artichoke bottoms
1¼ pounds fresh shrimp, cooked, shelled, and cleaned
1 teaspoon fresh lemon juice
2¼ cups shredded iceberg lettuce
6 ½-inch-thick slices tomato, peeled
3 hard-boiled eggs, sieved
12 pimiento strips (optional)

In a small mixing bowl combine 1¼ cups mayonnaise, chili sauce, chives, parsley, tarragon, ¼ teaspoon salt, and the pepper. Mix the dressing thoroughly and taste to correct seasoning.

Prepare artichoke bottoms according to the Boiled Fresh Artichokes recipe (*see Index*). Set aside to cool.

Reserve 6 shrimp for garnish. Toss the remaining shrimp with the lemon juice and ½ teaspoon salt in a large mixing bowl. Add the remaining 3 tablespoons mayonnaise and stir gently until the shrimp are well coated with the mixture.

To assemble, construct the salad on individual chilled salad plates. Place a thin layer of shredded lettuce, 3–4 inches in diameter, in the center of each plate. Place a tomato slice in the center of the lettuce. Arrange an artichoke bottom on top of the tomato and spoon equal amounts of the shrimp mixture into the slight hollow of each artichoke bottom. Sprinkle the sieved egg around the exposed circle of lettuce and garnish each mound with a whole shrimp. If desired, cross 2 strips of pimiento on each. Serve the salad chilled and pass the dressing separately.

NOTE: The salad components may be prepared early in the day or several hours before serving. However, *do not assemble* the salad until ready to serve. This salad may also be made with fresh Dungeness crab and garnished with crab legs.

GREEN GODDESS SALAD

SERVES 6–8

1½ tablespoons minced scallions, including tops
2 tablespoons minced fresh parsley
1 tablespoon minced fresh tarragon or ½ teaspoon dried
1 tablespoon snipped fresh chives
1 tablespoon fresh lemon juice
2 tablespoons tarragon vinegar
2 tablespoons heavy cream
5 tablespoons chopped anchovy fillets
1½ cups mayonnaise, preferably homemade (*see Index*)
6–8 cups bite-sized pieces of assorted salad greens: romaine, endive, escarole, and chicory
1 clove garlic, split

In a 1-quart jar place the scallions, parsley, tarragon, chives, lemon juice, vinegar, cream, and anchovies. Shake vigorously to blend the ingredients well. Stir in the mayonnaise, blending well. Shake the jar vigorously for about 30 seconds or until the ingredients are well mixed. Chill the dressing at least 4 hours, or until serving time.

Wash and pat try the assorted salad greens. Tear the greens into bite-sized pieces. Place the greens in a large salad bowl, cover, and chill well for 2–3 hours in the refrigerator so that they are very crisp.

When ready to serve, rub a large salad bowl with the cut clove of garlic. Place the greens in the bowl and pour the chilled dressing over the greens, tossing briskly. Serve the salad at once from the large bowl onto individual chilled salad plates.

SHREDDED ZUCCHINI SALAD

SERVES 4–6

¼ cup mayonnaise, preferably homemade (*see Index*)
¼ cup sour cream
1 tablespoon fresh lemon juice
1½ tablespoons Dijon mustard
4 cups shredded zucchini
1 cup cherry tomatoes, halved
Bibb lettuce leaves
Watercress
Pimiento strips (optional)

In a small mixing bowl place the mayonnaise, sour cream, lemon juice, and mustard and combine thoroughly with a wire whisk. Chill covered for 1 hour. The dressing may be stored in a covered jar in the refrigerator for up to 4 hours or until serving time.

When ready to serve, pour the dressing over the zucchini and the tomatoes, and toss lightly. Mound on a bed of chilled lettuce leaves and watercress. Garnish with pimiento strips if desired.

NOTE: The zucchini and the tomatoes may be prepared up to 1 hour before serving and kept in separate plastic bags in the refrigerator until ready to toss with the dressing. If the zucchini retains too much moisture, place it in a strainer for a few minutes before assembling the salad.

WATERCRESS AND WALNUT SALAD

SERVES 6

⅔ cup imported olive oil
⅓ cup red wine vinegar
1 teaspoon Dijon mustard
¼ teaspoon salt or to taste
¼ teaspoon pepper or to taste
2 bunches watercress, torn into
  pieces
1 head Boston lettuce, torn
  into pieces
1 avocado, peeled and sliced
2 green apples, peeled and
  sliced
¼ cup chopped walnuts

Place the oil, vinegar, mustard, salt, and pepper in a 1-pint covered jar or cruet and shake vigorously for 15 seconds. Chill in the refrigerator until ready to use.

In a large salad bowl place the watercress, lettuce, avocado, apples, and walnuts. Shake the dressing again, pour it over all, and toss the salad lightly. Serve at once.

NOTE: Do not peel the avocado until the final moment, as it tends to darken.

MARINATED CABBAGE SALAD

SERVES 6–8

1 large white cabbage
1 green bell pepper
1 medium purple onion
1 cup sugar
¾ cup salad oil
1 cup white wine vinegar
1 teaspoon whole celery seed
1 teaspoon whole mustard seed
1 tablespoon salt

Tear cabbage into bite-sized pieces and slice the green pepper and the onion into very thin rings, separating the rings. Remove and discard any seeds from the pepper. In a large mixing bowl or deep salad bowl place a layer of torn cabbage, sliced green peppers, and onions. Repeat 2 more times, ending with the onion.

In a 1-quart jar combine the sugar, salad oil, vinegar, celery seed, mustard seed, and salt. Shake vigorously for 30 seconds or until combined well. Pour over layered cabbage mixture. Cover and chill at least 4 hours. Periodically toss the mixture to marinate the ingredients evenly.

When ready to serve, toss the greens well in the dressing mixture and using a slotted spoon, place individual servings on chilled salad plates. Discard any extra dressing mixture.

NOTE: This colorful cabbage salad is a nice accompaniment to barbecued meat or ham and can be held well in the refrigerator for up to 24 hours.

FRESH CRANBERRY SALAD

SERVES 8

must be prepared 24 hours in advance

1 quart fresh cranberries, washed and hulled
2 cups sugar
1 pound Tokay grapes, quartered, unpeeled, seeds removed
1 pint heavy cream
1 cup chopped pecans
2 bunches Bibb lettuce

With a meat or food grinder set at medium, grind the cranberries and place in a medium-sized mixing bowl. Add the sugar and stir well to blend. Place the cranberry mixture in a colander to drain overnight, discarding the juice.

The next day, mix the cranberries and grapes in a large bowl and refrigerate 2–4 hours or more. Just before serving, whip the cream until fairly stiff, fold the whipped cream and pecans into the cranberry-grape mixture, and place on Bibb lettuce leaves for individual salads. Serve at once.

NOTE: In many homes this has become the traditional Christmas Eve salad. It is good with turkey and prime rib. Always allow a little extra for Santa!

ARTICHOKE BOTTOMS STUFFED WITH RATATOUILLE

SERVES 6–8

1 medium onion, minced
1 clove garlic, minced
3 tablespoons olive oil
1 medium zucchini, cut into ¼-inch slices
1 medium eggplant, peeled and cut into 1-inch cubes
1 medium green pepper, seeded, sliced into ¼-inch strips
1 pound, or 2 cups, firm ripe tomatoes, peeled and seeded
¼ cup chopped fresh parsley
1 teaspoon dried basil
1 teaspoon dried oregano
1 teaspoon salt
1 9-ounce jar well-drained artichoke bottoms or 6–8 fresh artichoke bottoms
Watercress and parsley sprigs

In a 12-inch skillet or deep casserole sauté the onion and garlic in the oil over low heat until softened, about 5 minutes. Stir frequently. Add the zucchini, eggplant, green pepper, tomatoes, parsley, basil, oregano, and salt, stirring gently to mix. Cover the skillet and simmer the vegetables for 30 minutes or until tender. Be sure to stir the vegetables occasionally to prevent them from burning or sticking to the bottom of the pan. Remove the cover and cook the ratatouille over high heat until the liquid has been considerably reduced, stirring occasionally. Do not allow the vegetables to scorch. Remove the ratatouille from the skillet and transfer it to a large flat Pyrex dish to cool at room temperature for 1 hour. Cover and chill for a minimum of 2 hours.

If you are using fresh artichokes, prepare the bottoms as directed in the Boiled Fresh Artichokes recipe (*see Index*).

When ready to serve, fill the artichoke bottoms with the ratatouille mixture. Place on a chilled serving platter and garnish with crisp sprigs of watercress and parsley.

NOTE: The ratatouille may also be served as a hot vegetable course. If so, remove it from the skillet and transfer it to a 1-quart baking dish. Bake covered at 350° for 15 minutes. The hot ratatouille is delicious with lamb or barbecued turkey.

CHICKEN SALAD

SERVES 6

4 whole chicken breasts
1 stalk celery
2 tablespoons butter
1 cup almonds, blanched
2 red apples
2 tablespoons fresh lemon juice
¼ pound bacon
1–1½ cups mayonnaise, preferably homemade (see Index)
2–3 tablespoons curry powder
¼ cup chopped celery
2 heads Bibb lettuce, separated
Watercress or parsley sprigs

Place chicken breasts in a large saucepan over medium heat with water to cover, approximately 2 quarts. Add the celery stalk to the chicken and simmer for 25–30 minutes. Remove the breasts from the liquid and set aside to cool. Discard the liquid.

In a small 6-inch skillet melt the butter over medium heat, add the almonds, and sauté them until golden brown, 3–4 minutes, stirring constantly. Remove the almonds from the skillet with a slotted spoon and place on paper towels to cool and drain.

Peel, core, and chop the apples into fine pieces. Place in a bowl and sprinkle with lemon juice to prevent discoloration. Skin and bone the cooked chicken and cut into bite-sized cubes. Set aside. In a 10-inch skillet fry the bacon until crisp, remove from the pan, and set aside on paper towels to drain. Crumble the bacon and set aside. In a small bowl mix together the mayonnaise and curry until well blended.

In a large mixing bowl combine the chicken pieces, almonds, apple, celery, and curry-mayonnaise mixture. Toss lightly to coat. Serve either as individual salads on beds of Bibb lettuce or on a large chilled platter decorated with the Bibb lettuce leaves. Garnish with the crumbled bacon and the watercress sprigs.

SWEET PEPPER SALAD

9 green bell peppers, cored,
   seeded, and thinly sliced
¼ cup imported olive oil
⅔ cup imported olive oil
⅓ cup red wine vinegar
1 teaspoon Dijon mustard
¼ teaspoon salt or to taste
¼ teaspoon pepper or to taste
1 red onion, thinly sliced and
   separated into rings
12 ripe olives, sliced
½ cup sliced fresh mushrooms

In a 12–14-inch skillet sauté the pepper slices in ¼ cup olive oil over medium-high heat for 10–15 minutes or until the rings are limp, stirring often. With a slotted spoon, remove the pepper slices from the skillet. Drain well and cool for about 15 minutes.

In a small covered jar blend together ⅔ cup oil, the vinegar, mustard, salt, and pepper and shake well.

In a large mixing bowl combine the cooled pepper slices, the red onion rings, olives, and mushrooms. Pour the dressing over the pepper mixture and allow to marinate covered 2–4 hours in the refrigerator.

NOTE: This salad is unusually different and delicious with a barbecued steak, lamb chops, or broiled chicken.

CAESAR SALAD

1 clove garlic, split
3 small heads romaine lettuce
Salt and pepper to taste
¼ teaspoon dry mustard
¼ teaspoon Worcestershire
   sauce
2 tablespoons fresh lemon juice
2 tablespoons olive oil
4 anchovy fillets, cut into
   ¼-inch pieces
1 egg
1 cup Croutons II (see Index)
3 tablespoons freshly grated
   Parmesan cheese

Rub the inside of a wooden salad bowl with the garlic and set aside. Wash the romaine thoroughly and remove all outside leaves. Pat the remaining leaves dry with a paper towel and cut crosswise into slices, about 1 inch wide. Refrigerate the leaves in the salad bowl.

In a small bowl blend well the salt, pepper, mustard, Worcestershire, lemon juice, olive oil, and anchovies.

Meanwhile, place the egg in a small saucepan with enough water to cover, place over high heat, and allow to come to boil. Remove the pan from the heat and allow the egg to sit in the hot water for 2 minutes. Remove immediately from the water and set aside.

To serve, break the coddled egg over the greens, add the salad dressing, and toss lightly. Add the croutons and 2 tablespoons of the cheese. Toss again. Serve the salad on chilled plates garnished with the remainder of the cheese.

COBB SALAD

1⅓ cups salad oil
⅔ cup white wine vinegar
1 clove garlic, split
1 teaspoon salt
½ teaspoon pepper
1 teaspoon sugar
1 teaspoon dry mustard
1 teaspoon paprika
1 teaspoon Worcestershire sauce
½ head iceberg lettuce, very finely chopped
½ bunch watercress, finely chopped
1 small bunch chicory, very finely chopped
2½ tablespoons minced fresh chives
3 small tomatoes, peeled, seeded, and finely chopped
2½ cups cooked, cooled, and finely diced white chicken meat
6 slices bacon, cooked crisply, drained, and finely crumbled
2 hard-boiled eggs, finely diced
3 ounces bleu cheese, crumbled
1 avocado, peeled and diced

Early in the day, combine oil, vinegar, garlic, salt, pepper, sugar, mustard, paprika, and Worcestershire in a covered 1-quart jar. Shake the jar vigorously and refrigerate. It will keep for several days.

Place the vegetables, chicken, bacon, eggs, cheese, and avocado in a large salad bowl. Remove the dressing from the refrigerator and shake vigorously. Remove the garlic and pour ½ the dressing over the salad. Toss the entire salad lightly but thoroughly. Add more dressing if desired. Serve at once.

NOTE: All of the finely chopped ingredients (except for the avocado) may be prepared several hours before serving and held in plastic bags in the refrigerator. This salad is especially nice for a luncheon, as it is an entire meal. It can easily be doubled.

FRESH MARINATED VEGETABLE SALAD   SERVES 6

1½ cups thinly sliced fresh
   mushrooms
1½ cups cherry tomatoes,
   halved
1½ cups thinly sliced zucchini
1½ cups thinly sliced carrots,
   peeled
1½ cups thinly sliced scallions,
   including tops
1½ cups thinly sliced green
   pepper rings
1½ cups broccoli flowerettes
1½ cups cauliflower flowerettes
1 clove garlic, split
1 teaspoon salt
½ teaspoon freshly ground
   pepper
½ teaspoon dry mustard
1 teaspoon chopped fresh
   chives
2 tablespoons red wine vinegar
1 tablespoon fresh lemon juice
2 tablespoons olive oil
Watercress sprigs
Spinach leaves

Prepare the mushrooms, tomatoes, zucchini, carrots, scallions, green pepper, broccoli, and cauliflower and set aside. Rub a large salad bowl with the garlic.

Combine the remaining ingredients except the watercress and spinach and shake well in a covered cruet for 30 seconds.

Place the vegetables in the salad bowl and pour the dressing over them. Cover the bowl and marinate the vegetables for at least 2 hours in the refrigerator. Serve (drained) with watercress and young tender spinach leaves on a large platter or on individual chilled salad plates.

NOTE: This salad is a delightful carry-along accompaniment for a warm summer evening picnic.

MARINATED RED ONIONS   SERVES 4–6

2 cups very thinly sliced
   red onions
½ cup olive oil
2 tablespoons fresh lemon
   juice
1 teaspoon salt
⅛ teaspoon pepper
¼ teaspoon paprika
½ teaspoon sugar
¼ cup crumbled bleu cheese

Place the thinly sliced onions in a 2–3-quart saucepan. Pour boiling water over the onions and allow them to sit for 2–3 minutes. Drain the onions thoroughly in a colander.

In a 1-quart jar mix the olive oil, lemon juice, salt, pepper, paprika, sugar, and cheese. Shake vigorously until well blended.

Place the onions in a 2-quart bowl and pour the dressing over the onions. Cover and refrigerate for at least two days. They are a refreshing, crisp side dish in place of a green salad.

CUCUMBER SALAD WITH YOGURT

2 cups cucumber, peeled,
  seeded, and diced
1½ teaspoons salt
2 cups plain yogurt
1 clove garlic, crushed
1 tablespoon white wine
  vinegar
¼ teaspoon dried dill weed
1 tablespoon olive oil
1 tablespoon finely chopped
  scallions (whites only)
1 tablespoon chopped fresh
  mint
Lettuce leaves
1 cup seedless green grapes

Place the diced cucumber in a small mixing bowl. Stir in 1 teaspoon salt and mix well. Cover and refrigerate for 1 hour. Remove the cucumber mixture from the refrigerator and drain off any excess liquid.

In a larger mixing bowl combine the yogurt with the garlic, vinegar, ½ teaspoon salt, dill, oil, scallions, and mint.

Add the diced cucumber. Stir well. Reserve 2 tablespoons of grapes and gently fold the remainder into the cucumber mixture. Cover and refrigerate for 1 hour. Serve in lettuce cups on a chilled plate. Garnish with the reserved grapes.

CELERY ROOT JULIENNE

must be prepared 24 hours in advance

2 small celery roots
2 tablespoons fresh lemon
  juice
2 teaspoons salt
3½ tablespoons Dijon mustard
3 tablespoons boiling water
⅓ cup light olive oil
3 tablespoons white wine
  vinegar
¼ teaspoon salt or to taste
¼ teaspoon freshly ground
  white pepper or to taste
Bibb lettuce leaves
2½ tablespoons minced fresh
  parsley
2½ teaspoons minced fresh
  chives
Cherry tomatoes (optional)

With a very sharp knife, peel the celery roots on a firm cutting board. Cut them into small, even, julienne strips, about 2 inches long and ⅛ inch thick. Place the strips in a small mixing bowl with the lemon juice and 2 teaspoons salt. Thoroughly mix the strips, lemon juice, and salt and marinate at room temperature for at least 1 hour.

Place the mustard in a large warmed bowl, add the boiling water a few drops at a time, whipping constantly with a wire whisk. Continue to whip, adding the oil, a drop or two at a time. The dressing should be thick. Beat in the vinegar with the whisk, a drop or two at a time. Season the dressing with ¼ teaspoon salt and pepper or to taste.

Gently mix the marinated julienne strips with the dressing. Cover the mixture and place in the refrigerator overnight.

Serve the celery root on a bed of Bibb lettuce on a shallow chilled serving platter. Sprinkle with the fresh parsley and chives and, if desired, surround the celery root with plump cherry tomatoes.

COLD SPICED MEXICAN TOMATOES

1½ cups vegetable oil
1 cup white wine vinegar
¼ cup sugar
1 clove garlic, minced
8 ounces green chile salsa
½ teaspoon dried oregano
⅛ teaspoon celery seed
¼ teaspoon salt or to taste
⅛ teaspoon pepper or to taste
6 scallions, including tops,
    finely chopped
½ cup finely chopped celery
4 small tomatoes, unpeeled,
    cored, and finely chopped
4 ounces green chiles, diced
    (optional)
6 tomatoes, unpeeled, cored,
    and cut into wedges
Lettuce leaves
12–16 anchovy fillets
¾ cup minced parsley

In a 1-quart jar blend the oil, vinegar, sugar, garlic, salsa, oregano, celery seed, salt, and pepper by shaking approximately 30 seconds to combine the ingredients well. Using a medium-sized mixing bowl, combine the scallions, celery, small tomatoes, and green chiles with the oil and vinegar dressing and mix well. (The green chiles make it a spicier marinade.) Cover the bowl and refrigerate 6 hours.

Two hours before serving, add the tomato wedges to the marinade mixture, blend well, cover, and return to the refrigerator.

To serve, arrange lettuce leaves on salad plates, and using a slotted spoon, place a serving of the tomato mixture on each plate. Pour some of the marinade over each serving including some of the green onions, diced tomatoes, celery, and chiles. Over each serving, crisscross 2 anchovy fillets and sprinkle with fresh parsley.

NOTE: This spicy, colorful salad appeals to everyone. It accompanies Mexican food well, but is equally good with beef and lamb.

LAYERED SALAD

SERVES 6

1 cup mayonnaise, preferably
    homemade (*see Index*)
1–2 tablespoons white wine
    vinegar or cider vinegar
1 head iceberg lettuce, washed,
    drained, and shredded
2–3 scallions, including tops,
    minced
1 or 2 large carrots, peeled and
    grated
2–3 stalks celery, chopped
1½ cups cooked peas, well
    drained

Use a deep salad bowl or serving dish with fairly straight sides. Plan on having 2 layers of each vegetable in the serving dish.

In a small mixing bowl combine the mayonnaise with the vinegar and set aside. The consistency of the dressing should be thin enough to spread easily over the vegetable layers.

In the salad bowl place a thin layer of each vegetable using about ½ the total amount. Over these first layers of vegetables, spread ½ the dressing and sprinkle on top of the dressing 1½ teaspoons sugar. Again repeat the process using

3 teaspoons sugar
4–6 slices bacon, cooked and
  crumbled

the rest of the vegetables, dressing, and sugar. Sprinkle the crumbled bacon on top of the salad, cover, and allow to marinate in the refrigerator for several hours or overnight. To serve, do not toss, but serve the salad in layers with each portion.

NOTE: This salad must be prepared a day ahead or at least 6–8 hours in advance in order for the dressing to marinate the vegetables.

CELERY VICTOR

SERVES 8

4 celery hearts, of equal size
1 tablespoon fresh lemon juice
½ tablespoon salt or to taste
2 cups salad oil
¾ cup fresh lemon juice
1 cup white wine vinegar
1 clove garlic
2 tablespoons chopped fresh
  parsley
1 teaspoon dried oregano
Dash cayenne pepper
1 teaspoon dried thyme
1 bay leaf
¼ teaspoon salt
¼ teaspoon black pepper
Lettuce leaves
8 flat anchovy fillets
2 ounces pimiento, sliced

Wash, trim, and cut the celery hearts in half. Place the hearts in a 3-quart saucepan and cover with water. Add 1 tablespoon lemon juice and the salt. Bring to a boil over high heat, reduce heat, cover, and simmer for 8–10 minutes to parboil the hearts. Remove the hearts from the water and let drain in a colander.

Mix the oil, ¾ cup lemon juice, the vinegar, garlic clove, parsley, oregano, cayenne, thyme, bay leaf, salt, and black pepper vigorously in a 1-quart jar to combine well. Pour the marinade into the same saucepan and bring to a boil over high heat. Add the drained celery hearts, reduce the heat, and simmer in the dressing until tender, about 5–8 minutes, testing frequently with a fork. With a slotted spoon, remove the hearts from the hot marinade, cool to room temperature, then cover and chill for a minimum of 4 hours. Place the marinade in a small bowl, cover, and chill.

Before serving, remove the clove of garlic and discard. Place a celery heart on a lettuce leaf on individual salad plates. Garnish each heart with 2 strips of anchovy and fine slivers of pimiento. Serve with a few teaspoons of the oil-vinegar cooking marinade spooned over each heart.

MUSHROOM AND SCALLOP SALAD

SERVES 8

1½ pounds bay scallops
2 tablespoons minced onion
1 bay leaf
¼ teaspoon salt
¼ teaspoon pepper
3 tablespoons fresh lemon
  juice
½ cup olive oil
Salt to taste
Freshly ground pepper to
  taste
1 pound fresh mushrooms,
  trimmed and thinly sliced
4 tablespoons chopped fresh
  parsley

Combine the scallops, onion, bay leaf, and ¼ teaspoon each of salt and pepper in a 2½–3-quart saucepan and cover with water. Bring to a boil over medium heat and immediately turn off the heat and let the scallops stand for 5 minutes. Drain the scallops and onions in a strainer. Remove the bay leaf and place them in a medium-sized mixing bowl. In another medium-sized mixing bowl combine the lemon juice, olive oil, and salt and pepper to taste. Pour ⅓ of the dressing over the scallop mixture, toss, and cover. Add the mushrooms to the remaining dressing and toss to coat well. Cover and refrigerate both the scallop and the mushroom mixtures separately for 2–4 hours. When ready to serve, combine the scallops and mushrooms in a large salad bowl and garnish with the parsley.

NOTE: This salad is a delicious choice for a picnic. Spoon into a large pineapple that has been cut approximately 1 inch down from the stem, hollowed out, and drained. After filling, use the top (stem end) of the pineapple as a lid.

HOT POTATO SALAD

SERVES 10–12

10 white rose potatoes, peeled
1 pound bacon
1 large onion, chopped
Salt and pepper to taste
1 cup vinegar
3 tablespoons sugar

Put the potatoes in a large saucepan. Cover with water. Boil the potatoes for about 40 minutes or until tender, but not falling apart.

In a heavy 10–12-inch skillet cut the raw bacon into small pieces and fry until crisp. Remove the bacon from the pan with a slotted spoon, reserve the bacon fat, and set aside. Slice the cooked potatoes about ¼ inch thick. In a 10-inch casserole dish arrange ⅓ of the cooked potatoes. Cover with ⅓ of the onion and bacon and repeat the layers until all is used up. Salt and pepper to taste.

In a small saucepan combine the bacon fat, vinegar, sugar, and salt to taste. Bring to a boil and pour over the hot potato mixture and stir gently. Serve at once.

RICE SALAD WITH SHRIMP

2 cups converted white rice
¼ cup vegetable oil
⅓ cup white vinegar
½ teaspoon salt or to taste
¼ teaspoon pepper or to taste
¼ teaspoon dried tarragon
½ green pepper, seeded and
    finely minced
¼ cup minced fresh parsley
½ cup minced scallions,
    including tops
1 cup cooked green peas
½–1-pound cooked baby shrimp
½ cup sliced ripe olives
    (optional)
Watercress sprigs

Cook and steam the rice according to the package directions. While rice is still hot, place in a large mixing bowl and add the oil, vinegar, salt, pepper, and tarragon, tossing lightly to blend well. Cool to room temperature. When cool, add the green pepper, parsley, scallions, and peas, mixing in well. Cover the bowl and refrigerate for a minimum of 2 hours.

At serving time, pile the rice mixture on a chilled serving platter in the shape of a pyramid and garnish with baby shrimp and olives. As an alternate salad, the rice mixture may be mixed with the shrimp and used to stuff 6–8 medium-sized peeled and hollowed tomatoes. Garnish each serving with a crisp sprig of watercress.

NOTE: This salad is a nice accompaniment for a picnic or barbecue.

SEAFOOD SALAD

1 cup crab meat
1 cup cooked, shelled, and
    deveined medium-to-large
    shrimp
1 cup 1-inch-chunks fresh
    pineapple
2 tablespoons chutney
1 cup sliced celery
1 cup sliced scallions, including
    some of the tops
1 cup sliced water chestnuts
½ cup pine nuts or slivered
    almonds, toasted (optional)
1 cup mayonnaise, preferably
    homemade (see Index)
½ cup sour cream
1 teaspoon curry

In a large bowl combine the crab, shrimp, pineapple, chutney, celery, scallions, water chestnuts, and pine nuts or almonds, if desired, and toss together lightly. Cover and refrigerate. In a small pint bowl combine the mayonnaise, sour cream, and curry, blending well. Cover and refrigerate at least 2 hours.

One hour before serving, pour the mayonnaise mixture over the seafood and mix lightly but thoroughly. Return to the refrigerator for 1 hour to blend the flavors. Serve the salad surrounded by lettuce leaves or in Mandarin Salad Mold (see Index).

MOLDED SALMON SALAD

SERVES 6–8

1 pound fresh cooked salmon
  meat
½ cup mayonnaise, preferably
  homemade (*see Index*)
1 cup small curd cottage cheese
¼ cup sweet pickle relish
3 tablespoons Worcestershire
  sauce
¼ cup capers (reserve 2
  individual capers for
  decoration)
1 tablespoon grated onion
¼ teaspoon white pepper,
  lemon pepper, or Tabasco
  to taste
4 tablespoons fresh lemon
  juice
½ teaspoon dried dill weed
1 tablespoon unflavored
  gelatin
¼ cup water
¾ cup chicken broth
1 cucumber
2 tablespoons vinegar
2 tablespoons sugar
1 3-inch-long tomato strip,
  skin on
Watercress sprigs

In a large mixing bowl combine the salmon, mayonnaise, cottage cheese, relish, Worcestershire, capers, onion, pepper, lemon juice, and dill. Stir well, breaking down the salmon. Soften the gelatin in a small bowl in ¼ cup cold water. Heat the broth and dissolve the gelatin in it. Cool slightly and add to the salmon mixture. Put the mixture in a greased 4-cup fish mold and refrigerate 4 hours.

Peel and seed the cucumber. Chop the cucumber very finely, place in a small bowl, and add to it the sugar and vinegar. Refrigerate.

To serve, unmold the jelled salmon mold and surround it with the cucumber mixture. Make a face on the salmon using the capers for eyes and the tomato strip for a smile. Garnish the fish with sprigs of watercress. Place the salmon salad in the refrigerator for 5–10 minutes prior to serving.

BLENDER CUCUMBER SALAD RING

SERVES 6

2 cups plain yogurt
½ clove garlic
1 teaspoon salt
1 tablespoon fresh lemon juice
2 cucumbers, peeled and
  coarsely sliced
2 tablespoons unflavored
  gelatin

Place the yogurt, garlic, salt, and lemon juice in a blender and blend at low speed. Gradually add the cucumbers, blending until the mixture is smooth, about 1–2 minutes. In a small saucepan dissolve and melt the gelatin in ½ cup of the cucumber mixture over low heat. Stir and cook only until all of the gelatin is dissolved. Return the gelatin mixture to the rest of the cucumber

2 tablespoons finely chopped
  fresh mint
Bibb lettuce leaves
Mint sprigs

mixture and blend again for 30 seconds at low-medium speed. Stir in the chopped mint and blend with a fork quickly and lightly. Pour the entire cucumber-yogurt mixture into an oiled 1-quart mold. Chill at least 4–5 hours, until firm, in the refrigerator. Just before serving, unmold the cucumber ring on a chilled platter. Surround with Bibb lettuce leaves and garnish with mint sprigs. For a luncheon entree, fill the center of the ring with Chicken Salad (*see Index*).

COLD MOLDED BROCCOLI RING

SERVES 6–8

¼ teaspoon salt
3 cups fresh broccoli, heavy
  stalks removed
  (approximately 2–2½ pounds)
2½ envelopes unflavored gelatin
2 chicken bouillon cubes
½ cup cold water
2 tablespoons fresh lemon juice
1 cup milk
½ teaspoon Worcestershire
  sauce
½ cup sour cream
2 hard-boiled eggs, chopped
Lettuce leaves
Cherry tomatoes
Parsley sprigs
Lemon slices
Roquefort Dressing (*see Index*)

In a 2-quart saucepan bring 1 cup water and the salt to a boil. Place the broccoli, which has been washed and trimmed, into boiling salted water. Reduce heat to low, cover, and cook the broccoli until it is tender, about 8–10 minutes. Drain the broccoli well and reserve ½ cup of the cooking liquid. Chop the broccoli into small pieces. In a small bowl soften the gelatin and bouillon cubes in the cold water. In a 2½–3-quart saucepan heat the broccoli liquid over low heat and stir in the gelatin mixture until it is dissolved. Remove from the heat and add the lemon juice, milk, and Worcestershire. Chill until partially set, about 15–20 minutes. Gently fold in the sour cream, eggs, and chopped broccoli. Pour into a 6-cup ring mold, which has been lightly greased with vegetable oil. Chill and mold for at least 8 hours. When ready to serve, invert the mold on a bed of lettuce. Garnish with cherry tomatoes, parsley sprigs, and lemon slices. In the center, place a small bowl of Roquefort Dressing (*see Index*).

THOUSAND ISLAND MOLD
WITH FRESH SEAFOOD

SERVES 8

2 tablespoons unflavored gelatin
½ cup cold water
1½ cups mayonnaise, preferably
   homemade (*see Index*)
1 cup chili sauce
¼ teaspoon Tabasco sauce
½ teaspoon sugar
¼ teaspoon salt
6 hard-boiled eggs, sliced
1 cucumber, peeled, seeded,
   and finely chopped
1 cup thinly sliced celery
1½ pounds fresh crab meat or
   fresh shrimp, cooked, shelled,
   and cleaned
2 tablespoons fresh lemon juice
½ teaspoon lemon pepper
Watercress sprigs
Bibb lettuce leaves
¾ cup chopped fresh parsley

Soften the gelatin in the water and dissolve by stirring the gelatin in a double boiler over hot water for 3 minutes. When thoroughly dissolved, combine the gelatin, mayonnaise, chili sauce, Tabasco, sugar, and salt in a large mixing bowl, stirring to blend well. Chill in the refrigerator until slightly firm, approximately 30 minutes. When slightly firm, remove from the refrigerator and gently fold in the sliced eggs, cucumber, and celery. Pour the mixture into an 8-cup oiled ring mold and chill until firm, at least 4–6 hours.

In a small mixing bowl combine the seafood, lemon juice, and lemon pepper. Gently toss this mixture and set aside.

Before unmolding the salad ring, prepare a bed of crisp watercress and Bibb lettuce. Unmold the ring onto the lettuce, place the seafood mixture in the center, and garnish with the parsley.

NOTE: This makes a very elegant luncheon entrée.

MOLDED EGG RING

SERVES 8

12 hard-boiled eggs, peeled
2 envelopes unflavored gelatin
1½ cups water
¼ cup fresh lemon juice
½ cup chopped fresh parsley
½ cup chopped fresh chives
½ teaspoon dry mustard
1 teaspoon catsup
½ teaspoon salt
½ teaspoon Worcestershire
   sauce
Bibb lettuce leaves
Seafood Filling (*below*)
Watercress sprigs

Force the eggs while still warm through a medium-fine sieve and set aside.

In a small bowl soak the gelatin in ½ cup of cold water. Add 1 cup of boiling water and the lemon juice. Mix thoroughly and set aside to cool and thicken slightly, 15–20 minutes.

In a large mixing bowl combine the parsley, chives, dry mustard, catsup, salt, and Worcestershire. Gently add the sieved eggs and cooled gelatin. Blend all the ingredients quickly and place in an oiled 1-quart ring mold. Place the mold covered in the refrigerator and allow to chill for 3–4 hours.

When ready to serve, unmold the ring mold onto a large, chilled serving platter covered with lettuce leaves. Fill the center of the mold with Seafood Filling and garnish with sprigs of watercress.

SEAFOOD FILLING

1 cup mayonnaise
½ cup chili sauce
1 pound fresh shrimp, cleaned, shelled, and deveined
1 pound fresh crab meat

To prepare filling, place the mayonnaise, chili sauce, and fresh seafood in a large mixing bowl and combine gently.

NOTE: This mold is especially nice for a luncheon, as it may be made ahead. Only the filling remains, and should be prepared just before serving.

GOURMET BEEF SALAD VINAIGRETTE   SERVES 6–8

1½ pounds sirloin beef roast, cooked
½–¾ pound fresh mushrooms, halved
7 ounces artichoke hearts, halved
2–3 medium tomatoes, peeled and cut in wedges
2 heads Bibb lettuce, washed, drained, and chilled
2 tablespoons fresh lemon juice
¼ cup red wine
¼ cup red wine vinegar
½ teaspoon salt
¼ teaspoon lemon pepper
½ cup thinly sliced scallions, including tops
¾ cup salad oil
¼ teaspoon dry mustard
⅛ teaspoon rosemary
⅛ teaspoon sage
⅛ teaspoon thyme
⅛ teaspoon marjoram
⅛ teaspoon white pepper
Watercress sprigs

Carve the roast beef into slices ⅛–¼ inch thick, then cut slices into strips approximately 1 inch wide and 2–3 inches long. Place the meat in a large bowl in which the salad will marinate. Add the mushrooms, artichoke hearts, and tomato wedges to the beef and set aside.

In a separate small bowl combine the lemon juice, wine, vinegar, salt, lemon pepper, scallions, salad oil, dry mustard, rosemary, sage, thyme, marjoram, and white pepper. Blend thoroughly with a wire whisk and pour the marinade over the beef-tomato mixture. Cover and chill 2–6 hours. Stir the salad several times while marinating.

Line a serving dish or shallow platter with the lettuce. Remove the meat-tomato mixture from the bowl with a slotted spoon and arrange attractively in the center of the platter. Discard the marinade. Surround the salad with additional tomato wedges and garnish with sprigs of watercress.

AVOCADO RING MOLD

2½ envelopes unflavored
    gelatin
1 cup water
3 ripe avocados
1 cup mayonnaise, preferably
    homemade (*see Index*)
1 cup sour cream
2 tablespoons grated green bell
    pepper
2 tablespoons grated onion
¼ cup fresh lemon juice
1 teaspoon salt
¼ teaspoon white pepper
Dash Tabasco sauce
1 teaspoon Worcestershire
    sauce

Dissolve the gelatin in the cup of water, heating it gently over a double boiler. After it has dissolved, place the gelatin mixture over a large bowl filled with ice water. Stir until it is completely cool and starts to thicken, about 5 minutes. Remove from the ice water bowl and set aside.

In a medium bowl mash the avocados and add the other ingredients. Gently stir in the cooled gelatin mixture. Pour into an oiled 1½-quart ring mold. Cover the mold and refrigerate for 4–6 hours. Unmold the salad on a serving platter.

NOTE: The mold is delicious filled with Chicken Salad (*see Index*). This can be made a day ahead. If doubled, use 4½ tablespoons of gelatin.

MANDARIN SALAD MOLD

1 cup (1 11-ounce can)
    Mandarin oranges
½ cup syrup from the oranges
1 envelope unflavored gelatin
½ cup white wine
1 teaspoon powdered chicken
    stock base
½ teaspoon salt
½ teaspoon curry powder
¼ cup chopped chutney
1 tablespoon chopped scallions,
    including tops
1 cup sour cream
½ cup chopped celery
2 tablespoons wine vinegar

Drain the oranges, reserving the syrup, and set aside. Place ½ cup syrup, the gelatin, and wine in a 1½–2-quart saucepan. Stir over low heat until the gelatin is dissolved. Remove the pan from the heat. Add the chicken stock base, salt, curry powder, chutney, and scallions. Chill until only partially set, about 15–20 minutes. Blend in the sour cream and fold in the oranges, celery, and vinegar. Place the mixture in a 6-cup oiled ring mold and refrigerate until set, at least 4 hours. Unmold on a bed of watercress. Fill the center with Seafood Salad or Chicken Salad (*see Index*).

FRENCH DRESSING I

½ cup salad oil
¼ cup vinegar or lemon juice
1 teaspoon Dijon mustard
1 teaspoon salt
1 teaspoon freshly ground
    pepper
2 tablespoons freshly grated
    Parmesan cheese
1 clove garlic, crushed
¼ teaspoon sugar

Combine all the ingredients in a small mixing bowl and beat for 1 minute with a wire whisk. Pour into a pint jar or cruet, cover, and refrigerate for at least 2 hours. Shake well before serving.

NOTE: This is especially refreshing on fresh tomato slices or washed and chilled spinach greens.

FRENCH DRESSING II

2 teaspoons salt
1 teaspoon freshly ground
    white pepper
½ teaspoon freshly ground
    black pepper
¼ teaspoon sugar
¼ teaspoon dry mustard
1 teaspoon Dijon mustard
1 teaspoon fresh lemon juice
2 teaspoons minced garlic
5½ tablespoons tarragon vinegar
3 tablespoons imported olive
    oil
9 tablespoons vegetable oil
1 egg, beaten
½ cup light cream

Place all the ingredients, in the order given, into a 2-cup covered jar. Shake the jar well and chill the dressing several hours before serving.

NOTE: This dressing is especially nice on a mixture of crisp chilled greens or on a bed of endive, watercress, and avocado.

MEXICAN WHITE DRESSING

1 cup vegetable oil
1 teaspoon celery seed
1 small onion, grated
6 tablespoons sugar
½ cup white cider vinegar
1 teaspoon prepared mustard
1 teaspoon salt

Mix all the ingredients in a 1-quart covered jar and allow to stand at room temperature for 24 hours. Refrigerate 1 hour before serving. Shake well just before using. This dressing will keep for 1 week in the refrigerator.

NOTE: This dressing is especially good on mixed greens or individual servings of sliced avocado and grapefruit sections.

VINAIGRETTE DRESSING

MAKES 1¼ CUPS

½ teaspoon paprika
1 teaspoon salt
⅛ teaspoon pepper
½ teaspoon dry mustard
½ teaspoon sugar
1 tablespoon tarragon vinegar
2 tablespoons cider vinegar
⅓ cup olive oil
1 teaspoon minced onion
½ teaspoon mustard seed

Mix all the ingredients together in a 2-cup covered jar and shake vigorously. Chill the dressing well before using.

NOTE: This is a delicious, spicy dressing for mixed greens such as romaine, Bibb lettuce, chicory, or watercress.

ROQUEFORT DRESSING

MAKES 2 CUPS

3 ounces cream cheese, softened
⅓ cup crumbled Roquefort or bleu cheese
½ cup light cream
¼ teaspoon salt
¼ teaspoon Dijon mustard
½ cup mayonnaise, preferably homemade (*see Index*)
½ teaspoon Beau Monde seasoning

Combine all the ingredients in a blender and blend for 2 minutes at medium speed. Refrigerate in a covered jar at least 8 hours to enhance the flavor. Shake before using. The dressing will keep for several days in the refrigerator.

NOTE: This is especially nice when poured over crisp, chilled romaine lettuce and garnished with tomato wedges and slices of avocado. The dressing may also be used in the center of Cold Molded Broccoli Ring (*see Index*).

HERB FRENCH DRESSING

MAKES 1 CUP

¾ cup olive oil
2 tablespoons vinegar
1 tablespoon fresh lemon juice
1 teaspoon Dijon mustard
½ teaspoon salt
¼ teaspoon pepper
1 tablespoon finely chopped fresh parsley
1 tablespoon finely chopped fresh chives
1 teaspoon dried chervil

Combine all the ingredients in a covered 1-quart jar and shake until well blended. Refrigerate the dressing. Shake the jar briskly again just before serving.

CREAMY SALAD DRESSING

MAKES 1½ CUPS

¼ cup red wine vinegar
¼ cup half-and-half or light
  cream
¾ cup oil, preferably imported
  olive oil
1 heaping teaspoon salt
1 teaspoon freshly ground
  pepper
1 teaspoon minced garlic

Mix all the ingredients in a covered jar, bottle, or cruet. Shake the dressing vigorously and place in the refrigerator. Shake again thoroughly before using.

NOTE: This dressing is best made a day ahead so the flavors can mix thoroughly. It is a very piquant dressing on a salad with fresh spinach or watercress. It may be held in the refrigerator up to 1 week.

FRENCH CAESAR DRESSING

MAKES 1½ CUPS

¼ teaspoon minced shallots
¼ teaspoon minced garlic
½ teaspoon Worcestershire
  sauce
1 teaspoon Dijon mustard
¼ teaspoon sugar
Pinch monosodium glutamate
Pinch salt
Pinch pepper
1 egg yolk
⅛ cup cider vinegar
1 cup peanut oil
1 tablespoon olive oil

Mix together all the ingredients, except the peanut oil and olive oil, in a large mixing bowl. Add the oils gradually, beating constantly with a whisk. The consistency will be that of a Caesar dressing, thicker than a normal vinaigrette.

NOTE: This dressing tends to separate on standing; blend or beat before serving on tossed greens or cold vegetables.

LEMON DIJON DRESSING

MAKES ¾ CUP

1 egg
2 teaspoons freshly grated
  Parmesan cheese
½ teaspoon salt
¼ teaspoon pepper
2 tablespoons Dijon mustard
3 tablespoons fresh lemon juice
1 teaspoon Worcestershire
  sauce
1 teaspoon sugar
½ cup vegetable oil

In a small mixing bowl combine all the ingredients and beat vigorously with a wire whisk until completely blended. Place the ingredients in a covered pint jar or cruet and refrigerate for at least 2 hours. Just before serving, shake the jar vigorously.

NOTE: This dressing is particularly nice on romaine, Boston, or Bibb lettuce leaves. Since it contains no vinegar, it can be served with wine.

MEDITERRANEAN DRESSING

MAKES ¾ CUP

1 clove garlic, crushed
½ teaspoon salt
¼ teaspoon pepper
½ teaspoon grated lemon rind
¼ teaspoon paprika
2 tablespoons tarragon vinegar
½ cup olive oil
2 tablespoons sour cream

In a small mixing bowl combine the garlic, salt, pepper, lemon rind, paprika, and vinegar. Gradually add the olive oil, beating constantly with a wire whisk. When blended well, beat in the sour cream and mix thoroughly. Store the dressing in a covered ½-pint cruet in the refrigerator. Chill in refrigerator at least 2 hours before serving.

NOTE: This is a delicious dressing for sliced tomatoes or cold cooked vegetables.

FRENCH RÉMOULADE DRESSING

MAKES 2½ CUPS

1½ stalks celery, finely minced
⅓ cup finely minced fresh
   parsley
3 large shallots, finely minced
1 teaspoon salt
½ teaspoon freshly ground
   pepper
½ teaspoon dried basil
Pinch dried rosemary
Pinch dried marjoram
¼ cup snipped fresh chives
1⅓ cups salad oil
⅔ cup tarragon-flavored red
   wine vinegar

Combine all ingredients in a 3-cup container with a lid. Shake well to combine and let stand, covered, for 4–6 hours before using.

NOTE: This dressing is very nice on mixed salad greens, avocado halves, sliced tomatoes, or thinly sliced crisp cucumbers.

JAPANESE SALAD DRESSING

MAKES 1½ CUPS

1 cup Japanese rice vinegar
1 tablespoon sugar
1 tablespoon fresh lemon juice
1 teaspoon salt
2 tablespoons sake

Warm all the ingredients except the sake over low heat in a small saucepan, about 5 minutes or until the sugar dissolves. Stir occasionally and when the sugar has dissolved, add the sake. Remove from the heat and pour into a 1-pint glass container. Let the dressing stand at room temperature uncovered for 1 hour to cool. After 1 hour, cover the container and chill in the refrigerator before using, at least 2–3 hours. Shake well before serving.

NOTE: This is very nice on fresh salad greens or as a marinade on cooked vegetables.

PARSLEY SALAD DRESSING

MAKES 1 CUP

¾ cup olive oil
3 tablespoons fresh lemon juice
½ teaspoon Dijon mustard
½ teaspoon salt
¼ teaspoon freshly ground
    pepper
1 cup minced fresh parsley
1 clove garlic, crushed
    (optional)

Place all the ingredients in the jar of an electric blender. Blend at medium speed for 45 seconds. Taste and correct seasonings if necessary. This delicious dressing will keep in the refrigerator in a covered jar for 3–4 days.

NOTE: This is especially good on a mixed green salad.

SEAFOOD LOUIE DRESSING

MAKES ABOUT 4 CUPS

2 cups mayonnaise, preferably
    homemade (*see Index*)
1½ cups chili sauce
2 teaspoons fresh lemon juice
1 teaspoon horseradish
¼ cup finely chopped dill
    pickle
¼ cup finely chopped celery
½ teaspoon Worcestershire

Mix all the ingredients in a medium-sized mixing bowl until well blended. Store the dressing in a covered 1½-quart jar in the refrigerator.

NOTE: Serve with all types of shellfish, such as crab, shrimp, or lobster.

FRUIT SALAD DRESSING

MAKES 1½ CUPS

5 ounces light Karo syrup
1 cup sugar
½ cup boiling water
2 egg whites
2 tablespoons grated orange
    rind
½ teaspoon vanilla
⅔ cup mayonnaise, preferably
    homemade (*see Index*)

In a 1½–2-quart saucepan cook the syrup, sugar, and water over moderate heat until the mixture is at thread stage, about 238° on a candy thermometer, stirring occasionally. In a separate medium-sized mixing bowl beat the egg whites with an electric beater until they are stiff, about 3 minutes. In a slow, steady stream, pour the syrup into the egg whites while beating continuously on low speed. Cool the egg white mixture in the refrigerator for 30 minutes. Add the orange rind, vanilla, and mayonnaise and stir in thoroughly. Refrigerate the dressing until ready to use.

NOTE: This dressing is a delicious accompaniment to a chilled platter of canteloupe, watermelon, and fresh pineapple slices. It may be kept in the refrigerator 3–4 days; however, it tends to separate when cold. Always stir before serving.

CHAPTER III

THE REDWOOD EMPIRE

EGGS, CHEESE, RICE, & PASTA

NURTURED by the damp air from the sea, vast groves of *Sequoia sempervirens* thrive in the mountainous California coast line between San Francisco and the Oregon border. This particular species of conifer has distinguished these coastal counties with the name Redwood Empire because of its prolific growth among the rivers and streams and along the rocky coast line. The redwood, called "Palo Alto" by the early Spanish explorers, is the world's oldest living plant next to the bristlecone pine and, except for some parts of Southeast Asia, grows nowhere else in the world.

In spite of a colorful history that includes the stories of a Russian royal princess, a Russian count whose fiancée became a nun, the birth of a republic, and a lost cabin full of gold, the Redwood Empire is only vaguely understood historically, and, except by lumbermen, it is relatively unexploited.

At one time, this area was the most distant outpost of the Russian Empire, and later it became a mother lode country for the lumber industry. The Redwood Empire is now a retreat for knowledgeable vacationers aware that beneath a shroud of fog lie black sand beaches strewn with driftwood in exotic shapes, and that the redwood groves shelter masses of ferns and rhododendrons of incomparable beauty.

Drake's Bay had been discovered, named, and to some extent explored more than a quarter century before any white men settled above the 37th parallel on the East Coast of the United States. Sir Frances Drake, aboard the *Golden Hind*, landed at this small bay north of San Francisco in 1578 or 1579 during the expedition that took him as far north as the Oregon border in his search for the Northwest Passage. He called the area New Albion and stayed at Drake's Bay a month to make repairs on his ship before returning south. Sixteen years later Sebastián Cermeño was ordered to search for a safe harbor on the California coast while on his way home from Manila to Acapulco. Cermeño brought his two-hundred-ton galleon, the *San Augustin*, into Drake's Bay, where she was wrecked by sudden winds that slammed her into the shore and broke her to pieces. Using timbers salvaged from the galleon, the crew constructed a small launch and were finally able to reach Mexico. No doubt there were other alien visitors to those northern latitudes, too, although no one knows who they were, but the discovery of a cache of Ming porcelain in a coast Miwok Indian burial ground is evidence that at least some China traders or Chinese visited the area in the early days.

Although the Spanish had planned to found missions north of San Francisco, and so might have been the first settlers of this part of California, the northern missions were delayed by apathy and economics until after the Russians had founded a permanent settlement. By the end of the eighteenth century, the Russian-American Fur Company was well established in Alaska and in the Aleutian Islands. The furs, usually traded with the Indians and Eskimos for trinkets, were shipped to Canton in exchange for silks and ivories, which were sold in Atlantic ports. This northern territory was rich in furs but poor in food for those accustomed to a European diet. When in 1806 Count Nikolai Rezanov, the Czar's chamberlain, went to Sitka on a mission for the Czar, he found the colonists to be in a deplorable state. They were sick with scurvy and fever, and many were starving. An American ship provided temporary relief for the unfortunates, but the count endeavored to find a permanent solution to their problem. Accordingly, he sailed south to attempt negotiations with the Spanish—all the while knowing that any trade was forbidden under Spanish law.

Though Spanish prejudice and law were against him, Count Rezanov succeeded in his mission. He secured permission for a Russian colony to be founded about eighty miles north of San Francisco. Whether the count's success in negotiation was contingent upon his successful wooing of Concepción Argüello, or whether it was true love on both their parts, must be left to speculation. The count met the beautiful and influential young Spanish lady at the Presidio of San Francisco, and in due time became engaged to marry her. Then he left San Francisco and his bride-to-be, never to return. Concepción waited for him, and waited. Eventually, she retired to the Convent of St. Catherine across the bay in Benicia and became a nun. It was not until several years had passed that she finally heard of her intended's death in Siberia shortly after he had left her.

In 1809 another Russian, named Ivan Kuskov, sailed south from Kiska to complete the project started by Count Rezanov. Reaching Bodega Bay, some sixty miles north of San Francisco, Kuskov stayed with his men for eight months, exploring the area and establishing friendly relations with the Indians. After sowing and harvesting a wheat crop, the Russians returned to Alaska with the grain and two thousand sea otter and seal skins. Three years later, Kuskov returned to California, this time

as governor of the Russian settlement to be established here. He came quietly, discreetly, and without ceremony. He took possession of the land for Russia and made a permanent settlement eighteen miles north of Bodega Bay. A large wooden fort was built on a high bluff overlooking the ocean. This northern settlement later became Fort Ross, a corruption or Anglicization of the word "Russe," or "Russian."

The Russian settlement was not entirely successful. However, Fort Ross, with its cannon and impressive fortifications, became the center of Russian activity. Cucumbers, potatoes, cabbages, beets, and grains such as wheat and barley were grown in the area around the fort. Fruit trees were planted, and horses, cattle, and sheep were raised. Fort Ross was comprised of at least sixty buildings, including a chapel, blockhouses, officers' quarters, and a barn accommodating two hundred cows. There was a boat landing and boathouse as well, plus facilities for building ocean-going vessels. The Russians at Fort Ross were the first to use the redwoods commercially. They cut and split the trees and built prefab houses for export. Although trade with the Spanish was forbidden by Spanish law, it was mutually advantageous and flourished.

The Princess Helena de Gagarin, who came to Fort Ross in 1841, easily qualifies as one of the most glamorous of California's early visitors. She was a niece of the Czar of Russia and bride of Count Alexander Rotcheff, who was then governor general of Siberia and of the Russian colonies of the North Pacific. The Princess Helena had read the accounts of a Russian navigator named Otto von Kotzebue, and, fired by his enthusiasm, she undertook to see the interior of California for herself. She came to Fort Ross and planned an expedition inland. It was a rugged trip for a lady. The route followed old Indian trails to Santa Rosa by way of Petaluma to the base of Mount St. Helena. The princess climbed the five-thousand-foot mountain, raised the Russian flag, placed a memorial plaque, and christened the mountain St. Helena in honor of the patron saint of the Russian czarina. Coincidentally, the mountain is supposed to have been named already by an earlier visitor, a Spanish friar who thought that the mountain resembled St. Helena lying on her bier.

The Russians were never completely successful in California, and they were destined not to remain. In December 1823 President Monroe promulgated his famous Doctrine, and in 1841 the Czar ordered the withdrawal of his subjects from California. The order was probably occasioned more by the decline of the fur harvest than by fear of avenging American armies, however. The sea otter, most highly prized of the fur-bearing animals of California, was by then nearly extinct, leaving little reason for the Russians to remain. When the Russians left, John Augustus Sutter bought the entire property upon which Fort Ross had stood for thirty thousand pesos.

The events that took place in northern California in the spring of 1846 should be reason enough to give Sonoma and northern California a place of prominence in American history. Citizens of all nations had come to California and liked it, but the balance of power, numerically speaking, was on the side of the Americans. One such group of Americans, having been here all of ten

years, had intermarried with the Californios or Mexicans and were considered long-time residents. They owned land and had a vested interest in keeping the status quo. The majority of the Americans, those who came to California by wagon train, were frontiersmen and settlers who were interested in grabbing the best free land they could get. These new settlers wanted California for the United States of America. Many had pre-empted lands from the rightful owners, thus creating problems for the Mexican authorities.

Amid the mounting pressures and tensions of these times, a group of Americans in the Sacramento Valley decided to rise up in open rebellion against the Mexican authorities. Desiring independence for California, about thirty of these insurgents arrived at General Mariano Vallejo's Sonoma home in the early hours of the morning of June 14, 1846. Included in this band of frontiersmen were William B. Ide, Robert Semple, Captain Ezekiel Merritt, and Captain John Grigsby. After much discussion and many bottles of aguardiente, they arrested Vallejo, who, curiously enough, had only recently advocated annexation to the United States. Within a few hours, he was on his way, under guard, to Sutter's Fort.

William Todd, one of the rebels and a nephew of Mary Todd Lincoln, designed a flag suitable for the occasion. Inspired by the flag of Texas, he contrived a star out of various scraps of material and placed it in the upper left-hand corner of a piece of unbleached muslin. In the center, Todd placed the figure of an animal representing a grizzly bear, under which he printed "California Republic." (A few years later, this banner, with some minor changes, became the official flag of California.) It was a great day for the Bear Flaggers, as they came to be known. William B. Ide read a proclamation in the plaza at Sonoma, reciting the settlers' grievances and urging all good citizens to unite and establish a republican form of government unshackled by the laws of Mexican tyranny. Thus the Bear Flag Republic was born.

On July 7, 1846, Commodore Sloat sailed into Monterey Harbor and raised the American flag. Thus, after three weeks, the California Republic was dissolved.

A large part of the subsequent exploration of the extreme north of California may be attributed to "Lost Cabin" legends. Crescent City, the northernmost city in California, according to early accounts, was founded by a prospector lured by tales of a lost cabin full of gold. The story had several versions and brought fortune seekers from the East as well as from other parts of California. Essentially, it was a romantic saga of a miner who had struck it rich and had buried a fabulous treasure of gold in the cellar of his cabin. Shortly thereafter, savage Indians burned the cabin, leaving the miner for dead. When the miner regained consciousness, he had lost his memory and wandered, eventually, back to civilization. After a time, his reason returned, and with it the memory of his lost treasure. He tried to find the location of the cabin again, but couldn't. Hundreds of other people tried, and although they never found the treasure, they found a rich land in which to settle. The hoard of gold, if it ever existed, is still there.

Actually, the wealth of this northern area of California lay not in gold, but in lumber. In 1851 Henry Meiggs, while searching for a Chinese silk ship run aground on the Mendocino coast, discovered the great lumber potential of the redwood and formed the California Lumber Company, a successful enterprise for fifty years. He put in the first sawmill in Mendocino, and as the lumbering business became more prosperous, small towns sprang up overnight on the rugged coast line, each town having its own sawmill. As there were no harbors, many mills operated greased chutes to run the logs from the high cliffs to the ships offshore. On this dangerous rocky shore line, there were also problems of loading and unloading. Slings were used to carry passengers and cargo to the waiting ships. Tides and reefs were constant aggravations. From 1850 to 1857 there were 113 shipwrecks, but still the lumber industry prospered.

A typical lumber town of the 1870s consisted of a group of crude redwood shanties. Two or three Chinamen at the stove provided food for the loggers. They ate good bread, meat, beans, dried apples, cakes, and pickles. Camp was divided into crews, each with twenty to twenty-six men and a team of eight to ten oxen. In the team were choppers, team masters, and chain tenders. With redwood trees over three hundred feet high and up to fourteen feet in diameter, it is no wonder that it took two choppers one day to fell a tree. It could be a dangerous occupation, but many fared well, saved their pay, and later became farmers.

At Fort Bragg, on the Mendocino coast, the Union Lumber Company built the famous "Skunk Line" railroad to receive the logs from Willits. This railroad still runs through some of the most scenic areas in the state and remains a popular tourist attraction.

The appeal of the Redwood Empire also drew some famous writers to the area. Bret Harte came to Arcata in 1857 to work for the *Northern Californian*, the only local newspaper. He loved the rugged coast line and tall redwoods. Through his prolific writings and lecturing, he created the stereotype of the western miner. To the Easterners he told of the early pioneer life, Indian uprisings, and the fervent search for gold by the California miners.

Another famous name from this northern country is Jack London. Born in San Francisco in 1876, he worked variously as an oyster pirate, a Klondike miner, a tramp, and finally a journalist. He fell in love with the Redwood Empire. With the proceeds from his best seller, *Call of the Wild*, he purchased land in the heart of the redwoods and built "Wolf House." Claiming it would last a thousand years, he spent a fortune on the construction of his castle. After three years, it was finally completed. On the eve of moving in, it burned to the ground—set afire by an arsonist. Part of the foundations remain today on a hillside overlooking the valley of Glen Ellen.

In 1892 John Muir, and enthusiastic explorer of the redwood country, joined with twenty six other California wilderness lovers in creating the Sierra Club. Its purpose is to enjoy and explore the mountains of the Pacific Coast and to enlist the support of people and government in preserving the forests. In 1907 William Kent, an ardent admirer of Muir's work, donated to the federal government a magnificent redwood grove of three hundred acres just north of San Francisco. This grove is still known as the Muir Woods National Monument.

The Redwood Empire has not changed much since its pioneering days. The picturesque old lumber towns are still full of Victorian houses with their red roofs and white sidings. There are old schoolhouses and churches on the hillsides. Towering above them all—still unchanged through thousands of years—are the magnificent redwoods, preserved in all their beauty and grandeur to endure for generations to come.

EGGS PETALUMA

6 eggs

3 tablespoons butter or
   margarine

3 tablespoons flour

2 cups milk

1 cup grated Swiss cheese

Salt to taste

2 shallots, chopped

¼ cup butter or margarine

¼ pound fresh mushrooms,
   chopped

½ cup half-and-half

¼ cup dry vermouth

Salt and pepper to taste

1 egg yolk

Place the eggs in a large saucepan and cover with cold water. Over medium heat bring the eggs to just below a boil and let cook for 10–15 minutes, turning a couple of times to center the yolks. Drain and cover with cold water immediately. When able to handle, peel eggs and slice in half lengthwise. Remove yolks and sieve finely, set aside.

In a medium saucepan over moderate heat melt the 3 tablespoons butter and stir in the flour. Slowly add the milk and cook, stirring constantly, over medium heat until thick and bubbly, approximately 3–5 minutes. Add ½ cup cheese and salt to taste and set aside to cool while preparing the mushroom sauce.

Cook the shallots in a medium-sized saucepan over moderate heat in the ¼ cup butter until tender, 5 minutes. Add the mushrooms and continue cooking for another 5 minutes. Remove from heat, pour in the half-and-half and vermouth, return to heat, and simmer 10 minutes longer. Add the reserved egg yolks, salt, and pepper to taste and blend carefully. Stuff this mixture into the hollowed-out egg whites and put the 2 halves together, making 6 whole eggs again.

To assemble, beat the 1 egg yolk into the cooled cheese sauce until well blended and smooth. Pour a thin layer of the cheese sauce onto the bottom of 6 ramekins or small flameproof bowls. Place 1 egg in each ramekin and cover with the remaining sauce, divided evenly between the ramekins. Divide and sprinkle the remaining ½ cup cheese on top of each ramekin. (The eggs may be prepared ahead up to this point and refrigerated. When ready to serve, place in a 400° oven for 20–30 minutes or until warmed through, and then under the broiler until the cheese on top is lightly browned.) Broil for 15 minutes or until bubbly and golden in color. Serve for a delightful brunch with Canadian bacon and muffins.

HUEVOS RANCHEROS

Oil (preferably olive)

2 cups minced onion

2 large cloves garlic, crushed

2 1-pound-12-ounce cans
  Italian plum tomatoes,
  sieved

4–8 ounces green chiles,
  drained, seeded, and minced
  (the amount of chiles used
  depends on degree of hotness
  desired)

1 teaspoon sugar

1 teaspoon salt

¼ teaspoon pepper

¼ teaspoon ground coriander

12 corn tortillas

12 eggs

1 ripe avocado, peeled and
  thinly sliced

Heat 3 tablespoons oil in a large skillet. Add the onion and garlic and cook over low heat until transparent, about 5 minutes. Stir in the tomatoes, chiles, sugar, salt, and pepper. Bring to a boil. Reduce the heat to low and simmer uncovered for 1 hour, stirring occasionally. Stir in the coriander and keep the sauce hot.

In a small heavy skillet place oil to a depth of ⅛ inch and heat over medium-high heat. Fry tortillas 1 at a time for about 1 minute per side or until lightly browned, adding more oil as needed. Place 2 tortillas side by side on each of 6 heated plates.

With a large spoon make 12 hollows in the tomato sauce. Drop 1 egg into each hollow and poach until cooked as desired. Place 1 egg on each tortilla. Spoon the sauce around each egg and garnish with avocado slices.

NOTE: Rather than poaching the eggs, they may be fried in a separate skillet, continuing as above.

HUEVOS MEXICANOS CON TORTILLAS

4 tablespoons oil

9 corn tortillas, cut into
  chip-sized pieces

1 cup chopped onion

12 eggs, lightly beaten

½ pound Cheddar cheese

4 ounces diced green chiles

Salsa Olvera (*below*)

1 cup sour cream

½ cup chopped ripe olives

1 cup chopped avocado

SALSA OLVERA

8 ounces tomato sauce

¼ cup vinegar

2 tablespoons brown sugar

½ cup chopped onion

½ cup chopped green pepper

⅛ teaspoon chili powder

Melt the oil in a 10–12-inch skillet. Sauté the tortilla chips and onion over low heat until soft, about 10 minutes. Pour the eggs over the tortilla chip mixture and stir over low heat until cooked. Grate the cheese and add with chiles just before serving and stir to blend well. Place on a serving platter and pass individual bowls of Sauce, sour cream, olives, and avocados to be spooned over the eggs. A good dish for brunch or a light supper.

To prepare sauce, place the sauce ingredients in a medium-sized saucepan and simmer over low heat for 15–20 minutes, stirring occasionally.

NOTE: For a spicy variation use Mexican Salsa (*see Index*) as a substitute for Salsa Olvera.

SPINACH AND EGGS

2 pounds fresh spinach or
  2 10-ounce packages frozen
  chopped spinach
½ teaspoon white pepper
¼ teaspoon ground nutmeg
½ cup heavy cream
8 teaspoons butter or margarine
8 slices prosciutto or cooked
  ham
8 eggs
Salt and pepper to taste

Thoroughly wash the spinach and remove stems. Cook in the water that clings to the leaves for 4–5 minutes. (If using frozen spinach, cook according to directions on package.) Drain the spinach thoroughly and purée in blender or force through a sieve. Mix in the pepper, nutmeg, and 4 tablespoons of the cream.

Melt 1 teaspoon butter in each of 8 custard cups or individual baking dishes. Spread 2 tablespoons spinach in each cup, place a piece of prosciutto on the spinach, and top with the remaining spinach. The cups can be set aside at this point for a couple of hours to finish cooking later.

Make a slight impression in the center of each spinach-filled cup. Break an egg into each, discarding ½ the white. Season each cup with salt and pepper and then top each egg with ½ tablespoon of the heavy cream. Bake in a preheated 400° oven for 8 minutes or until the eggs are cooked as desired. Serve immediately for a different and delightful breakfast or brunch entree.

HANGTOWN FRY

½ pound bacon
6–8 oysters, shucked and
  patted dry
2 eggs, beaten
10–12 soda crackers, finely
  crushed
6 eggs
¼ cup heavy cream
¼ cup chopped fresh parsley
¼ cup freshly grated Parmesan
  cheese
Salt and pepper to taste
2 sprigs parsley

In a 10–12-inch ovenproof skillet fry the bacon over medium heat until crisp. Remove the bacon with a slotted spoon and set aside. Remove all but 6 tablespoons of the bacon grease. Dip the oysters first into the beaten eggs and then into the cracker crumbs. Fry in the bacon grease over medium heat about 1 minute per side or until golden brown.

In a medium-sized mixing bowl beat together the 6 eggs, heavy cream, chopped parsley, cheese, salt, and pepper. Pour over the oysters in the skillet and reduce the heat to low. Scramble the eggs, lifting the cooked eggs with a spatula and tilting the pan to let the uncooked egg roll underneath. When the eggs are set but still moist, place under the broiler to brown lightly. Transfer eggs to a heated platter, garnish with the parsley sprigs, and serve with the bacon.

TAHOE BRUNCH

must be prepared 24 hours in advance

12 slices white bread, crusts removed

2–3 tablespoons butter or margarine, softened

¼ cup butter or margarine

½ pound fresh mushrooms, trimmed and sliced

2 cups thinly sliced yellow onions

Salt and pepper

1½ pounds mild Italian sausage

¾–1 pound Cheddar cheese, grated

5 eggs

2½ cups milk

3 teaspoons Dijon mustard

1 teaspoon dry mustard

1 teaspoon ground nutmeg

2 tablespoons finely chopped fresh parsley

Butter the bread with the softened butter and set aside. In a 10–12-inch skillet, melt the ¼ cup butter and brown the mushrooms and onions over medium heat for 5–8 minutes or until tender. Season to taste with salt and pepper and set aside. Cook the sausage and cut into bite-sized pieces. In a greased 11 × 7-inch shallow casserole, layer ½ of the bread, mushroom mixture, sausage, and cheese. Repeat the layers, ending with the cheese. In a medium-sized mixing bowl mix the eggs, milk, both mustards, nutmeg, 1 teaspoon salt, and ⅛ teaspoon pepper. Pour over the sausage and cheese casserole. Cover the casserole and refrigerate overnight.

When ready to bake, sprinkle the parsley evenly over the top of the casserole and bake uncovered in a preheated 350° oven for 1 hour or until bubbly Serve immediately with a fruit salad and crusty bread.

NOTE: For a milder variation, substitute 1⅓ cups chopped scallions for the yellow onions and ¾–1 pound sliced American cheese for the Cheddar cheese.

CHEESE AND LEEK PUFF

must be prepared 24 hours in advance

2–3 tablespoons soft butter or margarine

6 slices white bread, crusts removed

1 pound sharp Cheddar cheese, grated

4 tablespoons diced leeks (whites only)

4 eggs

2 cups milk

¾ teaspoon dry mustard

¾ teaspoon salt

Pepper to taste

1 teaspoon Worcestershire sauce

Butter the bread slices and cut into 1-inch cubes. Place the cubes on the bottom of a lightly greased 2-quart casserole. Spread the cheese on top and sprinkle with the leeks. In a quart mixing bowl combine the eggs, milk, mustard, salt, pepper, and Worcestershire, mixing well. Pour this mixture over the cheese and refrigerate covered overnight.

The following day, remove the casserole from the refrigerator and let it stand at room temperature for 30–60 minutes. Bake uncovered in a preheated 350° oven for 30–40 minutes or until lightly browned and puffed. Serve at once.

BLENDER CREPES

1½ cups milk
¼ cup cold water
1¾ cups flour
4 eggs
¾ teaspoon salt
4½ tablespoons melted butter
Oil

Place all the ingredients except the oil in a blender jar and blend for 1 minute at high speed. Scrape down the sides of the jar with a rubber spatula. Blend for an additional 3 minutes at high speed. Refrigerate the batter for at least 2 hours before making the crepes.

Put ¼ teaspoon oil in a 6–7-inch crepe pan or skillet and swirl around to coat the pan. Heat the skillet over moderate heat. Pour a small amount of batter (a little less than ¼ cup) into the well-heated and oiled skillet and swirl the batter around to coat the bottom of the pan, pouring off any excess batter. Cook the crepe for 1 minute or until slightly browned. Turn the crepe and lightly brown the other side for about 30 seconds. Remove the crepe to a piece of waxed paper and continue to make as many crepes as needed. Add additional oil to the skillet if needed to prevent the crepes from sticking to the pan. Cover each cooked crepe as it is made with a piece of waxed paper.

NOTE: The crepes may be made several days ahead and stored, tightly wrapped, in the refrigerator; or they may be frozen for several weeks. Any remaining batter may be stored, covered, in the refrigerator for 1 week.

SALMON SOUFFLÉ

5 tablespoons butter
6 tablespoons flour
1¼ cups milk
6 eggs, separated
1 cup smoked salmon, bones
   removed
4 ounces whipped cream cheese
   with chives
2 teaspoons fresh lemon juice
1½ teaspoons salt
¼ teaspoon cream of tartar

Collar a 2-quart soufflé dish with a 2-inch waxed collar and butter the collar. Set the dish aside. In a small saucepan melt the butter. Remove from heat and add the flour. Add the milk and place over medium-high heat and bring to a boil, stirring. Reduce the heat to low and simmer, stirring constantly from bottom of pan, for 1 minute.

In a large mixing bowl beat the egg yolks with a wire whisk. Add the cooked mixture slowly, so yolks will not curdle. Add the salmon, cheese, and lemon juice, combining well.

In a medium-sized mixing bowl beat the egg whites with the salt and cream of tartar until stiff, but not dry. Thoroughly add $\frac{1}{3}$ of the egg whites to the salmon mixture. Fold in remaining egg whites until just barely combined. Pour into the prepared soufflé dish. This may be held in the refrigerator for up to 4 hours before baking. If baked immediately after preparing, cook in a preheated 350° oven for 40 minutes. If refrigerated first, cook in a 350° oven for 55 minutes. Serve at once.

NOTE: An excellent cheese soufflé is made by substituting $\frac{1}{2}$ pound grated Cheddar cheese for the smoked salmon.

CRAB SOUFFLÉ SERVES 4

$\frac{1}{4}$ cup butter or margarine
3 tablespoons flour
1 cup milk
4 eggs, separated
$\frac{1}{2}$ cup grated Cheddar or Monterey Jack cheese
1 teaspoon salt
Dash ground nutmeg
Dash cayenne pepper
$\frac{3}{4}$ cup (6 ounces) crab meat
$\frac{1}{8}$ teaspoon cream of tartar

In a large saucepan melt the butter and blend in the flour. Cook over low heat for 2 minutes, stirring constantly. Remove the pan from the heat and slowly add the milk, using a wire whisk to blend well. Return the pan to the heat and cook over low heat until smooth and thickened, approximately 5 minutes. Add the egg yolks, 1 at a time, beating after each addition, and continue cooking over low heat, stirring, until sauce is thick and comes to a boil. Stir in the cheese, salt, nutmeg, and cayenne, heating until the cheese melts. Cool slightly, about 10 minutes, and add the crab.

In a medium-sized mixing bowl beat the egg whites with the cream of tartar until stiff but not dry. Fold the egg whites into fish sauce until just barely combined. Pour the mixture into a 1-quart buttered soufflé dish and set into a pan of hot water. Bake in a preheated 325° oven for 45 minutes and serve at once.

NOTE: If more convenient, this may be cooked in a 300° oven for 1 hour.

CAMEMBERT SOUFFLÉ

3 tablespoons butter or
  margarine
3 tablespoons flour
1 cup hot milk
1 cup finely diced Camembert
  cheese
4 egg yolks, lightly beaten
Pinch salt
Pinch cayenne pepper
6 egg whites, stiffly beaten
¼ cup freshly grated Parmesan
  cheese

In a large saucepan melt the butter. Remove the pan from heat and stir in the flour. Cook over low heat, stirring with wire whisk, for 2–3 minutes, until smooth and bubbling. Remove from heat and gradually add milk, stirring constantly. Cook over low heat for 5 minutes, stirring constantly, until sauce is smooth and thick. Add Camembert and cook, stirring until cheese is almost melted. Remove the sauce from the heat. Cool slightly. Beat egg yolks with salt and cayenne and add to the cheese mixture. Cool completely. Fold in the beaten egg whites.

Butter a 2-quart soufflé dish. Pour grated Parmesan into the dish and shake around until the dish is lined with cheese. Pour out any excess cheese. Put soufflé mixture into the dish. Tie a paper collar around the soufflé dish extending upward from the rim of the dish 2–3 inches. Place in a preheated 350° oven and cook 35–40 minutes. Serve at once.

NOTE: To get a crown, run a knife around the soufflé making a ring about 2 inches from outside edge.

GRITS SOUFFLÉ

4½ cups water
½ teaspoon salt
2 teaspoons sugar
1 cup hominy grits (quick-
  cooking)
¼ pound butter or margarine,
  cut into pieces
4 eggs slightly beaten
¼ teaspoon garlic powder
Dash Tabasco sauce
2 cups grated Cheddar cheese
⅓ cup bread crumbs
½ teaspoon paprika

In a heavy 3–4-quart saucepan bring the water to boiling and add salt, sugar, and grits. Cook 3–5 minutes, stirring constantly. Remove the saucepan from heat and add butter, eggs, garlic powder, Tabasco, and cheese. Stir well to blend thoroughly. Pour into a 2½-quart greased casserole. Sprinkle with bread crumbs and paprika. Bake uncovered in a preheated 350° oven for 1 hour. Serve at once.

MUSHROOM SOUFFLÉ

3 tablespoons butter or
  margarine
½ pound fresh mushrooms,
  trimmed and sliced
3 tablespoons finely chopped
  scallions (whites only)
3 tablespoons flour
¼ cup sherry
½ cup milk
½ teaspoon salt
5 eggs, separated

Melt the butter over medium heat in a medium-sized saucepan. Add the mushrooms and scallions and simmer rapidly until all the liquid has evaporated, 10–15 minutes. Stir in the flour and gradually blend in the sherry, milk, and salt. Cook over medium heat until thickened, 3–5 minutes. Remove from the heat and carefully beat in egg yolks.

In a medium-sized bowl beat the egg whites until stiff. Thoroughly mix ½ the egg whites into the mushroom mixture and then carefully fold in the remaining egg whites. Pour the mixture into a well-buttered 2-quart soufflé dish. Bake in a preheated 375° oven for 40 minutes. Serve at once. The soufflé is good either as a light entree or as a side dish.

NOODLE SOUFFLÉ

¼ cup butter or margarine
3 tablespoons flour
1 teaspoon salt
¼ teaspoon white pepper
1½ cups milk
¼ cup heavy cream
1 cup freshly grated Parmesan
  cheese
3 egg yolks
½ pound narrow noodles,
  cooked and drained
5 egg whites, stiffly beaten

In a 2½–3-quart saucepan melt the butter and slowly blend in the flour, salt, and pepper. Cook 2 minutes over low heat, stirring so butter will not brown. Add milk and cream, stirring until it comes to a boil. Cook 5 minutes. Add cheese and stir until melted. Remove from heat.

In a large bowl beat egg yolks until thick and lemon-colored. Gradually add sauce, stirring constantly so eggs will not curdle. Mix in noodles. Taste for seasoning. Cool for 20 minutes and then add egg whites. Fold gently and place into a 2-quart buttered soufflé dish. Bake in a preheated 375° oven for 25 minutes or until set.

SOUFFLÉ MEXICANA

SERVES 8

4 4-ounce cans whole green
    chiles
2 cups grated Monterey Jack
    cheese
2 cups grated Cheddar cheese
6 eggs
1 cup flour
4 cups milk
Salt and pepper to taste

Butter bottom of a 3-quart soufflé dish. Rinse chiles free of seeds and cut into 1-inch pieces Layer the cheeses and chiles in bottom of soufflé dish. Beat together the eggs, flour, milk, salt, and pepper and pour over cheese and chiles (should fill dish about ½ full). Bake in a preheated 350° oven for 1 hour.

NOTE: This should be served with Guacamole (*see Index*), salted sour cream, and Mexican Salsa (*see Index*) or canned green chile salsa.

SPINACH AND CHEESE FRITTATA

SERVES 6–8

¼ cup butter or margarine
3 eggs
1 cup flour
1 cup milk
1 teaspoon salt
1 teaspoon baking powder
1 pound Monterey Jack cheese,
    grated
4 cups fresh spinach, washed,
    dried, and torn into
    bite-sized pieces

Melt butter in a 7 × 11-inch baking dish. Beat eggs and add remaining ingredients, blending well. Pour spinach mixture over the melted butter Bake in a preheated 350° oven for 40–45 minutes, until golden brown. Cool 10 minutes and serve.

NOTE: This freezes very well.

SWISS FONDUE

SERVES 4

1 clove garlic
1 pound Swiss cheese, diced
Salt and pepper to taste
1¼–1½ cups white wine
5 or 6 teaspoons cornstarch
2 tablespoons kirsch
1 loaf French bread, cut into
    bite-sized pieces

Rub the inside of a ceramic cheese fondue pot with the garlic. Place the cheese in the pot along with the salt, pepper, and enough wine to almost cover the cheese. Place the ceramic pot over a larger pot filled with boiling water. Cook on the stove over medium heat until the cheese melts, stirring constantly back and forth—never around.

In a small bowl mix the cornstarch and kirsch together and add to the cheese, stirring to blend well. Cook for 2 more minutes. To serve, remove the fondue pot to a warmer at the table. Using fondue forks, dip the bread into the hot cheese. Serve with a green salad and white wine. Serves 8–10 when used as an hors d'oeuvre.

NOTE: For variety use ham, apple, or unpeeled pears cut into chunks in place of the bread.

MOZZARELLA MARINARA   SERVES 6

12 ounces mozzarella cheese
2 eggs, beaten
Flour
1½ cups dry bread crumbs
1 teaspoon salt
2 tablespoons freshly grated
   Parmesan cheese
Oil for frying
Marinara Sauce (*below*)
6 strips anchovy fillets, rinsed
   (optional)

MARINARA SAUCE
¼ cup olive oil
1 clove garlic, minced
¼ cup chopped onion
1 tablespoon minced parsley
½ teaspoon basil
½ teaspoon oregano
½ bay leaf
¼ teaspoon sugar
1 teaspoon salt
⅛ teaspoon pepper
2 cups peeled and chopped
   tomatoes, or canned
   Italian-style tomatoes,
   sieved
1 tablespoon tomato paste

Cut mozzarella into 3 × 2 × ½-inch pieces. Dip each piece into the eggs, then the flour, then into the eggs again, and finally into the bread crumbs which have been seasoned with the salt and Parmesan. Place the coated cheese pieces in a single layer on a plate and refrigerate for 30 minutes or longer.

When ready to serve, heat ½ inch oil over high heat in a 10–12-inch skillet. Fry the cheese until browned on one side, then turn and brown the other side. This may also be done, a few pieces at a time, in a deep fryer at 375° for approximately 2 minutes. Drain the cheese on absorbent paper and keep warm in a 250° oven until all the cheese has been fried. For each serving, pour 2 tablespoons of the Marinara Sauce on a small plate, place the cheese on the sauce, and top with additional sauce and 1 anchovy fillet. Serve at once. This makes a very unusual first course.

To prepare sauce, in a 10–12-inch skillet heat the oil over medium heat and add the garlic, onion, and parsley, cooking for 3–5 minutes Add the remaining sauce ingredients and simmer uncovered for 30 minutes.

ARTICHOKE PIE

1 9-inch pie crust

2 9-ounce packages frozen
artichoke hearts

4 tablespoons butter or
margarine

½ cup chopped onion

1 tablespoon flour

½ cup half-and-half

½ cup sour cream

4 eggs, beaten

Salt and pepper to taste

¼ teaspoon ground nutmeg

2 teaspoons minced fresh
parsley

½ cup shredded Cheddar
cheese

½ cup shredded Swiss cheese

¼ cup freshly grated Parmesan
cheese

Prepare pie crust according to directions for Basic Pie Crust (*see Index*).

Cook artichoke hearts as directed on the package. Set aside. Melt butter in a large skillet and add onion, cooking over medium heat until tender but not browned, about 5 minutes. Stir in flour until well blended, then add half-and-half. Cook, stirring, until thickened, 3–5 minutes.

In a small bowl combine the sour cream, eggs, salt, pepper, nutmeg, and parsley. Add to sautéed onions.

Place a layer of artichoke hearts on the bottom of the pie crust.

Sprinkle Cheddar over the top. Add another layer of artichokes and top with Swiss cheese. Pour egg mixture over layers and top with Parmesan. Bake in a preheated 350° oven for 45 minutes. Cut in wedges and serve at once.

CROQUE-MONSIEUR HAM AND CHEESE SANDWICH

1½ cups grated Swiss cheese

10 tablespoons heavy cream

Salt and pepper to taste

16 slices good white bread,
crusts trimmed

8 thin slices cooked ham,
trimmed same size as bread

3 eggs

4–6 tablespoons clarified butter

In a mixing bowl mash Swiss cheese and 6 table-spoons cream to make a thick, smooth paste. Season highly with salt and pepper. Spread cheese evenly on 1 side of all slices of bread. Top 8 slices of bread with ham and cover with remaining bread, cheese side down. Press sandwich together firmly.

Beat together eggs and 4 tablespoons cream until just combined. Season with salt and pepper. Dip each sandwich into egg mixture and let soak a few seconds. In a heavy 10–12-inch skillet or electric frying pan, fry over moderate heat in the clarified butter. Fry slowly enough to insure that cheese melts. Turning once only. Serve at once, cut in half.

MUSHROOM SOUR CREAM PIE

SERVES 6

1 9-inch unbaked pie shell
6 tablespoons butter or
    margarine
¾ pound small fresh mushrooms,
    sliced
½ cup chopped onion
½ teaspoon salt
¼ teaspoon paprika
⅛ teaspoon cayenne pepper
4 eggs
1⅓ cups sour cream

Prepare pie shell according to directions for Basic Pie Crust (*see Index*).

Melt the butter in an 8–10-inch skillet over medium-high heat and sauté the mushrooms and onion for 4–5 minutes. Add the salt, paprika, and cayenne and set aside.

Prick the sides and bottom of the pie shell with a fork and bake in a preheated 425° oven for 8 minutes. Remove from the oven and reduce the oven heat to 350°. Spread the mushroom mixture over the bottom of the pie shell, distributing evenly. In a small mixing bowl combine the eggs and sour cream, blending well. Pour over mushrooms. Bake the pie for 35–40 minutes or until the custard is firm. Remove from the oven and let stand for 5 minutes before cutting into wedges. May be served as a side dish or as the main course.

TOMATOES A QUESO

SERVES 6

4 medium onions, thinly
    sliced
3 tablespoons butter or
    margarine
5 or 6 large tomatoes, thickly
    sliced
1½ cups grated sharp Cheddar
    cheese (½ cup Monterey
    Jack cheese may be
    substituted for ½ cup
    Cheddar)
1 cup bread crumbs
Salt to taste
1 teaspoon paprika
2 eggs, beaten
1 cup sour cream

In a 10–12-inch skillet sauté the onions in the butter for 5 minutes over medium heat, not browning them. Grease a deep 2-quart casserole and arrange a layer of the tomatoes on the bottom. Sprinkle some cheese on top, followed by some of the bread crumbs, onion, salt, and paprika. Repeat layers until all the ingredients are used, ending with cheese.

In a small mixing bowl beat together the eggs and sour cream until smooth. Pour the sour cream sauce over the casserole and sprinkle with salt and paprika to add color. Cover and bake in a preheated 375° oven for 30 minutes, then uncover and bake 15 minutes longer or until puffed and brown.

NOTE: This is delicious served with barbecued meat.

CHILES RELLENOS

¼ pound Monterey Jack cheese
7 ounces whole green chiles
6 eggs, separated
3 tablespoons flour
¾ teaspoon salt
Oil for frying

Cut cheese into ½ × ½ × 2-inch strips and set aside. Remove the seeds and veins from the chiles, cut them in half lengthwise, and remove all the liquid by pressing between 2 sheets of paper toweling Lightly wrap each piece of chile around a strip of cheese and again press out any liquid that remains.

In a large mixing bowl beat the egg whites until stiff but not dry. In a small mixing bowl beat the egg yolks, flour, and salt together with a wire whisk. Stir approximately ¼ cup of the egg whites into the egg yolk mixture, mixing well. Fold this yolk mixture into the remaining egg whites until combined but still fluffy.

Pour the oil into a 10–12-inch skillet to the depth of 1-inch and heat over high flame until very hot (approximately 375°). Place 1 of the cheese-wrapped chiles on a large spoon and cover with about 2 tablespoons of the egg mixture. Gently drop the chiles into the hot oil, egg side down, and spoon about 2 more tablespoons of the egg mixture on the other side, so the entire chile is covered. Cook until golden brown, turn, and cook the other side. Remove with a slotted spoon, drain on paper towels, and place on a warm ovenproof serving dish. Continue until all the chiles are done and then place the dish in a pre-heated 400° oven for 3–5 minutes or until the crust is puffed. Serve with Tomato Sauce for Chiles Rellenos as an unusual first course or as part of a Mexican meal.

TOMATO SAUCE FOR
CHILES RELLENOS

¼ cup chopped onion
1 clove garlic, minced
1 tablespoon oil
1 cup peeled and finely chopped
  tomatoes
1⅔ cup chicken broth
⅓ cup water
2 chicken bouillon cubes
⅛ teaspoon dried oregano
1 tablespoon cornstarch

To prepare sauce, in a large saucepan cook the onion and garlic in 1 tablespoon oil over medium heat until tender, approximately 5 minutes. Add the tomatoes, chicken broth, water, bouillon cubes, and oregano and bring to a boil over high heat. Reduce the heat to low and simmer for 15 minutes. With a wire whisk blend in the cornstarch and continue cooking until the sauce has thickened. Serve over Chiles Rellenos.

TOMATO QUICHE

SERVES 6–8

1 9-inch unbaked pie shell
½ pound Swiss cheese, shredded
3 tomatoes, peeled, chopped,
  and drained
¼ cup chopped onion
Salt and pepper to taste
1 teaspoon dried basil
2 eggs
¾ cup milk
2 tablespoons grated Parmesan
  cheese

Prepare pie shell according to directions for Basic Pie Crust (*see Index*).

On the bottom of the pie shell sprinkle the Swiss cheese. Make a layer of tomatoes over this and top with onions. Sprinkle with salt, pepper, and basil.

Beat eggs and milk together and pour over tomatoes. Sprinkle the Parmesan on top. Bake in a preheated 350° oven for 45 minutes.

QUICHE LORRAINE

SERVES 8

1 9-inch unbaked pie shell
1 egg white, whipped until
  frothy
½ pound Canadian bacon,
  diced
1 onion, thinly sliced
1 cup grated Swiss cheese
¼ cup grated Parmesan cheese
3 eggs, slightly beaten
1½ cups half-and-half
¼ teaspoon nutmeg
½ teaspoon salt
⅛ teaspoon cayenne pepper

Prepare pie shell according to directions for Basic Pie Crust (*see Index*). Use either a pie plate or a quiche pan.

Prick sides and bottom of the pie shell. Brush the shell with a little of the whipped egg white and bake in a preheated 450° oven for 5 minutes.

In a heavy 8–10-inch skillet cook the bacon until crisp. Remove and drain. Remove all but 1 tablespoon of bacon fat. Cook the onion, separated into rings, in the bacon fat until transparent, 2–3 minutes. Spread cheeses, bacon, and onion in the partially baked pie shell. Combine the eggs, half-and-half, nutmeg, salt, and cayenne and strain over the cheese mixture. Bake in a preheated 450° oven for 15 minutes and then reduce heat to 350° and bake 10–15 minutes longer or until custard sets (when knife inserted 1 inch from the pastry edge comes out clean).

NOTE: When cut into smaller pieces, this may also be served as an hors d'oeuvre.

STEAMED RICE CHINATOWN STYLE

1½ cups long-grain white
   rice (not instant)
3 cups water

Wash the rice several times in cold water until the water runs clean. Place the rice in a large deep saucepan with a tight-fitting lid. Add the water (water should be ½ inch above rice) and soak overnight or all day (rice will be cooked in the same water).

To cook the rice, bring the water to a boil over high heat. Lower the temperature and simmer covered for about 20 minutes.

NOTE: This makes extra fluffy rice to be served with your favorite meat. Rice cooked this way can be held for several hours in the same pan. It also reheats beautifully; add a little water and warm over low heat.

HERB RICE

SERVES 8

¼ cup olive oil
¼ cup butter or margarine
1 cup diced celery
1 onion, finely chopped
2 cups wild rice, washed
1 teaspoon dried thyme
1½ cups beef or chicken broth,
   heated

Heat the oil and butter in a 1½–2-quart flame-proof casserole and stir in celery and onion. Sauté until tender, 2–3 minutes. Stir in rice and sauté 5–10 minutes longer. Add thyme and the hot broth. Cover and bake in a preheated 300° oven for 1 hour and 15 minutes.

NOTE: You may substitute brown rice for ½ the wild rice.

CURRY PILAF

SERVES 6–8

¼ cup butter or margarine
1 cup chopped onions
1½ cups rice
2 cans consommé
1 cup seedless white raisins
½ teaspoon curry powder
Salt and pepper to taste

Melt butter in a 2–3-quart flameproof casserole. Stir in onion and rice. Cook over medium heat until golden brown, about 5 minutes, stirring frequently. Add consommé, raisins, curry powder, salt, and pepper and mix well. Cover and cook over low flame for 30 minutes, or pour boiling consommé over rice, cover, and bake in a preheated 350° oven for 20–25 minutes.

LEMON RICE

¼ cup butter or margarine
1 cup thinly sliced celery
1 small onion, finely chopped
2 cups trimmed and sliced
  fresh mushrooms (optional)
¼ teaspoon dried thyme
1½ teaspoons salt
⅛ teaspoon white pepper
1½ cups water
Rind of 1 lemon, grated
  (approximately 2 teaspoons)
½ cup fresh lemon juice
1 cup long-grain white rice

Melt the butter in a heavy 12–14-inch skillet. Add the celery, onion, and mushrooms (optional) and sauté for 5 minutes over low heat. Add the thyme, salt, and pepper, stirring to blend in well. Remove from heat and set aside.

In a 2-quart saucepan combine the water, lemon rind, and lemon juice. Bring the mixture to a boil and add the rice and vegetable mixture. Bring to a boil again, stir, reduce the heat to low, cover, and simmer for 20 minutes. If a stronger lemon flavor is desired, more lemon juice and less water may be used. The total liquid volume should be 2 cups.

NOTE: This rice is delicious as a stuffing for trout or salmon or as an accompaniment for fish and poultry dishes. This recipe makes enough to stuff a 10-pound fish or bird.

ORANGE PILAF

3 tablespoons slivered almonds
1 cup finely chopped onion
¼ cup finely chopped green
  pepper
2 tablespoons butter or
  margarine
1 cup long-grain rice
1 cup orange juice
1 cup buttermilk
¼ teaspoon dried crushed
  oregano
½ teaspoon salt
2 oranges, peeled and cut into
  small pieces
Paprika

In a 400° oven bake the almonds for 5–10 minutes, shaking the pan occasionally to insure that they brown evenly.

In a 10–12-inch skillet over medium heat cook the onion and green pepper in the butter until tender but not browned, about 3–5 minutes. Add the rice and brown lightly, stirring constantly, for another 3–5 minutes. Add the orange juice, buttermilk, oregano, and salt. Stir once and bring to a boil over high heat. Cover and reduce heat, simmering the rice for 25 minutes or until it is tender and the liquid is absorbed. Stir the orange pieces and almonds into the cooked rice and heat through. Spoon into a serving bowl and sprinkle with paprika. Serve hot with veal, poultry, or lamb.

RICE PILAF

2 cups finely chopped onion
1½ tablespoons oil
2 cups long-grain white rice
2¾ cups chicken broth
2 chicken bouillon cubes
1⅓ cups dry vermouth
1½ tablespoons salt
Pepper to taste

In a 10–12-inch skillet over medium heat sauté the onions in the oil until transparent but not browned, about 5 minutes. Add the rice and cook another 5 minutes, stirring frequently. Spoon the rice and onions into a lightly buttered 2-quart casserole, with a cover, and stir in the broth, bouillon cubes, vermouth, salt, and pepper. Cover and bake in a preheated 350° oven for 35–40 minutes or until all the liquid is absorbed.

NOTE: This rice would be delicious served with the Leg of Lamb Stuffed with Spinach (*see Index*).

GREEN RICE

SERVES 8

2½ cups water
2 teaspoons salt
1 cup rice
4 eggs, separated
1 green pepper, finely chopped
1 small onion, finely chopped
½ cup finely minced fresh
   parsley
5 tablespoons freshly grated
   Parmesan cheese
1 teaspoon paprika
Salt and pepper to taste
1 cup heavy cream, whipped

Bring the water and salt to a boil and add the rice. Reduce heat to low and cover saucepan. Cook until tender, about 20–25 minutes.

Beat the egg yolks and combine with the green pepper, onion, parsley, cheese, paprika, salt, and pepper. Blend mixture with cooked rice. Fold in whipped cream. Beat egg whites until foamy and fold into mixture. Put into a well-greased 6-cup ring mold or 1½-quart casserole. Place in a pan of hot water and bake in a preheated 350° oven until set, about 50–60 minutes.

CHINESE FRIED RICE

SERVES 8

2½ cups water
1 teaspoon salt
1 cup raw rice
3 tablespoons oil
1 cup chopped onion
1 cup chopped celery

In a medium-sized saucepan bring the water to a boil. Add salt and rice, cover pan, and simmer over low heat until liquid is absorbed, approximately 20–25 minutes. Meanwhile, put oil in a large skillet and sauté the onion and celery until tender, about 5 minutes. Add the cooked rice,

2 cups trimmed and sliced
  fresh mushrooms
1 cup chopped water chestnuts
3 tablespoons soy sauce

mushrooms, water chestnuts, and soy sauce. Simmer over low heat, stirring occasionally, for 10 minutes.

NOTE: This is an excellent accompaniment to a Chinese dinner.

MEXICAN RICE

SERVES 8

1 large onion, chopped
4 tablespoons oil (preferably
  olive)
2 cloves garlic, minced
2 cups long-grained rice
1½ cups peeled and finely
  chopped tomatoes
4 cups beef consommé
1½ teaspoons cumin
Salt to taste

In a large skillet over medium heat cook the onion in the oil until tender but not browned, 3–5 minutes. Add the garlic and rice and cook another 3–5 minutes, stirring often, until rice is pale yellow. Add the tomatoes, consommé, cumin, and salt. Bring the mixture to a boil over high heat. Cover and simmer over very low heat until the liquid is absorbed and the rice is tender, approximately 20 minutes.

NOTE: This is an excellent complement to Chicken Breasts con Rajas (*see Index*).

SPINACH AND RICE

SERVES 8

3 bunches fresh spinach or
  3 9-ounce packages frozen
  chopped spinach
2 onions, chopped
1 clove garlic, chopped
¼ cup oil
1 cup rice
2½ cups water
Salt and pepper to taste
¼ cup fresh lemon juice
3 tablespoons chopped fresh
  mint

Wash and dry spinach and tear into bite-sized pieces. (If frozen spinach is used, thaw and drain, squeezing out all excess moisture.) In a 3–4-quart heavy saucepan with a cover, brown the onion and garlic in the oil for about 3–5 minutes over moderate heat, stirring occasionally. Add the rice. Cook 1 minute longer. Add the water, salt, and pepper and cook covered for 25 minutes over low heat. Add the spinach, lemon juice, and mint and mix thoroughly. Cook 10 minutes more or until done. Serve at once.

RISOTTO ALLA MILANESE

2 cups trimmed and sliced
fresh mushrooms
8–9 tablespoons butter or
margarine
6–7 cups chicken broth
½ cup minced onion
2 cups long-grain rice
½ cup dry white wine
⅛ teaspoon saffron
½ cup freshly grated Parmesan
cheese

Sauté mushrooms over moderate heat in 2 tablespoons butter for 5 minutes and set aside. Heat broth in a saucepan and bring to a simmer.

In a heavy 3-quart flameproof casserole melt 4 tablespoons butter and sauté onion over medium heat, stirring, for 8–10 minutes or until golden. Add rice and sauté, stirring, for 2 minutes, adding more butter if necessary, until the rice is well coated with butter. Add wine and cook uncovered over moderate heat until wine is nearly absorbed. Add 2 cups hot broth and cook uncovered, stirring occasionally, until liquid is almost absorbed. Add 2 more cups hot broth and repeat.

Meanwhile, add the saffron to 2 cups hot broth and let it steep a few minutes. Pour this over rice and cook, stirring occasionally, until stock is absorbed. The rice should be tender by now. If it is not, add more hot broth (½ cup at a time) until rice is tender. With a fork, stir in the sautéed mushrooms, 2–3 tablespoons butter, and the grated cheese. Mix very gently, until rice is creamy. Serve at once.

BROWN RICE AND PINE NUT CASSEROLE

½ cup pine nuts
¼ cup butter or margarine
1 cup brown rice, rinsed and
drained
½ cup bulgur (cracked wheat)
1 large onion, chopped
1 cup minced fresh parsley
6 tablespoons finely minced
fresh chives or scallions
¼ teaspoon salt
¼ teaspoon pepper
3 14-ounce cans regular-
strength beef or chicken
broth

Sauté the pine nuts in a medium-sized skillet with 2 tablespoons butter over moderate heat until browned, approximately 5 minutes, stirring occasionally. To the same skillet add and melt the remaining butter. Add the rice, bulgur, and onion. Brown for about 10 minutes, stirring frequently. Spoon this mixture into a 2-quart casserole. Add ¾ cup parsley, the chives, salt, and pepper. Bring broth to a boil and stir into rice mixture. Bake uncovered in a preheated 375° oven for 1 hour and 15 minutes. Garnish with the remaining parsley.

CHILE RICE CASSEROLE

2½ cups water
1 cup raw rice
2 cups sour cream
Salt to taste
¼ pound Monterey Jack cheese,
  grated
7 ounces diced green chiles
3 tablespoons butter or
  margarine
¼ cup freshly grated Parmesan
  cheese (more if desired)

In a medium-sized saucepan bring the water to a boil. Add the rice, cover pan, and simmer over low heat until the liquid is absorbed, approximately 20–25 minutes. Let the rice cool. Mix the cooked rice with the sour cream and salt. In the bottom of a greased 1½-quart casserole spread ½ the rice mixture. Sprinkle the grated Jack cheese and chiles on top and then add the rest of the rice. Dot with butter and sprinkle with the Parmesan. Bake uncovered in a preheated 350° oven for 30 minutes.

NOTE: This is a wonderful accompaniment to barbecued meat.

WILD RICE WITH MUSHROOMS AND ALMONDS

¼ cup butter or margarine
1 cup wild rice, well rinsed
  and drained
¼ cup slivered almonds
2 tablespoons chopped onion,
  chives, scallions, or green
  pepper
½ pound fresh mushrooms,
  trimmed and sliced
3 cups chicken broth

Over moderate heat place the butter, rice, almonds, onion or alternative, and mushrooms in a heavy skillet and cook 8–10 minutes, stirring almost constantly. Transfer to a 2-quart casserole and add the broth. Cover tightly and bake in a preheated 325° oven for 1½–2 hours.

NOTE: You may substitute brown rice for ½ the wild rice.

BULGUR PILAF

1 cup sliced fresh mushrooms
½ cup butter or margarine
¼ cup chopped onion
2 cups bulgur (cracked wheat)
1 teaspoon salt
Freshly ground pepper to taste
1 teaspoon fresh lemon juice
4 cups chicken stock or broth

In a small skillet sauté the mushrooms over moderate heat in 4 tablespoons butter for 5 minutes and set aside. Over a low flame melt the remaining butter in a heavy 2½–3-quart skillet with cover and add the chopped onion. Let it cook for 2–3 minutes, stirring occasionally, and add the bulgur, stirring until the grains are well coated with butter. Add the salt, pepper, lemon juice, and stock. Bring to a boil, lower heat, and cover the pan. Cook gently for 13–15 minutes until the wheat is done and liquid absorbed. Remove from heat, fold in the mushrooms and serve.

BARLEY CASSEROLE

SERVES 6–8

½ cup butter or margarine
2 medium onions, coarsely
  chopped
¾ pound fresh mushrooms,
  trimmed and sliced
1½ cups pearl barley
2 cups chicken or beef broth
1 teaspoon salt
⅛ teaspoon cayenne pepper
½ cup chopped fresh parsley

Over medium heat melt the butter in an 8–10-inch skillet and stir in the onion. After 5 minutes add the mushrooms and sauté for another 5 minutes or until the onions are golden and the mushrooms tender. Add the barley and cook, stirring occasionally, until the barley is light brown, 5–10 minutes. Transfer the mixture to a 2-quart lightly greased casserole and add the broth, salt, cayenne, and parsley. Cover and bake in a preheated 350° oven for 50 minutes or until the barley is tender and all the liquid is absorbed.

NOTE: This is delicious served with grilled meat or poultry.

SPINACH GNOCCHI

SERVES 6–8

2 pounds fresh spinach or
  2 10-ounce packages frozen
  chopped spinach
1 pound ricotta
1 cup freshly grated Parmesan
  cheese
1 egg, lightly beaten
1 cup soft bread crumbs
  (2–3 slices bread)
2 tablespoons flour
¼ teaspoon freshly grated
  nutmeg
Salt and pepper
½ cup butter, melted

Thoroughly wash and drain the spinach. Cook the spinach in the water that clings to the leaves for 4–5 minutes. Squeeze all the water from the spinach and chop finely, or blend for a few seconds in a blender. (If using frozen spinach, cook according to the directions on the package.) Place the spinach in a bowl and mix in the ricotta, ½ cup Parmesan, egg, bread crumbs, flour, nutmeg, and salt and pepper to taste.

In a large pot bring 6–8 quarts water and 1 tablespoon salt to a simmer over moderate heat. Roll 1 tablespoon of the spinach mixture at a time between the floured palms of the hands into small cylinders, approximately 1½ inches in length. Coat the gnocchi lightly with flour and gently drop, a few at a time, into the simmering salted water. Cook uncovered until the gnocchi rises to the surface of the water, then cook 1 minute longer. Lift the gnocchi from the water with a slotted spoon onto a warm flameproof serving dish which has been lightly buttered on the bottom. Cover with the melted butter and sprinkle the remaining ½ cup with Parmesan. Place in the center of a preheated 400° oven for 3–4 minutes. Serve at once.

GNOCCHI À LA ROMAINE

1 quart milk
½ cup butter or margarine
1 cup hominy grits (quick-
  cooking)
1 teaspoon salt
⅛ teaspoon pepper
⅓ cup butter or margarine,
  melted
1 cup grated Gruyère or
  Swiss cheese
⅓ cup freshly grated Parmesan
  cheese

In a heavy 3-quart saucepan bring the milk to a boil. Add the ½ cup butter cut into pieces so it will melt faster. Gradually stir in the grits. Cover the pan and reduce heat to low. Cook 3–5 minutes, stirring occasionally. Remove from the heat, season with the salt and pepper, and then beat hard with an electric mixer for 5 minutes, until the grits take on a creamy appearance. Pour into a buttered 13 × 9 × 2-inch casserole. Chill for at least 1 hour to allow it to set. Cut into 1½ × 2-inch rectangular pieces. Place them one over another like rows of fallen dominoes in a buttered 13 × 9 × 2-inch casserole which may be brought to the table. Over this pour the melted butter and sprinkle with the grated cheeses. (May be done to this point and refrigerated until ready to bake.) At serving time place in a preheated 400° oven for 25–30 minutes and then, if wanted, under the broiler just long enough to obtain a light brown crust. Serve at once.

REFRIED BEANS (Frijoles Refritos)

must be prepared 24 hours in advance

1 pound dried pinto or pink
  beans
2 onions, diced
1 clove garlic, minced
2 teaspoon salt
1½ teaspoons pepper
¾ cup butter or margarine
1 cup grated Monterey Jack
  or Cheddar cheese

Soak the beans in 5 cups cold water overnight in a large saucepan. The next day add the onions, garlic, salt, and pepper to the beans and water. Bring to a boil. Reduce the heat to low and simmer slowly until the beans are tender, about 3 hours. Mash the beans with a potato masher and add the butter, mixing well. Continue cooking, stirring occasionally, until the beans are thickened and the butter absorbed, 5–10 minutes. Taste and add more salt and pepper if needed.

Spread the beans in a shallow 13 × 9-inch casserole and sprinkle the cheese on top. Bake in a preheated 350° oven for 15 minutes. An excellent side dish for Huevos Rancheros (*see Index*) and other Mexican foods.

NOTE: Prior to final baking of the beans, the dish can be refrigerated covered for 1–2 days.

ENCHILADAS RANCHERAS

SERVES 6 (2 ENCHILADAS PER SERVING)

¼ pound Cheddar cheese,
  finely grated
1 pound Monterey Jack cheese,
  finely grated
2 scallions, including some of
  the tops, finely chopped
¼–⅓ cup butter or margarine,
  softened
Oil
12 corn tortillas (*see Index*)
Ranchera Sauce (*below*)
1 cup grated Monterey Jack
  cheese
Sour cream
Guacamole (*see Index*)
Scallions, sliced (optional)
Ripe olives, sliced (optional)

RANCHERA SAUCE
¼ cup oil
½ cup chopped onion
1½ stalks celery, chopped
1 green pepper, chopped
¼ cup flour
½ teaspoon dried marjoram
½ teaspoon salt
¾ teaspoon pepper
1½ teaspoons garlic powder
½ teaspoon dried oregano
½ teaspoon monosodium
  glutamate
2½ cups water
3 teaspoons chicken stock
  base
2 cups peeled and chopped
  fresh tomatoes

Mix the ¼ pound Cheddar and 1 pound Jack cheeses, 2 chopped scallions, and the butter until well blended. Divide mixture into 4 equal portions and then form each portion into 3 individual sticks the length of a tortilla, making 12 cheese sticks in all. Set aside.

In an 8–10-inch skillet pour ¼ inch oil and heat over medium-high heat. Soften tortillas, 1 at a time, by placing in the hot oil for a few seconds on each side. Remove quickly and drain on paper towels. Place a cheese stick on each tortilla and roll up the tortilla. Place the rolled tortillas side by side, seam down, in a 9 × 13-inch baking dish. Cover the enchiladas with Ranchera Sauce and top with the 1 cup Jack cheese. Bake in a preheated 450° oven until the sauce is bubbly and the cheese melted, approximately 15 minutes. If preferred, place under the broiler, watching carefully, until cheese is melted.

Serve enchiladas on warm plates with the sour cream on one side and the guacamole on the other. You may wish to garnish the sour cream with the sliced scallions and the guacamole with the sliced olives.

To prepare sauce, in a 10–12-inch skillet heat ¼ cup oil over medium heat. Cook the onion, celery, and green pepper in the hot oil until the vegetables are soft and the onion is transparent, 3–5 minutes. Combine the flour, marjoram, salt, pepper, garlic powder, oregano, and monosodium glutamate in a medium-sized mixing bowl and slowly add the water, mixing until smooth. Pour the flour mixture into the vegetables and add the chicken stock base and tomatoes. Cook over medium heat, stirring occasionally, until mixture boils and thickens. Reduce heat and simmer approximately 1 hour.

SOUR CREAM ENCHILADAS

1 pint cottage cheese
2 8-ounce packages cream
    cheese
1 pint dairy sour cream
1 clove garlic, crushed
1 teaspoon salt
1 4-ounce can green chile salsa
½ cup lard or oil
12 corn tortillas
1 pound Monterey Jack cheese,
    cut into finger-sized strips
1 4-ounce can diced green
    chiles
¾ cup chopped scallions

In a large bowl blend and beat until smooth the cottage cheese, cream cheese, sour cream, garlic, salt, and chile salsa. In a heavy 8–10-inch skillet melt the lard over moderate heat until well heated, about 1 minute. Holding tortillas with tongs, dip into the hot oil for a few seconds on each side until limp. Drain tortillas on paper toweling. Place 1 strip of cheese in center of each tortilla, add 1–2 teaspoons diced green chile and 1 large tablespoonsful of cream mixture. Roll tortillas and place seam side down in a 13 × 9 × 2-inch casserole. Cover with remaining cream mixture and chopped scallions. Bake in a preheated 350° oven for 20 minutes. Serve at once.

PASTA

7 quarts water
2 tablespoons salt
1 pound pasta

In a deep pot bring the water to a full boil and then add the salt. Keep the water boiling (if necessary, turn up the heat) and gently add the pasta. Push the pasta down so that it is totally underwater. Stir with a wooden fork to separate the strands as they cook. After the first 3 minutes of cooking, test the pasta often by tasting. It is ready when it is bitable and has no flour taste— al dente.

NOTE: If using freshly made pasta, you will need to test sooner and more often, as it cooks faster.

PASTA MOLTO FACILE

¼ pound butter (no substitute)
4 cups quartered fresh
    mushrooms
1 clove garlic, minced
2¼ cups chopped fresh parsley
12 ounces thin, narrow noodles
1 pint sour cream
½ cup freshly grated Parmesan
    or Romano cheese plus
    ¼ cup freshly grated
    Parmesan cheese

In a large skillet slowly melt the butter (do not brown) and cook mushrooms over low heat until just done, about 5 minutes. Add garlic and cook an additional minute. Add 2 cups parsley and cook for another 2 minutes. Cook noodles during above procedure. Drain and rinse briefly in very hot water. Return to pan in which they were boiled. Pour mushroom mixture over noodles, toss lightly, add the sour cream and the ½ cup cheese, and toss lightly again. Place on platter, surround with the remaining parsley and sprinkle with the ¼ cup Parmesan. Serve very hot.

TOMATO SAUCE FOR SPAGHETTI

SERVES 6

5 tablespoons olive oil
1 cup finely chopped onion
1 large clove garlic, minced
¼ cup chopped fresh mushrooms
¾ pound ground round or
    chuck
29 ounces tomato sauce
6 ounces tomato paste
6 ounces water
3 tablespoons white or red wine
1 teaspoon sugar
1 stalk celery, finely chopped
1 tablespoon fresh chopped
    parsley
Salt to taste
1 small bay leaf
1 tablespoon dried basil
1 teaspoon dried oregano

Heat 4 tablespoons (¼ cup) olive oil in a small skillet. Add the onion and garlic and cook over medium heat until transparent but not browned, 5–10 minutes. Remove the onion and garlic with a slotted spoon and set aside. In the same skillet add the remaining tablespoon oil and sauté the mushrooms for 5 minutes. Set these aside with onions. To the same skillet, still on medium heat, add the meat and sauté until brown, stirring to break up the pieces.

Meanwhile, in a large heavy saucepan heat the tomato sauce, tomato paste, water, and wine. To this add the onions, mushrooms, meat, sugar, celery, parsley, salt, bay leaf, sweet basil, and oregano. Cover, and simmer for 2 hours at 200° on top of the stove. Remove the bay leaf.

NOTE: This sauce may be served over hot pasta immediately or cooled and frozen for future use.

CLAM BAVETTE

SERVES 4–6

1 pound fresh clams or 2
    8-ounce cans minced clams
4 tablespoons butter or
    margarine
4 tablespoons olive oil
2 cloves garlic, minced
3 shallots, chopped
½ cup dry white wine
¼ cup chopped fresh parsley
1 pound bavette or linguini
    (fine noodles)
½ cup freshly grated Parmesan
    cheese
½ cup freshly grated Romano
    cheese

Scrub the clams thoroughly and steam them in a covered pot over a high heat with ¼ cup water. When shells open, drain them in a colander that is lined with cheesecloth and placed over a bowl to catch the juices. Shell clams, rinsing out any sand, and set aside in a separate dish. Save clam juices for later use. If using canned clams, reserve the liquid.

In a heavy medium-sized skillet melt the butter over low heat. Add the olive oil, garlic, and shallots and simmer until soft and transparent, 5–10 minutes. Set aside. Can be refrigerated at this point for up to 6 hours and finished later.

Just before serving combine the clams, reserved juices or liquid, wine, parsley, and the garlic mixture and reheat. Cook the pasta until al dente. Drain the pasta immediately and pour on a warmed serving platter. Cover with the clam sauce and cheeses. Toss carefully and serve at once.

SPAGHETTI WITH CRAB SAUCE

SERVES 8

2 tablespoons minced celery
2 tablespoons minced fresh
  parsley
1 large clove garlic, minced
2 small yellow onions, chopped
  (about 1 cup)
⅓ cup olive oil
1½ cups solid-pack tomatoes
6 ounces tomato paste
1¼ cups water
½ teaspoon paprika
2 teaspoons salt
½ teaspoon pepper
½ teaspoon dried basil
¼ teaspoon dried oregano
Pinch sugar
1 pound crab meat, shelled
  and washed
½ cup dry sherry
1 pound spaghetti
1 cup freshly grated Parmesan
  cheese

In a large skillet, using low to moderate heat, sauté celery, parsley, garlic, and onion in oil until lightly browned, about 10 minutes. Add tomatoes, tomato paste, water, paprika, salt, pepper, basil, oregano, and sugar. Turn heat to low and simmer uncovered 1 hour. Add well-drained crab meat and sherry. Simmer until it bubbles, approximately 5–10 minutes. Cook spaghetti and drain. Place pasta on a heated platter. Cover with sauce and garnish generously with cheese. Serve at once.

LINGUINI ALLA PESTO

SERVES 4 (8 WHEN A SIDE DISH)

4 small bunches fresh basil
  or 2 bunches fresh parsley
1 cup olive oil
2 cloves garlic, peeled
½ teaspoon salt
1 tablespoon toasted pine nuts
4 tablespoons freshly grated
  Parmesan cheese
4 tablespoons freshly grated
  Romano cheese
1 tablespoon salt
1 pound linguini noodles

Wash basil or parsley and dry well. Remove stems. Place in a blender with the oil, garlic, ½ teaspoon salt, pine nuts, and cheeses and reduce to a semi-liquid, or grind these ingredients in a mortar.

In a large saucepan bring 6–8 quarts water to a boil. Add the 1 tablespoon salt and the noodles and cook 8–10 minutes, testing often. Drain and pour pesto sauce over and mix well. Serve at once.

CANNELLONI

6 tablespoons olive oil
2 cups minced onion
3 cloves garlic, minced
2 cups peeled and chopped
   fresh tomatoes
½ teaspoon dried oregano
½ teaspoon dried basil
Salt and pepper to taste
1½ pounds ground beef
1 cup cooked chopped spinach,
   well drained
1 egg, beaten
9 tablespoons freshly grated
   Parmesan cheese
6 tablespoons butter or
   margarine
6 tablespoons flour
3 cups milk
12 to 14 Pasta Shells (*see Index*)
½ pound shredded Monterey
   Jack cheese

In a large saucepan heat 4 tablespoons oil over medium heat and cook 1 cup onion and 2 cloves garlic for 5 minutes or until tender. Stir in the tomatoes, oregano, basil, and salt and pepper to taste and simmer over low heat for 30 minutes, stirring occasionally. Set the tomato sauce aside.

In a 10–12-inch skillet heat the remaining 2 tablespoons oil over medium heat and cook the remaining 1 cup onion and 1 clove garlic until tender, about 5 minutes. Add the ground beef and cook, stirring to crumble, until browned.

Remove all excess oil and fat. Cool slightly, 5–10 minutes, and then blend in the spinach, egg, 6 tablespoons grated cheese, and salt and pepper to taste. Set the meat and spinach filling aside.

To prepare the cream sauce, melt the butter in a medium-sized saucepan over medium heat and blend in the flour until smooth. Slowly add the milk, stirring with a wire whisk, until thickened and smooth, 3–5 minutes. Stir in the remaining 3 tablespoons cheese and ¼ cup of the meat and spinach filling. Season to taste with salt and pepper.

To assemble, grease a shallow 7 × 11-inch baking dish and pour in the tomato sauce. Spoon some of the meat mixture in the center of each shell, dividing it evenly between all the shells, roll up, and place seam side down on top of the tomato sauce. Pour the cream sauce over the cannelloni and top with the Jack cheese. (The cannelloni may be covered and refrigerated at this point for as long as 24 hours before baking. Bring to room temperature before baking.) Bake in a preheated 350° oven for 30 minutes or until bubbly and the cheese is melted. Serve with a large salad, garlic bread or bread sticks, and red wine.

PIZZA

2 envelopes dry yeast

2 teaspoons sugar

2 cups warm water

1½ teaspoons salt

6 cups flour (approximately), sifted

¼ cup olive oil

Pizza Sauce (*below*)

½ pound imported prosciutto

2 pounds pepperoni, sliced

2 pounds mozzarella, thickly sliced

PIZZA SAUCE

1 small onion, very finely chopped

3 cloves garlic, finely chopped

3 tablespoons olive oil

4 cups Italian pear-shaped tomatoes, drained

12 ounces tomato paste

1 tablespoon dried oregano

½ teaspoon dried basil

½ teaspoon dried thyme

½ teaspoon crushed dried red pepper

1 teaspoon dried parsley

¼ teaspoon pepper

In a large mixing bowl dissolve the yeast and sugar in ½ cup warm water (110–120°) for 10 minutes. Mix the salt and 1½ cups warm water and stir into the yeast. Add and work in as much flour as the yeast will take. Turn out on a floured breadboard and knead, as you work in the ¼ cup olive oil, for 10 minutes. The dough should be smooth and elastic, with blisters on the surface. Place dough in a large greased bowl and cover loosely with a clean cloth. Set the bowl in a warm spot and let it rise until double in bulk (30–45 minutes).

To prepare sauce, in a large saucepan sauté the onion and garlic in the olive oil over medium heat until soft and golden, approximately 5 minutes. Chop the tomatoes and add to the onion mixture along with the tomato paste, oregano, basil, thyme, pepper flakes, parsley, and pepper. Cook, still over medium heat, for 10–15 minutes or until it reaches the desired consistency.

When the dough has risen, punch it down with a fist.

On a floured surface roll and stretch the dough to fill either 1 rimmed greased cookie sheet or 2 14-inch greased pizza pans. Spread Pizza Sauce over the dough and top with the prosciutto and pepperoni. Cover the entire surface with the mozzarella. Bake in a preheated 450° oven for 20–30 minutes or until the crust is browned and the top is melted and bubbly. Serve with a large green salad and crusty Italian bread.

NOTE: Italian pizza traditionally has a thicker, more breadlike crust, which is what you achieve by using the cookie sheet. If you want a thinner crust, use the 2 pizza pans.

MANICOTTI

ITALIAN TOMATO SAUCE

¼ cup olive oil

1 cup finely chopped onion

1 clove garlic, crushed

1 2-pound 3-ounce can Italian-
style tomatoes

6 ounces tomato paste

1½ cups water

2 tablespoons chopped fresh
parsley

2 teaspoons sugar

1 teaspoon dried oregano

½ teaspoon dried basil

1 tablespoon salt

¼ teaspoon pepper

PASTA SHELLS

5 eggs

1¼ cups unsifted flour

¼ teaspoon salt

1¼ cups water

1 teaspoon butter or margarine

MANICOTTI FILLING

2 pounds ricotta

8 ounces mozzarella cheese,
diced

⅓ cup freshly grated Parmesan
cheese

2 eggs

1 tablespoon chopped fresh
parsley

1 teaspoon salt

¼ teaspoon pepper

2 tablespoons freshly grated
Parmesan cheese

To prepare sauce, pour the oil into a 6-quart kettle and over medium heat sauté the onion and garlic until browned, about 5 minutes. Add the tomatoes, including the juice, tomato paste, 1½ cups water, 2 tablespoons parsley, the sugar, oregano, basil, 1 tablespoon salt, and ¼ teaspoon pepper, mashing the tomatoes and mixing well. Bring to a boil over high heat. Reduce heat and simmer covered for 1 hour stirring occasionally.

To prepare shells, in a medium-sized mixing bowl combine the 5 eggs, flour, ¼ teaspoon salt, and 1¼ cups water. Beat until smooth with an electric mixer. Melt the butter in a 7-inch skillet over medium heat. Pour in 2 tablespoons batter, rotating pan quickly, and cook until the top is dry but the bottom is *not* brown. Turn the shells out on a wire rack to cool. Continue, adding more butter to skillet if needed, until all the batter has been used.

To prepare filling, in a large bowl combine the ricotta, mozzarella, ⅓ cup Parmesan, 2 eggs, 1 tablespoon parsley, 1 teaspoon salt, and ¼ teaspoon pepper, beating with a wooden spoon until well blended.

To assemble, spoon a layer of tomato sauce on the bottom of 2 13 × 9 × 2-inch baking dishes. In the center of each shell place about ¼ cup of the filling and roll up. Place shells seam side down in a single layer in the baking dishes. Cover with the rest of the sauce and sprinkle with the 2 tablespoons Parmesan. At this point the dishes may be refrigerated for a day before baking. Bake uncovered in a preheated 350° oven for 30 minutes. Serve with a green salad and bread sticks or French bread.

LASAGNA BOLOGNESE

MEAT SAUCE BOLOGNESE

1 cup chopped onion

1 clove garlic, minced

½ cup chopped celery

2 tablespoons butter

1 pound mild Italian sausage

1 pound ground round beef

2 tablespoons olive oil

½ cup dry white wine

2 cups chopped tomatoes,
  peeled and seeded

3 tablespoons tomato paste

2 cups beef stock

1 bay leaf

½ teaspoon sugar

½ teaspoon dried oregano

⅛ teaspoon allspice

Salt and pepper to taste

BESCIAMELLA

(ITALIAN BECHAMEL SAUCE)

3 tablespoons butter

6 tablespoons flour

2 cups milk

1 cup heavy cream

1 teaspoon salt

Dash nutmeg

1 pound lasagna noodles
  (preferably green)

1 pound mozzarella cheese,
  grated

½ cup freshly grated Parmesan
  cheese

To prepare meat sauce, combine the onion, garlic, and celery and sauté over low heat in 2 tablespoons butter until golden, 8–10 minutes, stirring frequently. Remove to a heavy 3–4-quart saucepan. In same frying pan sauté the sausage and ground round in the olive oil until lightly browned. Stir to break up lumps. Remove excess grease. Add the wine to the meat and boil, stirring constantly, until wine is almost evaporated. Add meat to saucepan with onion mixture and add the tomatoes, tomato paste, stock, and seasonings. Simmer, partially covered, for 1 hour, stirring occasionally.

To prepare Besciamella, melt 3 tablespoons butter in a heavy 2–3-quart saucepan, over low heat. Stir in the flour and cook slowly 2–3 minutes, stirring constantly. Pour in the milk and cream slowly, stirring with a whisk to obtain a smooth sauce. Heat to boiling, stirring constantly, until sauce thickens. Remove from heat and add 1 teaspoon salt and the nutmeg. Set aside. (Makes 3 cups).

Butter a 9 × 13 × 3-inch baking dish. In a large 6–8-quart pot cook the lasagna. When cooked, drain and cover lasagna with cold water, then lift out strips and drain on paper towels.

To assemble, spread a layer of meat sauce on bottom of baking dish to about ¼ inch deep. Over this lay ⅓ of the noodles, then ⅓ of the Besciamella and ⅓ of the mozzarella. Repeat 2 more times; layering the meat sauce, noodles, Besciamella, and ending with the mozzarella. Sprinkle top with grated Parmesan and bake in a preheated 350° oven until bubbly, about 30 minutes. Can be frozen.

CHAPTER IV

SAN FRANCISCO

SEAFOOD & FISH

Duing the limbo hours of Sunday morning when it is too late for bed and too early for tennis, when bars and churches alike are closed, San Francisco revellers sometimes repair to Fisherman's Wharf for Hangtown Fry. Viewed objectively, this gastronomic nightmare hardly beckons weary head or jaded stomach, and had it been called Fourteen-Karat Omelette or Eggs and Oysters Jake, it would probably have faded into oblivion long ago. This delicious mixture of fried oysters and eggs originated, as some tell, in Hangtown, now known as Placerville. The story goes that an old, dirty '49er came into town, plunked his gold nuggets on the bar, and ordered the most expensive meal in the place. The chef checked his kitchen and found some six-dollar-apiece oysters, which had been shipped in barrels from the East Coast, which he combined with the scarce delicacy of fresh eggs. The result was Hangtown Fry.

Names are important, and San Franciscans have always had a flair for naming: Cliff House, Russian Hill, Maiden Lane, Nob Hill, Portsmouth Square, Golden Gate, and other romantic names that befit one of America's favorite tourist cities. From Steiner Street to Post to Powell to Union Square, and from Sansome Street to Market Street to the Embarcadero, the city abounds with memorable names, reflecting the personalities of the first Americans who came there to begin the transformation of Yerba Buena (meaning "good herb") into dynamic San Francisco.

The beginnings were inauspicious. The Spanish found it by mistake after long believing that no such place existed.

In 1597 a small bay to the north, now called Drake's Bay, became the original San Francisco Bay. Its location was subsequently forgotten. Junípero Serra wanted a mission to be established at San Francisco to honor the founder of his order, and Don Gaspar de Portolá found the place, though quite by accident, while looking for Monterey. The mission of San Francisco de Asis was founded in 1776, but it was not a great success. Mission Dolores, as it came to be called, in honor of Our Lady of Sorrows, was an unfortunately appropriate name. Although four thousand Indian converts had their names in the mission records, very few were faithful. Many ran away, remembering their carefree lives before the padres came. Many more sickened and died. The climate with its fogs and bone-chilling winds, combined with measles and other white man's diseases, proved fatal to many. The steep hills and sandy soil were unsuitable for agriculture.

The Presidio, or military post, was located some distance from the mission on a sandy knoll overlooking the bay. During the Mexican period, the Presidio went from neglect to partial ruin. Neither the mission nor the Presidio was influential during Spanish rule, and when this rule ended, the settlement sank into near oblivion. Although nearby rancheros raised cattle, and traders came to barter for their hides and tallow, the little settlement of Yerba Buena, so called because of the pungent shrubs growing on the shore, remained—even after the secularization of the mission lands—remote from foreign influence. The Mexican authorities were anxious to avoid outside contact, but because the government at Monterey imposed heavy duties on imports, foreign ships chose to anchor off Yerba Buena Cove rather than at Monterey. The Monterey governor was apparently annoyed by the smuggling that occurred to the north, but did little about it. By the 1830s Yerba Buena was gaining prominence as an international port.

The Mexican hold over the northern settlements had always been tenuous at best, and the best was past. Foreigners came, settled, and built houses. In the summer of 1836 there were only three houses. The 1844 census listed four trading posts, several grocery stores, one restaurant, two grog shops, a blacksmith, and three carpenters. There were about twenty houses, all owned by foreigners. In that year the government at Monterey ordered the building of the Custom House. This proved to be a futile gesture. Smuggling continued. The foreign population increased, and soon it was far larger than the Spanish-Mexican population. England, France, and Russia eyed the colony with proprietary interest, and so did the United States.

The Treaty of Guadalupe Hidalgo, in which Mexico formally ceded California to the United States, was not signed until February 2, 1848. At that time Yerba Buena was a small village with two hotels, two incompleted wharves, and 812 people. Then, in the spring of 1848, Captain John Sutter spread the word from Sacramento that gold had been discovered in the Sierras. In San Francisco people were generally disinterested and skeptical about a remote discovery. The first store proprietor to receive gold in exchange for purchases offered value equal to eight dollars per ounce. To the storekeeper it was merely a curiosity. To the editors of the *Californian* the news of the discovery was worth a short paragraph on the back page.

Sam Brannon, owner of the *California Star*, was a different kind of newspaperman. He sent his editor to Sutter's settlement, New Helvetia, to investigate. Then Sam Brannon went to see for himself. When he returned, he loudly proclaimed his findings the length of Montgomery Street, waving a bottle of nuggets and shouting, "Gold! Gold on the American River!" Almost overnight the town emptied. Merchants quickly sold out their stocks of shovels, pans, flour, and salt pork, and joined the exodus.

For several months, San Francisco was virtually a ghost town. Ships sat at anchor with no one to unload them. The few men who remained in town commanded kingly wages (by those days' standards) for whatever work they deigned to do. Goods and services had never before brought such prices. In most cases, they still don't. When the daily wage is ten or twenty dollars, six dollars is a lot to pay for a breakfast of ham, eggs, and coffee. The menu in a typical pioneer eating house in the fall of '48 consisted of:

Bean soup	$1.00
Hash (low grade)	.75
Hash (18K with beef)	1.00
Beef with 1 potato	1.50
2 Potatoes	.50
2 Potatoes (peeled)	.75
Baked beans (plain)	.75
Baked beans (greased)	1.00

As the summer of 1848 ended, many of the prospectors returned to San Francisco. Some had their fortunes made, and others, disappointed in the gold fields, were perspicacious enough to see the commercial opportunities inherent in a gold rush. Prospectors swarmed to California. They came from the eastern states, from Honolulu, from Europe, and even from the Orient. By 1849 the population had grown to forty thousand. Food came from a distance, too. In their eagerness to reach the bonanza, farmers had left some crops to rot in the fields and still others unplanted. Prices for goods imported from the Hawaiian Islands, Oregon, and the Far East were astronomical, not because of the distances from which they came, but because of their scarcity. Services, too, were so scarce that it was not unusual for the most fastidious residents to send their laundry by clipper ship to Honolulu or even to China.

San Francisco was a boomtown. Its boomtown aspects were most evidenced in the rate at which money changed hands. They were high flyers, those '49ers. Gambling establishments flourished, even with rents as high as $180 a day. Real estate changed hands quickly, and at prices that often wouldn't be matched again for a hundred years. Hotels, restaurants, rooming houses, bordellos, and saloons burgeoned. The restaurant fare became a great deal more sophisticated and began to offer gourmet foods and delicacies such as duck, venison, partridge, quail, trout, salmon, lobster, wines, and liqueurs, all at a high cost. Speculators bought and sold mining stocks on the street corners. Men drank, gambled, and sometimes shot each other. In all this, it was a boomtown, but with a difference. Just as San Francisco is today one of the world's most cosmopolitan cities, it was then, surely, the world's most cosmopolitan boomtown.

The hills of San Francisco became littered with tents and makeshift houses made of packing crates. The polyglot newcomers came, bringing with them the customs of many different lands and cultures. Each brought his own culinary heritage, too. This, combined with the varied origins of the actual foodstuffs that came to San Francisco, laid the foundations that helped San Francisco become a gourmet's paradise. Restaurants have been unusually important to San Francisco since that time.

The population then was overwhelmingly male. They lived in hotels, in rooming houses, in shacks. Rather than do home cooking, most people ate out; and they spent most of their evenings out, looking for entertainment and companionship. Many of these men were not only literate but cultured. Inevitably culture came to San Francisco. Men who are accustomed to amenities, and who can afford them, usually arrange to have them. During the period 1850–1900 many famous restaurants sprang up, numbering between two and three hundred. The prices were high, but the restaurants offered the finest. There was a great variety of foods. In 1870 a visitor wrote, "It is possible in San Francisco to dine in any language; to eat the especial dishes of any civilized country." Concerts, plays (including Shakespeare's *Richard III*), vaudeville shows, and circuses came to town. Jenny Lind came and so did Edwin Booth and Lola Montez. Theaters proliferated. It is said that between 1850 and 1859 over eleven hundred different dramatic pieces were produced in San Francisco. Writers, artists, actors, and all sorts of creative people loved the atmosphere in this new dynamic city. The frontier town had become the city.

A silver boom followed the gold rush. During the 1860s an enormous amount of money flowed into San Francisco as a result of the rediscovered silver in the Comstock Mines. Over the next twenty years the money amounted to nearly $300 million.

In 1869 the railroad was completed over the Sierras, joining San Francisco to the eastern states. The back-breaking work of completing the Central Pacific Railroad was done by thousands of Chinese who had immigrated to San Francisco. Within a few years a Chinatown was born—its shops adorned with Chinese signs and flags—a city within a city. It remains to this day the largest concentration of Chinese outside the Orient.

From that time on, San Francisco became a city in a class by itself, unchallenged by any other port on the Pacific and rivaled only by New Orleans. Excellent restaurants, long a tradition, thrived and grew. All types and varieties of foods were available. As San Franciscans enjoyed eating out, there also developed the tradition of the "Cocktail Route." This was the path that emerged by traveling to and from famous bars—from the Reception Saloon to the Occidental Bar to the Bank Exchange—all offering gourmet food and abundant free lunches. The Bank Exchange offered the famous San Francisco drink Pisco Punch. Known also as "the nectar of the gods," with a strong kick, it assumed a great mystique when the owner of the bar took the recipe with him to his grave.

Some of the famous restaurants of that period were the Maison Riche, Poulet d'Or (still in existence, but now called The Poodle Dog), the Maison Dorée, and of course the Palace Hotel. The Palace claimed it could prepare any dish regardless of origin, and among its repertoire were Palace Court Salad, Green Goddess Salad, Oyters Kirkpatrick (named for the first general manager), Oyster Omelette, and Pudding à la Sultan.

In April 1906 San Francisco suffered a severe earthquake. The resulting fire destroyed over thirty thousand buildings and covered four square miles. As the city was rebuilt there developed a great mixture of architectural styles and materials—all jumbled together but with a distinct California flavor. One architectural feature used extensively was the bay window. Theoretically it offered a view and allowed more sun to enter the room through the early morning fog.

San Francisco was and is a beckoning city, sensually appealing, full of sights and sounds and smells. The plaintive wail of the fog horn, the strident clang of the cable cars, the muffled clip-clop of the mounted policemen in the city's many parks, are sounds of San Francisco. The redolence of carnations and kelp and ginger and firecrackers denotes various districts of the city, even in the dark.

San Francisco is a good place to be hungry. The appetites generated by the climate account in part for the excellence of the cuisine. San Franciscans have always loved good food and their many outstanding restaurants. They can claim such specialities as sourdough bread, Celery Victor, chicken in the shell, shrimps à la Bordelaise, Irish coffee (first introduced to America in San Francisco), and numerous Chinese dishes. The various neighborhoods—French, Russian, Chinese, Japanese, Armenian, Greek, German, Jewish, Indian, Mexican, Italian—have little bakeries and markets catering to the local tastes. Fish is plentiful and fresh, except in neighborhoods where dried eel, shrimp, and squid are delicacies. Shrimp tempura, curried shrimp, or shrimp cocktail eaten from a paper cup at Fisherman's Wharf are all typical of San Francisco. Dungeness crab, petrole sole, abalone, rex sole, bay shrimp—together with such famous recipes as Oyster Loaf, crab Louis, fresh poached salmon, and, of course, Cioppino (seafood stew adapted by the local Italian fishermen)—tempt even a seafood hater. Probably nowhere in the world is seafood prepared in so many different ways in a given day.

Whatever external changes may befall San Francisco in the future, the essence of the city, the spirit of its people, will not change. Traditions have long been part of San Francisco's way of life. Comfort, ease, and luxury are hallmarks of San Francisco. However the sky line or shore line may change, there will always be a special feeling to this city. There will always be music, art, and church bells. There will always be a memorable meal.

HINTS FOR COOKING FISH

LEAN, MILD FIRM-FLESH FISH
  Halibut
  Sole
  Rockfish (red snapper)
  Lingcod
  Pacific cod
  Sea bass
  Sand dab

These fish are best when broiled, sautéed, poached, or when whole, baked.

FATTER FISH
  Salmon
  Swordfish
  Albacore
  Mackerel

These fish are best when barbecued, poached, broiled, or baked.

PAN-SIZED WHOLE FISH
  Mackerel
  Smelt
  Surfperch
  Trout

These fish are best when butter-sautéed, fried, oven-fried, broiled, or barbecued.

SPORT FISH
  Bonito
  Sheepshead
  Kelp bass
  Sand bass
  Striped bass
  Sierra

These fish with the exception of bonito may be prepared as you would any other lean whitefish. Bonito is similar to albacore, though stronger in flavor.

SHRIMP RUSSIAN HILL

6 tablespoons butter

4 pounds medium raw shrimp, peeled and deveined

1 cup thinly sliced fresh mushrooms

4 tablespoons dry sherry

½ cup thinly sliced green pepper

2 tablespoons tomato paste

1⅓ cups light cream

½ cup sour cream

½ teaspoon salt

1 tablespoon cornstarch

3 tablespoons cold milk

2 large onions, thinly sliced

Melt 4 tablespoons butter in a large heavy skillet over moderate heat. Place the shrimp in the skillet. Toss and stir the shrimp in the foaming butter until pink, about 2–4 minutes. Remove the shrimp from the butter with a slotted spoon and place on a platter. Add more butter to the skillet if necessary (there should be about 2 tablespoons melted butter in the skillet). Sauté the mushrooms in the butter over low heat for 5 minutes or until soft and tender. Add the sherry and green pepper to the skillet and sauté over moderate heat for 5 additional minutes. Turn the heat to low and slowly add the tomato paste, light cream, and sour cream, stirring well after each addition. Blend the mixture over a low flame and add salt to taste. Return the shrimp to the sauce and simmer over a *very* low flame for 15 minutes, stirring occasionally. Dissolve the cornstarch in the cold milk in a small cup and add to the shrimp mixture. Cook, stirring over low heat for a few minutes, until the mixture thickens.

If necessary, add more milk and cornstarch, in the same proportions, until the mixture is thick and creamy. Remove from heat. In another 10–12-inch skillet melt 2 tablespoons butter and sauté the onion over moderate heat until crisp and browned, being careful not to burn them. Remove the onions with a slotted spoon and add to the shrimp mixture. This dish may be prepared ahead and reheated, carefully, over low heat.

NOTE: This is a delicious luncheon dish served with almond rice pilaf and a crisp green salad. Accompanied by a green vegetable, such as broccoli or green beans, it also makes an unusual main course.

CHINESE SKEWERED SHRIMP

SERVES 6

30 large raw shrimp or prawns
⅔ cup dry sherry
⅔ cup soy sauce
⅔ cup olive or peanut oil
½ teaspoon powdered ginger
¼ teaspoon grated lemon peel
1 clove garlic, crushed
2 6½-ounce cans water chestnuts
30 fresh mushrooms, stemmed
½ pound bacon, cut into
   2 × 2-inch squares

Shell and devein the shrimp. In a 2-3-quart bowl combine the sherry, soy sauce, oil, ginger, lemon peel, and garlic. Place the raw shrimp in the bowl and marinate in the mixture, stirring occasionally. This may be done in the refrigerator for 2 hours or at room temperature for 1 hour. Thread the shrimp on metal skewers (5 per skewer), alternating with water chestnuts, mushroom caps, and bacon squares. This may be done ahead and refrigerated covered for several hours.

Place the skewers over medium coals on the barbecue, turning frequently and basting with the marinade. Cook for approximately 6–8 minutes or until shrimp are pink. Serve hot from the grill over rice pilaf and garnished with fresh or broiled tomatoes. The skewers may be made smaller and served as an hors d'oeuvre or first course. Guests may assemble their own from bowls of all the ingredients for an entertaining and sociable appetizer or dinner.

SHRIMP AU GRATIN TIBURON

SERVES 4–6

6 tablespoons butter
3 tablespoons finely chopped
   onion
¼ cup flour
¼ teaspoon dry mustard
½ teaspoon salt
⅛ teaspoon white pepper
1½ cups milk
1 cup grated Swiss cheese
2 tablespoons dry white wine
   or vermouth
1½ pounds shrimp, peeled,
   deveined, and cooked
½ pound fresh mushrooms,
   thinly sliced
½ cup soft bread crumbs
Parsley sprigs

Melt 3 tablespoons of the butter in a heavy 12–14-inch skillet or heavy 3-quart saucepan. Sauté the onion in the butter over low heat, stirring often, for 3–4 minutes or until soft and tender. Stir in the flour, blending until smooth, and cook over low heat for 3 minutes. Add the mustard, salt, and pepper. Cook, stirring constantly, over moderate heat until mixture is bubbling. Add the milk slowly, stirring constantly. Cook over moderate heat, stirring, for a few minutes until the mixture thickens and bubbles. Add ¾ cup of the Swiss cheese, stirring until melted and blended. Add 2 tablespoons white wine and blend. Add the shrimp to the sauce and remove from heat. In a heavy 10–12-inch skillet melt 2 tablespoons butter and sauté the sliced mushrooms over moderate heat for 3–5 minutes or until soft and tender. Remove the mushrooms with a slotted spoon and add the mushrooms to the shrimp sauce. Turn the mixture into a buttered shallow 2-quart baking dish. Combine the breadcrumbs and remaining $\frac{1}{4}$ cup Swiss cheese and sprinkle over the top of the dish. Dot with remaining 1 tablespoon butter. Bake in a preheated 400° oven for 10 minutes or until the sauce is bubbly and the top is lightly browned. Serve at once, garnished with parsley.

NOTE: This dish also can be cooked in individual shells or ramekins and served as a first course or luncheon dish.

SHRIMP IN FOIL

SERVES 2–4

$\frac{3}{4}$–1 pound raw medium to large shrimp, peeled and deveined
$\frac{1}{3}$ cup butter
1 cup thinly sliced fresh mushrooms
$\frac{1}{4}$ cup finely minced onion
$\frac{1}{4}$ cup finely chopped parsley
$\frac{1}{2}$ teaspoon salt
$\frac{1}{2}$ teaspoon Worcestershire sauce
Dash Tabasco sauce

Cut 2 12 × 12-inch squares of heavy-duty foil. Wash and dry the shrimp and divide into 2 equal portions. Place $\frac{1}{2}$ the shrimp on $\frac{1}{2}$ of each foil square. Melt the butter in a 1-quart saucepan over low heat. Add the remaining ingredients and stir over the heat for a few seconds. Pour $\frac{1}{2}$ the mixture over each portion of shrimp. Fold the foil over the shrimp and seal each package with a double fold on 3 sides, forming a triangle.

Place the foil packages on the barbecue over medium coals for 10–15 minutes. The foil packages will swell up but will not burst if properly sealed.

When ready to serve, place the foil packages on a warm plate, cut an X in the top of each package, and eat the shrimp and mushrooms out of the foil. This recipe may also be prepared by baking in a preheated 350° oven for 20 minutes.

NOTE: This is an unusual and delightful dish for a picnic or summer barbecue. It may also be served as a first course by dividing the shrimp into 4 equal portions.

SCAMPI

2 pounds large raw shrimp
1 cup melted butter
½ cup olive oil
½ cup vermouth
1 tablespoon finely minced
   garlic
1 teaspoon salt
½ teaspoon white pepper
1 tablespoon monosodium
   glutamate
Juice of 2 lemons
4 tablespoons chopped fresh
   parsley
¼ cup finely chopped scallions,
   including tops
¼ cup freshly grated Parmesan
   cheese
1 tablespoon capers, chopped
2 tablespoons cognac

Wash shrimp well and remove the shells, leaving the last segment of the tail shell intact. Devein and rinse again. Pat dry with paper towels and set aside.

Combine butter, oil, vermouth, garlic, salt, white pepper, monosodium glutamate, lemon juice, and parsley in blender. Cover and blend at high speed for 10 seconds. Arrange shrimp in an attractive pattern in a large flameproof shallow serving dish. Pour the marinade over shrimp and let them stand at room temperature for 1 hour.

Sprinkle scallions, cheese, and capers over shrimp. Place shrimp in a preheated broiler 3–4 inches from the flame for 5 minutes or until browned. Turn shrimp over and broil for 1–2 minutes until brown and firm to the touch. Do not overcook. Six to 8 minutes total cooking time should be enough. To serve, warm cognac in a very small pan. Ignite the cognac with a match and pour over the shrimp. Serve at once while still flaming, accompanied by Lemon Rice or Rice Pilaf (*see Index*).

OYSTER LOAF

1 round loaf French bread
1 clove garlic, split
4 tablespoons butter, melted
Salt and pepper to taste
2 dashes Tabasco sauce
1 teaspoon Worcestershire
   sauce
1 teaspoon sherry
2 eggs, beaten
½ cup flour
1 cup yellow corn meal or
   bread crumbs
2–3 dozen oysters
¼–½ cup butter

Cut the top off the bread so it forms a lid. Hollow out the inside, making a basket, leaving about ½-inch crust all the way around. Remove excess bread from the top crust or lid. Rub the inside of the loaf with split clove of garlic and brush inside and out with melted butter. Toast in a preheated 400° oven until crisp, 15–20 minutes. Remove and turn oven down to 300°.

In a small bowl add salt, pepper, Tabasco, Worcestershire, and sherry to beaten eggs. Place the flour and corn meal or bread crumbs in separate small bowls. Dip oysters first in flour, then in egg mixture, and finally in corn meal or bread crumbs.

Catsup
Lemon wedges

Melt the butter in a heavy 10–12-inch skillet and fry the coated oysters until brown and crisp. Fill the loaf with hot fried oysters and put the lid on top. Heat in oven at 300° for 10 minutes or until ready to serve. Cut in slices and serve with catsup and lemon wedges.

NOTE: The amount of oysters to buy varies according to the size of the oysters and the size of the loaf of bread. You want the "basket" of bread filled to the top with oysters.

OYSTERS KIRKPATRICK

SERVES 4–6

Rock salt
12 fresh oysters in their shells
4 tablespoons butter
4 slices bacon
½ cup catsup
1 tablespoon Worcestershire sauce
2 tablespoons dry sherry
Dash Tabasco sauce
⅓ cup freshly grated Parmesan cheese

Place a layer of rock salt at least ½ inch thick in a large shallow flameproof casserole. Open oysters and set them on the half shell on the rock salt. Dot each oyster with a small amount of butter. Place the oysters under a preheated broiler for 5–8 minutes, until the edges of the oysters start to curl. Remove the oysters from the broiler.

Cut the bacon strips into thirds. Sauté the bacon in a heavy 12-inch skillet over moderate heat until partially cooked but not crisp. Remove bacon from the skillet and drain on paper towels.

Combine the catsup, Worcestershire, sherry, and Tabasco. Place ⅓ slice of bacon on each oyster. On top of the bacon, spoon about 1 tablespoon of the catsup mixture. Sprinkle each oyster with cheese and place under the broiler again for 2–4 minutes or until cheese slightly melts and sauce cooks and bubbles. Serve at once as a first course or appetizer.

NOTE: If desired, individual servings may best be accomplished by covering individual ramekin or gratin dishes with ½-inch layer of rock salt and placing 2 or 3 oysters in each dish. Proceed as already described. Dishes must be flameproof.

OYSTERS ZELLERBACH

SERVES 2

1½ cups chopped cooked spinach, drained
1 tablespoon minced or grated onion
3 tablespoons sour cream
1 teaspoon salt
¼ teaspoon ground nutmeg (or less if desired)
¼ cup freshly grated Parmesan cheese
¼ cup fresh soft bread crumbs
½ cup melted butter
1 10-ounce jar western oysters, drained

In a small bowl combine the spinach, onion, sour cream, ½ teaspoon salt, and nutmeg. Spread the mixture in a small buttered shallow casserole or flameproof platter. The spinach mixture should be about 1 inch thick. In a small bowl combine the Parmesan, ½ teaspoon salt, and bread crumbs. Place the melted butter in another small bowl. Proceed by dipping the oysters first in the cheese and crumb mixture, then in the melted butter, and finally in the crumb mixture again.

Make indentations in the spinach for each oyster with the back of a tablespoon. Space these identations evenly and attractively. Place 1 oyster in each indentation. Sprinkle the leftover melted butter and crumb mixture on top of the oysters. Bake the oysters in a preheated 375° oven for 10 minutes. Place the platter under the broiler and broil for 3–5 minutes or until browned and bubbling. Serve at once with a green salad and warm French bread or as an elegant first course.

SCALLOPS AMANDINE

SERVES 6–8

2 pounds scallops
¼ cup flour
¼ cup dry bread crumbs
1 teaspoon seasoned salt
2 tablespoons oil
6 tablespoons clarified butter
½ cup slivered almonds
½ cup dry white wine or vermouth
3 tablespoons fresh lemon juice
2 tablespoons finely chopped fresh parsley
Lemon wedges

If using frozen scallops, thaw completely. Rinse, drain, and pat dry. Cut the large scallops in half so that the pieces are of uniform size.

In a small bowl combine flour, bread crumbs, and seasoned salt. Coat the scallops with this mixture. Heat the oil and 3 tablespoons of the clarified butter over moderately high heat in a heavy 10–12-inch skillet until butter stops foaming. Sauté the scallops until golden brown and tender, approximately 5–10 minutes. Stir to brown evenly. Remove the scallops to a heated platter. Keep warm. Add the rest of the butter and the almonds to the skillet. Cook over moderate heat, stirring constantly, until the almonds are golden brown, being careful not to burn the almonds or the bits in the pan. Add the nuts to the scallops. Add the wine to the skillet and continue to cook, loosening the browned bits from the bottom of the pan. Stir the lemon juice into the skillet, and pour over scallops and nuts. Sprinkle with parsley and garnish with lemon wedges. Serve at once. Can be served in shells or individual ramekins.

LOBSTER COQUILLE VÉRONIQUE

SERVES 8 AS FIRST COURSE

8–16 small baby lobster tails
Salt
White pepper
Monosodium glutamate
1 1-pound can white seedless grapes, drained
2 tablespoons butter
3 tablespoons finely chopped shallots
½ cup dry white wine or vermouth
1 cup heavy cream
2 teaspoons flour
2 teaspoons butter, softened
½ cup Blender Hollandaise Sauce (*see Index*)
2 tablespoons finely chopped scallions (whites only) or chives
¼ teaspoon Worcestershire sauce
Dash Tabasco sauce
1 tablespoon fresh lemon juice

Shell the lobster tails and cut into bite-sized pieces. Defrost thoroughly if frozen and drain on paper toweling. Sprinkle the lobster with salt, pepper, and monosodium glutamate. Place 4 or 5 grapes in each of 8 scallop shells or ramekins. Melt 2 tablespoons butter in a 12-inch skillet and add the lobster. Cook and stir over moderate heat for 1 minute. Add the shallots and cook, stirring, for 1 minute longer. Add the wine and ¼ cup cream and cook gently over low heat until slightly reduced and thickened, about 6–8 minutes. Remove the lobster from the sauce and divide it evenly among the shells or ramekins. Mix the flour and softened butter to a smooth paste and add to the pan drippings. Cook, stirring, over moderate heat for 3–4 minutes until the sauce is slightly thickened. Stir in ¼ cup cream. Add ½ cup Blender Hollandaise Sauce. Whip the remaining ½ cup cream in a small bowl until it is stiff and fold it gently into the sauce. Add the scallions, Worcestershire, Tabasco, and lemon juice. Blend and remove the pan from the heat. Correct the seasoning if necessary. (This recipe can be prepared ahead several hours to this point.)

When ready to serve, pour the sauce over the lobster and top with 3 or 4 more grapes. Place the shells or ramekins under the broiler for 4–5 minutes or until sauce is lightly browned and the coquilles are bubbling. Serve at once as a delicious first course, for a formal dinner party.

LOBSTER WITH CAVIAR CREAM SAUCE

SERVES 8

4 California lobsters, cooked and split, or 8 California lobster tails
1 tablespoon salt per 1 quart water
2 tablespoons butter, melted
Caviar Cream Sauce (*below*)
16 avocado slices
Lemon wedges

Steam or boil the lobsters or lobster tails if they are not precooked. Bring a large kettle of water to the boil, adding 1 tablespoon salt for each quart of water, and drop the lobsters into the kettle. Bring the water again to the simmer, cover the kettle, and simmer for about 7 minutes for 1-pound lobsters or about 10 minutes for 2-pound lobsters. When cooked, remove the lobsters from the simmering water, plunge into cold water, and drain. Most lobster tails come to the markets uncooked and frozen, so they must be thawed and cooked as described above. Whole lobster is usually cooked before freezing and shipping, so it need only be thawed. To prepare the lobster tails for eating after cooking, it is necessary to clip the tough cartilage away from the underside of the lobster, exposing the tender meat. With scissors, snip along the outside edges of the tail and gently remove the undershell, leaving the tail intact. Set aside.

To serve, brush the lobster tails with the melted butter and place them on a rack 5–6 inches from a preheated broiler for 1 minute or until lightly browned. Remove the lobster from the broiler and coat each tail or half with a layer of the Caviar Cream Sauce. Again place the baking sheet under the broiler and broil for 1–2 minutes, or until the sauce is bubbling and lightly browned. Place 2 avocado slices on top of each lobster tail and return to the broiler for an additional 15 seconds. Serve at once, garnished with lemon wedges.

CAVIAR CREAM SAUCE
1 cup sour cream
2½ tablespoons fresh lemon juice
2 tablespoons lumpfish caviar
½ cup heavy cream
Dash hot-pepper sauce
½ teaspoon salt

To prepare sauce, combine the sour cream and lemon juice in a small mixing bowl. Place the caviar in a small strainer and rinse under cold water until the water turns clear, to remove the black dye. Add the caviar, well drained, to the sour cream. In another small bowl beat the cream until it is stiff and add it to the caviar mixture, folding it in gently. Add the hot sauce and the ½ teaspoon salt and blend gently but thoroughly.

CRAB AND ARTICHOKE CASSEROLE

1 pound crab meat
4 tablespoons butter
3 tablespoons flour
1 cup milk
½ cup chicken broth
¾ cup grated mild Cheddar
    cheese
2 tablespoons Worcestershire
    sauce
¼ cup sherry (optional)
2 9-ounce packages frozen
    artichoke hearts, cooked
    and drained
4 hard-boiled eggs, sliced
2 tablespoons freshly grated
    Parmesan cheese
8 small whole crab legs

Prepare the crab by defrosting if frozen. Pick the crab meat apart and drain on paper towels. Some frozen crab has a rather strong iodine flavor and odor. If this is noticed, the crab meat should be placed in a large strainer and rinsed under cold water before being drained.

Place 3 tablespoons butter in a 1–2-quart saucepan and melt over low heat. Add the flour gradually to the butter, cooking and stirring over medium heat for 3 minutes until the roux is smooth and bubbling. Slowly blend in the milk and chicken broth and mix well. Add the Cheddar, Worcestershire, and optional sherry. Cook the cheese mixture over moderate heat until the sauce is well blended and the cheese is melted. When the sauce is smooth and bubbling, spoon about ⅓ of the mixture into the bottom of a 1½-quart casserole. Layer ½ each of the artichoke hearts (reserving 8 for garnish), eggs, and crab meat on top of the sauce. Repeat the layers, using the remaining artichoke hearts, eggs, and crab meat. Top with the remaining ⅓ sauce. Sprinkle with Parmesan and bake uncovered in a preheated 350° oven for 30 minutes or until browned and bubbling. Just before serving, melt 1 tablespoon butter in a small skillet and gently stir in the 8 crab legs and the 8 artichoke hearts. Cook and stir over moderate heat until heated through, about 3–5 minutes. Remove the skillet from the flame and keep warm. When ready to serve, garnish the casserole with artichoke hearts and crab legs.

NOTE: This makes a lovely luncheon dish accompanied by a crisp green salad and a chilled white wine such as Chenin Blanc.

CRAB ENCHILADAS SAN FRANCISCO SERVES 6

Salsa con Tomatillos (*below*)
½ cup oil or lard (more may
  be necessary)
6 corn tortillas
1½ cups flaked crab meat
6 tablespoons finely minced
  onion
½ pound Monterey Jack
  cheese, grated
Sour Cream Sauce (*below*)
Pitted ripe olives
Avocado slices
Tomato wedges

SALSA CON TOMATILLOS
2 10-ounce cans tomatillos
  (tomates verdes)
½ cup oil or lard
2 corn tortillas
2 fresh or canned Jalapeño
  chiles, finely chopped
½ cup chopped onion
2 tablespoons chopped fresh
  coriander leaves (cilantro),
  stems removed
1 clove garlic, crushed
1 teaspoon salt
Pinch sugar

Prepare the Salsa con Tomatillos and reserve. Place the ½ cup oil or lard in a heavy 12-inch skillet and heat over moderate heat until quite hot. Quickly fry the 6 tortillas in the oil (8–10 seconds) until they are soft. Remove the tortillas from the oil and place on paper towels to drain. When ready to assemble the enchiladas, dip the tortillas into the Salsa con Tomatillos using tongs. This softens the tortillas and makes them pliable. Place approximately ¼ cup crab meat in the center of each tortilla. Place 1 tablespoon minced onion on top of the crab and spread 1 or 2 tablespoons Salsa con Tomatillos over the onion and crab meat. Roll the enchiladas carefully and place them seam side down in a shallow baking dish large enough to hold them in 1 layer (approximately 8 × 12 inches). Cover the enchiladas with the remaining Salsa con Tomatillos and sprinkle them with the cheese. The dish may be prepared ahead to this point and held, covered, in the refrigerator. When ready to serve, bake at 400° for 10–15 minutes or until the dish is hot and bubbling. To serve, garnish each enchilada with several tablespoons of Sour Cream Sauce. On the top of each enchilada, place alternating sections of olives, avocado slices, and tomato wedges. Delicious served with Tostada Salad or Spinach Salad (*see Index*).

To prepare Salsa con Tomatillos, place tomatillos and their juice in a blender jar. Blend till smooth.

Heat ¼ cup oil or lard in a 10-inch skillet and fry the tortillas over moderate heat for 1–2 minutes or until crisp but not brown. Remove from oil and drain on paper towel. When cool enough to handle, crumble the tortillas into the blender jar with the tomatillos, stir with a spoon, and let soften for a few minutes. Blend until smooth.

Heat the remaining ¼ cup oil or lard in a 2-quart saucepan over moderate heat and add the chiles and onion and cook, stirring, for 3–4 minutes or until soft but not browned. Add 2 tablespoons (or more if desired) coriander, garlic, salt, and sugar. Cook, stirring, over moderate heat for 3–4 minutes. Add the blended tomalltio mixture to the saucepan and cook, stirring over moderate heat, for 4–5 minutes. If sauce seems too thick, a small amount of water may be added. If a smoother sauce is desired, all ingredients may be returned to the blender for a few seconds after cooking. Correct the seasoning. Add more salt and sugar if necessary. Sauce will be spicy and have a rather unusual flavor due to the coriander. Salsa may be prepared in advance and refrigerated or frozen.

To prepare Sour Cream Sauce, place sour cream in a small mixing bowl. Add all the other Sour Cream Sauce ingredients and stir well to combine. Serve as a garnish for crab enchiladas. Sauce may be doubled if desired and the additional sauce served separately as an accompaniment to the enchiladas.

SOUR CREAM SAUCE
1 cup sour cream
2 tablespoons minced fresh coriander leaves (cilantro), stems removed
1½ tablespoons finely minced onion
½ teaspoon salt
1 small clove garlic, crushed

SAN FRANCISCO DEVILED CRAB

SERVES 6

4 tablespoons butter
1 tablespoon vegetable oil
¾ cup finely chopped onion
½ cup finely chopped celery
3 tablespoons flour
1½ cups milk
1 cup light cream
1½ teaspoons dry mustard
¼ teaspoon Tabasco sauce
1 teaspoon Worcestershire sauce
¼ cup dry sherry
2 tablespoons fresh lemon juice
2 tablespoons chopped fresh parsley
3 hard-boiled chopped eggs,
1 pound Dungeness crab meat, flaked
Salt and white pepper to taste
½ cup freshly grated Parmesan cheese

In a 10–12-inch skillet combine 3 tablespoons butter and the oil and sauté the onion and celery over low heat for 4–6 minutes or until soft. Add the flour, a little at a time, and cook, stirring, for 3–4 minutes. Meanwhile, heat milk and cream in a small saucepan. Add the heated milk gradually to the onion mixture, stirring constantly.

In a small bowl combine the dry mustard, Tabasco, Worcestershire, sherry, lemon juice, and parsley. Add this mixture to the onion mixture in the skillet, stirring well. Bring to a simmer and stir until the sauce thickens, about 3–4 minutes. Add the chopped eggs and crab. Taste for seasoning, adding salt and pepper to taste.

Divide the mixture between 6 scallop shells or ramekins. Dot them with the remaining butter and cover with the cheese. Place them in a preheated 375° oven for 15 minutes or until they are lightly browned and bubbling. Serve as a first course or luncheon dish.

NOTE: This can also be served as a main course by placing the crab mixture in a shallow casserole and accompanying it with Sourdough Bread and Fresh Spinach Salad (see Index).

CRAB MOUSSELINE IN ARTICHOKE BOTTOMS

8 large fresh artichoke bottoms,
  cooked
1 pound Dungeness crab meat,
  cooked
3 tablespoons butter
½ pound fresh mushrooms,
  thinly sliced
2 tablespoons fresh lemon juice
¼ teaspoon garlic salt
2 tablespoons cognac
2 cups Blender Hollandaise
  Sauce (*see Index*)
½ cup heavy cream

Prepare the artichoke bottoms according to the directions for Boiled Fresh Artichokes (*see Index*). They may be prepared in advance and refrigerated. Shred the crabmeat and place on paper toweling to drain. If you are using frozen crab, some brands have a rather strong iodine flavor and should be rinsed in a large strainer and drained well on paper toweling.

Melt the butter in a heavy 10–12-inch skillet over moderate heat. Add the mushrooms and sauté over low heat for 2–3 minutes, stirring frequently. Add lemon juice and garlic salt and continue to cook over low heat for 2–3 minutes more. Add the crab and cognac and cook for 3–5 minutes more or until most of the liquid has evaporated. Remove from heat, set aside, and keep warm.

Prepare the Blender Hollandaise Sauce and keep warm. In a mixing bowl whip the cream until it is stiff. Fold the cream into the hollandaise. Gently blend 1 cup of the hollandaise mixture into the crab. Evenly divide the crab mixture into each artichoke bottom, shaping with a spoon to form a mound. Place the artichoke bottoms with the crab on a flameproof serving platter and gently spoon the remaining hollandaise mixture over each mound of crab. Try to prevent the sauce from running onto the platter. The mixture should be fairly stiff, so this should not be difficult.

Place the platter under a preheated broiler and broil for 2–4 minutes or until the sauce is golden brown and bubbling. Remove and serve at once.

NOTE: This is a beautiful and delicious luncheon dish. If served as a first course, use 12 smaller artichoke bottoms and smaller portions of the crab mixture, which would make 12 first-course servings.

DIVER'S REWARD   (Abalone Amandine)

4 abalone steaks
1 cup milk
½ cup flour
Salt and pepper
½ cup corn meal
¾ cup butter
Juice of 1 lemon
¼ cup finely chopped fresh
    parsley
½ cup slivered almonds (or
    more if desired)

Place the abalone steak on a board and with a thin, sharp knife, cut it across the grain into slices about ¼–½ inch thick. Pound each slice firmly with a wooden mallet or rolling pin, turning it from side to side during the pounding. Hit the abalone with a light, steady motion. (When pounded properly, it should feel soft and velvety. If the abalone is pounded too hard, it will break down. If pounded too gently, it will be tough.)

Place the milk in a large shallow bowl. In another large shallow bowl combine the flour, seasoned with salt and pepper, and corn meal. Melt ½ cup butter over moderate heat in a heavy 12–14-inch skillet. While the butter is melting, dip each abalone steak first into the milk, then the flour mixture, so that each piece is well coated. When the butter in the skillet has stopped foaming, quickly sauté each steak on each side, no more than 15–20 seconds per side. (Overcooking will cause abalone to be tough.) As each steak is sautéed, remove from the skillet and place on a warm platter. When all the steaks are sautéed, sprinkle the lemon juice over all the steaks and sprinkle them with the parsley. Place the platter in a warm (140°) oven.

In a heavy 10-inch skillet melt ¼ cup butter and sauté the almonds over moderate heat for 4–6 minutes or until they are golden brown, stirring constantly. Remove the platter from the oven, pour the almonds and butter over the abalone, and serve at once.

ABALONE WITH CUCUMBER SOUBISE SAUCE SERVES 8

8 abalone steaks, thinly sliced
   and pounded
1 cup flour
½ teaspoon salt or to taste
¼ teaspoon white pepper or to
   taste
2 tablespoons butter

CUCUMBER SOUBISE SAUCE
2 tablespoons butter
2 tablespoons finely minced
   onion
2 tablespoons flour
1 cup Fish Stock (*see Index*)
1 large cucumber, peeled,
   seeded, and chopped
   (1½ cups)
1 teaspoon chopped chives
¼ cup fresh lemon juice
Dash Angostura bitters
Dash paprika
1 teaspoon cream-style
   horseradish
1 tablespoon Dijon mustard
¼ cup dry white wine
¼ cup cream
1 ounce cognac

Prepare abalone steaks as detailed in Diver's Reward (*see Index*) by pounding them until they are very pliable. Dip the steaks lightly in the flour, coating both sides. Salt and pepper to taste. Melt the butter in a heavy 12-inch skillet and sauté the abalone over moderately high heat for 15–20 seconds on each side. Remove the fish with a spatula to a warm platter and serve at once, accompanied by Cucumber Soubise Sauce.

To prepare sauce, melt the butter in a heavy 12-inch skillet. Add the onion and cook over low heat for 3–4 minutes or until tender. Add the 2 tablespoons flour and cook, stirring, over moderate heat for 3–4 minutes or until smooth and bubbling. Add the stock and stir until thick and creamy, about 2–3 minutes. Add the cucumber, chives, lemon juice, bitters, paprika, horseradish, mustard, and wine. Cook for several minutes over moderate heat, stirring constantly. Sauce may be prepared ahead to this point and refrigerated for up to 4 hours. When ready to serve, heat the sauce and add the cream and cognac over low heat, stirring.

NOTE: The sauce is equally delicious served with poached or barbecued salmon or trout or with Catalina sand dabs.

FILLET OF SOLE PACIFICA SERVES 6

½ pound fresh salmon
1 tablespoon cream
¼ teaspoon salt
Pepper to taste
12 small narrow fillets of sole
3½ tablespoons butter
¼ cup thinly sliced fresh
   mushrooms

Skin, bone, and finely chop the salmon. Place the fish in a small bowl and add the cream, salt, and pepper. Blend these ingredients with a fork until smooth. Place the sole fillets on a board and spread a rounded tablespoon of the salmon mixture over the fillets, covering 3/4 of each fillet. Melt 2 tablespoons butter in a heavy 12-inch skillet and sauté the mushrooms over moderate

2 teaspoons finely chopped
  scallions (whites only)
1 cup dry white wine or
  vermouth
1 cup clam juice or fish stock
1½ tablespoons flour
2 tablespoons fresh lemon juice
1 cup cooked shrimp
3 tablespoons finely sliced
  scallions, including tops

heat for 3–5 minutes or until tender, stirring constantly. Divide the mushrooms evenly and spread them over the salmon mixture on the fillets. Gently roll the fillets, working toward the end that does not have the filling on it. Fasten the fish rolls with toothpicks and place them, seam side down, in a large shallow buttered baking dish.

Sprinkle the fish rolls with 2 teaspoons chopped scallions. Mix the wine and clam juice or fish stock together in a small bowl and pour the mixture over the fish. It should barely cover the fillets. If necessary, add more juice and wine in the same proportions. Cover the pan with foil and bake in a preheated 350° oven for 20–30 minutes or until the fish flakes when tested with a fork. Remove the fish gently with a slotted spoon, placing on a flameproof serving platter. Remove the toothpicks carefully and place the platter in the oven to keep warm.

Pour the cooking liquid into a 1½-quart saucepan and bring it to a boil over high heat. Reduce the stock until it measures ½ its original volume, approximately 6–8 minutes. In a heavy 2-quart saucepan melt 1½ tablespoons butter and stir in the flour, blending over low heat until smooth. Cook and stir for 3–4 minutes until sauce is smooth and bubbling. Stir the fish stock into the butter-flour mixture slowly, stirring, and cook over a low flame for 3–5 minutes or until thick and smooth. Add the lemon juice, stir in the shrimp, and taste for seasoning.

Preheat broiler.

Ladle the sauce over the fish and place the platter under the broiler for 3–4 minutes or until lightly browned and bubbling. Sprinkle with 3 tablespoons sliced scallions and serve at once.

NOTE: This recipe serves 12 as a first course.

FILLET OF SOLE WITH ASPARAGUS MALTAISE

SERVES 8

16–24 asparagus spears,
  trimmed
8 fillets of sole
⅓ cup melted butter
Maltaise Sauce (*below*)
2 tablespoons grated orange
  peel

Bring a 4-quart kettle of water to a boil. Drop the trimmed asparagus spears into the water, a few at a time, and boil for 6–7 minutes or until barely tender. Remove the asparagus from the water with a slotted spoon and drain on paper toweling. Place 2–3 asparagus spears on each fillet of sole, lengthwise. Roll the fillet around the asparagus and place in a shallow 2-quart casserole, seam side down. Pour the ⅓ cup melted butter over the fillets.

Cover the casserole with foil and bake in a preheated 350° oven for 20 minutes. Remove the casserole from the oven and drain all the juices from the fish. Set aside to keep warm.

When ready to serve, pour the Maltaise Sauce over the fillets and place under the broiler for 3–5 minutes or until golden brown and bubbly. Garnish the fillets with the 2 tablespoons grated orange peel.

MALTAISE SAUCE
3 egg yolks
2 tablespoons fresh orange
  juice
2 tablespoons grated orange
  peel
¼ teaspoon salt
Pinch white pepper
½ cup melted butter (1 stick)

To prepare sauce, place the 3 egg yolks, orange juice, 2 tablespoons orange peel, salt, and pepper in the blender jar. With the lid on, blend at high speed for 1 second. Turn the blender off. Remove the center portion of the blender lid, turn to high speed, and slowly pour ½ cup hot, melted butter into the blender. If the blender does not have a removable center in its lid, make a foil lid with a 2-inch hole in the center, as the mixture will splatter. The sauce may be held until serving time by placing it in the top of a double boiler over hot, not boiling, water. Stir occasionally.

NOTE: One fillet makes an unusual and interesting first course. For a main course, plan on 2–3 fillets per serving, depending on the size of the fillets. The recipe and the sauce may easily be doubled. To double the sauce recipe, remove the mixture from the blender and place in a heavy 1-quart saucepan. Over very low heat add an additional

½ cup butter very slowly, 2 tablespoons at a time, stirring constantly. The sauce may be kept warm by setting the pan in a larger pan of hot water.

FILLET OF SOLE STUFFED WITH SHRIMP   SERVES 8

2 tablespoons butter
4 shallots, finely chopped
4 tablespoons slivered almonds
24 large cooked shrimp,
  finely chopped
16 large fresh mushrooms,
  finely chopped
3 cups Mornay Sauce for Fish
  (*see Index*)
8 large fillets of sole
  (approximately 6 ounces
  and 3 inches wide apiece)
Salt and pepper to taste
2 tablespoons chopped fresh
  parsley (optional)

Melt the butter in a heavy 12-inch skillet and add the shallots and almonds. Sauté over moderate heat for 3–5 minutes or until almonds are light golden brown and shallots are soft. Add the chopped shrimp and mushrooms to the skillet and cook over moderate heat, stirring, for 3–5 additional minutes. Remove from heat and set aside. Add 3–4 tablespoons Mornay Sauce for Fish to the mushroom and shrimp mixture in the skillet.

Spread the fillets of sole on a flat surface and cover them with a ¼–½-inch-thick layer of the mushroom-shrimp mixture. Salt and pepper each fillet to taste. Carefully roll each fillet from the end and secure with a toothpick. Butter a shallow 2–3 quart baking dish and place the rolled fillets in the dish, seam side down. Pour approximately 1½ cups Mornay Sauce over the fish, spreading the sauce evenly. Bake in a preheated 350° oven for 20–25 minutes. Reserve the remaining Mornay Sauce to be heated and served separately accompanying the fish. If after 20 minutes the fish is not lightly browned and bubbling, place the dish under the broiler for 4–5 minutes. Serve at once with additional heated Mornay Sauce. Dish can be garnished with chopped parsley.

NOTE: This entree can be prepared ahead 2–3 hours and refrigerated. If this is done, however, dish must be removed from refrigerator 30 minutes before baking and allowed to come to room temperature.

MOUSSELINE OF SOLE AND CRAB
WITH SHRIMP SAUCE

SERVES 6

¾ pound fillet of sole
¼ pound fresh crab meat
  (frozen may be used)
2 eggs, separated, plus 2 egg
  yolks
1¾ cups heavy cream
3 tablespoons flour
1 teaspoon salt
⅛ teaspoon nutmeg
2 tablespoons fresh lemon juice
1 tablespoon brandy
Shrimp Sauce (*below*)
Parsley sprigs

Cut the fillet of sole into large chunks and place in a blender jar. Rinse, drain, and flake the crab and add to the blender jar. Blend the fish at high speed until it is puréed, about 1 minute. Place the puréed fish in a medium mixing bowl and add 4 egg yolks, beating until smooth. Beat in ¾ cup cream, flour, salt, nutmeg, lemon juice, and brandy. Place 1 cup cream in a small mixing bowl and beat until stiff. Fold the whipped cream into the fish mixture gently, until the 2 are well blended.

Divide the mixture between 6 1-cup ramekins or soufflé dishes. Place the ramekins in a pan of hot water 2 inches deep and bake in a preheated 350° oven for 25 minutes or until puffed and golden brown. Remove from oven and set aside to cool for 5–10 minutes. Invert the mousselines on individual serving plates and top with Shrimp Sauce. Serve the mousselines immediately after they emerge from the oven, as they are beautiful and look like soufflés. Garnish with parsley sprigs.

NOTE: This recipe will be adequate for a luncheon for 6. If it is desired as a first course, the recipe will serve 12 if divided between 12 ½-cup ramekins or soufflé dishes. However, there will not be room in the ramekins for the sauce, which is a necessary addition to the flavors, so serve the sauce on the side, and each guest may add his own after eating a few bites of the mousseline.

SHRIMP SAUCE
2 cups Fish Stock (*see Index*)
2 egg yolks
2 teaspoons cornstarch
½ cup heavy cream
1 tablespoon dry white wine
  or sherry
½ cup small cooked bay
  shrimp

To prepare sauce, place Fish Stock in a 1-quart saucepan. It is important to use high-quality fish stock, as this is what flavors the sauce. Bring the stock to a boil and boil uncovered until the volume is reduced by ½. This takes about 6–8 minutes. Measure the liquid every 3–4 minutes, and when it measures 1 cup, remove it from the heat.

In a small mixing bowl beat egg yolks until light and lemon-colored. Blend in the cornstarch and ½ cream, beating constantly. Add the hot stock to the mixing bowl, beating continuously. Place the mixture back in the saucepan and cook over low heat, stirring constantly, until thick and creamy. Add the wine and cook for 30 seconds. Add the bay shrimp and serve the sauce immediately. The sauce may be doubled. It may also be made ahead several hours and refrigerated. If this is done, however, wait until just before serving to add the shrimp.

NOTE: The sauce is also delicious served with halibut and other sole dishes.

REX SOLE

½ cup flour
½ teaspoon salt or to taste
¼ teaspoon pepper or to taste
½ cup milk
2 pounds rex sole or sand dabs
¼ cup oil
¼ cup butter, melted
Lemon wedges
½ cup chopped fresh parsley

Place the flour, seasoned with salt and pepper, and the milk in 2 separate shallow dishes. Dip sole in milk first, then flour. Shake off excess flour.

In a heavy 12-inch skillet heat the oil over high heat until hot but not smoking. Add the sole and brown quickly, 2–3 minutes per side. Add more oil if necessary. Remove pan from heat and let fish stand, covered to keep warm, for 15 minutes. Bone by slicing lengthwise along the backbone. Lift off the fillet and remove dark skin. Arrange fillets on heated plates. Pour melted butter over the fish, garnish with lemon wedges, and sprinkle with chopped parsley.

8 small narrow fillets of sole

8 thin slices fresh smoked
salmon or lox

1 cup finely chopped pistachio
nuts (almonds may be
substituted)

½ cup finely minced onion

4 teaspoons finely chopped
fresh dill

Salt to taste

White pepper to taste

1 package phyllo dough
(*see page 26*)

¼ cup fresh sweet butter,
melted (more may be
necessary)

1 cup fresh unseasoned bread
crumbs

Besciamella (*see Index*)

Fresh dill or watercress sprigs

Wash and dry the fillets of sole and lay them on a breadboard, skin side down, with the small end facing you. Top each fillet with a very thin slice of smoked salmon, running the length of the fillet. Sprinkle each fillet with 2 tablespoons pistachio nuts, 1 tablespoon minced onion, and ½ teaspoon fresh dill. Salt and pepper each to taste. Roll the fillets, starting with the small end, and set aside on a platter, seam side down.

Unroll phyllo dough, remove 4 sheets, and keep well covered with a damp towel (they dry out easily). Wrap remaining dough tightly in plastic wrap and replace in refrigerator or freezer for future use. On the breadboard cut a single sheet of dough in half lengthwise and brush it with melted sweet butter. Sprinkle sheet lightly but completely with bread crumbs. Place 1 rolled fillet of sole, seam side down, in the center of the prepared phyllo dough, about 3–4 inches from the bottom edge. Fold the bottom edge of phyllo up over the fillet. Brush the newly exposed outside surface with melted butter and sprinkle with bread crumbs. Fold outside edges inside as if wrapping a package. Butter and crumb lightly all newly exposed surfaces. Gently roll the fillet up inside the phyllo, buttering each newly exposed surface. When finished, check roll to see that entire surface has been well buttered. Place the rolls, when completed, seam side down on a buttered baking sheet. Repeat procedure for each fillet. This recipe may be prepared ahead to this point and refrigerated, tightly covered with a damp towel.

Place rolls in a preheated 400° oven and reduce heat immediately to 275°. Bake for 15–18 minutes or until light golden brown. Serve on a hot plate, topped with Besciamella and garnished with a sprig of fresh dill. If dill is unavailable, watercress may be substituted. Allow 1 per person for a first course or appetizer, and 2 if served as a main course.

BAKED STUFFED SALMON

1 ¾-pound whole salmon, boned
1 cup packaged herb-seasoned stuffing mix
½ cup hot water
2 tablespoons capers, drained and chopped
2 tablespoons chopped fresh parsley
3 strips bacon, minced
¼ cup finely chopped onion
½ cup butter, melted
½ teaspoon salt
¼ teaspoon finely ground pepper
Lemon slices
Parsley sprigs
Cucumber Sauce (*see Index*)

Rinse and thoroughly dry the salmon, inside and out. In a 2-quart mixing bowl combine the stuffing mix, hot water, capers, and chopped parsley. Toss lightly with a fork until the mixture is moist and blended. Place the minced bacon in a heavy 12-inch skillet and sauté over medium heat for 4–6 minutes or until bacon is tender. Add the onion and sauté for 3–5 minutes more until bacon is crisp, stirring frequently. Add the bacon, onion, and pan drippings to the stuffing mixture in the mixing bowl. Toss lightly with a fork to combine. Brush the inside of the salmon with the melted butter and sprinkle lightly with salt and pepper. Fill the cavity of the fish loosely with the stuffing mixture. Skewer or sew the opening shut.

Line with heavy foil a shallow baking dish or a pan large enough to accommodate the fish. Place the fish on the baking pan and bake in a preheated 425° oven for 25 minutes or until fish flakes easily when tested with a fork. Remove from oven and keep warm. When ready to serve, the skin can be removed easily, leaving head and tail intact. Coat the fish with Cucumber Sauce, garnish with lemon slices and parsley and serve at once.

NOTE: This is a spectacular dish for a buffet dinner. The salmon also can be prepared according to directions, tightly wrapped in foil, and barbecued over medium coals for 25–30 minutes and is equally delicious. If barbecue is a covered type, turning is not necessary. Otherwise, the salmon should be turned after 10 minutes.

BARBECUED BUTTERFLY SALMON

SERVES 8–12

1 6–8 pound salmon
3 tablespoons butter, melted

Trim the salmon of head, tail, and back fin. Butterfly from the stomach side, and bone, leaving the skin intact.

Lay the salmon open, skin side down, on a large piece of heavy-duty foil. Cut the foil to follow the outline of the fish, allowing an extra 2–3 inches around the edges. Brush the salmon with the melted butter. Cover the fish with another large piece of foil, shaped to form a dome. Seal the edges of the foil all the way around by double folding the top and bottom edges together.

Place the salmon on the barbecue, about 8 inches above hot, gray-colored coals. The coals should be arranged so that they cover all areas below the fish. Cook the salmon for 45 minutes, then test it. When done, it will flake easily when tested with a fork. If not fully cooked after 45 minutes, reseal the foil and continue cooking, testing every 10 minutes. When the fish is done, remove it carefully from the barbecue, supporting it with the foil and a large spatula. Slip the fish onto a large platter and remove the top piece of foil.

SOY BUTTER SAUCE

¾ cup butter
2 cloves garlic, crushed
1½ tablespoons soy sauce
1½ tablespoons English dry mustard
½ cup sherry
3 tablespoons catsup

To serve, lift pieces of the fish from the foil with a spatula. The skin of the fish will adhere to the foil. Pass Soy Butter Sauce separately.

To prepare sauce, in a small saucepan melt the ¾ cup butter over low heat. Add the garlic, soy sauce, dry mustard, sherry, and catsup. Keep warm over low heat until ready to serve, or prepare earlier in the day and reheat slowly. This is also delicious served with barbecued chicken.

SALMON POACHED IN CHAMPAGNE

SERVES 8–12

1 5–6-pound salmon
Lemon Rice (*see Index*)
3 lemons, very thinly sliced
3 strips bacon
¼ pound fresh mushrooms, stemmed

Wash and dry the salmon, inside and out. Make Lemon Rice and stuff the cavity of the fish loosely with the rice.

Place a large piece of heavy foil in the bottom of a baking dish large enough to hold the fish. Place

1 "split" bottle California
  champagne
Watercress sprigs
Sour Cream Dill Sauce (*see
  Index*)

the fish in the dish on top of the foil. Skewer the opening of the fish shut with wooden picks. Lay ⅔ of the lemon slices over the salmon. Place the bacon strips on top of the lemon slices. Scatter the mushroom caps around the edges of the salmon Pour the champagne over all. Loosely cover the fish with another large piece of heavy foil and seal the edges by folding them together. Place the fish in a preheated 400° oven and bake for 25–35 minutes or until the fish flakes easily when tested with a fork.

When ready to serve, remove the foil from the salmon and remove the fish to a large serving platter. Discard the fish broth and garnish the platter with the mushrooms, the remaining lemon slices, and watercress. Serve at once accompanied by Sour Cream Dill Sauce.

COLD POACHED SALMON   SERVES 8

8 salmon steaks
3 black peppercorns
1 bay leaf
2 slices lemon
¼ cup dry white wine or
  vermouth
2 cups water
1 teaspoon salt
3 sprigs fresh dill weed or
  1 teaspoon dried
Lettuce leaves
Verde Sauce or Cucumber
  Sauce (*see Index*)
Hard-boiled eggs, sliced
Tomato wedges
Cucumber slices

Rinse and dry the salmon steaks. Combine the peppercorns, bay leaf, lemon slices, wine, water, salt, and dill. Bring to a simmer in a 14-inch skillet. Gently place the salmon steaks into the simmering liquid. Cover the pan and simmer gently over low to moderate heat for 10–15 minutes or until the fish flakes easily when tested with a fork. Remove the salmon from the liquid with a slotted spoon and drain on paper toweling.

Place the steaks in a shallow 9 × 13-inch dish, cover with foil or waxed paper, and refrigerate until ready to use. The salmon may be prepared 4–6 hours before serving. Line a large platter with lettuce leaves, arrange the salmon steaks over the lettuce, and coat with Verde Sauce or Cucumber Sauce. The platter may be garnished with sliced eggs, tomato wedges, and cucumber slices.

NOTE: This is a wonderful hot weather luncheon or supper dish.

SALMON VÉLOUTÉ CREPES SERVES 6

12–14 Blender Crepes (*see Index*)
1 1-pound can salmon
3 tablespoons butter
3 tablespoons flour
⅔ cup scalded milk
2 egg yolks
½ teaspoon salt
¼ teaspoon white pepper
1 teaspoon grated fresh onion (or ½ teaspoon onion powder)
¼ teaspoon dried oregano
½ cup grated Swiss cheese
Watercress sprigs
Cucumber slices

Have crepes prepared ahead and stacked. Drain the salmon, reserving ½ cup of the liquid. Place the salmon in a small mixing bowl and remove the bones. Flake the salmon with a fork. Melt the butter in a 1-quart saucepan over low heat. Add the flour and cook, stirring constantly, for 3–4 minutes until the mixture is frothy. Add the milk and reserved salmon liquid and stir constantly over moderate heat until mixture thickens and is smooth. Remove the pan from heat.

In a small mixing bowl beat the egg yolks slightly. Add a little of the hot sauce to the yolks and stir to blend well. Add egg yolk mixture to remaining sauce in the saucepan and blend in well.

Stir in the salmon, salt, pepper, onion, and oregano and blend well. Place about 3 tablespoons of sauce mixture in the center of each crepe. Roll up the crepes and place seam side down in a buttered shallow 3-quart baking dish. Sprinkle the top of each crepe with the cheese. Bake in a preheated 375° oven for 10–15 minutes or until heated through. Serve at once, garnished with sprigs of watercress and cucumber slices.

NOTE: This dish can be prepared several hours in advance and refrigerated. Remove from refrigerator 30 minutes before baking. Salmon crepes are an unusual and interesting luncheon dish or first course.

CHARCOAL-BROILED SALMON EN BROCHETTE SERVES 8

8 salmon steaks
24 large fresh mushrooms
24 small boiling or pearl onions
6 green peppers
24 cherry tomatoes
2 cups olive oil

Cut the salmon steaks into 2 × 2-inch chunks, removing skin and bones. Cut the stems from the mushrooms so that they are even with the cap. Save stems for another use. Place the onions in a 3-quart kettle of boiling water and boil for 5 minutes. Drain and cool. Cut the root end from

1 cup dry white wine
½ cup fresh lemon juice
1 teaspoon salt
¼ teaspoon pepper
2–3 tablespoons fresh dillweed
  or 2–3 teaspoons dried
2 cups Hollandaise Cucumber
  Sauce (*see Index*)

the onion and lightly squeeze from the stem end. The outer skin of the onion should slide off. Reserve the centers. Seed and remove the veins from the green pepper and cut the flesh into 2 × 2-inch squares. Place alternating squares of salmon, mushrooms, tomatoes, onions, and peppers on long, slender metal skewers. Place skewers in a shallow baking pan, large enough to hold all in 1 layer.

In a 2-quart mixing bowl combine the olive oil, wine, lemon juice, salt, pepper, and dill. If dried dill is used, crush between fingers before adding. Pour the marinade over the salmon skewers and place in the refrigerator for 8 hours, turning occasionally. Grill over medium coals on the barbecue, turning frequently and basting with the marinade, for 8–10 minutes. Serve at once with Rice Pilaf accompanied by Hollandaise Cucumber Sauce.

RED SNAPPER WITH SHRIMP

SERVES 4–6

2 tablespoons butter
1 clove garlic, crushed
2 cups small shrimp, peeled,
  deveined, and cooked
1 cup toasted bread cubes
Salt and pepper to taste
2 pounds red snapper fillets
8 ounces tomato sauce
½ cup dry vermouth
1 teaspoon sugar
⅛ teaspoon cayenne

Melt the butter in a heavy 12-inch skillet. Add the garlic to the butter and cook gently over low heat for 2–3 minutes. Add the shrimp, bread cubes, and salt and pepper to taste. Combine these ingredients gently and quickly. Remove the pan from heat.

Arrange ½ the fish fillets on the bottom of a buttered shallow 2-quart baking dish. Top the fish with an even layer of the shrimp and bread cube mixture. Arrange the remaining fish fillets over the shrimp and sprinkle the fish lightly with salt. In a small bowl combine the tomato sauce, vermouth, sugar, and cayenne and pour over the fish. Bake uncovered in a preheated 350° oven for 30 minutes, basting occasionally. Serve with Rice Pilaf and Fresh Spinach Salad (*see Index*).

RED SNAPPER VERACRUZANA

SERVES 6–8

3 pounds red snapper fillets
(6–8 fillets)
1 teaspoon salt
½ cup fresh lime juice
¼ cup olive oil
2 cloves garlic, crushed
2 onions, thinly sliced
12 small tomatoes (or 6 large)
1 tablespoon tomato paste
1 large bay leaf
½ teaspoon dried oregano
18 green olives, pitted and cut
in half
2 tablespoons capers, minced
2 green chiles, seeds removed
and cut in strips (*chiles
jalapeños en escabeche*
preferred)
¼ cup fresh lemon juice

Place the red snapper in a shallow 2-quart casserole. Rub the fish with salt and lime juice. Prick the fish with a fork to aid in penetration of the lime juice and marinate for 3–4 hours, turning occasionally. Place the olive oil in a heavy 12-inch skillet. Add the garlic and onion to the skillet and sauté them over moderate heat for 3–5 minutes or until they are tender. Peel, seed, and coarsely chop the tomatoes. Add the tomatoes, tomato paste, bay leaf, oregano, olives, capers, chiles, and lemon juice to the skillet. Cook, stirring, over moderate heat for 10–15 minutes until the mixture is thick and some of the liquid has evaporated.

Place the red snapper fillets in a shallow baking dish large enough to hold them in 1 layer (approximately 3-quart) and cover them evenly with the tomato sauce. Bake uncovered in a preheated 325° oven for 20–30 minutes or until the fish flakes easily when tested with a fork. Serve with Spanish rice and a crisp green salad.

NOTE: This dish makes an unusual and interesting fish entree.

GOLDEN GATE HALIBUT

SERVES 4

6 tablespoons butter
2 pounds halibut or other
fine-grained whitefish
Salt and pepper
6 carrots, peeled and thinly
sliced
1 onion, finely chopped
1 shallot, finely chopped
1 leek, white part only,
finely chopped
½ cup Fish Stock (*see Index*)
1 cup Blender Hollandaise
Sauce (*see Index*)

Melt 3 tablespoons butter in a heavy 12–14-inch skillet over low heat. Place the fish in the skillet and sauté gently over low heat for about 20 minutes, turning it once. (If using sole or thinner fish, reduce cooking time to 15 minutes.) Do not let the fish brown. Season the fish to taste with salt and pepper.

Meanwhile, in another heavy 12–14-inch skillet melt 3 tablespoons butter and sauté the carrots, onion, shallot, and leek over medium heat for 8–10 minutes or until soft and tender. Season the vegetables to taste with salt and pepper. Remove the pan from the heat, drain the excess butter, and set aside.

Place the Fish Stock in a 1-quart saucepan and reduce, by boiling, to ¼ cup. Remove the pan from heat. Add the slightly cooled stock to the Blender Hollandaise Sauce.

Place the vegetables on the bottom of a flameproof shallow 1–2-quart casserole. Cover the vegetables with the fish. Coat the fish evenly with the hollandaise mixture. Place under the broiler for 3–5 minutes or until lightly browned and bubbling. Serve at once accompanied with Lemon Rice (*see Index*) and a crisp green vegetable.

FILLET OF FISH FLORENTINE
SERVES 6

6 fish fillets (salmon, trout, sole, turbot, or halibut), 2–2½ pounds total
1½ cups dry white wine
2 egg yolks
1 cup cream
1 tablespoon flour
1 tablespoon butter, at room temperature
¼ teaspoon dried basil
¼ teaspoon dried dill weed
⅛ teaspoon ground nutmeg
2 tablespoons fresh lemon juice
⅔ cup freshly grated Parmesan cheese
Salt and pepper to taste
2½ cups chopped fresh cooked spinach or 2 packages frozen chopped spinach

Place the fish in a heavy shallow casserole and poach the fish fillets in wine gently, over low heat, about 6–10 minutes, depending on thickness. Remove the fish, drain well, and set aside. Combine the egg yolks and cream in a small bowl and blend well. Thicken the wine stock by slowly adding the egg yolk mixture, stirring constantly.

In another small bowl blend the flour and butter thoroughly to make a *beurre manie*. Add the basil, dill, and *beurre manie* to the wine stock, stirring and cooking slowly, still over very low heat, until thickened. Add the nutmeg, lemon juice, and cheese, reserving 2–3 tablespoons of the cheese as a final topping, and stir until the cheese has melted. Season with salt and pepper to taste.

In a 1½–2-quart saucepan cook the spinach, either fresh or frozen, in a small amount of water and drain well, squeezing as much water as possible from the spinach. Place it in a greased shallow 2-quart casserole. Add ½ the wine-cheese mixture, then the fillets, and finally the remaining wine-cheese mixture. Sprinkle the remaining cheese on top and bake in a preheated 350° oven for 20–30 minutes. Finish this dish by placing it under the broiler for 1–2 minutes or until lightly browned. Serve with fresh French bread and a crisp green salad.

FILLET OF HALIBUT EN CROUTE
WITH LEMON DILL SAUCE

6 tablespoons butter
½ pound fresh mushrooms,
   finely minced
1 medium onion, finely chopped
4 tablespoons finely chopped
   fresh parsley
1 cup butter, softened
1 8-ounce package cream
   cheese, softened
2 cups flour
8 serving-size pieces halibut
   steak, 1 inch thick
1 egg
1 teaspoon water
Fresh dill or parsley sprigs

Place 2 tablespoons butter in a heavy 12-inch skillet and melt over low heat. Add the mushrooms and onion and sauté for 10 minutes over low-moderate heat or until all the liquid has evaporated and the mixture is pastelike, stirring frequently. Add the chopped parsley and sauté for 2 more minutes, continuing to stir. Set aside.

In a large mixing bowl mix together the 1 cup softened butter and cream cheese with a fork until smooth. Add the flour to the butter-cheese mixture and combine lightly with a fork. Do not stir the flour into the butter mixture; instead, use a cutting motion to blend. It should be somewhat mealy in texture, but hold together when formed into a ball. Divide the dough into 8 equal parts and wrap each in waxed paper. Refrigerate the dough for 2 hours or overnight.

Melt 4 tablespoons butter in a heavy 12–14-inch skillet over low heat. Pat the pieces of fish dry with paper towels. Heat the butter over moderate heat until the foaming subsides. Quickly sauté the fish about 1 minute on each side to seal them. Remove the fish steaks to a platter lined with paper towels to drain.

For each serving, roll out on a lightly floured pastry cloth a portion of the dough large enough to enclose a fish steak. Place 1–2 tablespoons of the mushroom filling on the center of each round of pastry. Place the fillet over the mushroom mixture. Fold the pastry up around the fish as though you were wrapping a package. Cut off the excess dough. Gently turn the fish, placing each piece seam side down on an ungreased baking sheet. Extra dough may be cut into flower shapes to decorate the tops if desired. Beat the 1 egg and the 1 tablespoon water in a small cup until blended. Brush this mixture evenly over the top and sides of the pastry. Prick the pastry in several places with a fork and bake in a preheated 425° oven for 20–30 minutes or until pastry is well browned. Remove the fish from the baking sheet and place them on a warm serving platter. Garnish the platter with fresh dill or parsley sprigs and serve at once, accompanied by Lemon Dill Sauce.

LEMON DILL SAUCE
½ cup butter
¼ cup flour
2 cups Fish Stock (*see Index*)
½ teaspoon salt
⅛ teaspoon white pepper
¼ cup fresh lemon juice
2 tablespoons finely chopped
    fresh dill weed or 1
    tablespoon dried

To prepare sauce, melt the ½ cup butter over low heat in a heavy 1½-quart saucepan. Add the flour slowly, stirring, and cook for 3 minutes. Add the stock and bring to a boil over moderate heat, stirring constantly until it is thick and creamy. Reduce the heat, add the salt, pepper, lemon juice, and chopped dill and simmer, stirring, for several minutes. Correct the seasoning if necessary and set aside. The sauce may be made early in the day, held in the refrigerator, and reheated.

LEMON SOY SWORDFISH STEAKS　　　SERVES 8

⅓ cup soy sauce
1 teaspoon grated lemon peel
¼ cup fresh lemon juice
1 clove garlic, crushed
2 teaspoons Dijon mustard
½ cup salad oil
8 small swordfish steaks
    (or 4 large ones, cut in half)
Lemon wedges
Parsley sprigs

Combine the soy sauce, lemon peel, lemon juice, garlic, mustard, and oil in a small bowl, blending well. Place the swordfish steaks in a shallow 9 × 13-inch baking dish. Pour the soy sauce marinade over the fish, pricking the fish thoroughly with a fork to assure penetration of the marinade. Turn the fish occasionally, again pricking it with a fork. Let the fish marinate for 1–3 hours in the refrigerator.

To cook, place the fish on a preheated broiler pan. Broil 5–6 minutes on each side or until fish flakes easily when tested with a fork. This swordfish can also be barbecued on a charcoal grill over moderate coals for 5–6 minutes on each side. During the cooking, brush the fish often with the marinade sauce. Serve at once, garnished with lemon wedges and parsley.

NOTE: This is delicious accompanied with Avocado Butter (*see Index*).

COLD POACHED RAINBOW TROUT

3 cups clam juice

3 cups dry white wine or
vermouth

2 tablespoons finely chopped
fresh dill weed or 2 teaspoons
dried

2 tablespoons finely chopped
fresh parsley

2 tablespoons finely chopped
fresh chives

8 rainbow trout, cleaned,
heads and tails intact

Lettuce leaves

4 hard-boiled eggs, sliced

1–2 cucumbers, peeled and
thinly sliced

2 cups Sour Cream Dill Sauce
(*see Index*)

2 tomatoes, cut in wedges

In a large shallow kettle, big enough to hold all of the fish, combine the clam juice, wine, dill, parsley, and chives. Bring to a simmer over low heat and gently add the trout. Poach for 5 minutes or until they flake easily when tested with a fork. (Large trout will take a little longer.) Remove the trout to a large plate with a slotted spoon, drain, and cool. Discard the stock.

Bone the trout without disturbing the head and tail. This is most easily accomplished by inserting a sharp knife at the head end under the backbone and cutting between the ribs and the flesh, releasing the bones from the fish back. Repeat on the other side of the fish. With scissors or a sharp knife. snip the backbone at the head and tail and gently ease bones free from fish. Trim off the fins. Chill the trout covered in the refrigerator. When ready to serve, carefully place the boned trout on a bed of lettuce on a large serving platter. Cover trout with alternating slices of hard-boiled egg and cucumber and cover with Sour Cream Dill Sauce. Garnish edge of platter with more cucumber, egg slices, and wedges of tomato.

NOTE: This is a delicious hot weather luncheon or supper dish.

TROUT IN CREAM

8 trout, cleaned

¼ teaspoon salt

¼ teaspoon white pepper

¼ cup fresh lemon juice

3 tablespoons butter

⅓ cup dry vermouth

1 cup heavy cream

2 teaspoons dried tarragon

1 cup fresh soft bread crumbs

¼ cup butter, melted

1 cup finely chopped fresh
parsley

Wash and dry the trout thoroughly. Sprinkle on all sides with salt, pepper, and lemon juice. In a heavy 12-inch skillet melt 3 tablespoons butter over low heat and place the trout in the skillet. Brown on both sides, approximately 3–5 minutes, over moderate heat.

Place the trout in a single layer in a shallow 9 × 13-inch baking dish. Cover with the vermouth, pour the cream over the fish, and sprinkle it with the tarragon. Cover the baking dish and bake in a preheated 350° oven for 30 minutes or until the fish flakes easily when tested with a fork, basting occasionally.

Remove the fish from the oven and cover with bread crumbs. Pour melted butter over the bread-crumbs and place under a preheated broiler for 3–5 minutes or until the crumbs are lightly browned. Garnish with the chopped parsley and serve at once.

NOTE: This is a delicious first course when served with a dry white wine.

FISHERMAN'S WHARF TROUT

SERVES 6

6 trout, cleaned and washed
Salt and pepper
¼ cup butter, softened
1 cup cooked and finely
   chopped spinach
¼ cup grated onion
1 egg
¼ cup milk
¾ cup toasted bread crumbs
½ cup shredded Swiss cheese
2 tablespoons butter
1½ cups Tartar Sauce for Fish
   or 2 cups Hollandaise
   Cucumber Sauce (*see Index*)

Wash the trout and pat dry with paper towels, inside and out. Sprinkle the inside of the fish with salt and pepper. Combine the ¼ cup butter, spinach, and onion and spread the mixture inside the cavity of each fish. Place the egg, milk, and 1 teaspoon salt in a 1-quart mixing bowl and beat until well mixed.

In another small bowl combine the bread crumbs and cheese. Dip each fish into the egg mixture and then roll it in the crumb-cheese mixture so that both sides of the fish are well coated with crumbs. Place the fish in a buttered shallow baking dish, in a single layer, sprinkling any of the crumb mixture remaining over the fish. Dot the fish with the 2 tablespoons butter. Bake in a preheated 500° oven for 15–20 minutes or until fish are tender and browned. Trout will be very crisp, similar to pan-fried, but much easier to prepare. Serve with Tartar Sauce or Hollandaise Cucumber Sauce.

ESCABECHE

8 small Pacific mackerel or
  sierra (white sea bass or
  lingcod may be substituted
  or any firm-fleshed whitefish)
1 cup flour
5 tablespoons butter
5 tablespoons corn oil
½ teaspoon salt
¼ teaspoon pepper
½ cup fresh orange juice
½ cup fresh lime juice
½ cup olive oil
1 onion, finely chopped
2 whole green chiles, seeded
  and finely chopped
2 cloves garlic, crushed
2 medium tomatoes, skinned,
  seeded, and chopped
½ teaspoon dried oregano
Pinch cayenne
½ cup chopped fresh coriander
  leaves (cilantro)

Wash the fish thoroughly and dry with paper towels. Place the flour in a bowl and roll the fish lightly in it, coating all sides. Shake off any excess flour. Melt the butter and corn oil in a heavy 12–14-inch skillet over moderate heat. When the foaming has subsided, sauté the fish for 3–4 minutes per side or until lightly browned. Remove the fish with a slotted spoon to a platter lined with paper towels and drain well. Salt and pepper the fish.

Arrange the fish in a shallow 2-quart baking dish and set aside. Combine the orange juice, lime juice, olive oil, onion, chiles, garlic, tomatoes, oregano, and cayenne in a small mixing bowl. Stir until well blended. Pour this sauce over the fish, pricking the fish with a fork in several places to aid in penetration of the marinade. Place the dish in the refrigerator covered for 24 hours. Turn the fish occasionally and prick with a fork. When ready to serve, place the fish on a serving platter, coat with the marinade, and garnish with chopped coriander leaves according to taste.

NOTE: This is a most unusual and delicious dish with a Mexican flavor. It makes a delightful hot weather entree or an addition to a buffet table.

BARBECUED ALBACORE WITH LEMON BUTTER

8 albacore steaks (¼–½ pound
  each)
8 slices bacon
⅔ cup butter
2 cloves garlic, crushed
6 tablespoons fresh lemon juice
2 tablespoons soy sauce
3 tablespoons finely chopped
  fresh parsley
½ teaspoon salt

Carefully remove the skin and dark areas from the albacore steaks. Wash the fish under cold water and pat dry with paper towels. Re-form the fish into steaks and wrap bacon around the outside edge to hold the fish in shape. Secure the bacon with a toothpick.

In a small saucepan melt the butter. Add all the other ingredients (except the lemon wedges and parsley sprigs) to the butter. Heat over moderate heat to simmering, stirring well to blend the

¼ teaspoon white pepper or to
   taste
Lemon wedges
Parsley sprigs

ingredients. Grill the fish over medium coals on the barbecue, turning frequently and basting often with the lemon butter. The sauce can be kept warm by placing the saucepan on the edge of the barbecue grill. Cook the fish for 10–15 minutes or until it flakes easily when tested with a fork. Remove the fish to a heated platter and brush generously with the lemon butter. Garnish the platter with lemon wedges and parsley sprigs and serve at once. If desired, Avocado Butter (*see Index*) can be served with this dish.

FISH STOCK

2 tablespoons butter
1 onion, thinly sliced
16–18 parsley stems (no leaves)
1 stalk celery, quartered
¼ cup diced carrots
4 pounds fish bones and
   trimmings (whitefish
   preferred)
3 tablespoons fresh lemon juice
2 cups dry white wine or
   vermouth
2 quarts cold water
2 teaspoons salt
4 black peppercorns

In a heavy 4–6-quart steel or enameled saucepan melt the butter. Add onion, parsley stems, celery, and carrots and sauté over low heat until limp but not brown, about 3–4 minutes, stirring frequently. Add fish bones, trimmings, and lemon juice and cook for 5 minutes. Add the wine and simmer uncovered 20 minutes. Add water, salt, and peppercorns, raise heat, and bring to boiling. Boil slowly at low-moderate heat for 45 minutes or until reduced by ⅓. Strain. Can be frozen in small quantities.

FISH POACHING LIQUID

1 quart water
1 onion, sliced
6 black peppercorns
2 allspice berries
3 tablespoons fresh lemon juice
1 bay leaf
1 teaspoon salt
½ cup dry white wine
¼ cup clam juice

Combine all ingredients in a large kettle. Bring the liquid to a boil, reduce the heat to simmer, and simmer gently for 20–30 minutes.

NOTE: You may add up to 2 quarts of water to the same ingredients if more liquid is necessary for the amount of fish to be poached. The recipe may be doubled or tripled and frozen for future use.

MORNAY SAUCE FOR FISH

2 tablespoons butter
¼ cup finely minced onion
2 tablespoons flour
1½ cups Fish Stock (*see Index*)
1½ cups light cream
¼ teaspoon salt
Dash white pepper
Pinch freshly grated nutmeg
2 egg yolks
¼ cup finely grated Swiss or
    Parmesan cheese

In a heavy 2-quart saucepan melt the butter and add the onion. Cook over a low flame, stirring, for 3–5 minutes or until the onion is soft but not browned. Stir in the flour and cook over low heat for 3–4 minutes. Gradually add the stock and cream, stirring vigorously. Add the salt, pepper, and nutmeg. Cook slowly, stirring frequently, over low heat for 30 minutes or until the liquid has the consistency of heavy cream.

Place the egg yolks in a small cup and add a little of the hot sauce to the yolks. Beat briefly with a fork and slowly add the yolk-cream mixture to the hot cream sauce, stirring constantly over low heat. Add the grated cheese to the sauce and heat just to the boiling point. The sauce can be made ahead and gently reheated, using low heat. It may also be doubled and frozen in small quantities for future use.

HOLLANDAISE CUCUMBER SAUCE

3 egg yolks
2 tablespoons fresh lemon juice
¾ cup butter
1 tablespoon hot water
½ teaspoon dry mustard
¼ teaspoon salt
2 tablespoons finely chopped
    fresh parsley
1 tablespoon finely chopped
    fresh chives
1 large or 2 small cucumbers,
    peeled, seeded, and diced

Combine in a blender the egg yolks and lemon juice. Turn the blender on high speed for 1 second. Turn the blender off. Melt the butter in a 1-quart saucepan over low heat, without browning. Add 1 tablespoon hot water to the egg yolks; turn blender on to high speed and immediately pour in the hot butter in a slow, steady stream. If the blender has a removable center in its lid, pour the butter through this opening. If not, make a lid from foil, cutting a 2-inch hole through which to pour, as the mixture will splatter. Turn the blender off and add the mustard and salt. Blend for 10 more seconds.

Remove the mixture to a small mixing bowl and add the parsley, chives, and cucumbers. The sauce can be kept warm over hot water but is better served at once.

NOTE: This is a delicious accompaniment to salmon, trout, or swordfish.

CUCUMBER SAUCE

2 large cucumbers
1 tablespoon salt
2 cups sour cream
2 cups mayonnaise
2 tablespoons cream-style
   horseradish
1 tablespoon tarragon vinegar
1 teaspoon grated onion
¼ teaspoon salt
Pinch white pepper

Peel the cucumbers and slice very thinly. Place the cucumbers in a 2-quart mixing bowl and cover with water. Add 1 tablespoon salt and stir well to combine. Soak for 30 minutes, drain, and dry the cucumbers on paper toweling. Combine the remaining ingredients in a 2-quart bowl. Add the cucumbers and stir gently to blend. Place the bowl covered in the refrigerator and let stand for several hours or overnight. The sauce will keep in the refrigerator for 3–4 days.

NOTE: This is a delicious sauce for cold poached salmon or trout as well as hot barbecued salmon. It also makes an excellent salad dressing.

SOUR CREAM DILL SAUCE

1½ cups sour cream
½ cup mayonnaise, preferably
   homemade (*see Index*)
1½ tablespoons chopped fresh
   dill weed or 1 tablespoon
   dried
1 teaspoon grated onion
½ cup finely chopped or grated
   hard-boiled egg
½ teaspoon salt or to taste
¼ teaspoon white pepper or to
   taste

Combine all ingredients in a 1-quart mixing bowl. Stir lightly with a fork until all ingredients are blended. Refrigerate until ready to use. Will hold for 24 hours.

NOTE: This is delicious served with salmon or trout.

AVOCADO BUTTER

½ cup softened butter
½ cup mashed ripe avocado
4 tablespoons fresh lemon juice
2 tablespoons finely chopped
   fresh parsley
1 teaspoon Worcestershire
   sauce
½ teaspoon garlic salt

Whip the butter with an electric mixer in a small mixing bowl until soft and creamy. Beat in the remaining ingredients. Refrigerate until ready to serve. The butter will hold about 1 hour.

NOTE: This is a marvelous accompaniment for any barbecued fish, particularly salmon or swordfish.

VERDE SAUCE

2 tablespoons fresh lemon juice
1½ cups spinach leaves, packed
½ cup watercress, packed
8–10 sprigs parsley
3–4 sprigs fresh chervil
  (optional)
6 sprigs fresh tarragon or 1
  teaspoon dried
1 cup mayonnaise
1 cup sour cream
1 teaspoon cream-style
  horseradish
1 tablespoon finely minced
  parsley
1 tablespoon finely chopped
  watercress

Bring 2 quarts water to a boil in a 3-quart sauce-pan. Add the spinach, ½ cup watercress, parsley, chervil, and tarragon and boil for 5 minutes. Remove from heat, strain, cool, and press out all the excess water.

In a 2-quart bowl combine the mayonnaise, sour cream, and horseradish and set aside. Force the cooled spinach mixture through a coarse strainer into a small bowl and add to the mayonnaise mixture. Stir to blend well. These ingredients may also be combined and blended for 2–3 minutes in a blender. Stir in the minced parsley and chopped watercress, cover, and refrigerate until ready to serve. The sauce will hold for 3–6 hours in the refrigerator. Serve with cold poached salmon or trout.

TARTAR SAUCE FOR FISH

¼ cup mayonnaise, preferably
  homemade (*see Index*)
¼ cup sour cream
¼ cup sweet pickle relish,
  drained
2 tablespoons finely minced
  dill pickle
1 teaspoon grated fresh onion
¼ teaspoon Worcestershire
  sauce
Dash Tabasco sauce
1 teaspoon fresh lemon juice
½ teaspoon cream-style
  horseradish (optional)

Combine all ingredients in a small mixing bowl and refrigerate for at least 1 hour. The sauce will keep in the refrigerator for 3–5 days.

NOTE: The sour cream may be omitted and the mayonnaise increased to ½ cup.

CHAPTER V

THE SIERRA NEVADA

POULTRY & GAME

Thrust up through eons of the earth's convulsions, this mighty range of snowcapped peaks and living glaciers, the Sierra Nevada, extends four hundred miles down the center of California. Crowned by Mt. Whitney, the highest peak in the continental United States, the majestic Sierras testify to their dramatic creation by an underlying fault shifting the earth's crust again and again.

In ages past, this range, a solid block of granite, tore loose from the adjacent land along its eastern flank and tilted up to form a towering escarpment—a formidable barrier, terrifying and heartbreaking to those courageous souls who later struggled west across the Great Plains.

During the Pleistocene Age the ice that formed in the Sierras carved out the basins for present-day lakes, the largest and deepest being Lake Tahoe. Today, as winter storms sweep down from the north bringing heavy falls of snow, the ice pack builds and the snow pack deepens. A fall of sixty feet of snow is not unusual, and at times one hundred feet has been recorded. In spring as the snows melt, the tiny waterfalls and gurgling streams pour down the gentle western slopes of these mighty mountains and become rivers, flowing through the lush green meadows dotted with tiny yellow flowers.

Sequoia gigantea, trees that were seedlings in the days of Caesar Augustus, tower over nearby stretches of smooth, weather granite. Dense forests are thick with firs, cedars, pines, and junipers. In the distance a meadowlark trills. A red-tailed hawk circles. Near Wilsonia, a U. S. Forest Service naturalist explains the secrets of Beetle Rock. A pack train and riders look down from Farewell Gap. An overheated timber rattlesnake slithers out of the sun. A man in a fire lookout station scans the horizon with binoculars. Back-packers rest beside Florence Lake. August in the Sierras is a time of peace and warmth and renewal, a time when man may linger in the fields and valleys and gaze in wonder at the surrounding beauty.

There are dangers there, too, to imperil the unwary or careless. Canyons are steep and shale is slippery. There is an abundance of wildlife—mountain lion, wildcat, deer, wolverine, coyote, and, of course, bear. Sudden, violent storms occur, and forest fires. The Sierras, like the ocean, demand caution and respect. Too often history has recorded the numerous immigrants and hunters alike who have starved or frozen to death in these rugged mountains. The tragedy of the Donner Party, who tried to cross this mighty range too late in the fall and were trapped by snow, remains a ghastly and gruesome reminder of the inherent dangers of the Sierras.

The history of the Sierra Nevada is a rich and colorful patchwork embracing the exploits of many nationalities. The many ghost towns of the Mother Lode country call to mind visions of rough and bearded miners, some from as far away as Chile and Australia. The snowshed-covered railroad tracks around Norden and Truckee remain a monument to the efforts of an army of pigtailed Chinese wearing coolie hats. The world-renowned enterprises of an Italian named Ghirardelli began in the tiny gold rush town of Hornitos.

"Snowshoe" Thompson, a Norwegian,

is another name in the Sierras. Few have ever heard of this intrepid man with his ten-foot-long skis fashioned from green oak (mistakenly called snowshoes, hence the nickname), but those who ride chair lifts at Mammoth, Heavenly Valley, or Sugar Bowl before whizzing effortlessly down the runs might do well to ponder his remarkable accomplishments. For twelve long winters—1855–67—Snowshoe made regular trips across the ninety-mile stretch of rugged mountains separating Placerville in California from the Carson Valley of Nevada. He was a letter carrier for the United States Post Office Department and the Sierras' first skier. His route, which took about five days for a round trip, was through the area traversed so unsuccessfully by the Donner Party nine years earlier.

As in other parts of California, there were Indians in the Sierras before the men appeared. They appear to have belonged to many different tribes and to have followed a primitive way of life. There is no evidence of farming or of permanent settlements. The Sierra Nevada adequately supports life for those who are sufficiently rugged and knowledgeable to take advantage of its bounty. There are piñon nuts, juniper berries, moss, edible fungi, and blackberries to eat. The Indians also ground up acorns to make porridge, bread, and a bitter coffeelike drink. There was abundant game. Mule deer, mountain sheep, squirrels, rabbits, porcupines, elk, bear, and quail must have provided meals for many Indians. Several species of trout are found in the lakes and streams. When the miners came, the Indians could not compete with them. These newcomers staked claims on what

had been free land for all. At first, the Indians fought as best they could to stop the desecration of their land and the plunder of their food supplies—the felling of acorn-bearing oaks and the sometimes profligate hunting and trapping. They were unsuccessful. Now they are gone.

The Spanish arrived in 1772. Captain Pedro Fages, while pursuing Indian bandits from the coast, reached the junction of the Sacramento and San Joaquin rivers. He explored only the foothills but looked at the great distant mountains ahead and called them *una gran sierra nevada*—a great snow-covered range. These mountains held no great attraction for the Spaniards, as they were neither hunters nor trappers.

Jedediah Smith was probably the first explorer in the Sierras. In 1827 he and his party of mountain men became the first white men to cross one of the high Sierra passes to the eastern deserts. He had reached California the previous year, trapping in the San Joaquin Valley. Shortly afterward, Russian explorers and French-Canadian and English trappers came to the area. In 1833 Joseph Walker brought more trappers to the area. Walker was the first man to lead a trapping expedition into California from east to west across the Sierras. In the course of his travels, he also was the first white man to see the Yosemite Valley. Within a few years, otters, fishers, martens, mink, and wolverine almost followed the Indians into extinction. They are rarely, if ever, found in the Sierras today.

Other notable Sierra explorers were John C. Frémont and Kit Carson. They explored the area around Donner Lake, as well as the Carson Valley, and later followed the American River into Strawberry Valley. This river begins near Donner Lake and runs from the Sierras to the Sacramento Valley.

Captain John Augustus Sutter is one of the more controversial figures in California history. The conflicting stories of his goodness and his villainy are no doubt both exaggerated. A Swiss businessman, he came to America in 1834 and received a land grant from the Mexican government in 1841, after first becoming a Mexican citizen. His nine-thousand-acre grant, the first of several, was near the junction of the American and Sacramento rivers. He was apparently able to understand and to adapt to the Mexican and Indian temperaments and ways of life, and to channel them into paths advantageous to himself without incurring their animosity. He called his homestead New Helvetia, in honor of his homeland and no doubt because of the similarities in topography. He built Sutter's Fort, which contained a cabinetmaker's shop, metal shop, saddlery, and rooms for a weaver and shoemaker. He also built a grist mill and distillery as well as storerooms, kitchen, and sleeping quarters. The fort measured 425 feet by 170 feet and had walls 3 feet thick. The furnishings were sparse, the dishes few, but the settlers fared well. Game was available in great variety and amounts so that the settlers, though short of recipes (meat was either roasted or fried with onions), were never hungry. Life was easy, prosperous, and harmonious for Indians and settlers alike for many years. Then the immigrants came.

The first overland migration of American settlers, the Bartleson-Bidwell party, came across the Sierras in 1841. They had abandoned their wagons before they reached the Humboldt Valley and, pressing on, were harassed by attacking Indians. In 1844 the first wagon train, called the Stevens Party, crossed the Sierras. With a great deal of luck and good planning, these settlers unloaded their wagons at Donner Lake and hand-carried the contents over the mountains. The cattle and oxen then hauled up the empty wagons over the huge granite boulders. This ingenious plan brought them safely to Sutter's Fort.

The Donner Party didn't fare so well. A group of ninety immigrants of all ages attempted to follow the Stevens Trail two years later. They were hampered by bad luck, poorly marked trails, Indian attacks, disease, and a naïve ignorance of frontier hardships. Without an able leader, they were unprepared for an early Sierra winter. Many starved (finally resorting to cannibalism) and perished in a makeshift camp at Donner Lake. When help finally arrived from Sutter's Fort in the spring, only half of the original party had survived. It has been called the worst disaster in the Sierras.

While John Sutter continued to expand his holdings and prosper in the peaceful Sacramento Valley, he decided to build a sawmill on the American River near Coloma. His partner, John Marshall, built the mill, receiving a share of lumber in pay, while Sutter supplied the men and materials. With the arrival of the new settlers, there was a great demand for lumber. On a cold January day in 1848, John Marshall found gold flakes in the millrace of the sawmill. There was much skepticism at first, but within a few months the gold rush was on resulting in one of the greatest migrations in history. One hundred thousand men came by foot, wagon, horse, or ship. The first ship of prospective diggers sailing into San Francisco from Panama was appropriately named *California*. The fare was exorbitant, and conditions on board were miserable. Living conditions at the diggings were no better. Miners stayed in flimsy tents, faced bitter cold winters, and fought hostile Indians. Scurvy was a problem, the main staple being flour and water baked in fire ashes. Potatoes were the only vegetable available. While only a few miners became wealthy, there are many legends of fabulous strikes. One nugget was said to have weighed twenty-four pounds. One tree stump yielded $5,000 worth of gold from its roots. As this was taking place, the city of Sacramento grew overnight around Sutter's Fort, becoming the center of transportation and communications for interior California. The Pony Express came, then the telegraph. In 1854 Sacramento became the state capital.

Most of those who came to the Sierras and the Sacramento Valley hoped to make their fortunes either from furs or from gold. Some made the trek merely out of a spirit of adventure, John Muir came to study and to savor. A naturalist and a conservationist in the 1860s and 1870s when conservation scarcely seemed necessary, he devoted himself to the exploration and study of what would now be called the ecology of the Sierra Nevada. Muir discovered living glaciers as well as birds, animals, and plants that he had never seen before. He kept diaries and made notes on his findings. His deep appreciation of the natural wonders he found impelled him to lay the groundwork for preservation of our forests and mountains and their inhabitants. Muir Woods National Monument, just north of San Francisco, is dedicated to his memory.

One of the most interesting and unusual of the early Californians was not a hero, but an outlaw, a sort of Jekyll and Hyde type of outlaw. His exploits covered a period of five years from 1877 to 1883. Charles Bolton of San Francisco was a gentleman. He was reputed to be a nonsmoking, nondrinking, God-fearing man with a substantial business interest in mines. He dressed richly and well, and frequented gatherings of San Francisco's high society. Black Bart was a gentleman, too, and was also financially tied to the mines. He was a stagecoach robber, operating in the gold rush country. His courteous "Will you please throw down your treasure box, sir" was the introduction to each of his twenty-eight successful robberies. Because he was a gentleman, he carried a neatly laundered handkerchief. At the scene of his last robbery, he dropped it by mistake. The laundry mark was traced to Charles Bolton. When he finally came to trial, his captors discovered that he had never even owned a single shell for the shotgun that he carried.

Leland Stanford, Mark Hopkins, Collis P. Huntington, Charles Crocker, and Theodore Judah brought a railroad to the gold country. Bret Harte and Samuel Clemens brought literary prowess. Lola Montez and Lotta Crabtree brought music and dancing. The Masons and the Odd Fellows brought fraternalism and lodges and resulting fellowship to lonely miners. E Clampus Vitus brought comic relief from the mystery and solemnity of the older fraternal organizations. Men came to the Sierras in droves. Few of them stayed after the lure of easy riches disappeared.

Today most of the people in the Sierras are visitors, hikers, skiers, and resort owners. Like a magnet, the Sierras draw them to its lakes, its trees, its valleys, and its eternal grandeur.

CHICKEN BREASTS IN GINGER CREAM

SERVES 8

¼ cup flour
½ teaspoon ground ginger
1 teaspoon salt
¼ teaspoon white pepper
4 large chicken breasts, split, washed, and dried
6 tablespoons butter
3 tablespoons flour
1¼ cups chicken broth
¾ cup light cream
2 tablespoons finely minced crystallized ginger
Parsley sprigs

Place the ¼ cup flour, ginger, salt, and pepper in a paper bag. Shake the chicken breasts in the paper bag, a few pieces at a time, and shake off any excess flour. In a 10–12-inch enameled skillet or casserole heat the butter until frothy and brown the chicken breasts skin side down over moderate heat for about 10 minutes. Turn the chicken and brown for 10 more minutes. Cover the pan and simmer until done, about 20 minutes more. Remove the chicken to a heated platter and keep warm in the oven. Add 3 tablespoons flour to the juice in the skillet and stir over low heat about 5 minutes. Add the chicken broth and cream. Stir until smooth and thickened. Season with salt and pepper and additional ground ginger if necessary. Pour the sauce over the chicken breasts on the platter and garnish with crystallized ginger and parsley sprigs. Serve with chutney and curried rice.

CHICKEN BREASTS CON RAJAS

SERVES 8

8 whole chicken breasts, boned and skinned
1½ teaspoons salt
½ teaspoon pepper
¼ cup butter
¼ cup oil
2 large onions, peeled and thinly sliced
8 ounces whole green chiles
½ cup Mexican Salsa (*see Index*)
¾ cup milk
1 pint sour cream
1 cup grated Cheddar cheese
1 cup grated Monterey Jack cheese

Cut the boned chicken breasts in half and season with 1 teaspoon salt and the pepper. Melt the butter and oil in a 10–12-inch skillet and sauté the chicken breasts lightly over moderate heat for 3–4 minutes on each side or until they are lightly browned. Remove the chicken from the pan. In the same pan sauté the onion for 5 minutes until soft but not browned. Slice the chiles into long strips and add ½ of them to the pan with the onion. Add the Mexican Salsa and cook over a low flame for 8–10 minutes or until the sauce is thickened slightly.

Meanwhile, place the remaining sliced chiles in the blender with the milk and ½ teaspoon salt. Blend at low speed until smooth. Add the sour cream and blend again. Place ½ the chicken breasts on the bottom of a 2-quart casserole.

Cover them with ½ the onion-chile mixture and ½ the sour cream sauce. Repeat the layers.

Mix the grated cheeses together and sprinkle on top of the chicken mixture. Bake uncovered in a preheated 350° oven for 30 minutes. Serve directly from the casserole.

NOTE: Depending upon individual tastes, you may want to increase the amount of green chiles to 12 ounces. This would then call for 6 ounces chiles to the onion-salsa mixture and 6 ounces to the sour cream mixture. This would make the recipe quite a bit "hotter."

CHICKEN WITH ARTICHOKES SERVES 8

2 15-ounce cans artichoke hearts or 1 package frozen artichoke hearts
4 whole large chicken breasts, split
1½ teaspoons salt
¼ teaspoon pepper
1 teaspoon paprika
¼ pound butter
½ pound fresh mushrooms, thinly sliced
3 tablespoons flour
⅔ cup chicken broth
3 tablespoons dry sherry
¼ cup finely minced fresh parsley

Drain the artichoke hearts well and set aside on paper towels, reserving for later use. Sprinkle the chicken breasts with salt, pepper, and paprika. In a 10–12-inch skillet brown the breasts in 4 tablespoons butter for 5 minutes per side, over medium heat.

Transfer the chicken to a large shallow casserole, preferably 13½ × 9 inches, that is suitable for serving. Add the other 4 tablespoons butter along with the sliced mushrooms to the pan in which the chicken was browned. Brown the mushrooms for about 2–3 minutes over medium-high heat. Sprinkle the flour on top, stirring constantly for 5 minutes so that the flour is completely mixed in. Slowly add the chicken broth and the sherry and simmer uncovered for an additional 5 minutes until the sauce thickens, stirring occasionally. Add the drained artichoke hearts to the sauce, stirring well. Pour the sauce over the chicken, cover the casserole with foil, and bake in a preheated 350° oven for 35–45 minutes. Sprinkle with the parsley and serve directly from the casserole, accompanied by white rice.

CHICKEN IN SHERRY HAM SAUCE

SERVES 6–8

½ pound fresh mushrooms,
  trimmed and thickly sliced
¼ cup oil
½ teaspoon salt
4 whole chicken breasts, split
  and skinned
½ teaspoon cayenne pepper
1 cup tomato sauce
¼ cup slivered smoked ham
½ cup dry sherry
2 teaspoons brown sugar
1 teaspoon grated orange peel

In a heavy 10–12-inch skillet sauté the mushrooms in oil over moderate heat for 5 minutes. Remove the mushrooms and set aside. Salt the chicken and place in the skillet. Sauté the chicken, adding more oil if necessary.

In a small bowl combine the cayenne, tomato sauce, ham, sherry, brown sugar, and orange peel. Mix well. Place mushrooms in the skillet with the chicken and pour the sauce over the chicken. Cover and simmer over low heat for 20–30 minutes. Transfer to a serving dish and serve at once, accompanied by Noodle Soufflé (*see Index*).

CHICKEN BREASTS WITH CUCUMBER

SERVES 8–12

1 large cucumber
½ cup chicken broth
½ cup dry white wine
6 whole chicken breasts, boned,
  skinned, and halved
1½ teaspoons salt
½ teaspoon pepper
6 tablespoons butter
2 tablespoons cognac
⅓ cup thinly sliced scallions
  (whites only)
1½ cups light cream
1 tablespoon grated lemon rind
2 tablespoons fresh minced
  parsley

Peel, halve lengthwise, and remove all seeds from the cucumber. Cut the halves into thin slices. Reserve ¾ of the slices.

In a large saucepan combine the remaining cucumber slices, chicken broth, and white wine. Bring the mixture to a boil, remove from heat, and let the cucumber slices steep in the liquid for 2 minutes. Strain the liquid, discarding the cucumber slices, and set aside.

Meanwhile, flatten the boned chicken breasts between waxed paper with a meat cleaver or rolling pin until they are ½ inch thick. Sprinkle lightly with ½ teaspoon each salt and pepper. In a 10–12-inch skillet sauté the breasts in the butter over low heat, turning frequently, for about 5 minutes. Pour the cognac over the chicken and ignite. When the flames subside, remove the chicken to a plate and keep warm.

Add the scallions to the skillet, cover, and cook them over low heat until tender but not brown, about 5–7 minutes. Return the chicken to the skillet along with the broth-wine mixture and cook covered for 5 minutes over low heat. Transfer the chicken to a serving platter and keep warm.

Over high heat, reduce the liquid in the skillet until it is almost a glaze, about ½ cup. Reduce the heat, stir in the cream, lemon rind, and 1 teaspoon salt. Simmer the mixture for 3–5 minutes or until slightly thickened. Stir and blend in the reserved cucumber slices. Pour the sauce over the chicken and sprinkle with minced parsley. Serve at once.

CHICKEN IMPERIAL

SERVES 8

2 cups dry bread crumbs
¼ cup minced fresh parsley
1 clove garlic, minced
1½ teaspoons salt
⅛ teaspoon pepper
1 cup butter, melted
1 tablespoon Dijon mustard
1 teaspoon Worcestershire sauce
8 whole chicken breasts, boned and halved
Parsley sprigs

In a medium-sized mixing bowl combine the bread crumbs, minced parsley, garlic, salt, and pepper. Mix together the melted butter, mustard, and Worcestershire. Dip the chicken pieces first into the butter mixture and then roll in the crumb mixture, making sure to coat all sides.

Place the pieces in a foil-lined shallow baking pan, just large enough to hold the pieces comfortably in 1 layer. Sprinkle the chicken with the remaining butter mixture and bake uncovered in a preheated 350° oven for about 1 hour or until the juices run clear when pierced by a fork. Arrange the chicken on a warm serving platter and garnish with parsley sprigs. Serve at once.

CHICKEN TARRAGON

SERVES 6

12 pieces chicken, combination of breasts, thighs, and legs
2 teaspoons salt
1 tablespoon oil
1 tablespoon butter
1 onion, thinly sliced
¾ cup chicken stock
½ cup dry white wine
1 bay leaf
1½ teaspoons dried tarragon
¼ teaspoon freshly ground pepper
1 cup sour cream

Season the chicken with the salt. Combine the oil and butter in a 10–12-inch skillet and brown the chicken and onion over medium heat for 5–7 minutes per side or until golden. Add the chicken stock, wine, and bay leaf. Cover and simmer until tender, about 25 minutes. Add the tarragon and pepper and continue cooking an additional 5 minutes. Stir in the sour cream and cook until the chicken is thoroughly heated. Do not boil the mixture after the sour cream has been added. Transfer the chicken and sauce to a serving dish and serve with Barley Casserole (*see Index*).

CHEESE-GLAZED CHICKEN

8 whole chicken breasts, boned,
    skinned, and halved
2 tablespoons flour
1½ teaspoons salt
1 teaspoon pepper
2 tablespoons butter
1 tablespoon oil
¼ cup dry sherry
1 teaspoon cornstarch
¾ cup half-and-half
⅓ cup dry white wine
1 tablespoon fresh lemon juice
½ cup grated Swiss cheese
1 teaspoon paprika

Place the chicken breasts in a bag with the flour, 1 teaspoon of salt, and pepper. Close the bag and shake the chicken until it is well coated. Heat the butter and oil together in a 10–12-inch skillet. Brown the chicken on all sides over moderate heat for 5–7 minutes per side. Add the sherry, cover, and simmer over low heat until tender, about 25 minutes. Blend the cornstarch with the half-and-half and the remaining ½ teaspoon salt. Stir the mixture into the pan drippings and continue cooking until the sauce thickens slightly, about 3–5 minutes. Add the wine and lemon juice and heat a few minutes more. Sprinkle the cheese over the top of the chicken. Cover the pan, remove the pan from the heat, and let stand for 15 minutes. (The recipe can be made up to this point and held in the refrigerator for up to 24 hours. Reheat the chicken in a 300° oven.)

Place the chicken under a preheated broiler to brown and glaze the top. Transfer the chicken to a casserole or shallow serving dish which is just large enough for the chicken to fit comfortably. Dust the chicken with the paprika and serve at once.

POULET AU CITRON

2 tablespoons grated lemon peel
¼ cup fresh lemon juice
2 cloves garlic, crushed
2 teaspoons dried thyme
1 shallot, finely chopped
1½ teaspoons salt
1 teaspoon pepper
2 2½–3-pound fryers, quartered
¼ cup butter, melted
2 lemons, thinly sliced
½ cup finely chopped fresh
    parsley

Combine the lemon peel, lemon juice, garlic, thyme, shallot, salt, and pepper in a mixing bowl. Place chicken pieces in a single layer in a shallow baking dish and cover with the lemon marinade. Turn chicken until it is thoroughly coated. Refrigerate covered in the marinade 3–4 hours, turning the chicken several times to marinate evenly.

Lift chicken from the marinade and drain well on paper towels, reserving the marinade. Place chicken in a single layer in a shallow 2-quart baking dish and brush with the melted butter.

Bake chicken uncovered in a preheated 425° oven for 25 minutes. Brush with reserved marinade, lower heat to 325°, and bake for an additional 30–35 minutes more or until chicken is browned and thoroughly cooked.

Remove chicken from oven and strain off as much grease as possible. Arrange the chicken on a serving platter. Surround with the lemon slices and sprinkle with the chopped parsley. Heat any remaining marinade and pass separately in a gravy boat.

MEXICAN CHICKEN WITH GRAPES

SERVES 8

3 tablespoons butter
3 tablespoons oil
2 2½–3-pound frying chickens, cut in pieces, washed and patted dry
1½ teaspoons salt or to taste
¼ teaspoon pepper or to taste
2 medium onions, thinly sliced
3 cloves garlic, crushed
3 large stalks celery, chopped
5 small tomatoes, peeled and coarsely chopped
¼ teaspoon dried thyme
¼ teaspoon dried marjoram
2 tablespoons flour
2 tablespoons butter, softened
½–¾ cup dry white wine
1 pound seedless grapes, halved

Heat the 3 tablespoons butter and the oil in a 3-quart flameproof casserole. Season the chicken with ½ teaspoon salt and the pepper and add to the casserole. Sauté over moderate heat 8–10 minutes, turning chicken once. Remove from the pan and set aside. In same oil, sauté onion, garlic, and celery over moderately high heat for 5–7 minutes or until limp, stirring frequently. Add the chopped tomatoes, thyme, marjoram, and 1 teaspoon salt, stirring to blend. Place the chicken in the tomato mixture, cover, and bake in a preheated 350° oven for 25–30 minutes. Remove chicken from sauce and place on a serving platter. Remove vegetable pieces with a slotted spoon and spoon over chicken pieces. Set aside and keep warm.

Deglaze the juices in the pan. In a small cup blend the flour and 2 tablespoons butter together to form a paste (*buerre manie*). Heat the juices over medium heat and add the *beurre manie*, stirring constantly, until blended and slightly thickened. Add the wine and simmer over low heat for 10 minutes. Add the grapes and simmer an additional 5 minutes. Spoon the hot sauce over the chicken and serve at once.

ITALIAN CHICKEN WITH ARTICHOKES

SERVES 8

2 6-ounce jars marinated
  artichoke hearts
4 tablespoons olive oil
¼ cup flour
2 2½-pound chickens, cut in
  serving pieces
6 tomatoes, peeled and
  quartered
4 small cloves garlic, minced
1 pound fresh mushrooms,
  trimmed and sliced
1 cup dry sherry
2 tablespoons minced fresh
  parsley
1½ teaspoons salt
¾ teaspoon pepper
1 teaspoon monosodium
  glutamate
1 teaspoon dried oregano
2 teaspoons dried basil
Parsley sprigs

Drain the artichokes, saving them for later, and combine ½ of their liquid with the oil in a 10–12-inch skillet. In a paper bag place the flour and chicken, a few pieces at a time. Shake and coat the chicken well. Brown the chicken on each side in the skillet over medium-high heat for about 5–7 minutes per side.

Transfer the chicken to a 3-quart casserole dish. Combine all the other ingredients except the artichokes and parsley sprigs in the browning skillet and simmer over medium-low heat for 10 minutes. Pour the sauce over the chicken and bake uncovered in a preheated 350° oven for 50 minutes. Add the artichoke hearts, adjust seasonings if desired, and bake uncovered for 10 more minutes. Serve the chicken on a deep platter with buttered vermicelli in the middle, surrounded by the chicken and sauce. Garnish with parsley sprigs.

CHICKEN CACCIATORE

SERVES 8

3 2½-pound chickens, cut into
  serving pieces
Salt and pepper to taste
½ cup olive oil
2 medium onions, sliced
1 large bell pepper, sliced
1 pound fresh mushrooms,
  trimmed and sliced
2 small cloves garlic, minced
½ teaspoon dried oregano
1 teaspoon dried rosemary
½ cup dry white wine
2 cups tomatoes, peeled and
  chopped
½ cup ripe olives, sliced

Wash the chicken pieces under cold water and pat with paper towels until completely dry. Season the chicken well with salt and pepper. Heat the oil in a heavy 10–12-inch skillet over moderate heat. Add the chicken, a few pieces at a time, and brown well on all sides, 2–3 minutes per side. Remove the chicken to a plate. Leave 4 tablespoons oil in the skillet. Sauté the onion, bell pepper, and mushrooms in the same skillet, stirring occasionally for 3 minutes. Stir in the garlic, oregano, and rosemary and cook for 1 minute. Add the wine to the skillet and cook another minute, stirring. Return the browned chicken, tomatoes, and olives to the skillet. Salt and pepper to taste. Cover and simmer over low flame until tender, about 30 minutes. Baste occasionally, turning and rotating pieces to cook evenly. The chicken is done when the juice runs clear after piercing with a fork. Arrange the chicken on a heated platter. Boil the sauce slightly until it thickens, taste for seasoning, pour over the chicken, and serve.

POULET VÉRONIQUE

SERVES 8

2 teaspoons monosodium glutamate
2 broiler-fryer chickens, cut into serving pieces
½ teaspoon paprika
1 teaspoon salt
½ cup butter
1 onion, finely chopped
1 clove garlic, minced
¼ pound fresh mushrooms, sliced, plus 8 large mushroom caps
4 tablespoons flour
1 teaspoon sugar
1 cup chicken broth
1 cup half-and-half
3 tablespoons fresh lemon juice
1 cup seedless white grapes
2 tablespoons butter
1 tablespoon oil
Parsley sprigs

Sprinkle monosodium glutamate over the chicken along with the paprika and salt. Melt ¼ cup butter in a 10–12-inch skillet. Add chicken and brown over moderately high heat for 2–3 minutes per side. Remove the chicken and set aside. To the skillet add the remaining ¼ cup butter, the onion, and garlic and cook over low heat for 5 minutes. Add the ¼ pound mushrooms (not the 8 caps) and cook over medium heat for 2 minutes longer, stirring to brown evenly. Blend in the flour and sugar and sauté over low heat for another 2–3 minutes, stirring often. Add the chicken broth, half-and-half, and lemon juice and bring to a simmer, stirring until the sauce thickens slightly. Return the chicken, cover, and simmer over low heat for 30 minutes or until tender. Uncover and add the grapes for the last 5 minutes of cooking.

In an 8-inch skillet sauté the mushroom caps in 2 tablespoons butter and 1 tablespoon oil over moderate to high heat for 2–3 minutes. Arrange the chicken on a heated serving platter and pour the sauce over it. Garnish with the sautéed mushroom caps and sprigs of fresh parsley.

CHICKEN WITH BRANDY

SERVES 8

2 2½-pound chickens, cut into
  serving pieces
1½ teaspoons salt
1 teaspoon pepper
¼ cup fresh lemon juice
3 tablespoons butter
2 tablespoons oil
¾ pound fresh mushrooms,
  sliced
3 scallions, including tops,
  finely chopped
1½ ounces brandy
1 cup dry white wine
3 large tomatoes, peeled,
  seeded, and chopped
½ cup chicken broth
1 tablespoon minced fresh
  parsley
1½ teaspoons dried tarragon
2 tablespoons flour

Rub the chicken pieces with a mixture of the salt, pepper, and lemon juice. Melt 2 tablespoons butter with the oil in a 10–12-inch skillet and brown the chicken on all sides over moderate heat, 5–7 minutes per side or until golden. Add the mushrooms and cook over moderate heat for 5 more minutes. Add the scallions, brandy, wine, tomatoes, chicken broth, parsley, and tarragon. Simmer gently, partially covered, for 25–30 minutes or until tender. Stir occasionally to mix the flavors.

Make a roux consisting of 2 tablespoons flour and the remaining 1 tablespoon butter. Work the mixture into a paste and add to the chicken and sauce. Stir constantly until the sauce thickens. Pour the chicken and sauce into a serving casserole and serve with plain wild rice.

CHICKEN À LA RITZ

SERVES 6

2 frying chickens, about 2½
  pounds each, cut into
  serving pieces
½ teaspoon salt
½ teaspoon pepper
4 tablespoons flour
4 tablespoons butter
1 tablespoon oil
½ pound fresh mushrooms,
  sliced
½ cup finely chopped scallions
  (whites only)
1 cup dry white wine
½ teaspoon dried basil
2 cups plus 1 teaspoon light
  cream
1 tablespoon fresh lemon juice

Season the chicken with salt and pepper and sprinkle with flour. In a 10–12-inch skillet sauté the chicken in the butter and oil for 10–12 minutes per side, using medium heat. Remove the chicken from the skillet with a slotted spoon and set aside.

Add the mushrooms and scallions to the skillet and sauté for 1 minute over moderate heat, stirring frequently. Return the chicken to the skillet. Add the wine and basil and simmer covered for 10 minutes. Add 2 cups cream and simmer uncovered for 15 minutes. Remove the chicken to a serving platter and keep warm. Add lemon juice to the cream sauce and correct seasoning, adding more lemon juice if necessary. Mix the egg yolks in a cup with 1 teaspoon cream

2 egg yolks, lightly beaten
Parsley sprigs

and add to the cream sauce. Cook for 2–3 minutes over low heat, stirring constantly, until the sauce thickens. Do not let it boil. Pour the sauce over the chicken, garnish with parsley, and serve at once.

CHICKEN WITH CASHEWS

SERVES 8

6 whole chicken breasts
6 egg whites, lightly beaten
6 tablespoons cornstarch
¾ teaspoon salt
1 large green pepper, cut into ½-inch pieces
¾ cup dry roasted cashews
6–8 scallions, whites only, thinly sliced
3 cloves garlic, minced
1 tablespoon ground ginger
2 cups corn oil

SAUCE CHOY
½ cup dry sherry
⅓ cup soy sauce
6 tablespoons water
6 tablespoons sugar
4 tablespoons cornstarch
3 tablespoons white vinegar
1 tablespoon oil
¾ teaspoon sesame seeds

The three parts to this dish—chicken mixture, cashew mixture, and sauce—should be assembled a few minutes ahead of time up to the cooking point and then stir-fried, preferably in a wok, just before serving. If a wok is not available, use a heavy 10–12-inch skillet.

Skin and bone the chicken and cut into ½-inch cubes. With your hands mix the chicken with the egg whites, 6 tablespoons cornstarch, and the salt in a large mixing bowl. Make sure the chicken is thoroughly coated. Set mixture aside. Mix together the green pepper, cashews, scallions, garlic, and ginger and set aside in a small bowl.

Pour the corn oil in the wok over medium heat, about 375°. Add the chicken mixture, stirring constantly to separate the pieces. Cook about 1 minute.

Lift the wok from the heat and place the chicken into a colander, draining the oil off into another pan. Set the cooked chicken aside. Discard all but 2 teaspoons of the oil and return that oil to the wok. Add the cashew mixture. Cook 1–2 minutes until the green pepper is just tender. Add the chicken and stir in the Sauce Choy. Bring to a boil for 1 minute, stirring constantly, coating the chicken and vegetables. Serve at once on a platter accompanied by Steamed Rice Chinatown Style (*see Index*).

To prepare sauce, in a small bowl combine all the sauce ingredients and mix well.

INDONESIAN CHICKEN

SERVES 7–8

must be prepared 24 hours in advance

- ½ teaspoon salt
- 8 whole chicken legs with thighs, separated
- 3 tablespoons butter
- 2 stalks celery, thinly sliced
- ½ red or green bell pepper finely chopped
- 2 onions, finely chopped
- 3 tablespoons all-purpose flour
- 3 cups chicken broth
- 1 cup cream-style peanut butter
- 1 teaspoon crushed dried red peppers
- 1 bunch scallions, including some of the tops, trimmed and thinly sliced
- 3 bananas, peeled and thinly sliced
- ½ cup coconut, toasted
- 3 tomatoes, cut in eighths
- 1 avocado, thinly sliced

Salt the chicken pieces and place in a shallow roasting pan. Broil under a preheated broiler until they are well browned, but not cooked through, about 8 minutes per side. Set the chicken aside after it is broiled.

Meanwhile, foam the butter in a 2–3 quart Dutch oven over moderate heat. Add the celery, bell pepper, and onion and cook covered until the vegetables are transparent and limp but not browned, about 4–5 minutes. Remove the Dutch oven from the heat. Stir in the flour, a little at a time, until all is used and the vegetables are sticky. Add the chicken broth, a little at a time, stirring to take out lumps. The mixture will resemble a thin soup after all the broth is added. Add any juices that formed in the roasting pan during the broiling of the chicken and heat the mixture to bubbling over a medium-high flame. Add the peanut butter and stir quickly to melt it and mix it through. The mixture may look curdled, but it will smooth out with perseverance. Add the dried pepper, but do not taste now, as it will be too hot.

Place the chicken in a 4–5-quart casserole dish and spoon the sauce over it. Cover and bake in a preheated 300° oven for 1 hour. Let the chicken cool and refrigerate it in the casserole for 24 hours. The flavors blend and improve immensely during this time.

An hour before serving, prepare the scallions, bananas, coconut, tomatoes, and avocado and reserve. Reheat the chicken in a 300° oven for 30 minutes or until it is completely heated through. Place the chicken on a deep serving platter and heap the condiments attractively over and around the chicken. Spoon the peanut sauce over all, condiments included, and serve with hot rice. Chutney may be offered also.

BROILED CHICKEN INDIENNE

4 small broilers, split
2 teaspoons salt
1 teaspoon pepper
2 tablespoons butter, softened
¾ cup oil
¾ cup chutney
5 tablespoons vinegar
2 cloves garlic, crushed
8 strips bacon

Wash the broilers and pat dry with paper towels. Sprinkle with 1 teaspoon salt and the pepper and rub with the softened butter. Place the oil, chutney, vinegar, 1 teaspoon salt, and garlic in the blender. Blend at medium speed for 30 seconds to make a smooth sauce and set aside. Lay the chickens in a large broiler pan, skin side down. Place in a preheated broiler for 7–10 minutes, until lightly golden, brush with the chutney sauce, and turn. Repeat the procedure with the skin side up, broil and baste with the chutney sauce until golden, about 15 minutes. Turn the oven to 350° and bake the chicken until tender, about 25 minutes. Arrange the chicken on a warm serving platter.

While the chicken is baking, cook the bacon slices until almost crisp. Curl the strips while they are still warm and pliable and set aside on paper towels to drain. Place a curl of bacon on each chicken half and serve immediately, accompanied by Curry Pilaf (*see Index*).

CHICKEN SAKE

1½ cups sake
5 tablespoons soy sauce
4 chicken breasts, boned, skinned, and cut into ¾-inch cubes
4 green bell peppers, seeded, scraped, and cut into ½-inch cubes
2 yellow onions, cut into ½-inch cubes
4 tablespoons oil

In a large mixing bowl combine the sake and 4 tablespoons soy sauce. Marinate the cubed chicken in this sauce for 8 hours at room temperature.

In a 10–12-inch skillet or wok heat the oil over a medium-high heat. Add the peppers and onion and sauté until they are just tender but not brown, about 3 minutes, stirring constantly. Drain the chicken, discarding the marinade, and add chicken to the peppers and onion. Sauté the chicken quickly, until it is just cooked through, about 3 minutes, stirring to prevent burning. Stir in 1 tablespoon soy sauce, transfer the chicken mixture to a serving platter, and serve at once with white rice and warm sake.

EAST INDIAN CHICKEN CURRY

SERVES 8

½ pound sweet butter
2 medium onions, chopped
2 large cloves garlic, minced
2 stalks celery, chopped
3 tablespoons chopped fresh
    parsley
1 large cucumber, peeled and
    chopped
2 apples, peeled and chopped
4 tablespoons flour
1 teaspoon nutmeg
1 teaspoon dry mustard
3–4 tablespoons curry powder
    or to taste
2 cups chicken broth
2 cups light cream
1 cup coconut milk
1½ teaspoons salt
1 tablespoon fresh lemon juice
6 whole chicken breasts,
    cooked, skinned, and cubed

In a 12-inch skillet melt the butter over moderate heat and sauté the onion, garlic, celery, parsley, cucumber, and apples until tender, about 3–5 minutes, stirring frequently. Add the flour, nutmeg, mustard, and curry powder and cook an additional 5 minutes, stirring often. Add the chicken broth, cream, coconut milk, and salt. Bring the mixture to a boil over high heat, reduce the heat, and simmer partially covered for 1 hour.

Pour the mixture through a large sieve into a bowl, making sure to squeeze all the juices from the cooked fruits and vegetables. Discard the vegetables, return the sauce to the skillet, add the lemon juice, and correct the seasonings if necessary. If more curry powder is desired, dissolve in a small amount of juice before adding.

Add the chicken to the curry sauce and simmer over low heat until the chicken is heated through, about 15 minutes, stirring well. Serve from a chafing dish with steamed rice and condiments.

Suggested condiments: chopped scallions, raisins, crumbled bacon, chopped hard-boiled eggs, shredded coconut, chopped cashews, Nectarine Chutney (*see Index*), and Peach Chutney (*see Index*). Place each condiment in a separate bowl for guests to serve themselves.

CHICKEN CREPES

SERVES 8

4 tablespoons finely chopped
    scallions, including tops
½ cup finely chopped celery
1 cup peeled and grated carrot
¼ teaspoon curry powder
½ cup butter
1¼ teaspoons salt
⅔ cup flour, sifted
3 cups light cream
⅔ cup dry white wine

In a 10–12-inch skillet sauté the scallions, celery, carrots, and curry powder in the butter for 8–10 minutes over moderate heat. Stir frequently. Blend in the salt and flour and cook for 2–3 minutes more, stirring constantly. Add the cream and wine, stirring until the mixture thickens, approximately 5–7 minutes. Add the lemon juice, water chestnuts, and chicken. Cook until the mixture is thoroughly heated. Remove from heat while filling crepes.

2 tablespoons fresh lemon juice

1 5-ounce can water chestnuts, drained and coarsely chopped

1 chicken breast, cooked, skinned, and shredded (2 cups)

16 Blender Crepes (*see Index*)

1 cup grated Gruyère cheese

To assemble the crepes, place a heaping tablespoon of the mixture on each crepe, roll the crepe, and place seam side down in a shallow 8 × 10-inch baking dish. Probably 2 baking dishes will be needed to hold all the crepes. Top the crepes with the remaining chicken mixture and the grated cheese. Bake uncovered in a preheated 350° oven for 15–20 minutes or until cheese is bubbly and crepes are heated through.

ROAST CHICKEN WITH PORT

SERVES 4

1 tablespoon butter

3 tablespoons oil

1 clove garlic, crushed

1 4–5-pound roasting chicken

4 tablespoons (¼ cup) cognac

½ teaspoon salt

¼ teaspoon pepper

⅓ cup port

½ cup consommé

½ teaspoon dried basil

½ teaspoon dried thyme

Heat the butter and oil in a medium-sized roasting pan or casserole on top of the stove. Add the garlic and brown the chicken on all sides over medium heat for about 10 minutes. Remove the chicken and most of the oil from the pan. Place the chicken on a rack and return it to the roasting pan. Pour 3 tablespoons of the cognac over the chicken, ignite, and wait for the flame to subside, about 1 minute. Salt and pepper the chicken and mix together the port, consommé, basil, and thyme in a small saucepan. Heat to simmer and pour over the chicken. Roast uncovered in a preheated 350° oven for about 20 minutes per pound, basting often with the pan juices. The juices should run clear when the breast is pricked lightly with a fork. If the juices are still pink, return to the oven for another 10–15 minutes. Place the chicken on a serving platter and keep warm. Strain as much of the grease from the roasting pan as possible. Add the remaining 1 tablespoon cognac to the pan drippings and boil the sauce down on top of the stove until it is slightly thickened. There should be about ½ cup of sauce. Cut the chicken into serving pieces and cover with the port sauce.

NOTE: This roast is delicious served with Brown Rice and Pine Nut Casserole (*see Index*).

ROAST CHICKEN WITH MINT SAUCE

1 5–5½-pound roasting chicken
Salt and pepper to taste
3 large bunches fresh mint,
    washed and dried
4 tablespoons butter
3 tablespoons butter, melted
Mint sprigs

MINT SAUCE
½ cup wine vinegar
½ cup dry white wine or
    vermouth
2 tablespoons minced shallots
¼ cup minced fresh mint leaves
½ teaspoon salt
¼ teaspoon freshly ground
    pepper
6 egg yolks
4 tablespoons cold butter
1 cup butter, melted

Rub the cavity of the chicken with salt and pepper. Stuff the chicken with the 3 bunches fresh mint leaves and the 4 tablespoons butter, which has been cut into bite-sized pieces. Pack the mint and butter in the cavity very tightly. Truss the bird securely. Brush the chicken completely with the 3 tablespoons melted butter. Place the chicken uncovered, breast side up, in a roasting pan and roast in a preheated 450° oven for 20 minutes. Reduce the heat to 350° and roast for an additional hour. Baste regularly with the pan juices. Pierce the chicken with a fork, and if the juices run clear, the chicken is done. Remove the chicken to a serving platter and keep warm, allowing the chicken to stand 10 minutes before carving. Remove the trussing. Garnish with the fresh mint sprigs and serve with Mint Sauce.

To prepare sauce, combine the vinegar, wine, shallots, 2 tablespoons mint leaves, salt, and pepper in a small saucepan. Bring to a boil over moderate heat and cook until liquid has reduced to 4 tablespoons. Cool and strain the mixture into the top of a double boiler.

In a small bowl beat the egg yolks until thick and creamy. Place the double boiler top over hot simmering water on low heat. Cut 2 tablespoons of the cold butter in small pieces and add butter and egg yolks to the mint mixture. Beat constantly with a wire wisk. Beat in the remaining cold butter, a little at a time, in small pieces. Slowly add the melted butter, stirring constantly. When all the butter is incorporated and the sauce is thickened, remove the pan from the heat and beat in the remaining 2 tablespoons mint leaves. Serve at once in a small sauce bowl.

NOTE: There will be very little sauce, but it is extremely rich, and each person will want only a spoonful or two.

GRANDMOTHER'S CHICKEN AND FLAT DUMPLINGS

1 large roasting chicken
3–3½ teaspoons salt
1 teaspoon pepper
3 sprigs parsley
1 stalk celery
¼ onion, peeled and sliced
1 cup flour
5 tablespoons softened butter
1 egg, beaten lightly
2 tablespoons flour
3 cups reserved chicken broth

Put the chicken, 1 teaspoon salt, pepper, parsley, celery, and onion in a 5–6-quart iron pot. Add enough water to cover the chicken, approximately 2½–3 quarts. Cover and bring the water to a boil over a medium-high flame. Reduce the flame and simmer for 45 minutes or until the chicken is tender. Remove the chicken to a large casserole and keep warm. Strain the chicken broth and return the broth to the same pot for cooking the dumplings. During the time the chicken is stewing, make the dumplings, which are really large, flat noodles.

In a large bowl combine the 1 cup flour, ½ teaspoon salt, 2 tablespoons butter, and the egg and work the dough with your fingers until the dough is stiff and sticks together. Roll the dough *very thinly*, between waxed paper, so the dumplings will be very flat, about ⅛ inch. Cut the dumplings into big 2-inch diamond shapes.

To cook, return the strained broth to a boil. Drop the dumplings a few at a time into the boiling broth, until all are added. Cook, stirring to keep them separate, for 15–20 minutes or until they are al dente. When they are tender, remove the dumplings with a slotted spoon and lay them over and around the cooked chicken in the casserole. Keep warm while making the gravy.

Make a roux of the remaining 3 tablespoons butter and the 2 tablespoons flour. Cook the roux slightly, about 2 minutes, in a 2-quart saucepan over low heat. Add the strained broth and heat slowly over a medium flame, stirring constantly with a wire whisk until the gravy is thick like a cream sauce. More broth may be added if desired. Add 1½–2 teaspoons salt and pour the gravy over the chicken and dumplings. There should be a great deal of sauce. Serve directly from the casserole.

NOTE: This recipe is very old-fashioned. The result is a simple, pure chicken flavor. All temptation to use wine and herbs should be resisted.

CHICKEN CROQUETTES
WITH WHIPPED LEMON DILL SAUCE

SERVES 8

must be prepared 24 hours in advance

3 tablespoons butter
3 tablespoons flour
¾ cup chicken stock
1 egg yolk
2 tablespoons heavy cream
¾ teaspoon salt
⅛ teaspoon cayenne pepper
2 teaspoons fresh lemon juice
1½ tablespoons chopped
    shallots
⅛ pound fresh mushrooms,
    chopped (½ cup)
2 tablespoons madeira
1½ cups finely chopped cold
    chicken
1 tablespoon finely chopped
    fresh parsley
½ cup flour
2 eggs
1½ tablespoons oil
½ cup bread crumbs
½ cup ground almonds
Whipped Lemon Dill Sauce
    (*below*)
Deep fat for frying

WHIPPED LEMON DILL SAUCE
3 egg yolks
1 tablespoon arrowroot
1 teaspoon salt
⅛ teaspoon cayenne pepper
1 cup chicken stock
2 tablespoons snipped fresh
    dill weed
1 tablespoon fresh lemon juice

Melt 2 tablespoons butter in a 1½-quart saucepan over low heat. Stir in 3 tablespoons flour and cook, stirring, for 2–3 minutes. Pour in the ¾ cup stock. Stir until the flour dissolves. Stirring constantly, bring mixture to a low boil until very thick. Simmer for 2 minutes. Remove saucepan from heat.

In a small bowl combine 1 egg yolk with cream. Blend egg mixture, a few tablespoons at a time, into the hot sauce. Heat to simmering for 10 seconds. Turn off heat. Season with the ¾ teaspoon salt, ⅛ teaspoon cayenne, and 2 teaspoons lemon juice. Set aside.

Heat 1 tablespoon butter in an 8–10-inch skillet and sauté the shallots for 1 minute. Mix in the mushrooms and cook for 8–10 minutes, stirring frequently. Pour in the madeira and cook until all of the liquid has disappeared. Set aside.

In a medium-sized bowl combine the chopped chicken, chopped parsley, the mushroom mixture, and the cream sauce. Spread this mixture in a 9 × 13-inch glass baking dish, ½ inch thick. Cover and chill overnight.

Several hours before serving, form the chilled chicken mixture into 1-inch-diameter balls. Roll in the ½ cup flour, shaking off any excess. In a mixing bowl beat the 2 eggs with oil. In another bowl mix the bread crumbs and almonds together.

Dip the croquettes first in the egg mixture, then roll in the bread crumb mixture. Place in a shallow baking pan, cover, and chill for at least 2 hours more. When ready to serve, fry the croquettes in deep fat at 375° until golden brown. Drain on paper towels. Serve with Whipped Lemon Dill Sauce.

To prepare sauce, combine the 3 egg yolks, arrowroot, 1 teaspoon salt, and ⅛ teaspoon cayenne in a medium-sized saucepan. Beat with a whisk, adding the stock a little at a time. Stir constantly over low heat until the sauce begins to thicken.

Do not boil or it will curdle. When thick, fold in the dill and 1 tablespoon lemon juice. This sauce may be made ahead and reheated in a double boiler over gently rolling water.

NOTE: This is an elegant luncheon dish accompanied by Stir-fried Broccoli (*see Index*).

MONTEZUMA PIE

SERVES 6

½ cup oil
18 corn tortillas
2 cups shredded cooked
  chicken
Green Chile Sauce (*below*)
1 cup sour cream
Tomatillo Sauce (*below*)
2 cups grated Cheddar cheese

Heat ½ cup oil in an 8-inch skillet over moderate heat. Fry 1 tortilla at a time for 15–20 seconds on each side until limp but not crisp. Drain the tortillas between paper towels.

Spread 6 tortillas on the bottom of a casserole 3½–4 inches deep and 10 inches in diameter. Spread ⅓ of the chicken, ⅓ of the Green Chile Sauce, ⅓ of the sour cream, ⅓ of the Tomatillo Sauce, and ⅓ of the cheese. Repeat the layers 2 times more. Bake uncovered in a preheated 350° oven for 25 minutes. Serve the casserole with rice and beer.

GREEN CHILE SAUCE
8 ounces whole green chiles
3 tablespoons oil
½ onion, thinly sliced
½ teaspoon salt

To prepare Green Chile Sauce, wash the chiles, remove the seeds, and dry the chiles thoroughly. In an 8–10-inch skillet heat the 3 tablespoons oil over medium heat. Slice the chiles into thin strips and cook them in the oil along with the onion slices and ½ teaspoon salt until the onions are limp, approximately 6–8 minutes.

TOMATILLO SAUCE
2 cups fresh tomates verdes or
  3 12-ounce cans tomatillos,
  drained
2 cloves garlic, minced
¼ teaspoon sugar
½ teaspoon salt
½ cup water
2 tablespoons chopped
  coriander leaves (cilantro)
½ cup chopped onion
2 tablespoons oil

To prepare Tomatillo Sauce, blend the tomates verdes, garlic, sugar, ½ teaspoon salt, water, coriander, and chopped onion in a blender at medium speed until smooth, about 30 seconds. Heat the 3 tablespoons oil over moderate heat in an 8–10-inch skillet and add the tomato mixture. Cook the mixture for 10 minutes, stirring occasionally.

ENCHILADA DE POLLO VERDE
(Green Chicken Enchilada)

1 cup shortening
12 corn tortillas
Salsa Verde (*below*)
3–4 chicken breasts, cooked, skinned, and shredded
1½ pounds Monterey Jack cheese, grated
2 7-ounce cans ripe olives, coarsely chopped
½ cup light cream
1 bunch scallions, whites only, chopped
1 cup sour cream

SALSA VERDE
2 12-ounce cans (tomates verdes) (tomatillos)
1 bunch coriander leaves (cilantro), chopped (about 1 cup)
3 chiles from can of *jalapeños en escabeche*, seeded and chopped
1 clove garlic, finely chopped
½ onion, coarsely chopped
3 tablespoons coarsely chopped fresh parsley
¼ teaspoon salt
Pinch sugar
2 tablespoons shortening

Heat 1 cup shortening in a heavy 10–12-inch skillet and dip a tortilla into the hot oil for a few seconds until it is limp. Then dip the same tortilla into warm Salsa Verde. Laying the tortilla on a flat surface, assemble the enchilada by putting 2 tablespoons chicken, 2 tablespoons grated cheese, and 1 tablespoon chopped olives in the center of the tortilla. Roll the tortilla up and place seam side down in a shallow 9 × 13-inch casserole dish. Repeat the process until all tortillas have been assembled into enchiladas.

Pour the cream around and under the enchiladas, lifting the edges with a spatula to permit the cream to run under. Cover enchiladas with the remaining salsa and grated cheese. Top with chopped scallions. Bake uncovered in a preheated 350° oven for 20 minutes. Pass sour cream separately in a small bowl and have guests put a spoonful on top of each enchilada if they desire.

To prepare Salsa Verde, drain the tomates verdes, reserving the liquid for use if the salsa is too thick, and place them, along with the remaining salsa ingredients, except the shortening, in a large mixing bowl. Pour ½ the mixture into the container of an electric blender and blend until smooth, about 45 seconds. Pour this into another large bowl and blend the second half of the mixture until smooth. Combine the mixtures.

In a heavy 10–12-inch skillet melt the 2 tablespoons shortening over medium heat and add the salsa. Bring the sauce to a boil, reduce the heat, and simmer for 5 minutes.

NOTE: The enchiladas should not be assembled more than 1 hour ahead of time, as they absorb liquid and become limp.

PERFECT PICNIC IN A BASKET

½ cup flour
1½ tablespoons sesame seeds
½ tablespoon dried thyme
¾ teaspoon dried tarragon
½ tablespoon poppy seeds
1 teaspoon salt
1 teaspoon pepper
8 chicken thighs
2 egg whites, lightly beaten
2 tablespoons butter
2 tablespoons margarine
1 round fresh sourdough bread

HERB AND SEEDS BUTTER SAUCE
4 tablespoons butter
3 tablespoons sesame seeds
1 tablespoon dried thyme
1½ teaspoons dried tarragon
1 tablespoon poppy seeds

In a small mixing bowl combine the flour, 1½ tablespoons sesame seeds, ½ tablespoon thyme, ¾ teaspoon tarragon, ½ tablespoon poppy seeds, salt, and pepper. Dip the chicken thighs in the beaten egg white and then coat each piece thoroughly in the flour mixture. Meanwhile, melt the 2 tablespoons butter and the margarine in a 10–12-inch skillet. Brown the chicken thoroughly, about 7 minutes per side, over medium heat. Put the chicken in a 3-quart casserole dish, cover, and bake 40 minutes in a preheated 350° oven.

To prepare the "basket," cut a large top in the bread round. Scoop out the inside of the loaf, leaving about ¾ inch of bread all the way around the edge. With a pastry brush, spread Herb and Seeds Butter Sauce over the entire inside of the loaf and the inside of the top. Place the loaf and top on a cookie sheet.

Put the chicken in the "basket" and return the chicken, basket, and top to the oven on the cookie sheet to bake for an additional 20 minutes, uncovered. Remove from the oven, put the top on, and wrap the basket in several layers of foil, surrounded by several layers of newspaper. It will remain very warm for several hours this way.

To prepare sauce, melt the 4 tablespoons butter in a small saucepan and add the remaining sauce ingredients. Use the sauce for Picnic in a Basket or, for delicious herb bread, brush over slices of hot French or Italian bread.

NOTE: When serving Picnic in a Basket, make sure each guest takes a large piece of bread with the chicken.

CREAMED CHICKEN EN PÂTE

¾ pound fresh mushrooms,
  sliced
4 tablespoons butter
5–6 shallots, finely chopped
2 stalks celery, finely chopped
2 tablespoons chopped fresh
  parsley
2 tablespoons flour
1 cup light cream, warmed
¼ cup white wine
¼ cup chicken broth
4 chicken breasts, cooked,
  skinned, and cubed
½ teaspoon salt
¼ teaspoon white pepper
8–10 individual pastry shells,
  baked

In an 8-inch skillet sauté the mushrooms in 2 tablespoons butter over a moderate flame for 5–6 minutes, stirring constantly. Remove the mushrooms from the skillet with a slotted spoon and set aside. Sauté the shallots, celery, and parsley in the same skillet, adding a little more butter if necessary. Cook the vegetables until transparent, about 5–6 minutes, over low heat, stirring frequently. Remove the skillet containing the vegetables from the flame and set aside.

In a 10–12-inch skillet blend the flour and remaining 2 tablespoons butter over very low heat for 10 minutes, stirring frequently. Add the warmed cream and bring to a boil over moderate heat. Add the wine and chicken broth, stirring constantly, until the sauce is the consistency of heavy cream. Add the sautéed vegetables, mushrooms, salt, pepper, and chicken, reduce the heat, and simmer for a few minutes until all ingredients are thoroughly heated. Serve immediately in individual pastry shells or over wild rice. Lemon-buttered broccoli and a fruit dessert are excellent accompaniments.

NOTE: This dish may be made the day ahead and reheated. If the sauce is too thick, add another ½ cup chicken broth.

HOT CHINESE CHICKEN SALAD

¼ pound butter
1 2½–3-pound broiler-fryer
  chicken
½ head iceberg lettuce, thinly
  shredded
1 bunch scallions, including
  tops, thinly sliced
1 small bunch coriander leaves
  (cilantro), chopped
¼ cup sesame seeds, toasted
2–3 ounces Chinese translucent
  noodles, fried (see Note)

Melt butter in a small roasting pan and brown the chicken well on all sides on top of the stove over moderate heat. Place chicken on a rack and roast, basting often, in a preheated 400° oven for about 1 hour or until juices run clear when pierced with a fork. Turn on all sides during roasting to ensure that the skin is crispy. Remove chicken from oven, let stand for 5 minutes to cool, and strip meat from carcass, including all the crispy skin. Place chicken meat in a large salad bowl, topped by lettuce, scallions, coriander, sesame seeds, and fried noodles. Pour Soy Lemon

Sauce over the salad, mix well, and serve at once while the chicken is still warm.

To prepare sauce, place all the sauce ingredients together in a small jar with a cover, shake well to blend, and let stand for about 1 hour. Shake again before mixing into the salad.

NOTE: The "translucent" noodles describe a variety of Japanese and Chinese noodles that resemble nylon fishing line. Any variety (rice, yam, or bean base) may be used, except the taro-based shirataki noodle. Follow directions on package for frying. If you are unable to find these noodles, toasted slivered almonds may be substituted.

SOY LEMON SAUCE

½ teaspoon dry mustard
½ teaspoon salt
1 teaspoon sugar
1 teaspoon grated lemon peel
2 teaspoons soy sauce
1 tablespoon fresh lemon juice
4–6 tablespoons salad oil

ROAST STUFFED DUCKLING

SERVES 4–5

1 5–6 pound domestic duckling
2 teaspoons salt
¼ teaspoon pepper
2 cloves garlic, minced
2 tablespoons olive oil
¾ cup finely minced onion
1 pound sausage meat
3 slices white bread, well
   toasted and diced
⅛ teaspoon crushed dried red
   pepper
½ teaspoon dried rosemary
½ cup chopped ripe olives
½ cup madeira

Wash and dry the duck thoroughly. Rub the duck inside and out with the salt, pepper, and garlic. Heat the olive oil in a heavy 10–12-inch skillet. Sauté the onion over medium heat for 5 minutes. Break up the sausage meat and add it to the onion to brown. Cook the sausage thoroughly for about 10 minutes and pour off all the fat. Remove the skillet from the heat and mix in the diced toast, red pepper, rosemary, and olives. Stuff the duck with the sausage mixture and skewer the duck closed. Place the duck on a rack in a roasting pan and roast for 30 minutes in a preheated 425° oven. Remove the roasting pan from the oven and pour off the fat. Reduce the oven to 350°.

Return the duck to the oven and roast for another 30 minutes and pour off all the fat again. Add the madeira, pouring it over the duckling, and continue to roast the duck for an additional 1½ hours or until the duck is tender, basting frequently with the wine. To serve, place the duck on a warm serving platter.

NOTE: An excellent accompaniment to the roast duckling is Gnocchi à la Romaine (*see Index*).

DUCK WITH PEACHES

6 fresh peaches, peeled and
  halved
¼ cup peach brandy
2 tablespoons brown sugar
2 4–4½-pound domestic
  ducklings
1 tablespoon salt
1 teaspoon pepper

Place peach halves, cut side up, in a shallow baking dish and sprinkle ¼ cup brandy and the brown sugar over them. Cover and let stand 4–6 hours. Drain peaches and set aside, reserving any juices for the Peach Brandy Sauce.

Rub cavities of ducks with 1 tablespoon salt and 1 teaspoon pepper. Place ducks on a rack in a shallow roasting pan and roast in a preheated 400° oven for 45 minutes. Pour off the fat from time to time. Cool ducks at room temperature for 3–4 hours.

About an hour before serving, cut the ducklings in half, and using a very sharp knife, remove the backbone, breastbone, and ribs. Cut into quarters. Place the ducks on a rack in the broiler pan, prick skin all over with a fork, and broil 10–15 minutes per side or until the skin is crispy and the fat has cooked out. Turn the ducks once or twice, again pricking thoroughly with a fork to release as much fat as possible from under the skin. Have the broiler heat moderate or place the ducks 7–8 inches below the flame so that the skin becomes crispy but not burned.

Meanwhile, heat the peaches a few minutes in a 350° oven until just warm. Reheat Peach Brandy Sauce.

Arrange the duck on a large platter. Slice the peaches and arrange them over and around the ducklings. Pour about ⅓–½ of the Peach Brandy Sauce over the ducklings and pass the rest separately.

PEACH BRANDY SAUCE
Peel of 1 orange, cut in slivers
Peel of 1 lemon, cut in slivers
¼ cup sweet butter
3 tablespoons flour
2 cups brown stock (4 beef
  and 4 chicken bouillon
  cubes dissolved in 2 cups
  water)
Juice of 1 orange
Juice of ½ lemon
½ teaspoon salt
½–¾ cup peach brandy
Juice from 6 drained peaches
  (optional)
¾ cup white port
Pepper to taste

To prepare sauce, cook the orange and lemon peel for 5 minutes in 1 cup boiling water in a small saucepan. Drain, discarding the water, and set the peels aside. Melt the butter in the top of a double boiler over boiling water, skimming off foam as it forms. Slowly stir in flour and cook, stirring, until the roux is lightly browned, 5–7 minutes. Remove from the heat and cool slightly. Add brown stock and cook, stirring, over a low heat until smooth. Add the peels, the juices of the orange and ½ lemon, ½ teaspoon salt, ½–¾ cup brandy, juice from peaches, and port. Cook over a moderate heat until it is reduced by ⅓. Strain sauce and season to taste with pepper. Set aside until ready to reheat just before serving.

NOTE: This elegant entree is delicious with wild rice.

WILD DUCK IN MADEIRA

SERVES 4

4 wild ducks, cleaned and
  halved
⅓ cup flour
2 teaspoons salt
1½ teaspoons pepper
¼ cup olive oil
1 large onion, finely chopped
2 cups madeira
½ cup sherry
4 tablespoons chopped fresh
  parsley
1 4-ounce can ripe olives,
  chopped
1 orange, thinly sliced
Watercress sprigs

Dust the duck pieces with flour seasoned with 1 teaspoon salt and 1 teaspoon pepper. Brown over medium heat in a 10-inch skillet in olive oil 5–7 minutes per side. Remove duck to a 3-quart baking dish. Simmer the onion in the same olive oil until golden. Add the madeira, sherry, parsley, olives, 1 teaspoon salt, and ½ teaspoon pepper. Cook for 1 minute, adjust seasoning, and pour over the duck meat. Bake uncovered in a preheated 350° oven for 40 minutes, basting occasionally with the sauce. Serve with Wild Rice with Mushrooms and Almonds (*see Index*) and garnish with orange slices and watercress.

BARBECUED WILD DUCK

SERVES 4–6

1 bottle red wine (⅘ of a quart)
½ cup water
2 teaspoons kosher salt
1 teaspoon pepper
Juice of 1 lemon
3 stalks celery, cut in large
  pieces
3 onions, 2 cut into cubes,
  1 very thinly sliced
6 wild ducks
1 orange, cut into slices
Watercress sprigs

In a large mixing bowl make a marinade of the wine, water, salt, pepper, lemon juice, celery, and onion. Cut the ducks in half and marinate them for 8–12 hours, turning them several times.

Wrap the duck halves in foil and barbecue them over very low coals for 15 minutes. Remove the foil and barbecue the ducks for an additional 15 minutes, basting often with the reserved marinade. To serve, place the ducks on a platter and garnish with orange slices and watercress.

NOTE: This recipe is particularly good for the tougher, less flavorful ducks.

DUCKLING WITH ALMOND GRAVY

2 4–4½-pound domestic ducks
2 teaspoons salt
½ teaspoon pepper
3 oranges
10 slices raisin bread, toasted
2 oranges, sectioned, seeds and
    membrane removed
1½ cups diced celery
2 teaspoons grated orange peel
¼ teaspoon dried thyme
Watercress sprigs
Orange slices

ALMOND GRAVY
1 cup water
1 cup fresh orange juice
2 tablespoons cornstarch
1 teaspoon molasses
2 teaspoons soy sauce
1 teaspoon salt
½ teaspoon pepper
½ cup almonds, slivered
2 tablespoons butter

Rinse, dry, and rub the ducks with 1 teaspoon salt and ½ teaspoon pepper. Cut the three oranges in half and reserve them for the basting juice while the ducks are roasting.

To prepare stuffing, cut the crusts off the toasted raisin bread and break the bread into small pieces in a large mixing bowl. Add the two sectioned oranges, celery, orange peel, 1 teaspoon salt, and thyme. Stuff the ducks with the mixture, skewer-closed, and truss.

Arrange the ducks on a rack in an open roasting pan. Roast in a preheated 325° oven for 2–2½ hours or until tender. Drain the fat every 30 minutes. Baste frequently by squeezing half an orange over the birds. Rub the skin with same orange half. Add the orange skins to the roasting pan to add flavor while roasting.

Remove the ducks to a serving platter and keep warm while making the gravy. To serve, garnish the serving platter with sprigs of fresh watercress and orange slices. Pour Almond Gravy into a gravy boat and pass separately.

To prepare gravy, drain the fat from the juices in the roasting pan, reserving 1 tablespoon fat. Add the water to the pan, scraping the browned bits from the bottom, and strain the sauce into a 2-quart saucepan. Mix the orange juice with the cornstarch in a small bowl and add to the juices. Cook over low heat, stirring constantly, until the sauce is as thick as heavy cream, about 8–10 minutes. Add the molasses, soy sauce, 1 teaspoon salt, and ½ teaspoon pepper. Cook for 3 more minutes and strain the gravy again. Meanwhile, in a small skillet sauté the almonds in the butter over medium heat for 2–3 minutes. Add the almonds to the gravy.

RED WINE DUCKS

2 tablespoons salt
4 wild ducks, cleaned and
  halved
3 tablespoons butter
1½ cups chicken broth
½ cup dry red wine
2 tablespoons tomato paste
1¼ teaspoons pepper
1 bay leaf
½ pound fresh mushrooms,
  sliced
5 teaspoons cornstarch
5 teaspoons dry sherry

Sprinkle the salt over the ducks. In a 5-quart Dutch oven brown the birds in 1 tablespoon butter, about 5 minutes per side. Set the ducks aside and discard the drippings. To the same pan add the broth, wine, tomato paste, pepper, and bay leaf, stirring to blend. Replace the ducks in the pan, cover, and simmer until tender when pierced by a fork, about 1½–2 hours. Remove the ducks to a serving platter and keep warm.

Skim the fat from the remaining liquid and reserve the liquid. In an 8–10-inch skillet melt 2 tablespoons butter and add the sliced mushrooms. Sauté over medium heat for 4 minutes. Combine the cornstarch and sherry and add to the sauce along with the mushrooms, and cook over low heat, stirring constantly, until the sauce thickens, between 5 and 10 minutes. Serve the ducks on a platter surrounded by wild rice. Pour the sauce into a gravy boat and pass separately.

CORNISH GAME HENS ESTERHAZE

6 slices crusty French bread,
  ½ inch thick
1 cup dry white wine
4 slices bacon, uncooked and
  finely chopped
Livers from the game hens,
  finely chopped
6 sprigs parsley, finely chopped
1 medium yellow onion,
  finely chopped
8 fresh mushrooms, finely
  chopped
2 eggs, lightly beaten
1 teaspoon salt
1 teaspoon pepper
4 1-pound Cornish game hens
4 tablespoons oil

Preheat oven to 400°. Soak bread in the wine in a medium-sized mixing bowl for about 10 minutes or until it is limp. Place the bacon, livers, parsley, onion, mushrooms, eggs, salt, and pepper in a large mixing bowl. Remove the bread from the wine, squeezing out all the excess moisture. Add the bread to the rest of the stuffing ingredients and mix well. Starting from the breast cavity, use the forefinger to separate the skin from the flesh on the breast and legs of the hens, taking care not to break the skin. Insert the stuffing between the flesh and skin of the birds, pressing the stuffing to distribute it evenly.

Reduce the oven heat to 350°.

Brush each hen with 1 tablespoon oil and place in an uncovered roasting pan. Bake for 1 hour. Split the birds with poultry shears and arrange skin side up on a warmed serving platter. Serve at once.

STUFFED CORNISH GAME HENS
WITH WINE SAUCE

3 tablespoons bacon drippings
1 cup finely chopped onion
½ cup finely chopped green
   pepper
6–8 slices bacon, cooked and
   crumbled
3 cups small dry bread cubes
1 cup pecans, finely chopped
3 teaspoons salt
½ teaspoon dried thyme
1 teaspoon dried sage
6 1-pound Cornish game hens
½ cup butter
½ cup white wine
1 clove garlic, crushed
Watercress sprigs

WINE CURRANT SAUCE
3 tablespoons flour
1 cup white or red wine
1 cup currant jelly
1 tablespoon dry mustard
1 teaspoon salt

Heat the bacon drippings in a 10–12-inch skillet over moderate heat and sauté the onion and green pepper for 5–7 minutes or until they are tender. Remove from heat. In a large bowl mix the bacon, onion, green pepper, bread cubes, pecans, 1½ teaspoons salt, thyme, and ½ teaspoon sage. Toss the ingredients lightly with a fork until they are well mixed. Loosely stuff the cavities of the hens. Close openings of hens with toothpicks and truss securely. Arrange the hens breast side up in a small roasting pan.

Melt butter in a small saucepan. Add ½ cup wine, garlic, 1½ teaspoons salt, and ½ teaspoon sage and cook over low heat for 2–3 minutes. Use for basting the hens, which roast in a preheated 400° oven for 1 hour. Baste every 10–15 minutes. When the hens are cooked, remove to a serving platter and keep warm in the oven while preparing Wine Currant Sauce. To serve, garnish the serving platter with sprigs of watercress. Drizzle a small amount of Wine Currant Sauce over the hens and serve the remaining sauce separately.

To prepare sauce, degrease the roasting pan and remove all but ⅔ cup of the drippings from the pan. Add 3 tablespoons flour. Cook over low flame, stirring constantly, until the mixture is smooth, approximately 3–5 minutes. Add the wine, jelly, mustard, and salt. Bring mixture to a boil, loosening the brown bits in the pan. Reduce heat and simmer 8–10 minutes or until the sauce is thickened.

TURKEY AND ASPARAGUS BAKE

SERVES 6–8

2 pounds fresh asparagus, trimmed

4–5 tablespoons oil or butter

3 pounds turkey breast, sliced and skinned

10 tablespoons butter

10 tablespoons flour

3½ cups chicken broth

1 cup sliced fresh mushrooms

Dash pepper

½ cup dry bread crumbs

4 tablespoons minced fresh parsley

4 tablespoons slivered toasted almonds

4 tablespoons melted butter

Cook the asparagus covered in a 10–12-inch skillet in a small amount of boiling, salted water for 10–15 minutes or until barely tender when the ends are pierced with a fork. Drain well and set aside. Meanwhile, in another 10–12-inch skillet heat the oil (or butter, if desired) and sauté the turkey slices 10–12 minutes per side or until cooked through. Set aside while making the mushroom sauce.

Add 10 tablespoons butter to the skillet and melt over low-moderate heat. Add the flour, stirring constantly for 2–3 minutes. Slowly add the chicken broth, stirring, and cook the mixture until it is thick and bubbly, about 5 minutes. Add the mushrooms and pepper. Place the cooked turkey slices in the bottom of a 3-quart casserole dish. Drizzle the turkey with ½ of the mushroom sauce. Arrange the asparagus spears on top of the sauce layer and cover with the remaining sauce.

In an 8–10-inch skillet over moderate heat combine the crumbs, parsley, almonds, and melted butter. Cook this mixture for 3–4 minutes or until well blended, stirring constantly. Sprinkle the bread crumb mixture over the top of the casserole. Bake in a preheated 325° oven for 20–25 minutes or until heated throughout and bubbling. This is delicious served with a green salad and fresh hot bread.

NOTE: This recipe can be prepared a day in advance and held in the refrigerator until needed. Increase the cooking time by 10–20 minutes. Have the casserole at room temperature before placing it in the oven.

TURKEY ENCHILADAS WITH SOUR CREAM   SERVES 6

8 ounces whole green chiles
1 large clove garlic, minced
2 tablespoons oil
1½ pounds fresh tomatoes,
    peeled, seeded, and chopped
2 cups coarsely chopped
    onions
2 teaspoons salt
½ teaspoon dried oregano
½ cup water
3 cups shredded cooked turkey
    or chicken
2 cups sour cream
1 cup grated Cheddar cheese
⅓ cup oil
12 corn tortillas

Remove and discard the seeds from the chiles and chop the chiles finely. In a 10–12-inch skillet sauté the chiles with the garlic in 2 tablespoons oil over medium-high heat, stirring often. Add the tomatoes, onions, 1 teaspoon salt, oregano, and water. Simmer uncovered until thick, stirring often, for about 30 minutes. Remove from heat and set aside.

In a large mixing bowl combine the turkey, sour cream, grated cheese, and remaining 1 teaspoon salt, mixing well. Heat the ⅓ cup oil in a heavy 8–10-inch skillet. Cook each tortilla briefly in oil, turning once. Place each tortilla between paper towels in a stack to remove excess oil. Fill each tortilla with 4 tablespoons of the turkey filling, roll up, and place side by side, seam side down, in a shallow 8 × 12-inch baking dish. This may require 2 baking dishes. Pour the sauce over the top of the enchiladas and bake in a preheated 350° oven until heated through, about 20 minutes. If the dish is prepared ahead and held in the refrigerator, the baking time will be 25–30 minutes. Reserve the sauce in a separate container and do not pour over the enchiladas until they are to be baked. Serve with refried beans and beer.

PHEASANT CALVADOS   SERVES 4–6

2 pheasants
⅓ cup flour
8–10 tablespoons butter
⅓ cup calvados or applejack
1 teaspoon salt
½ teaspoon pepper
½ cup dry white wine
1 cup half-and-half
3 egg yolks, beaten
6 green apples, thinly sliced
¼ cup sugar

Bone the breasts and the thighs of the pheasants. Discard carcass. Shake the pheasant pieces in flour. Melt 6–8 tablespoons butter in a heavy 10–12-inch skillet and sauté the pheasant pieces very gently until it is ivory, not golden. This will take 3–4 minutes over a medium flame.

Pour the calvados over the pheasant and flame. Turn the pheasant pieces once or twice as the flame subsides. Add the salt, pepper, and wine. Bring the mixture to a boil over medium-high heat, lower the heat, and simmer partially covered for 6–8 minutes. Be careful not to overcook.

Remove the pheasant to a serving platter and keep warm. Meanwhile, add a few more drops calvados to the pan. Mix the half-and-half and egg yolks together in a small bowl and slowly stir this mixture into the pan juices, stirring constantly over a medium flame. Cook long enough for the sauce to thicken, but do not allow it to boil. Pour the sauce into a sauceboat to be passed separately.

In another 10–12-inch skillet sauté the apple slices over medium-high heat in 2 tablespoons butter until they are golden, about 5 minutes. Sprinkle the sugar over the apples to glaze them. Surround the pheasant with the apple slices.

NOTE: This dish is delicious with wild rice.

BREAST OF PHEASANT WITH HORSERADISH AND CREAM
SERVES 6

3 pheasants
1 teaspoon salt
½ teaspoon pepper
¼ cup butter
1 onion, diced
½ cup dry white wine
½ pint sour cream
¾ tablespoon horseradish
Parsley sprigs

Remove, bone, and split the pheasant breasts, making 6 cutlets. Reserve the remainder of the pheasants for other use. Season the breasts with the salt and pepper. Melt the butter in a 10–12-inch skillet. Sauté the onion and the pheasant breast cutlets over medium heat for 5–7 minutes per side or until the pheasant is lightly browned. Remove the pheasant from the heat. Arrange the pheasant cutlets in a single layer in a shallow casserole dish and cover with the pan drippings. Roast in a preheated 350° oven for 15 minutes. Add the wine and roast for 5–10 minutes more or until just tender.

Remove pheasant to a warm platter. Stir the sour cream and horseradish into the pan juices, stirring constantly to blend and taking care that the sour cream does not separate. Heat thoroughly, but do not boil. Pour the sauce over the pheasant and garnish with the parsley sprigs. Serve with Wild Rice with Mushrooms and Almonds (*see Index*).

PHEASANT PÂTE DE FOIE GRAS

SERVES 4

must be marinated overnight

2 pheasants
1½ cups port
¼ cup olive oil
1 tablespoon butter, melted
2½ teaspoons salt
1 tablespoon butter
3 scallions, including tops,
    finely chopped
2 tablespoons pâté de foie gras
¼ cup brandy
¼ cup dry sherry
¼ teaspoon pepper

Place the pheasants in a bowl just large enough to hold them comfortably and cover with the port. Marinate the pheasants overnight in the refrigerator, covered.

Remove the pheasants from the wine, reserving it for later use. Place the birds in an uncovered shallow roasting pan and brush them with the oil and melted butter. Sprinkle with ½ teaspoon salt. Roast in a preheated 400° oven for 15 minutes. Remove the birds from the oven and cut the breast meat into strips ½ inch wide, discarding the carcasses. Set breast meat aside.

Melt 1 tablespoon butter in a 10–12-inch skillet, add the scallions, and cook for 1 minute over medium heat. Add the foie gras, brandy, and sherry. Cook for 2 minutes more, stirring constantly to blend in the pâté. Add the reserved port, 2 teaspoons salt, the pepper, and pheasant meat. Bring to a boil over high heat, cover, reduce the heat, and simmer for 6 minutes. Serve at once with brown or wild rice.

QUAIL

SERVES 4

8 quail
1 lemon
8 tablespoons (¼ pound) butter
2 carrots, coarsely chopped
2 stalks celery, coarsely chopped
1 large onion, coarsely chopped
Salt and pepper to taste
¼ teaspoon dried thyme
3 bay leaves
3 tablespoons flour
1½ cups chicken broth, heated
1 cup red wine
2 tablespoons brandy
2 beef bouillon cubes

Wash and dry the birds. Rub the birds with cut lemon. Brown the quail in butter over medium heat for 7 minutes per side, using a heavy 3-quart ovenproof pan. When browned, remove the birds to a warm platter. Brown the vegetables over medium heat in the same pan used to brown the birds, adding salt, pepper, thyme, and bay leaves. Brown the vegetable pieces well. Put the birds on top of the vegetables and place the ovenproof pan in a preheated 400° oven. Cook for 30 minutes.

Remove the birds from the pan to a covered serving dish (3-quart casserole) and keep warm while making the sauce. Stir 3 tablespoons flour into the vegetables and juices in the pan. Cook sauce gently over medium heat for a few minutes and add the hot chicken broth, wine, brandy, and bouillon cubes. Increase the heat and boil for 5 minutes. Strain the juice directly over the birds in the serving casserole. Serve at once with wild rice.

NOTE: You may also use squab or Cornish game hens, using only 4 birds.

PALOMAS BORRACHAS (Drunken Turtledoves)   SERVES 8

8 doves or 4 Cornish game hens, halved
½ cup oil
½ cup warm brandy
1 pint cherry tomatoes
2 slices white bread, well toasted and cubed
½ cup blanched and slivered almonds
1 clove garlic, crushed
1 tablespoon minced fresh parsley
2 cups dry red wine
¼ cup raisins
⅓ cup sliced ripe olives
3 teaspoons grated lemon rind
1 teaspoon salt
½ teaspoon pepper
2–3 dashes ground cloves
2–3 dashes ground cinnamon
8 strips bacon

In a large skillet brown the birds in the oil on all sides over moderate heat for 10 minutes. Pour the warm brandy over them; ignite the brandy and let flame for 1 minute. Extinguish the flame by covering the pan.

Remove the birds to an ovenproof 3-quart casserole. In the same browning pan sauté the tomatoes, bread cubes, almonds, garlic, and parsley for 5 minutes over low heat. Add the wine, raisins, olives, and lemon rind. Season the sauce with the salt, pepper, cloves, and cinnamon. Simmer for a minute to blend the flavors, and correct the seasonings if necessary. Place a bacon strip on each bird breast and pour the liquid over the birds. Cook uncovered in a preheated 325° oven for about 45 minutes, basting occasionally with the juices. Serve directly from the casserole accompanied by plain wild rice.

DOVE WITH MUSHROOM SAUCE

SERVES 4

8 doves, well cleaned
¼ cup flour
½ teaspoon salt
½ teaspoon pepper
¼ cup butter
1½ cups dry white wine
12 medium-large fresh
    mushrooms, sliced
1 cup seedless grapes
4 tablespoons chopped
    hazelnuts
Buttered toast

Shake the birds in a bag with the flour seasoned with the salt and pepper. Melt the butter in a 10–12-inch skillet and brown the birds on all sides for about 10 minutes. Add the wine and mushrooms to the skillet, cover, and simmer over low heat for about 30 minutes or until tender. Add the grapes and cook for an additional 3 minutes. Add the nuts and heat the mixture through, stirring gently. Serve on buttered toast with some of the sauce spooned over the birds.

NOTE: A nice accompaniment is Herb Rice (*see Index*).

VENISON WITH CHILE VERDE

SERVES 8

⅔ cup olive oil
4 pounds venison, cut in
    ½-inch cubes
6–7 cups tomatoes, peeled and
    coarsely chopped
2 large onions, finely chopped
2 cloves garlic, minced
7 ounces green chiles, diced
2 teaspoons crushed dried
    oregano leaves
1 teaspoon ground cumin
1 teaspoon salt
½ teaspoon freshly ground
    pepper
⅓ cup fresh lime juice (about
    3 limes)

Heat the olive oil in a heavy 10–12-inch skillet over moderate heat. Brown the venison, a few pieces at a time, removing the browned meat to a 5-quart Dutch oven. After all the meat is browned, add the rest of the ingredients to the Dutch oven, cover, and simmer over low heat, until the meat is tender, approximately 2 hours. Serve with refried beans and hot, buttered, and salted tortillas.

NOTE: The cooking time for venison stew may vary from 1½ hours (young buck) to 2½ hours (old buck). Test for doneness at 1½ hours. As with any stew, the flavor improves daily.

SEVENTEENTH-CENTURY HAUNCH OF VENISON

SERVES 8–10

1 venison haunch, about
  8–10 pounds (*see Note*)
Olive oil
1 onion, diced
1 bunch scallions, whites only,
  chopped
1 stalk celery, chopped
2 carrots, peeled and diced
3 shallots, chopped
1 leek, white part only,
  thinly sliced
3 tablespoons butter
1 teaspoon dried thyme
1 teaspoon dried marjoram
1 teaspoon dried oregano
1 teaspoon dried rosemary
1 teaspoon salt
½ teaspoon pepper
6 or 7 whole cloves
½–1 gallon red wine
¼ pound salt pork
1 clove garlic, slivered
½ cup red plum or
  chokecherry jelly
⅛ teaspoon ginger
Juice of 1 lime
½ cup sour cream
Jigger of brandy

Wipe the haunch with a damp towel, then rub thoroughly with the olive oil.

To prepare marinade, sauté the onion, scallions, celery, carrots, shallots, and leek in the butter over a moderate heat until the onions are clear. Add the thyme, marjoram, oregano, rosemary, salt, pepper, 3 cloves, and 2 cups wine. Simmer until the vegetables are tender, about 8 minutes. Put the marinade in blender and purée, adding more wine if the blender complains.

Place the haunch in a large roasting pan. Mix the purée with 1 quart more wine and pour mixture over the haunch. Marinate at room temperature, basting often, for 6–7 hours. Drain the marinade and reserve.

Just before cooking, lard the haunch with the salt pork and insert a few tiny slivers of garlic at intervals. Roast in a preheated 300° oven for 25 minutes per pound, basting frequently with the marinade. When roast is done, remove to a serving platter and keep warm while preparing the sauce.

To prepare sauce, melt the jelly in the marinade in a large saucepan along with the pan drippings. Bring the mixture to a simmer over medium-high heat and add the ginger, 3 or 4 cloves, and lime juice. When the sauce has thickened, add sour cream and heat thoroughly. Stir in the jigger of brandy and serve.

NOTE: Two shoulder roasts weighing 4–5 pounds each may be used in place of a haunch. This recipe is delicious with Wild Rice with Mushrooms and Almonds (*see Index*), cherry tomatoes, Zucchini Soufflé (*see Index*), tossed green salad, crusty bread, and good red wine.

SAUTÉED VENISON STEAKS OR CHOPS

SERVES 4

4 venison steaks or 8 venison
   chops
1 teaspoon salt
½ teaspoon pepper
4 tablespoons butter

HORSERADISH CURRANT SAUCE
2 tablespoons currant jelly
1 cup sour cream
2 tablespoons horseradish

Season the meat with the salt and pepper. Melt the butter in a 10–12-inch skillet and sauté the meat over a moderate-high flame for 4–5 minutes per side until the meat is medium rare. Serve with Horseradish Currant Sauce, passed separately in a gravy boat.

To prepare sauce, melt the jelly in a small saucepan over a low flame. Add the sour cream and horseradish and heat through thoroughly. More jelly or horseradish may be added according to individual taste preferences.

NOTE: This dish is delicious with wild rice.

CHAPTER VI
LOS ANGELES

MEATS

Los Angeles began with probably the largest name and the smallest population of any major city in the world. El Pueblo de Nuestra Señora la Reina de Los Angeles de Porciúncula—the City of Our Lady the Queen of the Angels of Porciúncula—was destined from the beginning to be called something shorter.

It was a small group of weary travelers who arrived at the present site of Los Angeles on a hot September day in 1781. They numbered forty-four in all: eleven men, eleven women, and twenty-two children. Traveling over a thousand miles up through the dry wastes of Baja California, they founded a settlement beside the Los Angeles River. The main purpose of the new colony was to supplement the production of food for the existing missions in order to cut down on the costly amount of imports.

These early settlers, or *pabladores* as they were called, were a sturdy people, all but two of them having a mixture of Indian, African, and Spanish blood. They possessed strength, self-reliance, endurance—necessary qualities for survival in this empty, semiarid land.

The first order of business in founding the settlement was to establish the location of the plaza, a central park measuring roughly two hundred feet by three hundred feet. Around the plaza, the pabaladores built their first shelters of tules, or rush, soon followed by sturdier houses of adobe with reed roofs and dirt floors. On the land surrounding the plaza they planted crops, built ditches for irrigation, and laid out vineyards. The little village, or El Pueblo, as Los Angeles was called for almost a hundred years, was well established. It was a peaceful and quiet time, and on Sundays the bells at San Gabriel Mission, nine miles away, could be clearly heard in the plaza, calling the pabladores to service.

Within ten years, the Pueblo was a successful farming country of 139 people. There were twenty-nine adobes with reed roofs now sealed over with tar from the nearby La Brea Tar Pits. The pabladores also had built a town hall, a small church, a soldiers' barracks, a guard house, and a granary, all enclosed by an adobe wall.

By 1822 the population had increased to nearly 1,000, and a new, larger plaza church had been built, along with a house for the priests and a cemetery. This same year marked the secession of Mexico from Spain and the subsequent rule of California by Mexico.

Now the little plaza began to change considerably. Large town houses, mostly one-story adobes, were built by the neighboring rancheros. There were the Lugos of Rancho San Antonio, the Carillos, whose great-grandson Leo would entertain Americans of future generations, and Francisco Avila, whose granddaughter Louisa would one day live on Rancho San Pasqual, the site of present-day Pasadena. Clustered around these larger homes were the simple adobes of the poor Indians and Mexicans that made up the preponderance of the population.

Life moved at an easy, relaxed pace. The plaza, with its children, dogs, and dust, was the social center of the Pueblo. On Sundays or holidays, following church service, there was often a bullfight or a horse race. The Californio as well as the Indian loved these exciting sports and the opportunity for gambling.

At this time, a system of land grants—carved out of the vast mission holdings—was developing that was to affect the pattern of life in California for many years to come. Soldiers, retiring from service at any of the four presidios or the existing missions, were given, upon request, large areas of land called ranchos. These early grants were comprised of lands immediately adjoining the Pueblo, and each covered thousands of acres. These grants were merely permission to use the land to build a house and run cattle.

In the semiarid climate the land was good primarily for grazing, so large land holdings were an economic necessity. As the herds of cattle, horses, and sheep increased, so did the wealth of the rancheros. Along with an abundant supply of meat, the cattle produced the hides necessary for making furniture, ropes, buckets, door hinges, as well as shoes and saddles. The ranchos also grew what crops were needed for food, thus becoming self-sustaining.

As the herds of the missions and ranchos increased, a brisk trade developed in hides and tallow with the ships from New England. What the trading ships could bring to these isolated outposts of civilization far outweighed the illegalities of such trading under Spanish rule. Hides became the principal export. They came to be called "Yankee bank notes" and served as currency to buy luxuries as well as necessities from the Boston ships. Spices, sugar, tea, and tobacco as well as nails, pots, pans, and various other cooking utensils were traded for these "notes."

In 1833 the missions were secularized, and their tremendous land holdings were released to the ownership of private individuals. This act was inducement for more sophisticated people to come from Mexico to obtain land. Also, there were foreigners, mostly Americans, who arrived, married into Spanish families, and obtained ranchos of their own. The newcomers, along with the more prosperous Spanish families, produced a higher cultural level and a more civilized socioeconomic structure. Richard Dana commented that to a way of life that had been easygoing and in many cases just plain shiftless was now added a dash of Yankee drive, ingenuity, and keen business competitiveness that would slowly change the pace of life in California.

Approximately eight hundred ranchos were created by the division of the mission lands. In order to receive a grant, a man had only to fulfill three requirements: be Catholic; build a house; and run cattle (at least 150 head branded with a recognized brand). This was the day of the famed Spanish don, a flamboyant and romantic period whose influence still continues. The don, hospitable to a fault, openhanded and hot-blooded, lived a feudal life on his rancho—the owner of vast lands and large herds—whose word was absolute law. Surrounded as a rule by a large family, and waited on not only by paisanos but by Indians, the don was the lord of all he surveyed.

The hacienda, or don's estate, operated in much the same way as the missions, for it too was self-sustaining. The adobe house was a beehive of activity with the dona supervising the children's activities as well as the sewing, weaving, candlemaking, and soapmaking. She also supervised the cooking, much of which was done outside in the ramada—a brush-covered pavilion. The don, riding on horseback, administered everything on the outlying rancho.

For diversion, there were occasional trips for the family away from the hacienda. When a Boston ship arrived, the family went to the harbor to see the treasures while the don oversaw the loading of the hides and tallow into carettas, or large trunks. A real bed, rugs to lay on the dirt floors, or a table and chair were often purchased to add to the simple, homemade furniture on the rancho. There were beautiful fabrics, fans, slippers, and ribbons for the ladies, while for the don there were handsome boots, a fine hat, or a jacket embroidered in gold and silver thread. Payment for these purchases was made in hide and tallow.

Occasional visitors to the ranchos were hospitably entertained and often the reason for a lavish celebration. Most of the cooking was done outdoors—a custom that has endured in California. Barbecues featured whole steers cooked over coals, an abundance of fruits and vegetables, and a choice selection of wines and brandies. Entertainment for the guests included turkey shoots, bull and bear fights, cockfighting, and the popular horse racing.

Annual roundups were scheduled to separate the cattle belonging to neighboring ranchos that had wandered far and wide over the unfenced plains. Rancheros on surrounding ranchos gathered at a chosen rancho, bringing their families and vaqueros. The cutting out and branding took place under the watchful eye of a Judge of the Plains, whose rulings were final. Evenings were given to music, dancing, and singing. These annual roundups are commem-

orated today when Los Rancheros Visitadores ride out from the Santa Ynez Mission for five days through the hills and valleys inland from Santa Barbara.

Mid-century events brought rapid changes to the splendid rancho life of the Pueblo. First came the war between Mexico and the United States, and in 1847 the subsequent defeat of the Californios. When the victorious Commander Stockton entered the City of the Angels and headquartered at the Avila adobe in the plaza, the quiet, peaceful life in the Pueblo was never quite the same again. Gold was discovered at Coloma in 1849. Prospectors from all over Mexico, South America, and the East streamed through El Pueblo, providing nothing but trouble. As thousands poured into the northern mines, the value of a steer, formerly worth only $1.50 as a hide, now brought up to $50 a head as food for the gold seekers. It was then that the earliest cattle drives started north, quickly making the ranchero a very wealthy man.

After statehood was achieved, events moved rapidly in the Pueblo. A county hospital was established, a hotel was built—the Bella Union—and a newspaper was founded, the *Los Angeles Star*, printed in both Spanish and English. In 1858 the first stage of the famous Butterfield Overland Mail arrived in the plaza. Americans were coming West, obtaining ranchos and creating a demand for goods.

Along with these signs of progress came the Pueblo's most violent days. Miners returning empty-handed from the mines, Indians drunk on aguardiente (a grape liquor), and undesirables driven out of San Francisco by the vigilantes drifted down to the village on the Los

Angeles River. Cattle rustling, gambling, robberies, and violent deaths were common occurrences. Los Angeles was typical of the worst of the Wild West, and the law, what little there was of it, tried to cope in two languages. In a population of about four thousand, there was an average of twenty to thirty murders a month, excluding lynchings.

Various rancheros were also affected by these changes. The United States Land Commission, sent West to review deeds of ownership, found that of the eight hundred grants extant, two hundred could not be confirmed to the ranchero for lack of ownership papers.

In the early 1860s a drought came that lasted over two years, during which time not a single drop of rain fell. The loss in herds was somewhere between one and three million head. The great cattle empire that was once California collapsed.

In the 1870s and the 1880s the Americanization of the Pueblo, now more often called Los Angeles, became apparent. The town had a harbor at San Pedro, opening up trade with the whole world. A railroad spanned the country, and Easterners were coming West by train, enticed by the glowing reports of climate and business opportunities. In 1887 the Santa Fe Railroad was completed to Los Angeles, and with it came the first population explosion due partly to a rate war between the existing railroads.

Another impetus to the population growth of Los Angeles was the success of the orange industry in Southern California. The first navel orange trees were planted near Riverside in 1871, by Mrs. Eliza Tibbetts. She received a gift of two small orange trees from a stock originating in Brazil. Planting them outside her kitchen door to protect them from rabbits, she irrigated them with her dishwater. Five years later, the trees bore delicious, thin-skinned navel oranges. They were a far superior fruit to the old mission oranges. Buds were transplanted from these two trees and the California orange industry was born. Within a few years, navel oranges were shipped east from groves in Los Angeles, Pasadena, Riverside, and other areas of Southern California.

Los Angeles was by 1890 a bustling town. Stores, banks, and a new hotel—the Pico House, with wooden bathtubs—were added to the scene. The growing city now boasted a Chamber of Commerce, a theater (the Merced), and even some raised wooden sidewalks. The population was a mixture of Mexican, American, a few Indians, and Chinese, these last developing a close neighborhood of their own off the plaza.

With the greater influx of Americans, Victorian houses appeared, replete with band-saw work, fish scales, and cupolas and surrounded by gardens and orchards. Los Angeles became very civilized. The Victorians of Los Angeles enjoyed the outdoor life and the gentle climate. They drove in buggies, surreys, and wagons for picnics at the seashore or the mountains. They often camped out and barbecued their meals just as their predecessors had done on the rancheros. Mexican cuisine endured, but as people from other parts of the world came to Los Angeles, the new settlers also contributed to the gastronomical riches of the city. The mild climate allowed an abundance of foods, such as avocados, olives, grapes, figs, dates, and all kinds of citrus fruit, to be produced. The well-indoctrinated beef-eaters of Los Angeles soon learned to enjoy the native abalone and the clawless lobsters of the Pacific. On the old ranchos, towns sprang up as agriculture flourished. Groves of citrus, walnuts, and pomegranate trees dotted the landscape, while Los Angeles reached out farther and farther for the all-important water to support its growing industries.

Since its founding in 1781 the Old Pueblo has changed radically from a dusty little plaza with its adobes to the megalopolis of today. Los Angeles now consists of many small communities within the boundaries of one city. There is an overlay of concrete, glass, papier-mâché, and plastic among the freeway interchanges, movie theaters built to resemble Chinese pagodas, and six-foot-high plaster doughnuts; but this is a façade. The true essence of Los Angeles, with its imitation Venetian canals, Scottish castles, and movie-set aspects, is the triumph of individual spirit. The city is a polyglot of individuals all contributing to the whole. Those who came to California and Los Angeles brought their dreams with them, and, in one form or another, many of their dreams may have come true.

STUFFED CHATEAUBRIAND
WITH MADEIRA SAUCE

1 4-pound chateaubriand
¼ pound fresh mushrooms,
  finely chopped
½ small onion, finely chopped
3 tablespoons butter
½ teaspoon flour
2 tablespoons brandy
1 4–5-ounce can pâté with
  truffles
¾ pound bacon

Make a 1¾-inch-deep slash on the top length of the meat to form a pocket. Do not cut through the two ends of the meat. In a heavy 8–10-inch skillet sauté the ¼ pound mushrooms and the onion in 3 tablespoons butter over medium heat for 3–5 minutes. Sprinkle the ½ teaspoon flour over the mixture in the pan and add the brandy, stirring until slightly thickened. Simmer for 5 minutes, stirring frequently. Add the pâté, stirring well to blend. Remove the skillet from the heat and cool slightly. Stuff the mushroom mixture into the cavity in the meat. Layer strips of bacon lengthwise over the top and bottom of the meat. Tie the meat securely with string every few inches to hold in the mushroom mixture. Barbecue over medium hot coals for about 45 minutes or until the meat thermometer registers 130°. Turn a few times while barbecuing to cook evenly. Place meat on a warmed serving platter, remove the strings, and slice thinly. Serve with Madeira Sauce Merrill.

MADEIRA SAUCE MERRILL
3 tablespoons butter
1½ tablespoons flour
¾ cup beef stock
1 teaspoon English gravy
  thickener (such as Bovril)
¼ cup madeira
1 teaspoon Worcestershire sauce
⅓ cup minced sautéed fresh
  mushrooms

To prepare sauce, in a heavy 1½–2-quart saucepan melt 3 tablespoons butter over medium-low heat. Add the 1½ tablespoons flour, stirring well, and cook for 5 minutes. Add the beef stock, gravy thickener, madeira, and Worcestershire. Cook over mediun heat 3 minutes. Stir in the mushrooms. Serve with chateaubriand. This sauce may be made early in the day and reheated.

CHILLED FILLET OF BEEF
WITH SOUR CREAM DRESSING

Salt and pepper
1 3-pound fillet of beef
4 tablespoons butter
1 carrot, finely chopped
1 leek, white part only, finely
  chopped
1 stalk celery, finely chopped

Salt and pepper the beef and dot with 2 tablespoons butter. In a small roasting pan melt the remaining 2 tablespoons butter and sauté the carrot, leek, and celery over low heat for 8 minutes. Add the beef and place the pan in a preheated 500° oven for 25 minutes. Remove the beef from the oven and cool for 1 hour in the pan juices.

1 tablespoon oil
1 clove garlic, crushed
¾ pound bacon, cut in 1-inch
  pieces
¼ pound fresh mushrooms,
  sliced
1½ cups sour cream
2 teaspoons prepared
  horseradish
1 tablespoon grated onion
1 tablespoon finely chopped
  fresh parsley
1 teaspoon dried thyme
1 teaspoon dried chervil

In the meantime make the dressing. In a heavy medium-sized skillet heat the oil and garlic over moderate heat for 1 minute, then add the bacon. Sauté the bacon until barely crisp. Remove the bacon and drain it on paper towels. Pour off all but 3 tablespoons of the fat and sauté the mushrooms in the remaining fat over moderate heat for 3–5 minutes. Drain the mushrooms and set aside.

After the meat has cooled, remove it to a cutting board. Pour the pan juices into a medium-sized mixing bowl and add the sour cream, horseradish, onion, parsley, thyme, and chervil, blending well. Add the bacon bits and mushrooms. Salt and pepper to taste.

To stuff, slice a 1-inch-wide, 1-inch-deep wedge along the top length of the fillet and remove the wedge. Fill the cavity evenly with 3 tablespoons of the dressing. Replace the wedge in the fillet. To serve, cut through the fillet in complete ¾-inch slices and serve accompanied by the additional dressing.

PEPPER STEAK

SERVES 4

4 sirloin steaks, approximately
  8 ounces each
1 teaspoon salt
2 tablespoons black peppercorns
2 tablespoons white peppercorns
4 tablespoons plus 1 teaspoon
  butter
1 tablespoon oil
1 teaspoon flour
¼ cup beef broth
2 tablespoons heavy cream
1 teaspoon Dijon mustard
½ cup brandy
Watercress sprigs

Sprinkle the steaks with salt on both sides. Place the peppercorns in a small plastic bag and pound with a hammer or rolling pin. Spread the crushed peppercorns on a cutting board and press one side of each steak in them. Melt the 4 tablespoons butter and brush the other side of each steak. Chill the steaks slightly to set the butter. When ready to serve, sauté the steaks in the oil in a large skillet, butter side down, for 5 minutes over moderate heat. Turn the steak and sauté 5 minutes on the other side. Remove the steaks to a serving platter and keep warm. To the pan add 1 teaspoon butter, the flour, beef broth, cream, Dijon, and brandy. Simmer, stirring for 3–5 minutes. Serve the sauce over the steaks. Garnish with watercress.

PERFECT BARBECUED STEAK

1 top sirloin steak,
approximately 2 inches thick,
2½–3 pounds
1½ tablespoons lemon pepper
4 tablespoons butter
1 clove garlic, halved
½ teaspoon Worcestershire sauce

Trim the steak, leaving about ¼ inch fat around the sides. The steak must be at room temperature. Sprinkle on both sides with the lemon pepper and rub in well. Have the barbecue coals flaming hot before cooking.

Place the steak on the barbecue grill 2–3 inches from the coals. Barbecue 6 minutes per side. The steak will flame and char, allowing the juices to be sealed in. Place the grilled meat on a warm, ovenproof platter and place in a preheated 300° oven for 15 minutes. Remove the meat and turn the oven to 250°. Rub both sides of the meat with the cut clove of garlic and smear both sides with 3 tablespoons of the butter. Place the remaining 1 tablespoon butter on top of the meat and sprinkle with the Worcestershire. Return to the oven for 10 minutes. Remove from the oven and let sit for 4–5 minutes before carving. Slice in thin strips and arrange strips on the platter, pouring the pan juices over the top. Serve at once.

NOTE: This steak will be evenly rare. For medium-rare steak, barbecue a total of 7–8 minutes per side.

FLANK STEAK STUFFED WITH ZUCCHINI

1 2–3 pound flank steak
1 clove garlic, crushed
2 tablespoons soy sauce
3 tablespoons red wine vinegar
1 tablespoon Dijon mustard
¾ cup peanut or salad oil
1 teaspoon freshly ground
pepper
½ teaspoon nutmeg
Zucchini Stuffing (below)
Parsley sprigs
10–12 cherry tomatoes

Score the steak and pound slightly.

Mix together the next 7 ingredients in a small bowl. Place the steak in a shallow roasting pan and cover with this marinade. Let the meat sit at room temperature for at least 4 hours, turning often.

Place the steak flat on a large cutting board and spread Zucchini Stuffing on the flank steak to within 1 inch from each side and roll jelly-roll fashion, tying with string to secure. Place the meat in a shallow roasting pan and baste with some of the marinade. Roast in a preheated 450° oven 20 minutes for rare, 35 minutes for medium-rare. Baste and turn meat 2 or 3 times during cooking. Slice in ½-inch slices through meat and stuffing. Arrange slices on a warm platter and garnish with parsley and cherry tomatoes. A nice accompaniment is Tomato Pie (*see Index*).

To prepare stuffing, cook the sausage meat in a heavy 10-inch skillet over medium-low heat, stirring occasionally, for 5–6 minutes. Pour off all but 1 tablespoon of the fat from the pan. Add the onion and sauté 5 minutes. Add the zucchini and sauté another 5 minutes. Remove the skillet from the heat. Add the salt, egg, bread crumbs, almonds, and 3 tablespoons of the marinade to the sautéed mixture.

ZUCCHINI STUFFING
½ pound bulk sausage meat
1 large onion, chopped
1½ cups grated zucchini
¼ teaspoon salt
1 egg, slightly beaten
½ cup fresh bread crumbs
¼ cup slivered almonds
3 tablespoons flank steak marinade (*above*) or beef broth

GOURMET FLANK STEAK   SERVES 4

1 2-pound flank steak
2 tablespoons butter, softened
2 tablespoons Dijon mustard
1 teaspoon curry powder
1 teaspoon Worcestershire sauce
¼ teaspoon salt
¼ teaspoon pepper
½ cup plus a dash madeira or dry sherry
1 cup sour cream
2–3 tablespoons brandy
¾ pound fresh mushrooms, sliced
2 tablespoons butter
2 tablespoons finely chopped fresh parsley

Place the flank steak in a flat dish. Mix the softened butter, mustard, curry powder, Worcestershire, salt, and pepper together to form a paste. Spread the mixture on top of the flank steak. Pour the madeira or sherry over the steak. Place the steak in the refrigerator for 6 hours or more. Remove the steak from the refrigerator to reach room temperature before broiling.

Place the meat in a preheated broiler pan and quickly brown each side, about 2–3 minutes per side. Remove the meat from the broiler and cut into thin diagonal slices. Place the meat on a heat-proof platter and keep warm. Blend the sour cream and brandy into the broiler pan juices. Sauté the mushrooms in 2 tablespoons butter in a small skillet over moderate heat for 5 minutes. Add a dash of the madeira or sherry. Add the mushrooms to the sauce in the broiler pan and pour over the steak slices. Place platter under the broiler for 1 minute longer. Serve garnished with parsley, accompanied by No-Fail Popovers (*see Index*).

POT ROAST MADEIRA

¼ cup fresh orange juice
1 6-ounce can frozen orange
    juice, thawed
1 tablespoon grated orange peel
2 medium onions, finely
    chopped
1½ teaspoons salt
½ teaspoon pepper
¼ teaspoon ground cloves
1 teaspoon ground coriander
¼ teaspoon ground cumin
1 teaspoon sugar
1 3½-pound chuck roast
1 tablespoon oil
1 tablespoon butter
2 tablespoons cornstarch
4 tablespoons water
2 medium oranges, thinly sliced
¼ cup madeira

Place the orange juices, orange peel, onions, salt, pepper, cloves, coriander, cumin, and sugar in the jar of an electric blender. Blend on medium speed until well mixed. Place the meat in a large bowl and pour the marinade over the meat. Marinate in the refrigerator 4–6 hours, turning the meat occasionally to marinate evenly.

When ready to prepare, scrape the marinade from the meat and reserve. Heat the oil and butter in a 6–8-quart Dutch oven over moderately high heat and brown the meat well on all sides, about 4–5 minutes per side. Pour the reserved marinade over the meat, bring to a boil, reduce heat, and simmer covered for 2½ hours or until fork-tender. Remove the meat to a platter and keep warm. Blend the cornstarch and water and add to the juices in the pot. Cook over medium-low heat for 5 minutes. Add the orange slices and madeira and simmer over low heat an additional 10 minutes. Slice the meat and arrange on the platter. Remove the orange slices from the sauce and set aside. Pour the sauce over the meat, arrange the orange slices around the platter, and serve at once.

BRANDY AND WINE POT ROAST

SERVES 8

1 teaspoon dried thyme
1 teaspoon dried rosemary
1 bay leaf
1 5–6-pound chuck roast
1 clove garlic, split
2–3 teaspoons brandy
3½ tablespoons flour
    (approximately)
1 teaspoon salt
¼ teaspoon pepper
2 tablespoons bacon fat
¼ cup brandy
10 pearl onions, peeled
10 carrots, peeled and
    quartered

Tie the thyme, rosemary, and bay leaf together in cheesecloth to make an herb bouquet. Set the bouquet aside. Rub the roast with garlic and brush with 2–3 teaspoons brandy. Dredge the meat with about 2 tablespoons flour, the salt, and the pepper. In a 5–6-quart Dutch oven melt the bacon fat and sear the roast over high heat until brown on all sides. Remove the pot from the flame. Pour the ¼ cup brandy over the roast and ignite. When the flame subsides, add the onions, carrots, green pepper, beef stock, and wine. Add the herb bouquet. Bring the mixture to a boil, turn to simmer, and cook covered for 1½ hours. Add the tomatoes and mushrooms and simmer for 45–60 minutes longer.

¼ cup diced green pepper
2 cups beef stock
2 cups dry red wine
6 tomatoes, peeled and
   quartered
½ pound fresh mushrooms,
   quartered
3 tablespoons water
1 cup sour cream

Place the meat on a platter, surround with the vegetables, and keep warm. Discard the herb bouquet. Strain the pan juices and return to the Dutch oven. In a small bowl mix 1½ tablespoons flour with 3 tablespoons water. Place the Dutch oven over moderate heat. Stir the flour mixture into the juices and cook 5–8 minutes or until thickened to a nice gravy consistency. Turn the heat to low, add the sour cream, and bring to a simmer. Pour some of the sauce over the meat and serve the rest in a small serving bowl.

BEEF STEW WITH DILL AND ARTICHOKES   SERVES 6

4–6 tablespoons vegetable oil
2 cloves garlic, split
2 large onions, sliced
2½ pounds stewing beef, cut in
   1½-inch cubes
⅓ cup flour
½ teaspoon salt
½ teaspoon pepper
½ teaspoon dried dill weed
1 cup burgundy
1¼ cups beef stock
18 fresh mushrooms, quartered
4 tablespoons butter
8 fresh artichoke hearts, halved,
   or 1 9-ounce package frozen
   artichoke hearts, thawed
2½ cups biscuit dough or enough
   to make approximately 16
   biscuits
¼ cup butter, melted
¼ cup freshly grated
   Parmesan cheese

Heat 4 tablespoons of the oil in a heavy 3-quart pot over moderate-low heat. Sauté the garlic and onion 6–8 minutes or until soft. Remove the onion and garlic with a slotted spoon and set aside. Dredge the meat in the flour, salt, and pepper. Brown the meat, ⅓ at a time, over moderate-high heat, using the cooking oil from the onion and adding 1–2 tablespoons more oil as needed. Remove the meat and set aside as you brown. When all the meat is browned, return it to the pan along with the onion and garlic. Add the dill, wine, and stock. Cover the pot and simmer approximately 2 hours or until the meat is tender.

Sauté the mushrooms in the butter over moderate-low heat approximately 2–3 minutes. Add the mushrooms and artichoke hearts to the meat. Remove the garlic halves and place the stew in a 2½-quart casserole. Cut the biscuit dough into rounds and place on top of the stew. Bake in a preheated 400° oven 20 minutes. Remove the casserole from the oven and brush the top with the melted butter and sprinkle with the cheese. Return to the oven for 5 minutes. Serve with additional biscuits and a tossed green salad.

BEEF RAGOUT

3 pounds boneless chuck, cut
　into 1-inch cubes
½ cup plus 2 tablespoons flour
1 cup beef broth
½ cup dry sherry
¾ cup finely chopped onion
1 teaspoon curry powder
½ teaspoon dried oregano
¼ teaspoon dried basil
1 clove garlic, crushed
1 bay leaf
⅛ teaspoon garlic salt
1 teaspoon freshly ground
　pepper
2 strips bacon
1 stalk celery
12 baby carrots
2 mint leaves, finely chopped
4 small tomatoes, peeled,
　seeded, and cubed
½ pound fresh mushrooms,
　sliced
1 cup tomato purée
½ cup finely chopped celery
½ cup finely chopped fresh
　parsley
1 teaspoon salt

Roll the beef in ½ cup flour to coat evenly. Place the meat, broth, sherry, onion, curry powder, oregano, basil, garlic, bay leaf, garlic salt, and ½ teaspoon pepper in a Dutch oven. Place over moderate heat and bring mixture to a boil. Add the bacon and celery. Cover and bake in a preheated 350° oven 1–1½ hours or until the meat is fork-tender.

Cook the carrots and mint in 1 cup water in a saucepan over medium-low heat for 10–15 minutes or until fork-tender. Drain and set aside. Remove the Dutch oven from the oven. Remove the celery stalk and bacon. Place the pot on the stove over moderate heat. Sprinkle the 2 tablespoons flour over the meat, stirring to blend. Add the tomatoes and mushrooms. Simmer for 10–15 minutes. Add the carrots, tomato purée, chopped celery, parsley, salt, and ½ teaspoon pepper. Stir to blend. Place in a warmed casserole dish and serve. Can be made a day in advance.

CARBONADES A LA FLAMANDE

1 7-bone roast or blade of beef,
　approximately 5–6 pounds
5 tablespoons butter or
　margarine
1 tablespoon olive oil
4 onions, diced
2 cloves garlic, crushed
2½ cups dark beer
1½ teaspoons dried thyme
2 bay leaves

Cut the beef into 1-inch cubes, saving the bones. In a Dutch oven brown the beef in 2 tablespoons of the butter and the oil. Remove the beef from the pot and set aside. In the same pot sauté the onion and garlic in 3 tablespoons butter over moderate heat for 3–5 minutes or until golden. Deglaze the mixture with 1 cup beer. Return the meat to the pot, stirring well. Add the bones, thyme, and bay leaves. Pour in 1 cup beer. Add the salt and pepper. Bring to a boil, reduce to a

1 teaspoon salt
½ teaspoon pepper
2 tablespoons plum, nectarine,
  or strawberry preserves
3 tablespoons cornstarch

simmer, cover, and simmer gently for 1½ hours or until tender. Remove the bones and cool the mixture at room temperature for 5 minutes. Stir in the preserves. Mix the cornstarch with the remaining ½ cup beer. Add this to the pot, stirring over moderate heat until thickened, about 3–5 minutes. Continue cooking 3 minutes. Serve with parsleyed new potatoes and glazed carrots.

WINE-COUNTRY STEW

SERVES 6

2–3 pounds top sirloin, cut in
  2-inch pieces
2 tablespoons bacon fat
¼ pound Westphalian ham, cut
  in 1-inch pieces
2 large onions, chopped
25 stuffed green olives, halved
5 cloves garlic, wrapped in
  cheesecloth
¾ teaspoon dried thyme
½ cup raisins, soaked in hot
  water for 5 minutes and
  drained
1 bottle (but not more than 3
  cups) Petite Sirah, Zinfandel,
  or any full-bodied red wine
2 tablespoons green peppercorns
  or 2 teaspoons freshly ground
  pepper
1 teaspoon salt
4 tablespoons brandy
¾ cup heavy cream
Flour and water

In a heavy 12-inch skillet brown the beef in the bacon fat over moderate-high heat for 3–5 minutes. Add the ham and onion and sauté 3–4 minutes or until golden brown. Place the meat, onion, and ham in a large Dutch oven. Add the olives, garlic, thyme, raisins, and wine. Cover and place in a preheated 350° oven for 40 minutes. Add the peppercorns, salt, brandy, and cream and cook 30 minutes longer. Strain the juices from the pot and reserve. Remove the garlic cloves and discard.

Arrange the meat mixture in a serving dish and keep warm. Return the juices to the pot. For each cup of juice mix 1½ tablespoons flour with 3 tablespoons water until smooth. Add this to the juices, stirring with a wire whisk over moderate heat 2–3 minutes or until thickened. Continue cooking over low heat for another 5 minutes. Pour over the meat and serve with a simple rice dish and a buttered vegetable.

ESTOFADO (Beef Stew) SERVES 4

3 tablespoons olive oil
1 large onion, finely chopped
2 pounds lean stewing beef, cut
 into 1-inch cubes
2 cloves garlic, crushed
3 tablespoons red wine vinegar
½ cup tomato sauce
1 cup red wine
1 bay leaf
1 teaspoon dried oregano
½ teaspoon salt
⅛ teaspoon pepper
1 cup green chile salsa or 1
 7-ounce can chile salsa
2 tablespoons finely minced
 fresh parsley

In a 10–12-inch skillet heat 2 tablespoons of the oil over moderate-high heat. Sauté the onion for 3–5 minutes, stirring constantly. Remove the onion from the pan with a slotted spoon and set aside. Add the remaining oil to the pan and heat. Place the meat in the pan and brown well, stirring frequently. Return the onion to the pan. Add the remaining ingredients. Bring the mixture to a boil over high heat, reduce heat, and simmer covered for 1½–2 hours or until the meat is fork-tender. Turn into a warmed serving dish and garnish with the parsley. Serve with warmed fresh Corn Tortillas (*see Index*).

ORIENTAL BEEF WITH VEGETABLES SERVES 4–6

Choose 1 or a combination of
 the following vegetables (you
 will need 4–6 cups of
 trimmed vegetables):
Chinese pea pods or snow peas
Onions, quartered
Broccoli, trimmed and cut in
 small pieces
Bean sprouts
Water chestnuts, sliced
Mushrooms, quartered
Green or red pepper, sliced
Carrots, quartered
Scallions, halved
1 2-pound flank steak
¾ cup peanut oil
¼ cup soy sauce
¼ cup dry sherry
1 tablespoon sugar
1 clove garlic, crushed

Have all the vegetables you will use trimmed and ready for quick cooking. Cut flank steak in half lengthwise and then on a slant into pieces 1½ inches long and ¼-inch thick. Combine ¾ cup peanut oil, the soy sauce, sherry, sugar, garlic, ginger, cornstarch, and water in a jar and shake well. Place the meat in a shallow dish, add the marinade, and marinate for at least 1 hour, turning meat often. Cook just before you are ready to serve.

Preheat wok or frying pan until very hot, then add 1 tablespoon oil per 1 cup vegetables. Add vegetables immediately, making sure they are dry of any water, and stir-fry for 3–5 minutes. Sprinkle vegetables with garlic salt while frying. Vegetables should still be slightly crisp. Remove the vegetables to a large platter and keep warm. Clean the wok with paper towel. Drain meat very well and reserve the marinade.

1 teaspoon finely grated fresh
  ginger
2 teaspoons cornstarch
¼ cup water
Peanut oil for frying
¼ teaspoon garlic salt per 1 cup
  vegetables

Reheat the wok until very hot and add 3 tablespoons oil. Add meat to the hot oil and stir-fry 2 minutes. Add the marinade and cook, stirring, over medium heat until thickened, about 2–3 minutes. Arrange the meat on the platter with vegetables and pour the sauce over all. Serve with Steamed Rice Chinatown Style (*see Index*).

CALIFORNIA CHILI   SERVES 8

4 medium tomatoes, peeled and
  coarsely chopped
1½ cups water
1 large onion, chopped
2 stalks celery, chopped
½ teaspoon salt
½ teaspoon pepper
1 medium onion, chopped
1 green pepper, seeded and
  chopped
2 cloves garlic, crushed
4 tablespoons lard or bacon
  drippings
2 pounds round steak, trimmed
  and cut into ¼-inch cubes
1 pound lean pork, cut into
  ¼-inch cubes
1 tablespoon flour
5 tablespoons chili powder
2 bay leaves
1 tablespoon salt
1 tablespoon brown sugar
1 tablespoon dried oregano
1 tablespoon red wine vinegar
1 cup pitted ripe olives,
  coarsely chopped
1 cup Monterey Jack cheese,
  grated

Simmer the tomatoes, water, 1 large onion, celery, ½ teaspoon salt, and pepper in a medium saucepan for 30 minutes covered and another 30 minutes uncovered. Set aside. In a large Dutch oven sauté the medium onion, green pepper, and garlic in the lard for 3–5 minutes over moderate heat. With a slotted spoon remove the vegetables from the pan and set aside. Add the meats to the Dutch oven and brown over moderate-high heat for 5–8 minutes. Add more lard if necessary. Add the flour to the browned meat, stirring well. Simmer for 2 minutes. Return the vegetable mixture to the Dutch oven and add the chili powder, bay leaves, 1 tablespoon salt, brown sugar, oregano, and vinegar. Add the tomato sauce. Cover and simmer over low heat for 2 hours. Add the olives and cheese and simmer covered for an additional 45 minutes, stirring occasionally. Remove bay leaves. Serve in chili bowls, with a side dish of finely chopped onions. Accompany with a tossed salad and Skillet Corn Bread (*see Index*).

NOTE: The flavor of this dish is enhanced if it is made 24 hours in advance.

BURGUNDY PATTIES WITH MUSHROOM SAUCE

SERVES 4

1 medium onion, finely chopped
1 clove garlic, crushed
2 tablespoons vegetable oil
2 pounds ground round steak
⅓ cup burgundy
2 tablespoons finely chopped
    fresh parsley
½ teaspoon salt
¼ teaspoon freshly ground
    pepper
1 tablespoon Dijon mustard
½ teaspoon monosodium
    glutamate

MUSHROOM SAUCE
2 tablespoons safflower oil
1 pound fresh mushrooms,
    trimmed and sliced
1 tablespoon flour
½ cup consommé
½ teaspoon meat extract
1 tablespoon finely chopped
    fresh parsley

In a heavy 8–10-inch skillet sauté the onion and garlic in oil over moderately low heat until soft and golden, approximately 4–5 minutes. Stir frequently.

Place the meat in a large bowl with the burgundy, 2 tablespoons parsley, salt, pepper, Dijon, and monosodium glutamate. Add the sautéed onion mixture to the meat and mix well. Form the meat into 6 patties. Place on a preheated broiler pan and broil 4–5 inches from the flame for 5 minutes on each side for medium-rare. Serve with Mushroom Sauce.

To prepare sauce, in a medium skillet with a cover heat the oil over moderate-low heat for 1 minute. Add the mushrooms and cook covered for 5 minutes. Sprinkle the flour over the mushrooms and stir well.

Add the consommé and meat extract and simmer for 10 minutes. Add the 1 tablespoon parsley and mix well. Serve over Burgundy Patties.

NOTE: The sauce is very low in calories. It is also delicious over steak or as a sauce for a cheese soufflé.

RAMS STEAK SANDWICH

SERVES 6

⅔ cup beer
⅓ cup oil
1¼ teaspoons salt
½ teaspoon pepper
2 cloves garlic, crushed
2 pounds flank steak
4 tablespoons butter
½ teaspoon paprika
3 cups sliced onion

Combine the beer, oil, 1 teaspoon salt, pepper, and garlic in a jar and shake well. Score the flank steak and place in a shallow dish. Pour the beer marinade over the meat and let sit at room temperature 4 hours. When ready to serve, melt in a medium saucepan the 4 tablespoons butter with the paprika and ¼ teaspoon salt. Add the sliced onion and cook over moderate-low heat 16–20 minutes or until tender. Keep warm.

6 tablespoons butter, softened

6 sourdough rolls, split

¼ teaspoon dried parsley

¼ teaspoon dried tarragon

¼ teaspoon dried thyme

¼ teaspoon dried oregano

1½ cups sour cream

2 tablespoons prepared horseradish

Mix the softened butter with the herbs and spread on each half of the roll. Wrap rolls in aluminium foil and bake in a preheated 350° oven for 20 minutes. Remove the steak from the marinade and broil 3–5 minutes on each side for medium-rare. Thinly slice the meat on the diagonal and keep warm. In a small saucepan heat the sour cream and horseradish over low heat until warm. To serve, place 2 roll halves on each plate open-faced. Place slices of meat on the rolls, cover with the onion mixture, and top with sour cream. Sprinkle with paprika and serve with ice-cold beer and Cold Spiced Mexican Tomatoes (*see Index*).

MEAT LOAF BOURGUIGNON   SERVES 6–8

2½ pounds lean ground beef

½ pound ground pork or sausage meat

2 large onions, chopped

3 cloves garlic, minced

½ cup minced fresh parsley

2 teaspoons dried oregano

2 teaspoons dried thyme

2 teaspoons nutmeg

2 teaspoons salt

1 teaspoon pepper

3 tablespoons teriyaki sauce or 1 tablespoon soy sauce

2 tablespoons Dijon mustard

1 cup dry red wine

2 cups crushed unsalted crackers

½ cup finely minced walnuts

2 eggs, slightly beaten

½ pound Cheddar cheese, cut in ⅛-inch slices

Parsley sprigs

Into a large bowl place all the ingredients except the cheese and parsley sprigs in the order given. Knead the mixture well to mix thoroughly. Divide the mixture in half and form each half into a compact loaf approximately 1½ inches in depth. Place the cheese on the top of one of the loaves and top with the other loaf. Pinch the loaves together well, to seal. Place in a shallow roasting pan and bake in a preheated 400° oven 1 hour. Remove from the oven. Slice the loaf and arrange slices on a warm platter. Garnish with parsley sprigs.

JOE'S SPECIAL—SAN FRANCISCO

SERVES 4–6

1 tablespoon olive oil
1 tablespoon butter
1 pound lean ground beef
1 small onion, finely chopped
2 bunches fresh spinach, cooked,
    drained, and chopped, or
    1 10-ounce package frozen
    chopped spinach, thawed
    and drained
½ teaspoon dried basil
¼ teaspoon dried marjoram
1 teaspoon salt
¼ teaspoon pepper
4 eggs

In a heavy 11–12-inch skillet heat the oil and butter over moderate heat. Swirl to evenly coat the bottom of the pan. Add the meat and cook 5–7 minutes or until browned. Stir occasionally to crumble the meat. Add the onion and cook until tender but not browned, about 3–5 minutes. Stir in the spinach, basil, marjoram, salt, and pepper. Beat the eggs and add to the meat mixture, stirring over moderate heat for 3 minutes or until eggs are set. Good as a "wee hours of the morning" breakfast.

CALF'S LIVER SAUTÉ

SERVES 4

4 slices calf's liver, cut ½ inch
    thick
2 tablespoons oil
2 tablespoons butter or bacon
    fat
½ cup California brandy
1 tablespoon butter
1 teaspoon tomato paste
2 teaspoons Dijon mustard
1 cup heavy cream
1 teaspoon finely minced garlic
2 tablespoons finely chopped
    fresh parsley

Rinse and pat the liver slices dry and brush with a little brandy (not the ½ cup) on both sides. Allow them to sit for 3 minutes. In a heavy frying pan, using moderate to high heat, heat the oil and 2 tablespoons butter just to the sizzle point. Add the liver slices and brown on each side about 1 minute per side. Heat the ½ cup brandy in a small saucepan. Remove the brandy from heat and ignite. Pour over liver slices. Remove the liver from pan and keep warm. To the pan add the 1 tablespoon butter, tomato paste, and mustard. Lower the heat and slowly blend in the cream. Add the minced garlic and parsley. Simmer for 3 minutes. Serve over the liver slices.

BARBECUED INDIAN VEAL

SERVES 6–8

1 cup imported olive oil
¼ cup fresh lemon juice
¼ cup white wine vinegar
2 tablespoons curry powder
2 cloves garlic, crushed
2 teaspoons turmeric
1 teaspoon salt
1 fillet roast of veal,
   approximately 4 pounds
1 lemon, thinly sliced
8–10 sprigs parsley

Most people do not realize that curry and veal are deliciously attracted to each other. This recipe combines them nicely.

In a medium-sized bowl mix together the oil, lemon juice, vinegar, curry powder, garlic, turmeric, and salt. If you are fond of curry, use a little more than 2 tablespoons. Marinate the veal in a shallow dish for at least 3 hours, turning the meat occasionally.

To barbecue, light the fire about 30–40 minutes before cooking the veal. The coals should be evenly heated and glowing. Cook the meat 6–8 inches from the coals for about 5–6 minutes per side or until tender brown on the outside. The inside should be pale pink, almost white. Place on a small warmed platter and garnish with the lemon slices and parsley sprigs. Cut in slices and serve at once.

VEAL PICCATA

SERVES 4

2 pounds boneless veal round
   (approximately 9–10 small
   pieces)
1 teaspoon salt
½ teaspoon pepper
3 tablespoons flour
¾ teaspoon dried oregano
3 tablespoons olive oil
2 cloves garlic, crushed
1 large onion, chopped
1½ cups beef broth
¼ cup fresh lemon juice
8 slices lemon, cut paper thin
2 tablespoons capers
¼ cup finely minced fresh
   parsley

Rub the veal pieces with the salt, pepper, flour, and oregano. Heat the oil over moderate-low heat in a 12-inch skillet. Add the garlic and onion and sauté for 3–5 minutes or until soft but not browned. With a slotted spoon remove the onion and garlic and set aside. Raise the heat to medium-high and brown the veal slices on both sides. Return the onion and garlic to the pan and add the broth. Bring to a boil, cover, then turn to simmer for 10–15 minutes. Stir in the lemon juice and coat the veal slices evenly with the juice. Arrange on a heated serving platter and garnish with the lemon slices, capers, and parsley. A nice accompaniment is Gnocchi à la Romaine (*see Index*).

BRAISED VEAL PAPRIKA IN DILL SAUCE   SERVES 6

2½ pounds veal shoulder or
  boneless round, cut into
  2-inch cubes
3 tablespoons oil
1½ cups finely chopped onion
2 cloves garlic, finely minced
3 tablespoons sweet Hungarian
  paprika
1 cup white stock
1 cup white wine
1 teaspoon salt
½ teaspoon pepper
3 tablespoons flour
½ pound fresh mushrooms,
  quartered
3 tablespoons butter
½ cup heavy cream
½ cup sour cream
3 tablespoons finely chopped
  fresh dill weed or 1 tablespoon
  dried
2 tablespoons minced fresh
  parsley

In a heavy 3–4-quart casserole or saucepan brown the veal in oil over moderate-high heat for 3–5 minutes. Remove the meat to a platter. Sauté the onion and garlic in the same saucepan over moderate heat for 8–10 minutes or until golden. Add more oil if necessary. Remove the saucepan from the heat and stir in the paprika, coating the onions well. Return the saucepan to the heat and add the stock and wine, deglazing the pan by scraping up any bits sticking to the bottom. Return veal to the pan and sprinkle with salt, pepper, and flour, stirring well. Reduce heat, cover, and simmer for 1 hour. Check the meat carefully. It should be fork-tender. If not, cook for an additional 8–10 minutes.

In a small skillet sauté the mushrooms in the butter over medium-low heat for 6–8 minutes and add to the veal mixture. Stir in the heavy cream, sour cream, and dill. Simmer for 3 minutes or until the sauce is thickened and smooth, stirring frequently. Arrange the veal on a warm serving platter and garnish with the minced parsley. A nice accompaniment to this dish is Noodle Soufflé (see Index).

LEMON VEAL SCALLOPS WITH AVOCADO   SERVES 4

1 pound veal scallops, 5 or 6
  slices, about ⅛ inch thick
1 egg, well beaten
2 tablespoons flour
3 tablespoons butter
1 tablespoon oil
¼ cup vermouth
½ cup chicken broth
3 tablespoons fresh lemon juice
¾ teaspoon salt
¼ teaspoon white pepper
¼ cup chopped fresh parsley
1 large or 2 small avocados

In a small casserole soak the veal scallops in the beaten egg for at least 1 hour. Remove to a plate and sprinkle evenly with the flour, patting gently into both sides of the meat with your hands. Discard any excess flour. In a 10–12-inch skillet, with a lid, melt the butter and oil over moderate-low heat. Sauté ½ the veal scallops at a time for about 3 minutes per side or until lightly browned and remove to a plate. After all the pieces are browned, return all the meat to the skillet. Add the vermouth and stir gently. Add the broth, 2 tablespoons lemon juice, salt, and pepper, stirring in well. The sauce will become creamy. Turn the heat to simmer, cover, and cook about 10–15 minutes. During the last 5 minutes, gently stir in the chopped parsley.

While the veal is cooking, peel the avocado, cut into 8 even slices, and sprinkle with 1 tablespoon lemon juice. Place the slices in a small ovenproof dish and bake in a preheated 300° oven for 5 minutes. Place the veal slices on a warm serving platter and surround with the avocado slices. Pour the sauce from the sauté pan over all and serve at once.

OSSO BUCO

SERVES 4–6

2 veal shanks, cut into 2-inch thick slices
Flour
Salt and pepper
4 tablespoons butter
1½ cups dry white wine
2–3 cups Italian plum tomatoes
1½ cup veal or chicken stock
3 cloves garlic, finely chopped
½ cup grated lemon rind
¾ cup coarsely chopped fresh parsley

In a large bowl dredge the shanks with flour, salt, and pepper. In a heavy 12-inch skillet melt the butter over moderate heat. Add the shank pieces and fry 5–6 minutes or until they are nicely browned on all sides. Remove the shanks and place in a large flameproof and ovenproof pot. Set the pot over low heat, add the wine, and simmer for 5 minutes. Add the tomatoes, stock, ½ teaspoon salt, and ¼ teaspoon pepper. Place the pot in a preheated 325° oven and cook for 1½ hours. Remove the pot from the oven, stir in 2 tablespoons flour to thicken the liquid, and return the pot to the oven for an additional 30 minutes. Remove the pot from the oven and place the shank pieces in a serving dish. Stir the garlic, lemon rind, and parsley into the meat mixture in the serving dish. This is traditionally served with Risotto alla Milanese (*see Index*).

SWEETBREADS IN MUSHROOM SAUCE

SERVES 8

4 pairs veal sweetbreads
1 tablespoon white wine vinegar
1 teaspoon salt
¼ pound butter
2 teaspoons arrowroot
1 tablespoon powdered
  mushrooms
2 teaspoons tomato paste
1 cup chicken stock
⅓–½ cup dry sherry
½ teaspoon Beau Monde
  seasoning
½ bay leaf
Toast triangles

Wash the sweetbreads and soak in a 3-quart enameled saucepan in cold water to cover for 30–40 minutes. Add the vinegar and salt. Bring to a boil and simmer covered 15 minutes. Drain and cover with ice water. When cool enough to handle, remove all the membrane and tubes. Cut into cubes.

Melt the butter in a 10–12-inch skillet. Brown the sweetbreads lightly, about 3–5 minutes, over moderate heat. Remove the skillet from the heat and place the sweetbreads onto a plate with a slotted spoon. Stir the arrowroot into the remaining butter in the skillet. In a small bowl combine the powdered mushrooms, tomato paste, and chicken stock. Add this to the butter and arrowroot mixture. Bring to a boil, then simmer over low heat, stirring constantly, until sauce thickens slightly and is smooth, about 5 minutes. Add the sherry, Beau Monde, bay leaf, and sweetbreads. Simmer slowly for 15 minutes. Remove the bay leaf. Serve on triangles of toast.

LAMB WITH ARTICHOKES

SERVES 8

1 6–7-pound leg of lamb
2 teaspoons salt
1 teaspoon pepper
2 teaspoons crushed dried
  oregano
8–12 fresh artichoke hearts or
  1 package frozen artichoke
  hearts
1 cup tomato sauce
1 clove garlic, finely chopped
1 cup dry white wine
Dash Tabasco sauce
1 teaspoon sugar
1 lemon, thinly sliced

Bring the lamb to room temperature. Rub salt, pepper, and oregano into the lamb. Roast the lamb on a rack in a roasting pan in a preheated 325° oven for 1½ hours.

Prepare fresh artichokes according to the Boiled Fresh Artichokes recipe (*see Index*). (Thaw frozen artichokes.) Set aside.

Combine the tomato sauce, garlic, wine, Tabasco, and sugar in a 1–2-quart saucepan and simmer for 10 minutes over low heat.

Remove the lamb from the oven. Drain the excess fat from the juices in the pan. Place the meat in the roasting pan without the rack. Lay the lemon slices on top of the lamb and surround with the artichoke hearts. Pour the mixture from the saucepan over the lamb and cook for an additional 1 hour, basting several times with the pan juices. Meat thermometer should register 165° for a slightly pink, juicy lamb. Place the lamb on a warm serving platter and let it rest for 15 minutes before serving. Skim the excess fat from the pan juices. Surround the lamb with the artichoke hearts and a few lemon slices. Pour the warm sauce over the meat before serving.

ROAST LEG OF LAMB WITH CURRANT SAUCE

SERVES 8–10

1 6–7-pound leg of lamb
1 jigger (1½ ounces) gin
2 tablespoons Dijon mustard
1 clove garlic, crushed
½ teaspoon dried rosemary
1¼ teaspoons salt
¼ teaspoon white pepper
2 tablespoons flour
½ cup currant jelly
1¼ cups water
¼ cup gin

Wipe the lamb well and place on a rack in a roasting pan, fat side up. Blend the jigger of gin, the mustard, garlic, rosemary, 1 teaspoon salt, and the pepper to make a paste. Spread the mixture over the lamb. For a pink and juicy lamb, roast the meat in a preheated 325° oven for approximately 2 hours or until a meat thermometer registers 165°. For a medium to well-done lamb, roast the meat 2½–2¾ hours or until thermometer registers 180°. Remove the lamb from the oven and place on a serving platter. Keep warm while making the sauce.

Remove the excess fat from the pan drippings. To the drippings add the flour, stirring well, and simmer 3 minutes. Add the currant jelly and water and heat, stirring, until the jelly is melted. Add ¼ teaspoon salt and the ¼ cup gin, stirring to blend. Cook, stirring constantly, over moderate-low heat until the mixture thickens and boils, approximately 2–3 minutes. Remove the sauce from the heat and serve with the lamb.

NOTE: A nice accompaniment to this is Wild Rice with Mushrooms and Almonds (*see Index*).

SADDLE OF LAMB EN CROUTE
WITH MADEIRA SAUCE

SERVES 6

1 2½–3-pound saddle of lamb
1 tablespoon butter, softened
8 frozen patty shells, thoroughly
  defrosted (*see Note*)
Duxelles (*below*)
1 egg, well beaten
1 teaspoon water
Madeira Sauce (*below*)

Bone, trim, roll, and tie the saddle of lamb. It should be about 3½–4 inches in diameter and 6–7 inches long. Place in a roasting pan and allow the meat to come to room temperature while preparing the Duxelles and Madeira Sauce. (These may be prepared the day before and refrigerated overnight.)

Rub the tied saddle with 1 tablespoon softened butter. Cook in the roasting pan in a preheated 425° oven for 35 minutes. Remove from the oven and set the pan on a rack to cool. Let the lamb cool for 1 hour. Remove the strings and discard. Add any juice that has dripped from the meat to the Madeira Sauce.

On a lightly floured breadboard, lay out the patty shells in a rectangular shape, overlapping the edges slightly. Roll out the dough into a rectangle approximately 12 × 14 inches and ¼ inch thick. It should be 3 inches wider than the roast and long enough to wrap around. Cover the top of the roast with half of the Duxelles, spreading it evenly with a knife down the sides. With a broad knife, press the Duxelles carefully onto the meat. Place the roast, with the Duxelles side down, into the center of the pastry dough. Spread the rest of the Duxelles over the remaining side and ends of the roast, pressing in carefully. Bring up the ends of the pastry and seal all the edges, enclosing the entire roast. Pinch pastry edges together and seal with a little water. Cut off the excess pastry from the ends and save for decoration. Place the roast seam side down in a slightly oiled roasting pan.

Cut out simple flowers and leaves from the remaining pastry dough. Place decoration on top of the roast, sealing with a little water. In a small cup mix the egg and water together. Brush the roast liberally with this mixture, covering the top, ends, and sides. Roast in a preheated 400° oven for 30 minutes. The lamb will be rosy pink. If you are using a meat thermometer, it will register 135°. If you like lamb cooked medium, cook it another 10 minutes or until the thermometer registers 145°.

Allow the lamb to rest for 10–15 minutes before carving. Heat the Madeira Sauce to a simmer. Place the lamb on a warm serving platter garnished with a bouquet of parsley and accompanied by the sauce. Cut into ¾-inch slices.

To prepare Duxelles, wash, trim, and dry the mushrooms. Chop very fine. Taking a handful at a time, place the mushroom pieces in a dish towel and twist into a tight ball, extracting as much juice as possible. Repeat until all the mushroom pieces have been squeezed and set aside. Heat the 3 tablespoons butter and the oil in a 10–12-inch skillet over moderately high heat, until the foam subsides. Add the mushrooms and cook, stirring, for 2–3 minutes. Add the scallions and shallots and cook another 2–3 minutes, stirring constantly. Add ¼ cup madeira, the thyme, and rosemary and cook over high heat for 1 minute to boil down the wine until most of the moisture has evaporated. Remove the skillet from the heat and add the pâté, mixing it thoroughly. Add the egg yolk, salt, and pepper. Taste for seasoning. Cool. Place in a small mixing bowl, cover, and refrigerate for at least 2 hours.

To prepare sauce, place the bouillon, red wine, parsley, onion, carrot, and bay leaf in a heavy 1½–2-quart saucepan. Bring to a boil over high heat, reduce the heat, and simmer for 30 minutes. The sauce should have reduced to approximately 1½ cups. Strain into another saucepan of the same size, pressing the vegetables in a strainer to extract all their juices. Add ½ cup madeira and heat over low heat. In a small bowl make a *beurre manie* by mixing together the flour and 3 tablespoons softened butter. Stir into the sauce with a whisk until thickened. Remove from heat. Taste for seasoning and cool. Refrigerate covered until ready to use.

NOTE: The frozen patty shells are preferred not only for their convenience but because the dough cooks evenly through to a lighter, flakier crust. You could use ¾ pound of your favorite puff paste recipe instead.

DUXELLES

¾ pound fresh mushrooms
3 tablespoons butter
1 tablespoon cooking oil
2 tablespoons finely minced scallions (whites only)
2 tablespoons finely minced shallots
¼ cup madeira
⅛ teaspoon dried thyme
⅛ teaspoon dried rosemary
⅓ cup canned pâté de foie Gras
1 egg yolk, slightly beaten
½ teaspoon salt or to taste
⅛ teaspoon pepper or to taste

MADEIRA SAUCE

2 cups rich bouillon or beef broth
½ cup dry red wine
3 sprigs parsley
½ onion, coarsely sliced
1 carrot, cut in 4 or 5 pieces
1 bay leaf
½ cup madeira
2 tablespoons flour
3 tablespoons butter, softened

LEG OF LAMB STUFFED WITH SPINACH   SERVES 4–6

1 6–7-pound leg of lamb
½ pound sausage meat
5 tablespoons butter
1 medium onion, finely chopped
1 cup Seasoned Bread Crumbs I
   (*see Index*)
½ cup chopped fresh spinach,
   cooked and drained
1 tablespoon finely chopped
   fresh parsley
1 egg, slightly beaten
½ teaspoon salt
⅛ teaspoon pepper
2 large onions, sliced
6 large carrots, quartered
Herb bouquet: 1 stalk celery,
   4 sprigs parsley, 1 bay leaf,
   and a pinch of thyme,
   wrapped in cheesecloth
3 tablespoons flour
1 cup beef stock
1 cup dry red wine
6 fresh tomatoes, peeled and
   chopped

Have the butcher bone the leg of lamb, reserving the bones. Roll and tie the lamb, leaving an opening at each end for the stuffing. You will stuff from each end to the middle.

In a medium saucepan cook the sausage for 2 minutes over moderate-high heat, stirring constantly. Drain on paper towel. In the same saucepan melt 1 tablespoon of the butter and sauté the chopped onion until soft, about 2 minutes. Remove from the heat and mix in the sausage, bread crumbs, spinach, parsley, egg, salt, and pepper. Stuff the mixture into the cavity of the lamb. Melt 1 tablespoon butter in a large roasting pan with a lid and place the onions and carrots in it. Add the herb bouquet. Place the lamb bones over the vegetables. Lay the lamb on top of the bones, skin side up. Spread 1 tablespoon butter on the lamb. Bake uncovered in a preheated, 425° oven for 30–40 minutes or until well browned. Remove the lamb from the pan and sprinkle 1 tablespoon flour over the vegetables. Add the stock, wine, and tomatoes. Return the lamb to the pan. Cover the pan, reduce the oven to 350°, and bake for an additional 1 hour, basting often. Remove from the oven and arrange the meat and vegetables on a serving platter and keep warm. Discard the bones. Over a high heat reduce the pan juices by ⅓. Blend 2 tablespoons butter and 2 tablespoons flour together in a small bowl and add gradually to the juices. Cook over medium heat for 5 minutes. Pour the sauce over the lamb and vegetables. Serve with Rice Pilaf (*see Index*).

BARBECUED BUTTERFLY LEG OF LAMB

SERVES 6–8

1 cup dry red wine
¾ cup beef stock
3 tablespoons orange
   marmalade
2 tablespoons red wine vinegar
1 tablespoon minced dried onion
1 tablespoon dried marjoram
1 tablespoon dried rosemary
1 large bay leaf, crumbled
1 teaspoon seasoned salt
¼ teaspoon ginger
1 clove garlic, crushed
1 6–7-pound leg of lamb, boned
   and butterflied

In a 2-quart saucepan combine all ingredients except the lamb and simmer uncovered for 20 minutes. Place the butterfly lamb in a medium-sized (9 × 13) roasting pan. Pour the hot marinade over the lamb and marinate at room temperature 6–8 hours, turning frequently. Barbecue over medium hot coals for 30–45 minutes or until meat thermometer registers 150–160°. Lamb will be cooked to medium. Slice fairly thin on a slight diagonal and serve with Curry Pilaf (*see Index*).

GRILLED LAMB CHOPS

SERVES 4–6

2 tablespoons cider vinegar
1–2 cloves garlic, crushed
¼ teaspoon curry powder
½ teaspoon dry mustard
⅛ teaspoon cayenne pepper
3 tablespoons oil
6 lamb chops, 1½ inches thick
6 sprigs parsley
12 cherry tomatoes

With a wire whisk beat together the vinegar, garlic, curry powder, mustard, and cayenne in a small bowl. Add the oil gradually, beating well. Brush the marinade over both sides of each lamb chop and let the chops stand at room temperature for at least 30 minutes.

To barbecue, place the chops about 6 inches above hot coals and grill for approximately 6–8 minutes per side. They should remain pink inside. To broil in the oven, place the chops in a broiler pan and broil 4 inches from the flame for approximately 5–6 minutes per side. Place the chops on a warmed platter and garnish with the parsley and cherry tomatoes. Serve with Green Rice (*see Index*).

5 pounds combination of lamb
   shoulder, neck, and breast,
   cut into 2-inch cubes (reserve
   the trimmed fat and 2 or 3
   bones)
1½ tablespoons sugar
¼ cup flour
2 teaspoons salt
1½ cups beef broth
1 cup chicken broth
¼ teaspoon dried thyme
½ teaspoon dried rosemary,
   crushed
1 bay leaf
2 bunches fresh baby carrots
10 small white boiling potatoes
12 small boiling onions
6 small turnips
5 small yellow crookneck squash
1½ cups tiny peas, fresh or
   frozen
¼ cup finely minced fresh
   parsley

Place the lamb fat in a large baking pan and render in a preheated 500° oven for 10 minutes, stirring twice. Remove the pan and reserve 3 tablespoons of the fat. Discard the remaining fat. Place the meat in the baking pan. Mix the fat with the meat. Sprinkle the sugar over the meat and bake for 20 minutes uncovered, to draw the juices from the meat. Drain the meat juices into a 1½–2-quart saucepan and set aside. Mix the flour and salt together and sprinkle, evenly, over the meat. Return the meat to the oven for 20 minutes, stirring occasionally. Reduce oven to 375°.

Bring the meat juices to the boil over high heat and boil until reduced to ¼ cup. Add the beef and chicken broth, thyme, rosemary, and bay leaf and stir to blend well. Pour the broth mixture over the meat and stir to loosen any particles of meat sticking to the pan. Place the reserved bones in the pan with the meat. Cover the pan with a lid or foil and bake in the oven for 1¼–1½ hours or until meat is very tender. With a slotted spoon place the meat in a large bowl. Discard the bay leaf and bones. Strain the lamb sauce into another bowl. Skim the fat from the sauce and add to the meat. Cool and refrigerate until ready to serve (up to 24 hours).

To assemble, degrease the navarin again. Place the navarin in a 5–6-quart casserole with a lid. Bake in a preheated 300° oven for 45 minutes, stirring occasionally.

To prepare vegetables, peel the carrots, potatoes, onions, and turnips. Cut the carrots into 1-inch pieces. Cut the turnips into 1-inch rounded pieces. Leave the potatoes and onions whole. Cook each of these vegetables separately in covered saucepans in boiling salted water to cover for 15 minutes or until just tender.

Cut the ends from the squash and cut in half lengthwise. Cook in a covered saucepan in boiling salted water to cover for 8 minutes or until fork-tender. Drain the vegetables and add to the meat. Return the casserole to the oven and cook for 45 minutes. If using fresh peas, cook in boiling salted water, covered, for 5–8 minutes. If using frozen peas, thaw and drain thoroughly. Stir the peas into the casserole. Return the casserole to the oven for 30 minutes. To serve, stir in the parsley. Baste the top of the stew with some of the juice. Serve with a light salad and Whole-wheat Sunflower Bread (*see Index*).

LAMB SHISH KEBAB

SERVES 8

⅓ cup vegetable oil
6 cloves garlic, finely minced
¾ cup finely minced onion
½ cup fresh lemon juice
¾ cup smooth peanut butter
⅓ cup brown sugar, firmly packed
⅓ cup soy sauce
2 cups water
1 beef bouillon cube
1 teaspoon crushed dried green chile pepper or red pepper
½–1 teaspoon freshly ground ginger
⅛ teaspoon ground coriander
1 6-pound leg of lamb, cut into 2-inch cubes
2 green bell peppers, halved and seeded
½ fresh pineapple, cut into 1½-inch chunks
½ pound thick-cut bacon, cut in 2-inch pieces
4 small onions, quartered

In a heavy 12-inch skillet heat the oil and sauté the garlic and onion over medium-low heat for 10 minutes or until lightly browned. Add the lemon juice, peanut butter, brown sugar, soy sauce, water, bouillon cube, crushed pepper, ginger, and coriander. Simmer for 15 minutes. Cool, about 20 minutes. Place the lamb in a large bowl and pour the marinade mixture over the meat, tossing the meat to coat evenly. Marinate at room temperature at least 4 hours. Place the bell pepper halves in a large saucepan. Pour boiling water over them and boil 5 minutes. Plunge the peppers into cold water. Quarter each bell pepper half and set aside.

When ready to cook, pour the marinade off the meat into a small bowl and set aside. On 12-inch-long skewers, thread the lamb, pineapple, bacon, onion, and green pepper, allowing about 4–5 pieces of lamb and 2 of each of the other ingredients for each skewer. Brush ⅓ of the marinade over the skewered meat and vegetables. To cook in the oven, place the skewers on a rack in a large broiler pan and bake in a preheated 400° oven for 25–30 minutes or until meat is still pink inside. To barbecue, place the skewers over glowing coals about 6 inches from the flame and cook 20 minutes, turning and basting frequently. Strain the remaining marinade and heat in a small saucepan 10 minutes. Serve as a sauce with the shish kebab.

NOTE: A nice accompaniment to this dish would be Bulgar Pilaf (*see Index*).

MOUSSAKA

3 medium eggplants
1 cup butter (or ⅔ cup butter
   and ⅓ cup oil)
3 large onions, chopped
2 pounds ground lamb
2 pounds ground veal
4 tablespoons tomato paste
½ cup red wine
½ cup minced fresh parsley
¼ teaspoon ground cinnamon
1¼ teaspoons salt
½ teaspoon pepper
½ cup butter
6 tablespoons flour
4 cups milk
4 eggs, beaten
⅛ teaspoon nutmeg, preferably
   freshly grated
2 cups ricotta (or small curd
   cottage cheese)
3 tomatoes, peeled and cored
1 cup dry bread crumbs
1 cup freshly grated Parmesan
   cheese

Cut the unpeeled eggplants into ½-inch-thick slices. Melt 2–3 tablespoons of the butter in a 10–12-inch skillet over moderate heat. Add a layer of eggplant slices and brown on both sides, 2–3 minutes per side. Remove the browned eggplant to a large bowl. Continue browning the eggplant slices, adding additional butter or oil, as the eggplant soaks it up quickly. In the same skillet melt 2 tablespoons butter and brown the onion for 3–5 minutes over moderate heat. Add the ground meats and brown over high heat, stirring to break up the meat.

Combine the tomato paste, wine, parsley, cinnamon, salt, and pepper in a large mixing bowl. Add the meat mixture and mix thoroughly. Return this mixture to the skillet and cook over low heat, stirring occasionally, for 10 minutes or until most of the moisture has evaporated. Return this mixture to the large mixing bowl.

Melt the ½ cup butter in a 1½-quart saucepan over low heat. Stir in the flour and cook, stirring, for 1–2 minutes. Bring the milk to a boil in a separate saucepan. Add the hot milk gradually to the flour and butter, stirring constantly. Bring to a boil over moderate heat, then set aside until cool. Stir in the beaten eggs, nutmeg, and ricotta.

Slice the tomatoes thinly. Melt 1 tablespoon butter in the same skillet used for the meat and sauté the tomatoes for 5 minutes over medium heat, stirring occasionally.

Butter a 6-quart casserole or two 3-quart casseroles.

To assemble, place a layer of bread crumbs, then eggplant, then meat mixture, then Parmesan, then tomatoes, making 2 or 3 layers of each. Pour the white sauce evenly over the top layer. Poke holes through the layers with a kitchen fork so that the sauce will gradually sink to the bottom.

Bake in a preheated 375° oven for 1 hour or until the top is puffed and golden. Cool for 20 minutes. Serve with a green salad and buttered Greek peta bread.

NOTE: This casserole may be made early in the day and reheated for 20 minutes just before serving. The recipe may also be halved.

LAMB CURRY   SERVES 6

3 tablespoons vegetable oil
½ green bell pepper, seeded and chopped
1 large yellow onion, chopped
1 clove garlic, crushed
¼ cup applesauce
2 tablespoons flour
3 tablespoons curry powder or more, depending upon the degree of hotness desired
1 cup beef consommé
½ cup dry red wine
⅛ cup lemon juice
½ cup raisins
4 cloves
1 bay leaf
2 cups 1-inch-cubes cooked lamb
¼ cup shredded coconut
1 tablespoon sour cream
Salt to taste
1 tablespoon peanut butter

In a heavy 12-inch skillet heat the oil over moderate heat and sauté the bell pepper, onion, and garlic until the onion is transparent, approximately 5 minutes. Stir in the applesauce. Sprinkle the flour and curry powder over the mixture in the pan and blend well. Cook 3 minutes over moderate-low heat. Slowly stir in the consommé, wine, and lemon juice, blending well. Stir in the raisins, cloves, and bay leaf. Simmer until the mixture thickens, stirring constantly, about 5 minutes. Simmer uncovered another 15 minutes, stirring occasionally to prevent sticking. The mixture should have the consistency of a thick sauce. This much may be done ahead of time and refrigerated up to 24 hours in advance. If refrigerated at this point, reheat sauce 10–15 minutes. When ready to serve, add the lamb, coconut, and sour cream. Heat 3–5 minutes, stirring well. Salt to taste. Just before serving, remove the cloves and bay leaf and add the peanut butter. Correct the seasoning. Serve with hot buttered rice and bowls of the condiments of your choice, each with its own spoon. A simple tossed salad with a light dressing of oil and lemon juice is all that is needed to accompany the curry.

Suggested condiments: chutney, bean sprouts, sliced grapes or bananas, shredded coconut, grated Cheddar cheese, mashed avocado, crumbled cooked bacon, or any of the following finely chopped: green onions, hard-boiled eggs, oranges, mangoes, water chestnuts, radishes, apples, raw mushrooms, walnuts, pecans, peanuts, pineapple, green pepper, tomatoes, sweet pickles, celery, carrots.

NOTE: This recipe is infinitely expandable simply by doubling or tripling the ingredients.

LAMB SHANKS WITH CHUTNEY

SERVES 4

4 meaty lamb shanks
2 tablespoons oil
2 fresh tomatoes, peeled, seeded, and chopped
2 teaspoons curry powder
½ teaspoon ground ginger
1½ cups beef broth
½ teaspoon salt
1 clove garlic, minced
1 medium onion, finely chopped
½ cup chutney
¾ cup rice
1 tablespoon minced fresh parsley

In a large heavy skillet brown the lamb shanks well in oil over moderate-high heat for 5 minutes. Place them in a 3-quart Dutch oven.

In a blender place the tomatoes, curry, ginger, broth, salt, garlic, onion, and chutney and blend on low speed for 30 seconds or until well mixed but not puréed. Pour this mixture over the lamb shanks. Over moderate-high heat bring to a boil, then reduce to simmer, and cook covered for 2 hours. Skim the fat, add the rice, replace the cover, and simmer 30 minutes longer or until rice is cooked. Garnish with the parsley and serve with Watercress and Walnut Salad (*see Index*).

BAKED PORK TENDERLOIN WITH MUSTARD SAUCE

SERVES 6

½ cup soy sauce
½ cup bourbon
4 tablespoons brown sugar
3 pork tenderloins, ¾–1 pound each

Prepare the marinade by mixing together the soy sauce, bourbon, and brown sugar. Place the pork in a shallow dish and pour the marinade over it, turning the meat occasionally for 2–3 hours at room temperature.

Bake the meat in a roasting pan in a preheated 325° oven for approximately 1–1¼ hours. The meat should be tender and the juices should run clear when the meat is pierced with a fork. Carve the meat into thin, diagonal slices and serve with mustard sauce.

MUSTARD SAUCE
1 tablespoon dry mustard
4 tablespoons Dijon mustard
2 tablespoons sugar
½ teaspoon salt
2 tablespoons vinegar
4 egg yolks, beaten
1 cup heavy cream
2 hard-boiled eggs, finely chopped

To prepare sauce, put the 2 mustards, sugar, salt, vinegar, and beaten egg yolks in the top of a double boiler. Cook over simmering water, stirring constantly, until thickened, approximately 10 minutes. Cool slightly. Stir in the cream and hard-boiled eggs. Serve the sauce at room temperature. (This sauce may be prepared ahead and kept in the refrigerator for up to 3 days. It is also delicious on ham.)

NOTE: A nice accompaniment would be Orange Pilaf (*see Index*).

CROWN ROAST OF PORK WITH CRANBERRY STUFFING AND MUSTARD SAUCE BALCHAN

SERVES 8–10

1 crown roast of pork, trimmed
    of any excess fat,
    approximately 18 chops
Cranberry Stuffing (*below*)
Orange slices or spiced peaches
Watercress sprigs
Mustard Sauce Balchan (*below*)

CRANBERRY STUFFING
4 cups wild rice, cooked to
    package directions
2 cups raw cranberries,
    coarsely chopped
½ cup butter, melted
3½ tablespoons sugar
2 tablespoons grated onion
1 teaspoon salt
½ teaspoon dried marjoram
1 clove garlic, finely minced
½ teaspoon pepper
½ teaspoon mace
½ teaspoon dried thyme
½ teaspoon dried dill weed

MUSTARD SAUCE BALCHAN
4 tablespoons pan drippings or
    4 tablespoons butter
4 tablespoons flour
1 cup dry white wine
½ cup chicken broth
¼ cup heavy cream
3 tablespoons Dijon mustard
1 teaspoon dry mustard
Salt and pepper to taste

Cover the bone ends of the crown roast with foil to prevent burning in the oven. Place a piece of foil around the bottom of the roast so the stuffing will not leak through. Place the roast on a rack in a large roasting pan. Roast in a preheated 350° oven 20 minutes per pound. One hour before the roast has completed cooking, fill the middle of the crown with Cranberry Stuffing, piling it quite high. Extra stuffing can be put in a buttered baking dish, covered, and heated 30 minutes. Return the roast to the oven and roast an additional 1 hour. If the stuffing becomes too brown, cover it with foil. Place roast on a platter, remove the foil tips, and decorate with paper frills. Garnish with the orange slices or spiced peaches and the watercress sprigs. Pass Mustard Sauce Balchan separately.

To prepare stuffing, in a large saucepan combine the stuffing ingredients and cook over medium-low heat 10–15 minutes or until heated thoroughly. Stir the mixture often. Allow the stuffing to cool.

To prepare sauce, in a medium saucepan blend the 4 tablespoons pan drippings or butter with the flour. Cook the roux over low heat 3 minutes. Add the white wine and cook until thickened, approximately 3 minutes. Add the chicken broth and cream and cook and additional 5 minutes. Stir in the Dijon mustard and dry mustard. Salt and pepper to taste.

NOTE: The roast can be kept warm in a 200° oven while preparing the mustard sauce.

WHISKEY-BRAISED PORK

SERVES 6

1 tablespoon oil
3 pounds boneless pork roast
4 tablespoons Dijon mustard
½ cup brown sugar
3 carrots, cut in ½ inch chunks
1 medium onion, quartered
2 stalks celery, cut in 2-inch
    pieces
1 or 2 bones from the roast
½ cup scotch or bourbon
½ cup vermouth
¾ teaspoon salt
½ teaspoon pepper
¾ cup sour cream
½ teaspoon salt
⅛ teaspoon pepper
1 tablespoon butter
1 tablespoon flour
2 tablespoons minced fresh
    parsley
½ teaspoon dried tarragon
2 tablespoons minced fresh
    chives
Watercress or parsley sprigs

In a large heavy casserole with a lid heat the oil over moderate-high heat until very hot. Quickly sear the pork on all sides until well browned. Remove the meat from the pan and spread it with 3 tablespoons mustard and the brown sugar. Return the meat to the pan and add the carrots, onion, celery, and bones. Over a very low heat pour the scotch or bourbon over the meat and flambé. When the flame dies, add the vermouth, ¾ teaspoon salt, and ½ teaspoon pepper. Place the meat covered in a preheated 375° oven for 1½–2 hours, turning the roast 3 or 4 times. When ready, a meat thermometer will register 160–170°. Place the pork on a serving platter and keep warm while making the sauce. Reserve the pan juices.

To prepare sauce, strain the pork juices and degrease. Set aside. Heat the sour cream, ½ teaspoon salt, and ⅛ teaspoon pepper in a saucepan over low heat for 2 minutes. Mix the remaining 1 tablespoon mustard, butter, and flour in a small bowl to make a paste. Add the flour mixture and pan juices to the sour cream and simmer for 2–3 minutes. Stir in the 2 tablespoons parsley, the tarragon, and chives. Slice the pork in ½-inch slices and arrange attractively on the platter. Pour the sauce evenly over the slices. Garnish with the watercress or parsley.

PORK CHOPS WITH FRESH APPLES

SERVES 6

3 large pippin apples
2½ tablespoons sugar
¼ cup butter, melted
1½ cups dry white wine
¼ cup apple brandy
1 teaspoon ground cinnamon
Salt and pepper
6 pork chops, 1 inch thick
5 tablespoons butter
2 tablespoons flour
1 beef bouillon cube
Parsley or watercress sprigs

Peel, core, and halve the apples. Place the apple halves on a cutting board flat side down. Slice each half as a shingle in 5 or 6 slices, not cutting completely through the apple. Grease a shallow baking dish and dust it with ½ tablespoon of the sugar. Place the apple halves in the dish and pour the melted butter, ½ cup wine, and ¼ cup brandy over the apples. Sprinkle with the remaining 2 tablespoons sugar and the cinnamon. Place in a preheated broiler 6–8 inches from the flame. Cook, basting often, for approximately 25 minutes or until apples are golden brown and tender. Keep warm.

In the meantime, salt and pepper the chops. In a 12-inch skillet melt 3 tablespoons of the butter and brown the chops on both sides over moderate-high heat 3–5 minutes per side. Add ½ cup wine and ¼ cup brandy. Bring to a boil, turn heat to low, and simmer the chops covered for 20 minutes or until tender. Remove the chops and place on a warm platter.

In the cooking skillet melt the remaining 2 tablespoons butter, stirring to loosen any particles in the pan. Add the flour, stirring until thick. Add the remaining ½ cup wine, ¼ cup brandy, and the bouillon cube. Simmer over low heat for 5 minutes. Salt and pepper to taste. To serve, place an apple half on each chop and pour the sauce over the top. Garnish the platter with parsley or watercress and serve with Red Cabbage (*see Index*).

PORK CHOPS CALVADOS

SERVES 6

6 tablespoons sweet butter
6 loin pork chops, ¾–1 inch thick, well trimmed
¾ teaspoon salt
¼ teaspoon pepper
1 pound Gruyère or Swiss cheese, finely grated
3 tablespoons Dijon mustard
8 tablespoons heavy cream
6 tablespoons calvados or applejack
2 tablespoons finely chopped fresh parsley

Melt the butter in a 12-inch flameproof and ovenproof skillet over moderate heat. Add the chops and brown on both sides, approximately 5 minutes per side. Season the chops with salt and pepper and place the pan in a preheated 350° oven. Cover and bake for 45 minutes.

Mix together the cheese, mustard, and 3 tablespoons of the cream. Remove the chops from the oven and spread the cheese mixture on the chops. Place the chops under the broiler, 3–5 inches from the flame and broil until the top is browned and bubbly, approximately 3 minutes. Remove the chops to a serving platter and keep warm. Add the calvados to the pan and stir over medium heat, scraping up any bits clinging to the bottom of the pan. Turn the pan to simmer, add the remaining 5 tablespoons cream, and cook approximately 3 minutes or until the sauce is slightly thickened. Remove the chops from the oven, pour the sauce over them, and sprinkle with the parsley.

SWEET AND SOUR RIBS

5–6 pounds pork spareribs
1 cup tomato sauce
⅔ cup dry sherry
⅔ cup honey
¼ cup cider vinegar
¼ cup soy sauce
2 tablespoons sesame seeds
2 cloves garlic, crushed
¼ cup finely chopped onion
¼ cup finely chopped celery
1 teaspoon salt
1 teaspoon Worcestershire sauce
¼ teaspoon pepper
Dash hot-pepper sauce
½ teaspoon ground ginger
8–12 red crab apples
2 oranges, thinly sliced

Place the ribs in a single layer in a large baking pan. Put the ribs in a preheated 450° oven for 30 minutes. Remove the ribs from the pan and drain on paper towels. Put the ribs in a large roasting pan, about 12 × 18 inches. Reduce oven to 350°.

In a medium-sized saucepan combine the tomato sauce with the remaining ingredients except the crab apples and oranges. Simmer the sauce uncovered for 20 minutes. Pour the sauce over the ribs in the baking pan. Cover the pan tightly with foil and place in the oven for 40 minutes. Remove the foil and turn the ribs several times, coating each rib evenly with the sauce. Return the baking pan to the oven and bake uncovered for 40 minutes longer, basting often. Place the ribs on a warm platter and pour the pan sauce over them. Garnish with crab apples and thin slices of orange.

FARMER-STYLE SPARERIBS

20 meaty farmer-style spareribs
1 onion
6 whole cloves
1 teaspoon dried rosemary
1 teaspoon dried thyme
1 teaspoon dried marjoram
1 teaspoon dried oregano
⅔ cup catsup
2 tablespoons soy sauce
½ teaspoon ground ginger
4 tablespoons honey
1 clove garlic, crushed

Place spareribs in a 6–8-quart pot. Cover with cold water and bring to a boil. Peel the onion and stud with the cloves. Add to the spareribs along with the rosemary, thyme, marjoram, and oregano. Simmer over low heat for 20 minutes. Drain the spareribs well.

In a small bowl make a marinade of the catsup, soy sauce, ginger, honey, and garlic. Mix well. Place the ribs in a single layer in a large roasting pan and cover with the marinade, turning ribs to coat evenly. Let stand at room temperature for at least 2 hours.

Cover the spareribs with foil and bake in a preheated 350° oven for 30 minutes. Remove the foil and bake an additional 30 minutes, basting frequently. Serve at once.

BRANDY-GLAZED HAM

1 10–12-pound smoked ham, with the bone in
6 cups dry red wine
6 cups water
2 tablespoons Dijon mustard
¼ teaspoon ground cloves
¼ teaspoon ground cinnamon
¼ teaspoon ground ginger
¼ teaspoon ground nutmeg
¼ teaspoon pepper
3 ounces currant, pomegranate, or other tart jelly
¼ cup scotch
¼ cup brandy
½ cup brown sugar, well packed

Place ham in a large heavy pot or Dutch oven with a cover and cover the meat at least halfway with the equal parts of wine and water. Bring the mixture to a boil over high heat, reduce the heat, cover, and simmer for 2 hours, turning ham after 1 hour to cover the other side with the liquid. In the meantime, in a saucepan combine the remaining ingredients and heat until thickened, stirring well to blend.

Remove the ham from the pot and trim off all but ¼ inch of fat. Score the ham well and place it on a rack in a baking pan with the scored side up. Cover with ⅓ of the glaze and bake in a preheated 325° oven for 1 hour, basting twice with the remaining glaze. Let ham stand approximately 30 minutes before slicing.

NOTE: Do not let the ham cool between the simmering and the baking steps. Simmering the ham in the wine gives it a nice color and delicious taste, eliminating most of the saltiness. A nice accompaniment to this dish is French Carrots with Celery (*see Index*).

COLD HAM MOUSSE

4 cups cooked ham, ground
1 large onion, diced
½ cup golden raisins
2–3 tablespoons dry sherry or madeira
1 teaspoon prepared horseradish
½ teaspoon ground nutmeg
2 teaspoons Dijon mustard
2 tablespoons unflavored gelatin
2 tablespoons cold water
1 cup chicken stock
1 cup heavy cream
2 tablespoons finely chopped fresh parsley

Put the ground ham, onion, and raisins through the finest blade of a meat grinder 3 times. Place the meat mixture in a large bowl and add the sherry or madeira, horseradish, nutmeg, and mustard. Bring the chicken stock to a boil. Soften the gelatin in the water and dissolve the gelatin mixture in the boiling stock. Beat the dissolved gelatin into the ham mixture. Cool at room temperature approximately 10–15 minutes.

In a small bowl whip the cream until stiff and fold it into the ham mixture along with the parsley. Turn the mixture into an oiled 5-cup mold. Chill until set, approximately 3 hours. Serve with very thin slices of French bread or rye bread. The mousse would be nice on a picnic with cheese, wine, and Basque Pickled Beans (*see Index*).

HAM AND ASPARAGUS CASSEROLE

½ cup butter
½ cup flour
3 cups light cream
1½ cups milk
½ cup chicken broth
1 cup grated Cheddar cheese
½ cup grated Paremsan cheese
¼ cup fresh lemon juice
3 tablespoons grated onion
2 tablespoons finely minced
    fresh parsley
2 tablespoons prepared mustard
¼ teaspoon dried rosemary,
    crushed
2 teaspoons salt
½ teaspoon pepper
1 cup mayonnaise, preferably
    homemade (*see Index*)
2 pounds fresh asparagus,
    washed and trimmed, or 2
    10-ounce packages frozen
    asparagus
6–10 ounces spaghettini
3 pounds ham, cut in 1-inch
    cubes

In a medium saucepan melt the butter. Blend in the flour and add the cream, milk, and chicken broth. Cook over medium heat for 5 minutes, stirring constantly. Add the cheeses and lemon juice and mix well until cheese is melted. Blend in the onion, parsley, mustard, rosemary, salt, and pepper. Remove the mixture from the heat and stir in the mayonnaise. Cool.

To cook the fresh asparagus, lay the spears in a 12-inch pan. Pour boiling water over asparagus to cover and boil 10–12 minutes or until barely tender. Cool. If using frozen asparagus, cook according to package directions and cool. Cook spaghettini according to package directions until tender. Drain and rinse well.

In a large bowl mix together the ham, sauce, and spaghettini. Butter a 13 × 9-inch baking dish. Arrange layers of asparagus and sauce, starting with asparagus and ending with the sauce. Bake uncovered in a preheated 350° oven for 30–40 minutes or until bubbly. This may be prepared 2 days in advance and kept in the refrigerator, or it may be frozen. To reheat, bake 30–35 minutes in a preheated 300° oven. Serve with Oatmeal Bread or Casserole Rye Bread (*see Index*).

2½ cups dry red kidney beans
   or 3 15¼-ounce cans
6 tablespoons butter
3 medium onions, sliced
1 large green bell pepper,
   chopped
1 clove garlic, minced
3 pounds fresh mild Italian
   sausage
2 cups dry red wine
1 bay leaf
3 whole cloves
3 tablespoons tomato paste
Salt and pepper

If using dry kidney beans, soak or cook according to package directions, about 2 hours before proceeding with the recipe.

In a large skillet melt the butter and add the onions and green bell pepper. Stir in the garlic and cook for 5 minutes. Add the beans, which have been thoroughly drained. Brown the sausage in a separate medium-sized skillet over moderate-high heat, stirring occasionally. Drain the grease from the skillet. Slice the sausage into bite-size pieces and set aside.

In a saucepan bring the wine to the boiling point with the bay leaf and the cloves. Stir in the tomato paste. Discard the bay leaf and the cloves. Keep warm. Place ⅓ of the bean mixture in a buttered 3-quart casserole with a cover. Sprinkle with salt and pepper. Add ½ of the sausage and ⅓ of the beans, sprinkled with salt and pepper. Add the remaining sausage, then the remaining beans, sprinkled with salt and pepper. Pour the hot wine mixture over the top. Cover the casserole and cook in a preheated 300° oven for 1 hour. Reduce the heat to 275° and cook for an additional 1 hour.

NOTE: Can be frozen or made the day before and reheated.

CHAPTER VII

THE MISSIONS

BREADS, CAKES, & COOKIES

IN a spring day in 1769, two ships set sail from Lower California bound for San Diego. One hundred days later, those of the company who remained alive struggled ashore to found the first white settlement in Alta California. Today, the journey could be made in a little over an hour. San Diego is now a thriving and progressive city, but when the first settlers arrived, they found little to sustain them except their courage and determination to settle California for the greater glory of God and in the name of the King of Spain.

At the same time, in 1769, a land party of soldiers commanded by Don Gaspar de Portolá headed north from Loreto, Mexico, bearing the flag of Imperial Spain. In this party was Father Junípero Serra, a determined Franciscan priest whose vision of Christianizing Alta California finally produced a chain of twenty-one missions, stretching up the coast from San Diego to Sonoma.

Father Serra was already fifty-five years old when he was chosen to undertake the journey. He was not robust and had been lame most of his life. Nevertheless, he traveled overland approximately six hundred miles, walking most of the way, to join the rest of the Spanish settlers who had come to San Diego by ship. Struggling north up the hostile and forbidding land of Baja California, he came with the flag and the cross, in Spain's age-old pattern of conquer and Christianize.

Arriving in San Diego on a warm and sunny summer day in July, Father Serra had a brushwood altar built, erected a cross, and after celebrating mass, founded the first of the famous California missions, San Diego de Alcalá.

In the following three years, Father Serra founded four more missions in the same humble manner. A site was chosen where there was water, wood, and Indians. As quickly as possible a crude stockade was built, then a shelter for the priests, and finally the planting was started. It was necessary for these missions to be self-supporting as soon as possible in order to survive. Sheep, cattle, seed grain, and cuttings needed to be cared for. Mexico was far away and supplies could never be counted on. In the first years of these early missions, it was a long, hard struggle to survive in these lonely outposts of civilization, and all too often they existed on the ragged edge of starvation.

There were two padres assigned to each mission plus six or seven soldiers for their protection and some neophyte Indians brought up from Baja California. These Indians performed various jobs for the missions such as herding animals, hunting, farming, and even established a form of crude translation between the local Indians and the padres. Little by little, many of the local Indians would agree to be baptized. They then were called neophytes and lived near the mission under its discipline.

From these modest beginnings grew the mighty missions. San Diego was followed by San Carlos Borromeo at Monterey, later moved to Carmel, then San Antonio de Padua, San Gabriel Arcángel, San Luís Obisbo de Tolosa, and San Francisco de Asis. Others followed as the years went by, and a mission chain was forged that stretched for 650 miles. Father Serra died in 1784, after founding fifteen mission. He is buried at the Carmel Mission, where he spent most of his later years.

The missions were built to an exact

plan. First, a chapel; then, following an age-old patio concept, adobe buildings were built to form a quadrangle (with the church usually in the northeast corner) around a protected inner patio or compound. The missionaries were not architects but adapted their memories of the churches in Spain and Mexico.

Indian neophytes were trained in making adobe bricks. These building materials formed the church and the surrounding rooms for weaving, spinning, tanning, sewing, candlemaking, cooking—every industry that would make and keep the mission as self-sufficient as possible.

As the groups of neophyte Indians at the various missions grew in number, so did the herds, the fields of grain, the orchards, the vineyards, and the vast lands under mission control. Mission San Gabriel, for instance, eventually claimed the lands from the mountains to the sea and from the deserts beyond San Bernardino to the borders of San Fernando Rey de España, the next mission to the west.

While the missions themselves were usually built near the sea, as they grew in size and their ranchos extended farther and farther from the mission church, an asistencia, or tiny chapel, was often built far inland. Here a priest came every few weeks to hold services, baptize children, perform marriages, etc., so that isolated groups of vaqueros or farmers were not entirely cut off from the civilizing effects of Christianity. About ten missions built asistencias, but only one of these remains today. It belongs to Mission San Luis Rey. Father Peyri, while senior padre there, founded San Antonio de Pala in 1815. This small chapel, situated in what was at that time the major grain-producing area of San Luis Rey, still serves the Pauma Indians as it did 150 years ago.

As time passed, Mexican artisans were imported to train the Indians in tilemaking, stonecutting, and other building arts. Four mission churches were built of cut stone by these artisans. Tiles for roofs and floors were made not only for the churches but for all the adobe buildings in the mission.

When these quadrangles were finally completed, the mission compound became a very busy community. Not only was the mission a religious center, but it was also a center for various trades and businesses. Here the cloth was woven for the garments for all the neophytes as well as the resident soldiers. The mission fed everyone who worked or lived there and often sent food to other missions in distress. Should one of California's four presidios be nearby, the mission was responsible for helping clothe and feed the soldiers and their families.

The kitchen of any mission was usually a small, smoky room opening onto an arcade where most of the cooking was done. Utensils were homemade from local woods such as manzanita or oak. Anything made of metal would have to be imported, so metal pots were cherished. Huge iron vats, traded by New England whalers, were sometimes found in a mission kitchen. These vats were invaluable for storing tallow. Meats were usually barbecued over open grills while other foods were cooked in beehive ovens.

As early as 1770 the missionaries were importing and planting trees. The first ones were probably the olive trees planted at the Mission San Carlos, but olive trees have come to be associated with nearly all the missions. They grow well in California, which is fortunate, for the early settlers used olive oil not only for cooking but for lighting too. The padres also planted many kinds of fruit trees. They also brought to California the first grapevines. As many as twenty-five types of chile peppers grew in the mission gardens, and while corn and beans were dietary staples, the salubrious climate allowed all the fruits and vegetables indigenous to Spain to flourish.

The corn tortilla, a thin corn-meal cake, was a staple food item. It was sometimes eaten plain, but was also the basis of other dishes, such as the many varieties of enchilada. *Atole*, or corn porridge, was used in many different dishes.

Mission cooking was usually done by Indian women supervised by a padre. These Indian neophytes learned to make vinegar, yeast, and cheese, to cure olives, to dry fruit, and to make the beef jerky that the padres carried with them on their journeys. A surprising variety of breads and cookies originated in the mission settlements, many of which are still popular in California.

As the missions grew and prospered, their menus also became more diversified, adding such items as *huevas de chile*, an egg in chile dish; *torrejas*, a corn dough fritter; *jiricalla*, the nearest thing to ice cream they had; *champurrado*, a thick, very sweet chocolate drink; and various *relleno* dishes, stuffed, roasted green chiles.

In the early 1800s a very brisk trade in hides and tallow developed with ships from Mexico and later the Boston ships from New England. This trade became the economic lifeblood of the missions. They eventually made brandy and wine to enhance their trading power. While the laws of Spain forbade trading with any but Spanish ships, the needs of the mission often demanded discreet smuggling. This was not only a rewarding business, but intellectually satisfying to these educated priests whose daily routine was prayer and hard work. A new face on the horizon bringing news of the outside world, a few new ideas, a third person with whom to share a leisure hour were treats beyond price.

The missions became the hotels of early California, and travelers up and down the coast were warmly welcomed. Many travelers of different nationalities left records in reports and diaries of the hospitable reception they received and of the charm and erudition of the priests. Often some form of entertainment was provided by the Indians for a guest. The Indians had a natural love of music and often enjoyed playing on homemade musical instruments.

At some missions the Indians were taught to sing church music, and often the choirs achieved a certain excellence of performance. It was a little bit of beauty in a strange land. The long nave of the church decorated with colorful Indian designs, with the choir singing in the light of flickering candles, brought comfort to soldiers and to travelers from faraway lands. At San Juan Bautista the padres developed a choir that achieved a good deal of fame. In 1829 a hurdy-gurdy was given to the mission and immediately became a very popular source of music. The Indians loved to crank out the tunes, and the sacred cloisters often rang out with the sprightly rhythms of "Lady Campbell's Reel," "Go to the Devil," and "A College Hornpipe." This same music barrel one time served as a strong defense when a tribe of warring Tulare Indians attacked the mission. The padre, dragging the organ out into the open, started cranking away while the neophytes began singing at the top of their lungs. The Tulares, dumbfounded at first, finally became so enchanted with the recital that they laid down their weapons and demanded more music, eventually joining in with the chorus in a rousing song.

Bells were also an important part of the furnishings of each mission. Not only did they call the parishioners to service, but they announced important events and tidings. Many, cast in the eighteenth century, still hang in the towers built for them. There are many interesting stories about the history of the mission bells. One of the bells, at the San Fernando Mission, was cast in Russian-ruled Kodiak, Alaska, in 1797. It was brought down from Sitka in 1806 by Count Rezanov to trade for food for the Russian colonies. It is believed he gave the bell to Argüello while he was courting Argüello's daughter, Concepción, in San Francisco. How it found its way so far south to San Fernando is a mystery.

Another bell, one from the original set at San Gabriel, had an equally interesting career. Somehow, it was removed from the church in 1870 by a high wind and landed in a passing buckboard. After this remarkable wind, the bell's history becomes somewhat vague until it turned up years later, at Lucky Baldwin's nearby ranch. In 1930, many years after Baldwin's death, it was restored to the San Gabriel Mission.

By the time Mexico gained independence from Spain in 1822, the missions were the main industrial plants in California, and the Indians were the work force. The missions conducted a flourishing trade with ships from the East Coast as well as foreign countries. Hides and tallow were exported, along with wine, brandy, and grains, which in turn would bring metal goods, glass, furniture, cloth, and many other items so badly needed in this isolated province. California was cut off from the rest of our land mass by the high and rugged Sierra Nevada and the searing sands of the vast Colorado desert. The sea was the one approach to California. But colonists came in great numbers, and sailors often jumped ship to stay. Hungry eyes focussed on the tremendous land holdings of the missions. A few land grants had been made to soldiers retiring from mission or presidio duty, but these grants were only permission to use the land. More people now wanted to own the land, and pressures built to secularize the missions, freeing thousands of acres from church control.

The missions were frontier institutions set up to last ten years, after which they were to be turned over to the Indians to administer as pueblos while the mission church remained as the parish church. Knowing the Indians were not yet capable of this responsibility, the padres fought long and hard against the threat of secularization, but to no avail. In 1833 the Secularization Act was passed, and one by one the mission lands were carved up and given as land grants to a new breed of colonist, one who was to become the famed ranchero. California was entering into a new era, the day of the don.

Mission buildings themselves were often sold or given over to administrators, many of them Yankees, who doubtless tried to keep some semblance of order and production. This was an impossible task, as the land that supported the missions had been sold, the trade that supplied them had diminished, and the Indian work force had disappeared. Slowly the mission buildings fell into ruin. Rancheros, building homes on their new ranchos, helped themselves to roof tiles, window sashes, doors, or anything in the old mission complex that wasn't nailed down. Once the protecting roofs were gone, the adobe buildings crumbled away—a little more with each rain—while bats, owls, and lizards took up residence in the now deserted compounds.

In some missions a lone padre struggled on devotedly. In Santa Barabara the wealthy and devout parishioners rallied and supported the mission, at least saving the church and the priest's home from destruction.

Today, the twenty-one missions are where they always had been. A few of the missions stand in preserved ruins, but in most cases the church has been restored. At some sites the entire compound has been reconstructed. Anyone wanting to spend several days on this odyssey can start at San Diego and travel northward along the El Camino Real, the Royal Highway, following the same route the padres took over two hundred years ago. For whatever remains today, each mission in its own way will forever recall the name of Father Junípero Serra and those cowled Franciscan priests whose sandaled feet walked the long trail for the colonization and Christianization of California.

HINTS FOR BAKING BREAD AND CAKES

1.   If you have an electric oven, a way to provide the perfect temperature and atmosphere for rising bread dough is to preheat the oven to "warm" setting, then turn it off while you prepare the dough. Place the mixing bowl of finished dough on a centered shelf in the oven. Place a container of warm water under the bowl, on a lower shelf, and close the oven door. The inside of the oven should be a humid 80° or 85°. While checking the rising process of the dough, replenish the water to maintain the proper oven temperature. (A gas oven will provide its own warm atmosphere with the pilot light.)

2.   The best test for judging if a yeast bread has risen enough to be "punched down" or baked (as the recipe requires) is to poke two fingers $\frac{1}{2}$ inch deep into the dough. If the holes made by your fingers remain, continue with the next step of your baking.

3.   Home-baked bread is often a bit difficult to slice thinly for sandwiches or toast. The bread may be frozen and will then slice easily. What remains of the loaf may be returned in airtight plastic wrap to the freezer *unsliced*, as slicing permits air circulation and will cause the bread to dry out more rapidly.

4.   In all baking, unbleached flour may be used interchangeably with "all-purpose" flour. Unbleached flour enhances the flavor, texture, and nutritional value of baked goods.

5.   The quality of any cake is improved when its ingredients are at room temperature when mixed. A quick way to bring eggs to room temperature is to submerge them in a bowl of very warm tap water for 7–8 minutes.

6.   The use of a Teflon-coated bundt pan usually eliminates the problem of removing the cake without damaging its shape and crust. The cake's crust will be slightly crisper, but the flavor, inside texture, and cooking time will remain the same. (The cooking time on a cupcake-size bundt *may* be slightly less; test the inside middle with a toothpick about 5 minutes before cooking time has ended.) Grease *and* lightly flour the bundt pan before use, and allow the cooked cake to stand in the pan 10 minutes before removing.

MONKEY BREAD

1½ packages active dry yeast
¼ cup lukewarm water (110°)
3 tablespoons granulated sugar
1 cup milk
1 cup butter
1 teaspoon salt
4–5 cups flour, preferably
   unbleached
3 eggs, beaten

In a small bowl soften yeast in warm water until dissolved. Stir the sugar into yeast mixture.

In a saucepan, scald milk. Place ½ cup butter and salt in a large mixing bowl and over this pour the scalded milk, mixing to melt the butter. Cool the milk mixture to lukewarm (110°) and add the yeast mixture. Beat about 2 cups of the flour into the milk mixture, then beat in eggs, blending thoroughly. Add the rest of the flour, about 1 cup at a time, beating to form a soft but nonsticky dough. Turn out on a floured breadboard and knead well, about 8–10 minutes. Place dough in a greased bowl, turning to grease top. Cover with a damp cloth and let rise in a warm (80–85°) draft-free place until doubled in bulk, about 1 hour.

Punch down dough and divide in half for easy handling. Melt the remaining ½ cup butter. Grease a 10-inch tube pan. Roll out each half of dough on a floured board to a thickness of ¼ inch. Cut the dough into diamonds 3 inches on a side, using a floured cookie cutter or a sharp knife. Dip each diamond in the melted butter and layer in the tube pan, points overlapping. There should be about 3 layers and the ring should be no more than ¾ full (or pieces of dough will fall off during baking). Drizzle any remaining butter over the batter. Cover the mold and let dough rise again until almost doubled, about 1 hour. The dough should not rise above the edge of the pan.

Bake in a preheated 375° oven for 45 minutes. Cool 5 minutes. Turn out on plate and serve warm. Allow guests to separate and pull off pieces with 2 forks.

NOTE: The bread may be reheated, wrapped in foil, at 325° for 15–20 minutes.

TARRAGON POTATO BREAD

MAKES 2 LOAVES

2½ cups flour (unbleached or all-purpose)
2 packages active dry yeast
1½ cups milk
2 tablespoons granulated sugar
2 teaspoons salt
2 tablespoons butter
1 10¾-ounce can condensed cream of potato soup
½ cup sour cream
½ cup finely chopped fresh chives
1 teaspoon dried tarragon, crushed
4 cups flour (approximately)

In a large mixing bowl combine 2½ cups flour and the yeast. In a medium saucepan scald the milk, remove from heat, and stir in sugar, salt, and butter. Cool the milk mixture to lukewarm (110°), then stir it into the flour-yeast mixture. Blend the soup, sour cream, chives, and tarragon into the flour mixture and beat the batter at medium speed on the mixer for 1–2 minutes or by hand vigorously, until well mixed and smooth. With a wooden spoon beat in enough of the remaining flour, ½ cup at a time, to form a stiff dough. Turn the dough out on a floured board and knead for 8 minutes, adding enough additional flour to keep the dough from being sticky. Place the dough in a large greased bowl, turning it to grease the dough's surface. Cover with a damp cloth and let rise in a warm, draft-free place for about 1 hour or until the dough has doubled in bulk.

Punch the dough down, cover with a damp cloth, and let rise 15 minutes. Divide the dough in half, shape as loaves, and place in 2 greased 9 × 5-inch loaf pans. Cover and let rise in a warm place for 30 minutes or until almost doubled. Bake the loaves in a preheated 400° oven for 30–35 minutes or until loaves sound hollow when tapped. Turn the loaves out on a rack to cool.

CARMEL LOG CABIN BREAD

MAKES 2 LOAVES

2 cups boiling water
1 cup rolled oats (not instant)
2 packages active dry yeast
¼ cup lukewarm milk (110°)
¼ cup molasses
2 teaspoons salt
1 tablespoon butter
5 cups flour

In a large bowl pour boiling water over rolled oats and let the mixture stand for 1 hour. In a small bowl sprinkle yeast over lukewarm milk and allow the mixture to soften for 5 minutes. Mix the molasses, salt, butter, and yeast mixture into the oat mixture. Blend the flour, 1 cup at a time, into the oat mixture, beating with a wooden spoon to make a stiff, elastic, but still sticky dough. Cover the bowl with a damp cloth, place in a warm (80–85°) draft-free place, and allow the dough to rise until doubled in bulk, about 1 hour. Beat the dough down, divide it between 2 greased 9 × 5-inch loaf pans, cover, and let rise again in a warm place until doubled, about 45–60 minutes.

Bake the loaves in a preheated 375° oven for 30 minutes, then decrease the oven to 300° and continue baking them for 15 minutes more or until they are dark brown and hollow-sounding when tops are tapped.

NOTE: This molasses-flavored bread is delicious used for sandwiches, especially ham, or when toasted for breakfast.

COTTAGE CHEESE DILL BREAD

MAKES 1 LOAF

1 package active dry yeast
¼ cup lukewarm water (110°)
1 cup creamed cottage cheese, heated to lukewarm
2 tablespoons granulated sugar
1 tablespoon instant minced onion
1 teaspoon salt
1 tablespoon plus 2 teaspoons butter, softened
¼ teaspoon soda
1 egg
2 teaspoons dill seed
2¼–2½ cups flour
¼ teaspoon coarse salt

In a warm cup combine yeast and water and set aside to soften for 5 minutes. In a large bowl combine the cottage cheese, sugar, onion, salt, 1 tablespoon butter, soda, and egg. Add softened yeast mixture to cottage cheese mixture and stir well. Add dill seed. Mix the flour into cottage cheese mixture 1 cup at a time, beating well after each addition, to form a stiff and elastic dough. Cover the bowl with a damp cloth and let rise in a warm (80–85°) draft-free place for about 1 hour or until doubled in bulk.

Stir the dough down and place in a greased, round 1½-2-quart casserole or 6-cup soufflé dish. Let rise again in a warm place for 30–40 minutes.

Bake in a preheated 350° oven for 40–50 minutes, until well browned and hollow-sounding when top is tapped. Brush top with remaining butter and sprinkle with coarse salt.

NOTE: This recipe may be doubled and placed in 3 standard loaf pans. Serve the bread with a hearty soup.

WHOLE-WHEAT SUNFLOWER BREAD

MAKES 2 LOAVES

3 cups lukewarm water (110°)
¾ cup honey, at room
  temperature
2 packages active dry yeast
¼ cup butter, softened
4 cups whole-wheat flour,
  preferably stone-ground
3–6 cups unbleached white flour
2 teaspoons salt
1 cup unsalted sunflower seeds

In a very large mixing bowl combine and mix the lukewarm water, honey, and yeast until the yeast is softened, about 5 minutes. Blend the butter, whole-wheat flour, 1 cup unbleached flour, salt, and sunflower seeds into the yeast mixture. Beat the mixture by hand (at least 100 strokes) or with an electric mixer on low speed for 7 minutes. Slowly add 2 or 3 cups unbleached flour, beating with a wooden spoon, until a stiff dough is formed.

Sprinkle 1 cup of the remaining flour on a breadboard, turn the dough out on the board, and knead, continuing to add flour if the dough is sticky. Knead 8–10 minutes or until the dough is smooth and elastic. Place it, smooth side down, in a greased bowl and turn the dough to grease its top. Cover the bowl with a damp towel and place it in a warm (80–85°) draft-free place until the dough has doubled in bulk, about 1 hour.

Knead the dough down for 1 minute, cover, and let rise in a warm place again, until doubled (probably less than the amount of time required for the first rising; it will vary with the temperature and brand of flour used).

Punch down a second time, divide the dough in half, shape in 2 loaves, and place in greased 9 × 5-inch loaf pans. Place in a warm place and allow to rise to the top of the pans (possibly 45 minutes). Bake the loaves in a preheated 350° oven for about 1 hour or until they are well browned and hollow-sounding when the tops are tapped. Turn loaves out on a rack to cool.

NOTE: This is an all-purpose bread, excellent as an accompaniment to soup or salad, toasted for breakfast, or used for sandwiches. The sunflower seeds add a tasty-chewy texture to the slices. If desired, a slightly denser and even more nutritious bread may be made by using entirely whole-wheat flour.

CASSEROLE RYE BREAD

MAKES 1 LARGE LOAF

3¾ cups flour (approximately; unbleached is best)
1½ cups rye flour
⅓ cup dark brown sugar, packed
2½ teaspoons salt
1 tablespoon caraway seeds
2 packages active dry yeast
1 cup water
1 cup milk
2 tablespoons butter

In a large container combine the 2 flours. In a large bowl mix 1½ cups of the flour, the sugar, salt, caraway, and yeast. In a medium saucepan combine the water, milk, and butter and heat slowly over low heat until lukewarm (110°). Gradually add the milk mixture to caraway mixture and beat 2 minutes at medium speed on an electric mixer (or briskly by hand). Add 1 cup more flour to the mixture or enough to make a thick batter and beat at high speed for 2 minutes. Add remaining flour or enough to make a stiff batter that clings together. Stir or knead in bowl until well mixed. Cover with a damp cloth and let rise in a warm (80–85°) draft-free place until doubled, about 45 minutes.

Stir batter down and beat well for 30 seconds. Turn into a greased 1½-quart casserole or soufflé dish. Cover and let rise 30 minutes. Bake in a preheated 400° oven for 45–50 minutes or until dark brown and hollow-sounding when tapped. Remove from dish and cool on a rack.

CARAWAY CHEESE BREAD

MAKES 1 LOAF

2 cups flour, sifted
2 teaspoons baking powder
½ teaspoon baking soda
¾ teaspoon salt
¼ pound Cheddar cheese, finely shredded
1 tablespoon caraway seeds
1 tablespoon vinegar
1 cup milk
1 egg, beaten
1 tablespoon butter, melted

In a large bowl sift together flour, baking powder, baking soda, and salt. Mix cheese and caraway into flour mixture, tossing lightly to distribute. In a small bowl mix together the vinegar, milk, and egg and add, along with the butter, to flour mixture, stirring just enough to moisten. Mixture will be lumpy. Pour batter into greased 9 × 5 × 3-inch loaf pan. Bake in a preheated 350° oven for 50 minutes or until a toothpick inserted in the center comes out clean. Cool in the pan 10 minutes, then turn out on rack and cool completely or serve warm with butter.

NOTE: The bread may be stored, foil-wrapped, in refrigerator for 1 week or in freezer for 3 months. Reheat, foil-wrapped, at 325° for 15–20 minutes.

OATMEAL BREAD

must be prepared 24 hours in advance

2 cups milk
1 tablespoon shortening
1 cup rolled oats
½ package active dry yeast
¼ cup lukewarm water (110°)
4 cups flour
¼ teaspoon baking soda
1½ teaspoons salt
2 tablespoons granulated sugar

In a medium saucepan scald the milk, remove from heat, and add shortening. Pour milk over rolled oats in a large bowl and let stand for 1 hour. In a small bowl or measuring cup dissolve the yeast in water and add to the oatmeal mixture. Sift together the flour, soda, salt, and sugar and slowly add to oatmeal mixture, beating with a wooden spoon until well blended. Cover the bowl with a damp cloth and let the dough rise overnight.

In the morning beat the dough down by hand or stir thoroughly. Do not knead. Place the dough in a greased 9 × 5-inch loaf pan and grease the top with butter. Cover and let rise again in a warm (80–85°) draft-free place until doubled in bulk, about 45–60 minutes. Bake in a preheated 350° oven for 30 minutes, grease loaf top with butter, and continue to bake 30 minutes longer. Turn the loaf out on a rack to cool.

MILD CHEESE BREAKFAST BREAD

2 cups sifted flour (unbleached
    is best)
½ cup granulated sugar
4 teaspoons baking powder
1 teaspoon salt
¼ cup butter
1 cup shredded Cheddar cheese
½ cup chopped walnuts
1 egg, beaten
1 cup milk

In a large bowl sift together the flour, sugar, baking powder, and salt. With a pastry blender or 2 knives, cut in the butter until mixture resembles coarse meal. Stir the cheese and nuts into flour mixture. Stir the egg and milk into flour mixture, mixing just enough to moisten the flour. Pour mixture into a 9 × 5 × 3-inch greased loaf pan. Allow to stand for 20 minutes. Bake in a preheated 400° oven for 40 minutes or until loaf shrinks from the edge of pan. Cool in pan for 10 minutes. Turn out on rack and continue cooling. Slice while still warm and serve with butter, or cool completely and store, foil-wrapped, in refrigerator.

NOTE: This bread may be reheated in foil at 325° for 15–20 minutes, or by the slice in a toaster oven.

WALNUT AND HERB QUICK YEAST BREAD

MAKES 1 LOAF

1 cup milk
2 tablespoons granulated sugar
1 tablespoon salt
2 packages active dry yeast
1 cup lukewarm water (110°)
3 tablespoons chopped fresh
    parsley
1½ teaspoons dried basil,
    crushed
1½ teaspoons dried tarragon
⅛ teaspoon garlic powder
4½ cups flour, sifted
¾ cup walnuts, coarsely chopped

In a small saucepan scald the milk. Remove from heat. Add the sugar and salt and cool the mixture to lukewarm. In a large bowl sprinkle yeast over warm water, stirring until dissolved, about 5 minutes. Blend the milk mixture into yeast mixture. Add parsley, basil, tarragon, garlic powder, and 3 cups of the flour to the yeast mixture and beat at medium speed on a mixer (or vigorously by hand) for 2 minutes. Add remaining flour and beat by hand until batter is satiny (batter will be sticky). Cover with a damp cloth and let rise in a warm (80–85°) draft-free place until doubled in bulk, about 45 minutes.

Add walnuts and stir batter down, beating vigorously with a wooden spoon for about 1 minute. Turn into a greased 1½-quart casserole or soufflé dish and let rise, in a warm place, to the top of the casserole for about 30 minutes. Bake in a preheated 375° oven for 1 hour. Turn out of the dish and cool on a rack.

NOTE: This bread is excellent with Italian foods, soups, or salads. It requires as little as 2½–3 hours in total preparation time.

GREEN CHILE CORN BREAD

SERVES 6–8

1 cup yellow corn meal
3 teaspoons baking powder
½ teaspoon salt
3 eggs
1 cup buttermilk
½ cup butter, melted
1 cup corn, fresh from cob or
    frozen (thawed and drained)
4 ounces chopped green chiles
2 cups shredded Cheddar cheese

In a large bowl mix together the corn meal, baking powder, and salt. In another bowl beat eggs until well mixed and mix in the buttermilk, butter, and corn. Blend egg mixture into the corn meal mixture. Pour ⅓ of the batter into a greased 8- or 9-inch square baking dish and over this, layer ½ the chiles and ½ the cheese. Pour the remaining batter into the pan and top with the rest of the chiles and the cheese. Bake in a preheated 350° oven for 45 minutes. Serve warm, directly from the pan, cut in 2-inch squares.

NOTE: This tasty bread may be served with steaks, roast beef, or Spanish omelets.

GOUGÈRE (Puffed Cheese Ring)   SERVES 6

1 cup milk
¼ cup butter
½ teaspoon salt
Dash cayenne pepper
1 cup flour, unsifted
4 eggs
1 cup shredded Swiss cheese

In a 2-quart saucepan place the milk, butter, salt, and cayenne. Bring the mixture to a full boil and over medium heat add the flour all at once. Cook and stir vigorously until mixture clings together and leaves the side of the pan, about 2 minutes. Remove the mixture from the heat, cool slightly, and beat in the eggs (by hand), 1 at a time, until the mixture is shiny, smooth, and thoroughly blended. Beat ½ the cheese into the batter. Allow the mixture to cool.

On a greased cookie sheet, using an ice-cream scoop or large spoon, make 7 equal mounds, arranged in a circle and touching each other. This should use about ¾ of the dough. With the remaining dough, make a small ball on top of each of the larger ones. Sprinkle the top with the remaining cheese. Bake in the middle of a preheated 375° oven for 45–55 minutes or until puffs are crisp and brown. (Do not open the oven while ring is puffing.) Serve hot with butter.

NOTE: This is an excellent accompaniment to Chicken Salad or Seafood Salad (*see Index*).

SWISS CHEESE BREAD   MAKES 2 LOAVES

1½ cups milk
¼ cup dark brown sugar, packed
2 teaspoons salt
3 tablespoons butter
2 packages active dry yeast
½ cup lukewarm water (110°)
2 cups rolled oats
¼ pound Swiss cheese, grated
4 cups flour (approximately)

In a 1½–2-quart saucepan scald the milk and add the brown sugar, salt, and butter. Remove from heat and cool to lukewarm. In a large warm bowl sprinkle the yeast over warm water, stir, and let soften for 5 minutes. Stir the lukewarm milk mixture into the yeast mixture. Mix in the oats, cheese, and about 2 cups of the flour, beating until thoroughly blended (about 2 minutes on an electric mixer). Beat in enough remaining flour to make a stiff dough that clings together. Turn the dough out on a lightly floured board and knead 8–10 minutes, adding more flour if dough is sticky, until it is smooth and elastic. Place in a greased bowl, turning the dough to grease the top, cover with a damp cloth, and let rise in a warm (80–85°) draft-free place until doubled in bulk, about 1 hour.

Punch the dough down, divide in half, and shape into 2 loaves. Place the loaves in 2 greased 9 × 5-inch loaf pans, cover, and let rise again in a warm place until doubled, about 45–60 minutes. Bake the loaves in a preheated 375° oven for about 35 minutes or until well browned and hollow-sounding when tops are tapped. Remove the loaves from the pans and cool on racks.

NOTE: This bread is delicious when sliced, toasted, and buttered as an accompaniment to a green salad or a soup.

MOIST ZUCCHINI TEA BREAD

MAKES 1 LOAF

must be prepared 24 hours in advance

2 eggs
⅓ cup salad oil
½ cup granulated sugar
1½ teaspoons maple flavoring
1 cup shredded zucchini (approximately 2 small zucchini)
1¼ cups sifted flour
¼ cup wheat germ
1 teaspoon salt
1 teaspoon baking soda
¼ teaspoon baking powder
½ cup finely chopped walnuts
3 tablespoons sesame seeds

In a large bowl beat the eggs with a mixer on low speed until blended. Add the oil, sugar, and maple flavoring. Continue beating until the mixture is thick and foamy. Stir the zucchini into the oil mixture. In another bowl combine and mix the flour, wheat germ, salt, baking soda, baking powder, and walnuts. Add the flour mixture to the oil mixture, stirring just enough to blend. Pour into a greased and lightly floured 9 × 5 × 3-inch loaf pan. Sprinkle the sesame seeds evenly over the top. Bake in a preheated 350° oven for 1 hour or until a toothpick inserted in the center comes out clean. Cool the loaf in the pan for 10 minutes. Turn the loaf out of the pan and cool completely on a rack. Wrap in foil and store 1 day before slicing.

NOTE: This bread keeps well refrigerated for 2 weeks or frozen for 3 months. The recipe may be doubled for 2 loaves.

ORANGE AND PRUNE TEA BREAD

MAKES 1 LOAF

must be prepared 24 hours in advance

1 cup pitted prunes
2 medium oranges
1 teaspoon baking soda
½ cup fresh orange juice
2 tablespoons butter, melted
⅔ cup granulated sugar
1 egg
½ teaspoon vanilla extract
2 cups sifted flour
2½ teaspoons baking powder
½ teaspoon salt
1 cup chopped walnuts

Place the prunes in a medium saucepan, cover with water, and simmer over low heat for 10 minutes. Drain, cool, chop the prunes, and set them aside.

Trim a thin slice from each end of the unpeeled oranges, cut them in half lengthwise, and remove the white cores. Cut the halves in wedges and purée them in the blender to make 1¼–1½ cups purée. Place the purée in a medium bowl and sprinkle with the soda. Bring orange juice to a boil in a small saucepan and pour over the purée. Set the orange mixture aside. In a large bowl blend together the butter, sugar, egg, and vanilla extract until smooth. In another bowl sift together the flour, baking powder, and salt and add to the sugar mixture, all at once, along with the orange purée. Blend until smooth. Add the prunes and nuts to the sugar mixture. The batter will be thick.

Pour batter into a greased 9 × 5-inch loaf pan and bake in a preheated 300° oven for 1 hour or until a toothpick inserted in the center comes out clean.

Cool in the pan on a rack for 10 minutes, turn the loaf out on the rack, and cool completely. Store 1 day before slicing.

NOTE: This bread, served with butter, makes a nice luncheon accompaniment. Store the bread, foil-wrapped, in the refrigerator for up to 2 weeks or in the freezer for 3 months. The recipe may be doubled.

DATE TEA BREAD

MAKES 1 LOAF

must be prepared 24 hours in advance

1 cup dates, pitted
2 tablespoons sweet butter,
  softened
¾ cup granulated sugar
1 egg

Simmer the dates with 1 cup water over low heat in a small saucepan for about 5 minutes or until dates are softened. Drain the dates and chop fine. In a large bowl cream the butter and sugar until fluffy. Add the egg and beat until blended.

1 ripe banana, mashed
1 cup flour
1 teaspoon baking soda
½ cup raisins

Stir in the banana. Sift together the flour and baking soda and add to the creamed mixture, stirring until well blended. Stir in the raisins and dates. Pour the mixture into a greased 8½ × 4½-inch loaf pan. Bake in a preheated 375° oven for 55–60 minutes or until a toothpick inserted in the center comes out clean. Remove the pan to a rack and cool for 10 minutes. Remove the loaf from the pan and cool completely on a rack. Wrap loaf in foil and store for 1 day before slicing.

NOTE: Keeps refrigerated for 3 weeks or frozen for 3 months. The recipe may be doubled for 2 loaves.

ORANGE COAST MARMALADE BREAD   MAKES 1 LOAF

must be prepared 24 hours in advance

1½ cups plus 2 tablespoons
   sifted flour
1½ teaspoons baking powder
¼ teaspoon salt
½ cup granulated sugar
1 egg
1 tablespoon butter, melted
½ cup milk
½ cup marmalade
½ cup chopped walnuts

Into a large bowl sift together the flour, baking powder, salt, and ½ cup sugar. In another bowl beat the egg and combine with butter and milk. In a small saucepan bring the marmalade to a simmer. Pour the milk mixture, all at once, into the flour mixture and stir gently, just enough to blend. Immediately stir in the simmering marmalade and nuts. Pour the batter into a greased 9 × 5 × 3-inch loaf pan and bake in a preheated 350° oven for 1 hour or until a toothpick inserted in the center comes out clean. Remove the pan to a rack and poke several holes in the loaf. Drizzle Orange Bread Pour over the warm loaf and allow it to cool in the pan 15 minutes. Remove the loaf from the pan and cool completely on the rack. Wrap in foil and store at least 1 day before slicing the bread.

ORANGE BREAD POUR
2 tablespoons orange juice,
   fresh or frozen
2 tablespoons orange liqueur
¼ cup granulated sugar

To prepare pour, heat orange juice, orange liqueur, and ¼ cup sugar together in a small saucepan over low heat, stirring until the sugar is dissolved.

NOTE: The bread keeps refrigerated 3 weeks or frozen for 3 months. The recipe may be doubled for 2 loaves.

VERY LEMON BREAD

must be prepared 24 hours in advance

¼ cup butter, melted
1 cup granulated sugar
3 tablespoons lemon extract
2 eggs
1½ cups sifted flour
1 teaspoon baking powder
1 teaspoon salt
½ cup milk
1½ tablespoons grated lemon
   rind
½ cup chopped pecans

LEMON POUR
¼ cup lemon juice
½ cup granulated sugar

In a large bowl mix the butter, 1 cup sugar, and the lemon extract. Beat the eggs into the butter mixture. In another bowl sift together the flour, baking powder, and salt. To the butter mixture add the flour mixture alternately with the milk, beating just enough to blend. Fold in the grated rind and nuts. Pour the batter into a greased and floured 9 × 5 × 3-inch loaf pan. Bake in a preheated 350° oven for 1 hour or until a toothpick inserted in the middle comes out clean. Cool 10 minutes. Remove the bread from the pan and while still warm drizzle Lemon Pour over the top and into the cracks that form while baking. Store, foil-wrapped, for 1 day before slicing.

To prepare pour, in a small bowl combine the lemon juice and ½ cup sugar and mix well.

SKILLET CORN BREAD

2 tablespoons butter
1¼ cups yellow corn meal
⅓ cup flour
3 tablespoons granulated sugar
1 teaspoon salt
1 teaspoon baking soda
2 cups milk
1 cup buttermilk
2 eggs

Place the butter in a 9- or 10-inch skillet (or square baking dish) and preheat in the oven for 5 minutes. Meanwhile, in a large bowl sift the corn meal, flour, sugar, salt, and baking soda. Stir 1 cup of the milk and the buttermilk into the corn meal mixture. Blend eggs into the corn meal mixture. Pour the batter into the hot skillet and carefully top the batter with the remaining 1 cup milk. *Do not stir*, as the milk will sink to the bottom and form a custard. Bake in a preheated 400° oven for 35 minutes.

Serve at once while still hot. This custard bread may be cut into wedges and served with butter and honey if desired.

BANANA TEA BREAD

2 cups granulated sugar
1 cup butter
6 ripe medium bananas, mashed

In a large bowl cream together the sugar and butter until fluffy. Add the bananas and eggs and blend. Sift together the flour, salt, and soda 3

4 eggs, well beaten
2½ cups sifted cake flour
1 teaspoon salt
2 teaspoons baking soda

times. Carefully blend the flour mixture into the banana mixture. Do not overmix. Pour the batter into 2 greased 9 × 5 × 3-inch loaf pans. Bake in a preheated 350° oven for 50–55 minutes or until a toothpick inserted in the middle comes out clean. Cool for 10 minutes. Remove the loaves from the pans and cool completely on racks before slicing.

NOTE: Loaves may be refrigerated, wrapped in foil, for 2 weeks or frozen for up to 3 months. The recipe may be halved for 1 loaf.

CRANBERRY BANANA BREAD

MAKES 1 LOAF

must be prepared 24 hours in advance

2⅔ cups granulated sugar
1 cup water
4 cups fresh cranberries
1¾ cups sifted flour
½ teaspoon salt
2 teaspoons baking powder
¼ teaspoon baking soda
⅓ cup butter, melted
2 eggs, beaten
½ cup chopped walnuts
1 cup mashed banana
¼ cup cranberry juice, reserved from cooked berries (optional)
2 tablespoons granulated sugar (optional)
2 tablespoons Grand Marnier (optional)

In a large saucepan bring 2 cups sugar and the water to a boil, stirring to dissolve the sugar. Add the berries and simmer over low heat for 10 minutes or until berries pop open. Cool. Drain the berries, reserving the juice and measuring 1 cup of berries for use in the bread.

Sift together the flour, salt, baking powder, and baking soda. In a large bowl combine ⅔ cup sugar, the butter, eggs, walnuts, banana, and berries. Add the flour mixture to the berry mixture, stirring until blended. Pour the mixture into a greased and lightly floured 9 × 5 × 3-inch loaf pan. Bake in a preheated 350° oven for 1 hour or until a toothpick inserted in the center comes out clean. If you wish to have a topping, combine the cranberry juice, 2 tablespoons sugar, and the Grand Marnier in a small saucepan and stir over low heat until heated through. Poke a few holes in the baked loaf and pour on the topping. Cool 10 minutes in the pan. Turn the loaf out on a rack and cool completely. Wrap in foil and store 1 day before slicing.

NOTE: The bread keeps refrigerated for 3 weeks or frozen for 3 months. The recipe may be doubled for 2 loaves.

SOURDOUGH FRENCH BREAD

allow at least 3 days for "starter" and bread

1 package active dry yeast
2 tablespoons lukewarm water
1 cup hot water
2 tablespoons granulated sugar
2 tablespoons butter
1½ cups Sourdough Starter
  (*below*)
2 teaspoons salt
2 teaspoons white vinegar
4–5 cups unbleached flour
1 tablespoon yellow corn meal
1 egg white
1 tablespoon cold water

To prepare bread, mix 1 package yeast and 2 tablespoons warm water in a warm cup and set aside to soften. In a large mixing bowl pour the hot water over the sugar and butter, stirring, to mix and dissolve them. Cool the butter mixture to lukewarm (110°) and add the yeast mixture, starter, and salt. Add the vinegar and 2 cups flour and beat vigorously by hand about 100 strokes or 1 minute on a mixer at medium speed until well blended. Stir in enough of the remaining 2–3 cups flour to make a firm, very stiff dough. Turn the dough out on a well-floured board and knead for 8–10 minutes or until dough is smooth and elastic. Work in enough additional flour so that the dough is not sticky.

Place the dough in a buttered bowl, turning to butter the top of the dough. Cover the bowl with a damp cloth and let rise in a warm place 1–2 hours or until doubled in bulk. Punch the dough down and let it rise again for 30 minutes. Turn out on a lightly floured board, divide in half, and let rest 10 minutes before shaping. To shape the loaves, roll each half back and forth gently, elongating it to about 14 inches. Grease a large cookie sheet and sprinkle it with corn meal. Place the unbaked loaves on the sheet and cover them lightly with clear plastic film. Let them rise in a warm place until almost doubled and puffy, about 1–1½ hours.

In a small bowl mix together the egg white and cold water and set aside. (Optional: Place a rimmed baking sheet or jelly-roll pan on the lowest rack of the oven and pour into it about ¼ inch of boiling water. This extra moisture during the baking will result in a chewier texture in the bread crust.) Carefully make 3 or 4 diagonal cuts ¼ inch deep across the top of each unbaked loaf, using a razor blade so that the bread won't fall. Gently brush the egg white mixture on the tops and sides of each loaf. Bake the loaves in a preheated 400° oven for 15 minutes, brush again with the egg white mixture, and continue baking for 25–35 minutes or until loaves are well browned and hollow-sounding when tapped. Cool the loaves on wire racks.

Sourdough French Bread will keep refrigerated for several days or can be frozen in airtight wrap for 1–2 months. Week-old sourdough is ideal for French toast.

SOURDOUGH STARTER

1 package active dry yeast
2 cups warm water (110°)
2 cups flour

To prepare starter, in a 1½-quart glass, pottery, or plastic (not metal) container, mix 1 package yeast, 2 cups warm water, and 2 cups flour until smooth. Cover the container with cheesecloth and let it stand at room temperature for 48 hours, stirring it down 3 or 4 times. The mixture should ferment, bubble, and smell slightly sour.

Before mixing the bread dough, stir and pour off as much starter as the recipe requires. Then replenish the remaining starter with equal amounts of flour and warm water (for example, 1 cup of each) and let the mixture stand a few hours until it bubbles again. Store the starter in a lidded plastic or glass container in the refrigerator for future use. When properly cared for, Sourdough Starter will improve with age.* Before using again, allow the starter to stand at room temperature for 4–6 hours.

*NOTE: Sourdough Starter is a live thing and should be cared for much the same as a house plant. If the starter is not used every week, then every 10 days to 2 weeks half of it should be discarded. The other half should be allowed to come to room temperature and fed with equal parts of flour and water. The mixture should then stand at room temperature and bubble before being returned to the refrigerator. Never add anything but flour and water (and up to ½ teaspoon sugar, if desired, to get the yeast going) to the starter. Since Sourdough Starter is by nature acidic, it should never be mixed or stored in a metal container. The fermentation process produces gases, so be sure to open and close a tightly sealed, refrigerated container at least once a month (or use a plastic container with a lid). At room temperature, the starter should *never* be tightly sealed, as it could explode.

CORN TORTILLAS

2 cups masa harina (a corn
flour; Quaker brand is
preferable)
1½ cups water (approximately)
Salad or olive oil (for greasing
the pan)
You will need a tortilla press
and waxed paper.

In a large bowl blend the masa and water together by hand, kneading slightly with the fingers until the dough forms a firm but soft paste. Divide and form the dough into 12 balls, 1½ inches in diameter, and cover with a damp cloth or paper towel.

Tear or cut waxed paper into 24 6–8-inch squares. Place 1 square of paper on the bottom plate of a tortilla press. Next, place 1 ball on top of the waxed paper, slightly to the rear of the center of the press. Flatten the ball slightly with fingers, place another square of paper on top, pull the top of the press down firmly, and mash the dough to a thickness of less than ⅛ inch, if possible. Open the press and gently pull only the top piece of waxed paper off the tortilla. (One of the secrets to a good tortilla is the proper consistency of the dough. If the dough is too dry, the uncooked tortilla will appear rather ragged around the edges. If the dough is too moist, the waxed paper will stick to the tortilla. Corrections may be made by the addition of more water or masa, as required.)

Into a medium-hot, seasoned, lightly oiled heavy iron pan or griddle, place the tortilla, paper side up. Leave the paper intact, and in a few seconds, as the tortilla heats, gently peel the paper off. Cook for about 1 minute (until the underside is dry but not browned), flip the tortilla with a spatula, and cook for 1 more minute. The tortilla is done when dry around the edges and should be removed immediately if it begins to bubble.

Immediately wrap the cooked tortillas, stacking them together as they are finished, in a fresh tea towel until they are cooled. (This will keep them moist and soft as the steam intermingles.)

NOTE: Store the cooled tortillas in airtight plastic wrap, refrigerated for 1 week or frozen for 3 months.

OVEN STRAWBERRY PANCAKES

SERVES 6

2 pints fresh strawberries
¼ cup brown sugar
3 tablespoons flour
½ teaspoon salt
1 cup half-and-half
8 eggs
3 tablespoons butter
Confectioners sugar
½ cup sour cream (optional)
1½ tablespoons granulated sugar
  (optional)

Hull strawberries, slice in half, place them in a medium bowl, and toss together with brown sugar. Set aside.

Combine flour and salt in a large bowl. Gradually beat in half-and-half. Beat eggs 1 at a time into flour mixture, blending until batter is smooth and thin. Place about ½ tablespoon butter in each o six 5–6-inch individual baking dishes (or Pyrex bowls). Place dishes on a baking sheet and preheat in the oven for 4–5 minutes. Remove them from the oven and place about ½ cup of batter in each dish. Bake in a preheated 450° oven for 15 minutes or until cakes are puffed and brown around the edges. Leave cakes in dishes, sprinkle with powdered sugar and pile with strawberries. Each cake may be topped with a spoonful of sour cream, sweetened with the granulated sugar. Serve at once.

NOTE: These are excellent for breakfast or brunch.

BRAN PANCAKES

SERVES 4–6

1 cup whole-wheat flour
1 cup whole bran cereal (such
  as All-Bran or Bran Buds,
  not flakes)
3 teaspoons baking powder
3 tablespoons brown sugar,
  packed
¾ teaspoon salt
½ teaspoon baking soda
1 cup milk
1 cup buttermilk
2 eggs, beaten
3 tablespoons butter, melted

In a large bowl combine and mix the flour, bran, baking powder, sugar, salt, and soda. Slowly blend the milk and buttermilk into the flour mixture. Add the eggs and melted butter and beat until blended. Fry the cakes on a greased, medium-hot griddle, turning them as the uncooked side appears dry. These cakes will brown faster than a regular pancake and may be cooked with slightly less heat—about 360° in an electric skillet—for a longer period of time. Serve the pancakes with butter and maple syrup or honey.

NOTE: For crunchier pancakes use the batter immediately; for smoother pancakes let stand for 20 minutes. Batter may be refrigerated for 5 or 6 days; you may wish to thin it after the first day.

GOLDEN HIND CRUMPETS

1 package active dry yeast
1 teaspoon granulated sugar
3 tablespoons lukewarm water
  (110°)
⅓ cup milk
1 egg
4 tablespoons butter, melted
1 cup flour, unsifted
½ teaspoon salt

In a medium-sized mixing bowl mix the yeast, sugar, and water and let stand for 5 minutes to soften yeast. Blend in the milk, egg, and 1 tablespoon of the butter. Add flour and salt, mixing until smooth. Cover the bowl with a damp towel and let stand in a warm (80–85°) draft-free place for 45 minutes or until dough is almost doubled in bulk. Brush 1 tablespoon of butter on the bottom of a large heavy frying pan. Brush the insides of four 3-inch-diameter flan rings or open-top cookie cutters or tuna cans (with tops and bottoms removed) with the remaining butter. Place the rings inside the frying pan and place the pan over medium heat until the butter is hot and sizzling. Reduce heat to medium-low and pour 2 or 3 tablespoons of batter into each ring. Fry about 6 or 7 minutes or until holes appear in crumpets and their tops are dry. Remove the rings and flip the crumpets, browning the other side lightly, about 3 minutes more. Repeat until the batter is used.

Serve the crumpets warm or cool them completely on racks and store them in airtight plastic bags in the refrigerator. Crumpets may be reheated in a toaster.

NO-FAIL POPOVERS

1 cup flour, unsifted
¼ teaspoon salt
1 cup skim milk or ½ cup
  regular milk and ½ cup water
3 eggs
½ cup grated Cheddar cheese
  (optional)
3–4 tablespoons butter

In a medium bowl mix the flour and salt. Slowly blend in milk. Beat eggs into the batter until well blended. Fold in cheese, if used.

Place 1–1½ teaspoons butter in the bottom of each of six to eight 6-ounce custard cups. Place the cups on a cookie sheet and place the cookie sheet in a preheated 375° oven to preheat for 3–5 minutes (until the butter is melted and the cups are hot). Remove the sheet and cups from the oven and fill each cup ½–⅔ full (you may or may not use all the cups, depending on how much you fill them). Return the cups on the sheet to the oven immediately and bake at 375° for 45–50 minutes until well popped and browned. Resist the urge to peek at them (unless your oven has a window) for the first 30 minutes of baking time.

Popovers should be served immediately while hot. With the oven turned off, the popovers may be allowed to wait for up to 10 minutes in the oven. This will cause them to dry out a bit in the middle. They do not reheat well. Serve with butter and preserves if desired.

SUPER-NATURAL BRAN MUFFINS

MAKES 24 PLUS

1 cup whole bran cereal (such as All-Bran or Bran Buds, not flakes)
1 cup boiling water
½ cup vegetable oil
1¼ cup "yellow D" sugar (found at health-food stores) or brown sugar, packed
¼ cup honey
2 eggs
2 cups buttermilk
2½ cups whole-wheat flour
2½ teaspoons baking soda
1 teaspoon salt
2 cups granola (plain or fancy)

In a 2–3-quart container or bowl with a cover stir together the bran and water. Let stand for 10 minutes or until the water is absorbed. Meanwhile, in another large bowl combine the oil, sugar, and honey and mix well. Beat the eggs into oil mixture. Add and mix in the buttermilk. Mix the oil mixture into bran mixture in the large container. In another bowl combine and mix flour, soda, salt, and granola. Slowly blend these ingredients into bran mixture. Cover and refrigerate the batter for several hours or overnight.

Remove enough batter to make desired amount of muffins. Spoon the batter into greased muffin tins, ½–⅔ full. Bake in a preheated 400° oven for 22–25 minutes or until well browned and a toothpick inserted in the center of a muffin comes out clean. Serve warm with butter.

NOTE: The remaining batter may be used as needed and will keep refrigerated, tightly sealed, for 4 weeks. The recipe may be doubled.

Variations: Before baking, add raisins, walnuts, and/or chopped, unpeeled pippin apples to the batter in whatever amounts desired.

For the 2 cups granola, you may substitute more bran or a combination of bran, oatmeal, and a small amount of wheat germ—all totaling 2 cups.

ORANGE SWEET ROLLS

1 package active dry yeast
¼ cup lukewarm water (110°)
1 cup granulated sugar
1 teaspoon salt
2 eggs
½ cup sour cream
½ cup butter, melted
3½ cups sifted flour
3 tablespoons grated orange
   rind
3 tablespoons butter, melted

In a large bowl dissolve the yeast in warm water. With an electric mixer, beat ¼ cup of the sugar, the salt, eggs, ½ cup sour cream, and 6 tablespoons of the melted butter into the yeast mixture. Gradually add 2 cups of the flour to the yeast mixture, beating until smooth. Knead the remaining flour into the dough. Cover the bowl with a damp cloth and let dough rise in a warm (80–85°) draft-free place until doubled, about 1½–2 hours. Turn dough out on floured surface and knead about 15 times. Divide dough in half. Roll out each half of the dough to a 12-inch circle. Combine ¾ cup sugar and the orange rind. Brush each half of the dough with 1 tablespoon melted butter and sprinkle each with ½ the rind-sugar mixture. Cut each half into 12 wedges. Roll the wedges up, starting with the wide end, and place them point side down, in 3 rows, in a greased 9 × 13-inch pan. Cover the rolls with a damp cloth and let rise in a warm place about 1 hour.

Brush the tops of the rolls with the last 3 tablespoons melted butter and bake in a preheated 350° oven for 30 minutes. Remove from oven. Pour Sour Cream Orange Glaze over the rolls. Serve warm with additional butter if desired.

SOUR CREAM ORANGE GLAZE
¾ cup granulated sugar
½ cup sour cream
3 tablespoons fresh orange juice
½ cup butter

To prepare glaze, combine ¾ cup sugar, ½ cup sour cream, 3 tablespoons orange juice, and ½ cup butter in a medium saucepan. Boil, stirring constantly, for 3 minutes.

BLUEBERRY BUCKLE

¼ cup butter, softened
¾ cup granulated sugar
1 egg
1½ cups sifted flour
2 teaspoons baking powder
¼ teaspoon salt
½ cup milk
2 cups fresh blueberries (frozen
   berries, thawed and drained,
   may be substituted)

In a large bowl cream together the butter and ¾ cup sugar until fluffy. Blend egg into creamed mixture. In another bowl sift together the 1½ cups flour, the baking powder, and salt. Add flour mixture alternately with milk to creamed mixture, beating after each addition. Gently fold the blueberries into batter. Pour batter into a greased and floured 8 × 8-inch square pan. Sprinkle evenly with Crumb Topping. Bake in a preheated 375° oven for 40–45 minutes or until a toothpick inserted in the center comes out clean. Place pan on a rack and cool.

Cut in squares and serve warm as a rich, delicious coffeecake or cooled, topped with whipped cream, for dessert.

CRUMB TOPPING
½ cup granulated sugar
⅓ cup flour
½ teaspoon cinnamon
¼ cup butter, cut up

To prepare topping, in a small bowl mix together ½ cup sugar, ⅓ cup flour, and the cinnamon. With 2 knives or a pastry blender cut the cut-up butter into sugar mixture until mixture resembles coarse meal.

VINEYARD COFFEECAKE

SERVES 10

¾ cup butter, softened
1 cup granulated sugar
2 eggs
2 cups sifted flour
¾ teaspoon baking soda
1½ teaspoons baking powder
1 cup buttermilk
1 teaspoon vanilla extract
½ cup golden raisins
⅓ cup semisweet chocolate chips
½ cup finely chopped walnuts
   or almonds
2 tablespoons sugar
1 teaspoon ground cinnamon

In a large mixing bowl cream the butter until light, slowly add 1 cup sugar, and continue to cream until well blended and fluffy. Blend in the eggs one at a time. In another bowl sift together the flour, soda, and baking powder. Mix the flour mixture, alternately with the buttermilk, into the creamed mixture, beginning and ending with the dry ingredients, blending well after each addition. Mix in the vanilla and lightly fold in the raisins and chocolate chips.

In a small bowl combine the nuts, 2 tablespoons sugar, and cinnamon. Pour ⅔ of the coffeecake batter into a greased and lightly floured 10-inch tube pan or 12-cup (standard) bundt pan, and top with ½ the topping mixture. Pour the remaining ⅓ of the batter into the pan and sprinkle over it the remaining topping. Bake in a preheated 350° oven for 45–55 minutes or until a toothpick inserted in the center comes out clean. Cool the pan on a rack for 10 minutes, then turn the cake out, flipping it over again so that the topping side is up, and cool a few minutes more. Serve the coffeecake warm with butter.

NOTE: This cake keeps well in the refrigerator, tightly wrapped, for up to 1 week. It may be reheated, loosely wrapped in foil, at 350° for about 15 minutes.

CHOCOLATE DUMP CAKE

2 squares unsweetened chocolate
½ cup butter
2 cups granulated sugar
½ cup buttermilk
1 teaspoon vanilla extract
1 cup warm water
2 cups flour
1½ teaspoons baking soda
½ teaspoon salt
2 eggs

Melt 2 squares chocolate and ½ cup butter in top of a double boiler set over simmering water and set aside. In a large mixing bowl combine the granulated sugar, buttermilk, and 1 teaspoon vanilla and blend at low speed with an electric mixer. Add the chocolate mixture to the buttermilk mixture, beating until blended. Beat the warm water into the chocolate mixture and beat at low speed until blended. In another bowl sift together the flour, baking soda, and salt. Add the flour mixture to the chocolate mixture and beat at low speed until blended. Add the eggs and beat at high speed for 2 minutes. Mixture will be thin.

Pour the batter into a greased and floured 9 × 13 × 2-inch pan. Bake in a preheated 350° oven for 50–60 minutes or until a toothpick inserted in the center comes out clean. Cool completely in the pan on a rack before frosting with Fudge Frosting.

FUDGE FROSTING
2 squares unsweetened chocolate
½ cup butter
½ cup brown sugar, packed
1 pound confectioners' sugar
⅓ cup sour cream
2 tablespoons light corn syrup
1 teaspoon vanilla extract
⅛ teaspoon salt
1 cup chopped walnuts

To prepare frosting, melt 2 squares chocolate and ½ cup butter in the top of a double boiler over boiling water. Keep the water boiling while adding the brown and confectioners' sugar, sour cream, corn syrup, 1 teaspoon vanilla, ⅛ teaspoon salt, and the walnuts. Cook only until dissolved. (Mixture will harden like fudge if overcooked.) Cover the top of the cake with the warm frosting, working rapidly before it cools and is hard to manage.

BRANDY APPLE SPICE CAKE

4 cups chopped baking apples
6 tablespoons brandy
2 cups granulated sugar
½ cup salad oil
2 eggs
2 cups flour
2 teaspoons ground cinnamon
2 teaspoons baking soda

Peel, core, and coarsely chop enough apples to measure 4 cups. As they are chopped, place them in a bowl with as much brandy as they will absorb (about 6 tablespoons).

In a large bowl beat together the sugar, oil, and eggs with an electric mixer until well blended. In another bowl sift together the flour, cinnamon, baking soda, salt, nutmeg, and cloves. Stir flour

1 teaspoon salt
1 teaspoon ground nutmeg
¼ teaspoon ground cloves
1 cup coarsely chopped walnuts
1 cup raisins, plumped
Whipped cream, slightly sweetened

mixture into oil mixture until blended. Fold in the apples, walnuts, and raisins. Pour batter into greased and floured 9 × 13 × 2-inch pan. Bake in a preheated 325° oven for 1 hour or until a toothpick inserted in the center comes out clean. Cool in the pan on a rack. Serve warm or cool, topped with whipped cream.

SUPER CHOCOLATE POUND CAKE

SERVES 12

6 ounces semisweet eating chocolate (common bar chocolate is suitable)
4 ounces milk chocolate
2 tablespoons water
1 cup butter, softened
2 cups granulated sugar
4 eggs
2 teaspoons vanilla extract
1 tablespoon brandy
2¼ cups flour
½ teaspoon salt
¼ teaspoon baking soda
1 cup buttermilk
½ cup chopped nuts (optional)

DARK CHOCOLATE POUR FROSTING
1 6-ounce package semisweet chocolate chips
2 tablespoons butter
2 tablespoons light corn syrup
3 tablespoons milk

In a medium saucepan melt together the chocolate and water over very low heat and set aside to cool. In a large bowl cream together the 1 cup butter and sugar until light and fluffy. Add eggs one at a time, beating after each addition. Blend in melted chocolate, vanilla, and brandy. Sift together the flour, salt, and soda. Add flour mixture alternately with the buttermilk to chocolate mixture, beginning and ending with flour, blending after each addition. Fold in the nuts if used.

Pour batter into a well-greased and floured 10-inch tube pan or 12-cup (standard) bundt pan. Bake in a preheated 325° oven for 1 hour and 20–35 minutes or until a toothpick inserted in the center comes out clean. Cool in the pan 10 minutes, turn out on a rack, and continue cooling for 20 minutes more. Place the cake on a platter and pour Dark Chocolate Pour Frosting over the cake while the cake is still slightly warm.

To prepare frosting, melt the chocolate chips and butter in the top of a double boiler over simmering water, stirring often. Stir in the corn syrup and milk and beat until smooth.

NOTE: The cake recipe may be halved and baked in a 9 × 5 × 3-inch loaf pan or a 6-cup mini-bundt pan. Bake at 350° for about 70 minutes for a loaf pan or 60 minutes for a mini-bundt pan. Frosting may be halved also (use ½ cup for 1 package of chocolate chips). Serves 6–8.

CHOCOLATE CHIP DATE CAKE

SERVES 12

1¼ cups water
8 ounces fresh dates, pitted and chopped (about 1½ cups)
1¼ teaspoons baking soda
1 cup granulated sugar
¾ cup butter, softened
2 eggs
1¼ cups sifted flour
½ teaspoon salt
1 teaspoon vanilla extract
½ cup oatmeal
1 12-ounce package mini-chocolate chips
1 tablespoon granulated sugar
¾ cup chopped walnuts

Simmer water, dates, and 1 teaspoon soda together in a small saucepan for 10 minutes; set aside to cool.

In a large bowl cream 1 cup sugar and the butter until fluffy. Blend in the eggs one at a time, beating after each addition.

In another bowl sift together the flour, ¼ teaspoon soda, and the salt. Blend the flour mixture into the creamed mixture. Stir in dates (including liquid), vanilla, oatmeal, and ½ the chocolate chips, mixing until blended. Spread the batter evenly into a greased and floured 9 × 13 × 2-inch pan.

Mix together the remaining chocolate chips, 1 tablespoon sugar, and the nuts and sprinkle evenly over the top of the uncooked cake. Bake in a preheated 350° oven for 35 minutes. Cool in pan. Serve warm or cool, cut in 2-inch squares.

The dates, having been cooked with soda, liquefy and blend into the batter to form a smooth, rich, moist cake.

MONTEREY SOUR CREAM COFFEECAKE

SERVES 8–10

½ cup butter, softened
1 cup plus 4 tablespoons granulated sugar
2 eggs
1 teaspoon vanilla extract
1 cup cake flour
½ cup all-purpose flour
1½ teaspoons baking powder
1 teaspoon baking soda
¼ teaspoon salt
1 cup sour cream
1½ teaspoons ground cinnamon
½ cup raisins
½ cup chopped walnuts

Grease and flour an 8- or 9-inch springform pan. In a large bowl cream together the butter and 1 cup sugar until light and fluffy. Blend in the eggs, 1 at a time, beating after each addition, and the vanilla. In another bowl sift together the flours, baking powder, baking soda, and salt. Slowly blend the flour mixture into the creamed mixture until smooth. Blend the sour cream into the batter, mixing well. Pour ½ the mixture into the prepared pan.

In another bowl mix together the cinnamon, 4 tablespoons sugar, and raisins, and sprinkle ½ of this mixture evenly over the batter in the pan.

Top with remaining batter, remaining cinnamon mixture, and the walnuts. Bake in a preheated 350° oven for 40–45 minutes or until a toothpick inserted in the center comes out clean. Cool in the pan on a rack for about 20 minutes. Serve warm, cut in wedges.

CLASSIC CARROT CAKE

SERVES 12

must be prepared 24 hours in advance

1¼ cups salad oil
1 cup brown sugar, packed
1 cup granulated sugar
4 eggs
1 cup all-purpose flour
1 cup less 2 tablespoons whole-wheat flour
1 teaspoon salt
2 teaspoons baking soda
2 teaspoons baking powder
2 teaspoons ground cinnamon
3 cups finely shredded raw carrots, packed
8½ ounces crushed pineapple, drained
½ cup finely chopped walnuts (optional)

LEMON CREAM CHEESE FROSTING
8 ounces cream cheese, softened
¼ cup butter, softened
2 cups confectioners' sugar
1½ teaspoons vanilla extract
1 tablespoon grated lemon rind

In a large bowl blend together the salad oil and brown and granulated sugars. Add eggs one at a time, beating until blended. In another bowl sift together both flours, salt, soda, baking powder, and cinnamon. Add the flour mixture, about ⅓ at a time, to the oil mixture, beating just enough to blend. Fold the carrots and then the pineapple into the batter. Add nuts if desired. Pour the batter into 2 greased and lightly floured 9-inch round cake pans. Bake in a preheated 350° oven for 35–40 minutes or until a toothpick inserted in the center of each comes out clean. Cool the cakes in the pans on a rack for 10 minutes. Turn cakes out on the rack and cool completely. Frost with Lemon Cream Cheese Frosting and allow the cake to rest for 1 day, if not previously stored, to improve flavor.

To prepare frosting, in a large mixing bowl mash the cream cheese, add the butter, and cream them together until well mixed and fluffy. Add the confectioners' sugar (sift it first if it is lumpy) to the cheese mixture and beat until well blended. Blend in the vanilla and lemon rind.

NOTE: Unfrosted, the cakes may be wrapped in airtight plastic wrap and refrigerated for 5–6 days or frozen for 2–3 months. If frosted, the cakes may be stored in refrigerator for a week or more.

NO-EGG CARROT CAKE RING
WITH LEMON SAUCE

¾ cup butter, melted and cooled
1 cup brown sugar, packed
1¼ cups shredded raw carrots
2½ teaspoons fresh lemon juice
1½ cups sifted flour
3 teaspoons baking powder
1 teaspoon ground cinnamon
½ teaspoon ground nutmeg
¼ teaspoon salt
½ cup raisins

LEMON SAUCE
1 tablespoon cornstarch
¼ cup granulated sugar
⅛ teaspoon salt
½ cup water
½ cup fresh orange juice (or ½
    cup additional water)
2 teaspoons grated lemon rind
5 teaspoons fresh lemon juice
3 tablespoons butter
Dash mace

In a large bowl combine the melted butter, sugar, carrots, and the 2½ teaspoons lemon juice and mix well. In another bowl sift together the flour, baking powder, cinnamon, nutmeg, and the ¼ teaspoon salt. Slowly add the flour mixture to the butter mixture, stirring until well blended. Stir the raisins into the batter. Pour the batter into a well-greased 4–5-cup ring mold or 6-cup mini-bundt pan. Bake in a preheated 350° oven for 45–50 minutes or until a toothpick inserted in the center comes out clean. Remove the pan to a rack and cool for 10 minutes. Invert the pan, remove the cake, and continue cooling on the rack for at least 30 minutes more before serving. Top each serving with Lemon Sauce.

To prepare sauce, in a small saucepan combine the cornstarch, granulated sugar, and the ⅛ teaspoon salt and gradually add the water and orange juice. Cook and stir the mixture over medium-low heat until thick and boiling. Reduce the heat to low and simmer the sauce, stirring, until almost clear, about 10 minutes. Remove sauce from heat and stir in lemon rind, the 5 teaspoons lemon juice, the butter, and mace. Cool at least 20 minutes. Makes 1¼ cups.

NOTE: This cake is tasty and refreshing without being too rich. It makes a delicious luncheon dessert or teatime snack.

SPICY PERSIMMON BRUNCH CAKE

1¼ cup puréed fresh persimmon
    (see Note)
1 teaspoon baking soda
½ cup butter, softened
1 cup granulated sugar
2 cups sifted flour
2 teaspoons baking powder
1 teaspoon ground cinnamon
¼ teaspoon salt

Stir together the persimmon and soda in a small bowl until blended and set aside. In a large bowl cream the butter and sugar until fluffy. Add the purée to the creamed mixture. Sift together the flour, baking powder, cinnamon, salt, nutmeg, and cloves. Gradually blend the flour mixture into the persimmon mixture. Add the nuts and rinds, beating just enough to blend. Batter will be stiff.

¼ teaspoon ground nutmeg
¼ teaspoon ground cloves
½ cup pecans, finely chopped
1 teaspoon grated orange rind
½ teaspoon grated lemon rind
Confectioners' sugar

Spoon the batter into a well-greased and floured 8 × 8 × 2-inch cake pan or 5-cup ring mold or 6-cup mini-bundt pan. Bake in a preheated 350° oven for 40–45 minutes or until a toothpick inserted in the center of the cake comes out clean. Cool the cake in the pan for 10 minutes and turn out on a rack to continue cooling another 20 or 30 minutes before serving (or serve the cake directly from the 8 × 8 × 2-inch pan). Sprinkle with confectioners' sugar and serve warm.

Cake may be baked earlier and reheated, wrapped in foil, for 15 minutes at 325°.

NOTE: A fresh persimmon should feel soft and jellylike when ripe. Cut it in half and scoop the flesh from the skin with a spoon. Then whirl the pulp in the blender until smooth. Use at once or freeze. The purée tends to turn brown if left, and a small amount of lemon juice may be added if desired, to prevent discoloration and enhance flavor.

APPLE CAKE WITH SHERRY CREAM SAUCE SERVES 12

½ cup vegetable oil
2 cups granulated sugar
2 eggs, beaten
2 teaspoons vanilla extract
2 cups sifted flour
2 teaspoons baking soda
¼ teaspoon salt
2 teaspoons ground cinnamon
1½ cups chopped walnuts
4 cups peeled, cored, and
    coarsely shredded tart apples
Confectioners' sugar for dusting

SHERRY CREAM SAUCE

3 egg yolks
6 tablespoons confectioners'
    sugar
4–5 tablespoons sherry
1 cup heavy cream

In a large bowl cream together the oil and granulated sugar. Blend the beaten eggs and the vanilla into sugar mixture. Sift together the flour, soda, salt, and cinnamon and blend into sugar mixture. Fold in the walnuts and then the apples. Pour batter into a greased and floured 10-inch tube pan or 12-cup (standard) bundt pan. Bake in a preheated 350° oven for 1 hour or until a toothpick inserted in the center comes out clean. Cool in the pan for 10 minutes, loosen sides, and carefully turn out on rack to cool completely. Dust with confectioners' sugar and serve topped with Sherry Cream Sauce.

To prepare sauce, in a medium bowl beat the 3 egg yolks until light. Stir in the 6 tablespoons confectioners' sugar and the sherry. Whip the cream until stiff and fold into yolk mixture. Chill well.

OATMEAL BUNDT CAKE

SERVES 12 GENEROUSLY

2½ cups boiling water
2 cups oatmeal (regular)
1 cup butter, softened
1 cup brown sugar, packed
2 cups granulated sugar
4 eggs
1⅔ cups flour (unbleached is
   preferable)
1 cup less 2 tablespoons
   whole-wheat flour
1 teaspoon salt
2 teaspoons baking soda
2 teaspoons ground cinnamon
2 teaspoons ground nutmeg
2 teaspoons vanilla extract
½–1 cup raisins (optional)

ORANGE CREAM CHEESE
FROSTING
3 ounces cream cheese, softened
¼ cup butter, softened
2 cups confectioners' sugar,
   sifted
½ teaspoon vanilla extract
1½ teaspoons grated orange
   rind

CURRENT BRANDY GLAZE
½ cup currant jelly
2 tablespoons granulated sugar
1 tablespoon brandy

In a large mixing bowl pour the boiling water over the oatmeal and let the mixture stand for 20 minutes.

In another large bowl cream the 1 cup butter until light; slowly add the sugars, continuing to cream until the mixture is fluffy and well blended. Beat in the eggs one at a time. In another bowl sift together the flours, salt, soda, cinnamon, and nutmeg. Blend the flour mixture into the creamed mixture. Stir in the oatmeal and the 2 teaspoons vanilla, mixing until blended. Mix the raisins, if used, into the batter until evenly distributed. Pour the batter into a well-greased and lightly floured 10-inch tube pan or 12-cup (standard) bundt pan. Bake in a preheated 350° oven for 1 hour and 10 minutes or until a toothpick inserted in the center comes out clean. Place the pan on a rack and cool 10–15 minutes. Loosen sides, turn cake out on rack, and continue cooling. Frost with Orange Cream Cheese Frosting or Currant Brandy Glaze.

To prepare frosting, in a large bowl mash the cream cheese, add the ¼ cup butter, and cream them together. Slowly add the confectioners' sugar, continuing to cream. Mix in the ½ teaspoon vanilla and the orange rind.

To prepare glaze, combine the jelly and sugar in a small saucepan over low heat until the mixture is melted. Increase the heat to medium-high and continue to cook the mixture for 2–3 minutes or until it coats a spoon (about 225°). Add the brandy and continue cooking over low heat for 1 additional minute. Cool the glaze slightly and pour it evenly over the cake.

NOTE: The Oatmeal Bundt Cake recipe may be cut in half to serve 6–8 people. Place the batter in a 5-cup ring mold or 6-cup mini-bundt pan and bake in a preheated 350° oven for 50–60 minutes or until the cake tests done.

ORANGE DATE HOLIDAY CAKE

SERVES 12

must be prepared 24 hours in advance

1 cup butter, softened
2 cups granulated sugar
4 eggs
4 cups flour
1 teaspoon baking soda
⅛ teaspoon salt
1¼ cups buttermilk
1 teaspoon lemon extract
1 tablespoon grated orange rind, packed
12 ounces pitted dates, chopped
1 cup pecans, chopped

ORANGE CAKE POUR
2 cups granulated sugar
1 cup fresh orange juice
2 tablespoons grated orange rind
¼ cup curaçao

In a large bowl cream the butter until light, slowly add the 2 cups sugar, and continue creaming until fluffy. Beat the eggs, one at a time, into the creamed mixture.

In another bowl sift all but 2 tablespoons of the flour, the soda, and salt. Add the flour mixture alternately with the buttermilk to the creamed mixture, beginning and ending with the flour and beating after each addition. Blend the lemon extract and the 1 tablespoon orange rind into the batter. Sprinkle the remaining 2 tablespoons flour over the chopped dates and toss lightly. Fold the dates and pecans into the batter, stirring just enough to distribute evenly. Pour the batter into a greased and lightly floured 10-inch tube pan or 12-cup (standard) bundt pan. Bake in a preheated 350° oven for 1 hour or until a toothpick inserted in the center comes out clean. Remove the pan to a rack, pierce the cake in a few places with a pick, and pour over it the slightly cooled Orange Cake Pour. Allow the cake to cool completely before removing it from the pan. Let stand for 1 day to develop flavor.

To prepare pour, in a 1½–2-quart saucepan mix the pour ingredients and bring to a boil over medium heat to dissolve sugar. Remove from heat and cool 2–3 minutes.

NOTE: This cake keeps well, foil-wrapped, in the refrigerator. It is particularly nice served at Christmastime.

LEMON MERINGUE LAYER CAKE

4 eggs, separated
⅔ cup granulated sugar
1 teaspoon lemon extract
1 cup sifted cake flour
⅛ teaspoon salt
2 tablespoons butter, melted
 and cooled

LEMON BUTTER CREAM FILLING
¼ cup butter
1 cup plus 2 tablespoons
 granulated sugar
1 egg plus 2 egg yolks (reserve
 2 whites for Meringue
 Frosting)
3 tablespoons fresh lemon juice
2 teaspoons grated lemon rind
6 tablespoons butter, firm but
 not chilled

MERINGUE FROSTING
2 egg whites
1 cup granulated sugar
¼ teaspoon cream of tartar
⅓ cup water

Butter and lightly flour an 8-inch round cake pan and set aside. In a large bowl beat the 4 egg yolks until they are thick and pale yellow. Slowly beat in the ⅔ cup sugar and the lemon extract. Sift together the flour and salt and lightly stir them into the yolk mixture. Stir in the cooled butter.

In a mixing bowl beat the 4 egg whites until stiff peaks form and gently fold them into the yolk mixture. Pour the batter into the prepared pan. Bake in a preheated 350° oven for 25–30 minutes or until the cake springs back when lightly touched and shrinks back from the edge of the pan. Remove the pan to a rack for 5 minutes, then turn the cake out on the rack and cool completely.

Cut the cooled cake horizontally into 2 layers. Spread ⅓ of the chilled Lemon Butter Cream Filling between the layers and frost the top and sides with the remaining filling. Chill the cake 2–3 hours.

Cover the cake completely with Meringue Frosting and place it in a preheated 450° oven for 10–15 minutes, until lightly browned.

To prepare filling, in the top of a double boiler cut the ¼ cup butter into small pieces and add the 1 cup 2 tablespoons sugar, egg plus egg yolks, lemon juice, and rind. Place over simmering water and beat the mixture with a whisk until it is the consistency of lightly whipped cream, about 10–12 minutes. Remove the pan from the heat and cool completely. Beat the 6 tablespoons butter, 1 tablespoon at a time, into the lemon mixture until smooth. Chill the mixture until it is of spreading consistency.

To prepare frosting, in a medium bowl beat the 2 egg whites until stiff peaks form and set aside. In a 1–2-quart saucepan over medium heat combine the 1 cup sugar and the cream of tartar in the water, stirring to dissolve. Cook the syrup until it forms a thread when dropped from a spoon (240° on a candy thermometer). Pour the syrup in a thin, steady stream over the egg whites, beating (with an electric mixer or rotary beater) until the mixture is cool and thick.

LEMONY PRUNE CAKE

SERVES 12–16

1 12-ounce package moist pitted prunes
1½ cups water
¾ cup butter, softened
1½ cups granulated sugar
4 eggs
1 tablespoon vanilla extract
1 tablespoon grated lemon rind
3 cups sifted flour
2 teaspoons baking powder
1 teaspoon baking soda
½ teaspoon salt
1 teaspoon ground cinnamon
1 teaspoon ground nutmeg
1 cup chopped walnuts

FLUFFY LEMON FROSTING
3 ounces cream cheese, softened
½ cup butter, softened
2 tablespoons milk
1 pound confectioners' sugar, sifted
2 teaspoons grated lemon rind
1 tablespoon lemon juice
1 teaspoon vanilla extract

In a medium saucepan simmer the prunes in the water uncovered over medium-low heat until tender, about 5 minutes. Purée the prunes and water in the blender and measure out 2 cups for use in the recipe. Set aside.

In a large bowl cream the ¾ cup butter until light, and slowly add the granulated sugar, continuing to cream until the mixture is well blended. Add the eggs, one at a time, to the creamed mixture and beat in a mixer at high speed until mixture is pale yellow, about 5 minutes. Mix in the 1 tablespoon vanilla, the 1 tablespoon lemon rind, and the puréed prunes.

In another bowl sift together the flour, baking powder, soda, salt, cinnamon, and nutmeg. Stir the flour mixture into the prune mixture and blend until smooth. Mix in walnuts and pour the batter into 2 greased and lightly floured 8-inch round cake pans. Bake in a preheated 350° oven for 35–40 minutes or until a toothpick inserted in the center comes out clean. Place the pans on racks and cool for 10 minutes. Remove the cakes from the pans and cool completely on the racks. Frost with Fluffy Lemon Frosting (it may be necessary to stabilize the layers atop each other with toothpicks).

To prepare frosting, in a large bowl cream together the cream cheese and butter and beat in the milk until mixture is light. Add the confectioners' sugar 1 cup at a time and blend. Beat in the 2 teaspoons lemon rind, the lemon juice and the 1 teaspoon vanilla.

ORANGE OAKS LAYER CAKE

5 egg yolks

1½ cups granulated sugar

¾ cup fresh orange juice (about 3 oranges)

1 tablespoon grated orange rind

2 cups cake flour

2 teaspoons baking powder

3 egg whites

¼ teaspoon salt

ORANGE CUSTARD

1 cup granulated sugar

4 tablespoons flour

2 teaspoons grated orange rind

½ cup fresh orange juice

1 teaspoon fresh lemon juice

2 teaspoons butter, cut up

2 eggs, lightly beaten

⅛ teaspoon salt

ORANGE BUTTER CREAM

⅞ cup granulated sugar

½ cup water

¼ plus ⅛ teaspoon cream of tartar

7 large or 8 small egg yolks

1½ cups sweet butter, slightly softened

2 tablespoons grated orange rind

2 tablespoons fresh orange juice

2 tablespoons Grand Marnier

Grease and lightly flour 3 9-inch round cake pans.

In a large mixing bowl beat the 5 egg yolks until pale lemon-colored. Slowly add the 1½ cups sugar to yolks, beating until blended and light. Blend the ¾ cup orange juice and 1 tablespoon orange rind into the yolk mixture. In another bowl sift together the 2 cups flour and the baking powder 3 times. Slowly add the flour mixture to the yolk mixture, blending lightly but thoroughly. In a medium-sized mixing bowl beat the egg whites and ¼ teaspoon salt until stiff but not dry peaks form. Carefully fold the egg whites into the batter, ½ at a time, lightly but thoroughly.

Divide the batter evenly among the 3 prepared pans. Bake in a preheated 375° oven for 20 minutes or until the cakes have slightly pulled away from the edge of the pans and spring back when touched. Place the pans on racks and cool for 10 minutes. Turn the cakes out on the racks and cool completely. Fill with Orange Custard and frost with Orange Butter Cream.

To prepare custard, in the top of a double boiler mix the Orange Custard ingredients in the order listed. Cook the mixture over simmering water, stirring constantly, until mixture thickens, about 15 minutes. Cool completely before spreading between cake layers.

To prepare butter cream, in a heavy 1–2-quart saucepan combine the ⅞ cup sugar, the water, and cream of tartar. Cook slowly over medium heat until sugar dissolves. Turn up the heat and boil the mixture, without stirring, until a candy thermometer reads 240° ("softball") or until it forms a thread when dropped from a spoon Remove the pan from the heat. In a mixing bowl beat the 7 or 8 yolks until thick and lemon-colored. Still beating, pour the syrup in a thin steady stream into the yolks. Continue beating until mixture is thick and cool, about 5–10 minutes. Keep beating while adding the sweet butter slowly in pats. Beat in the 2 tablespoons rind, 2 tablespoons juice, and the Grand Marnier. If the butter cream seems too soft to hold shape when spread, chill until it is the proper consistency.

FRESH RHUBARB CAKE

SERVES 8–10

¼ cup butter, softened
1½ cups brown sugar, packed
1 egg
1 teaspoon vanilla extract
2 cups flour
¼ teaspoon salt
1 teaspoon baking soda
1 tablespoon fresh lemon juice
1 cup milk
2 cups coarsely chopped fresh rhubarb (*see Note*)
¼ cup pecans or walnuts, chopped
¼ cup granulated sugar
1 teaspoon ground cinnamon

In a large mixing bowl cream the butter until it is light. Add the brown sugar slowly, continuing to cream, until the mixture is well blended and fluffy. Beat the egg and vanilla into the creamed mixture until blended.

In another bowl sift together the flour, salt, and baking soda twice. Combine the lemon juice and milk and add it alternately with the flour mixture to the creamed mixture, beginning and ending with the dry ingredients. Beat, after each addition, just enough to blend. Gently fold the chopped rhubarb into the batter, stirring just enough to distribute. Pour the batter into a greased and floured 9 × 13 × 2-inch pan, spreading evenly.

In a small bowl blend together the nuts, granulated sugar, and cinnamon and sprinkle evenly over the top of the batter. Bake in a preheated 350° oven for 45–50 minutes or until a toothpick inserted in the center comes out clean. Cool the cake in the pan at least 30 minutes, cut in squares, and serve.

NOTE: Fresh rhubarb should appear firm and very pink when selected. It may be stored in the refrigerator for up to a week. Do not use the leaves of the rhubarb, as they contain a toxic substance. This cake is suitable as coffeecake, tea cake, or dessert, topped with slightly sweetened whipped cream and dusted with cinnamon.

LEMON-LIME LAYER CAKE

2¼ cups flour

1½ cups granulated sugar

3 teaspoons baking powder

1 teaspoon salt

½ cup salad oil

5 egg yolks, at room
temperature

⅓ cup water

1 teaspoon grated lemon rind

1 teaspoon grated lime rind

¼ cup fresh lemon juice

2 tablespoons fresh lime juice

8 egg whites (1 cup), at room
temperature

½ teaspoon cream of tartar

LEMON FILLING

¼ cup fresh lemon juice

2 teaspoons grated lemon rind

2 cups granulated sugar

3 eggs, beaten

LIME CREAM FROSTING

3 egg yolks

⅓ cup granulated sugar

⅛ teaspoon salt

¼ cup fresh lime juice

1 cup heavy cream

2 teaspoons grated lime rind

In a large bowl sift together the flour, the 1½ cups sugar, the baking powder, and the 1 teaspoon salt. Make a well in the center of the mixture and add, in order, oil, egg yolks, water, 1 teaspoon each lemon and lime rinds, ¼ cup lemon juice and 2 tablespoons lime juice. Mix just until smooth and blended. In another large bowl beat the egg whites with cream of tartar until stiff peaks form. Gently fold the batter mixture into the beaten egg whites just until blended.

Pour the batter into a 10-inch ungreased tube pan and bake in a preheated 325° oven for 55 minutes. Increase the oven to 350° and continue baking for 10 minutes longer or until the cake springs back when touched and has begun to shrink back from the edge of the pan. Invert the pan on the neck of a bottle or a rack and cool completely, about 1 hour or more.

Run a knife around the sides of the cake and remove from the pan. Cut the cake horizontally in 3 equal layers. Spread Lemon Filling between the layers and frost with Lime Cream Frosting. The cake should be stored in the refrigerator.

To prepare filling, in the top of a double boiler combine Lemon Filling ingredients in the order listed. Cook over simmering water, stirring constantly, until mixture thickens to the consistency of honey, about 10–15 minutes. Cool completely before spreading between cake layers.

To prepare frosting, in the top of a double boiler combine the first four Lime Cream Frosting ingredients. Cook, stirring constantly, over hot (not boiling) water until mixture has thickened and mounds when dropped from a spoon, about 15–20 minutes. Refrigerate the mixture for about 1 hour. Whip the cream until stiff and fold, along with the 2 teaspoons lime rind, into the chilled egg mixture until well combined.

CHOCOLATE ALMOND TORTE

1 cup almonds, with skins
4 ounces semisweet baking
   chocolate
½ cup butter, softened
⅔ cup granulated sugar
3 eggs, separated
1 teaspoon vanilla extract
¼ cup fine melba toast crumbs
⅛ teaspoon salt
Chocolate Honey Frosting
   (*below*)
Blanched, slivered almonds
   (optional)

Butter the sides and bottom of an 8-inch round cake pan and line the bottom with buttered waxed paper. Grind the 1 cup almonds as fine as possible in a blender.

In a small saucepan melt the chocolate over low heat and set aside to cool. In a medium large bowl cream the ½ cup softened butter with the sugar until smooth and light. Beat the egg yolks until light and ribbons form when dropped from blades, about 5 minutes. Blend the yolks into the creamed mixture. Add the chocolate, ground almonds, vanilla, toast crumbs, and salt to the creamed mixture, blending after each addition. Beat the egg whites until they hold stiff peaks. Fold ⅓ of the whites into the chocolate mixture and then carefully fold in the remaining whites. Pour the batter into the prepared cake pan and bake in a preheated 375° oven for 25 minutes. Cool cake 10 minutes, turn out on rack, peel off the waxed paper, and cool completely. Frost with Chocolate Honey Frosting. Top may be garnished with slivered almonds which have been toasted lightly under the broiler.

CHOCOLATE HONEY FROSTING
2 ounces unsweetened chocolate
2 ounces semisweet chocolate
½ cup butter, softened
4 teaspoons honey

To prepare frosting, in a small saucepan melt the chocolates, butter, and honey over low heat, beating with an electric mixer until smooth. Remove the pan to a large bowl of ice and continue beating until frosting just barely begins to set and is spreadable. Frost the cooled cake immediately. (If this frosting can be caught just before it sets up, it may be *poured* on the cake directly, forming a handsome marble glaze. Either way, it has an unusually delicious flavor.)

ORANGE ALMOND TORTE

2 large navel oranges

8 ounces blanched almonds or 1½ cups ground almonds

6 eggs

⅛ teaspoon salt

1 teaspoon baking powder

1 cup granulated sugar

1 cup heavy cream

3 tablespoons confectioners' sugar

1 tablespoon Grand Marnier

Wash the oranges and place them, unpeeled, in a large saucepan with water barely covering them. Simmer the oranges over medium-low heat for 1½–2 hours or until they are very soft. Drain and cool the oranges. Cut them in half and remove the seeds and navel. Place the oranges, including rinds, in a blender and purée. Place the purée in a bowl and set aside. (This procedure may be done well ahead of baking time if desired.)

Prepare a 1½-quart, straight-sided soufflé dish or 9- or 10-inch springform pan by heavily buttering and flouring (shake out excess flour). Grind almonds in the blender to measure 1½ cups. In a large bowl beat the eggs until well blended and light in color. Add the salt, baking powder, sugar, puréed oranges, and ground almonds to the eggs. (If the orange skins are very thick, you may wish, after tasting the batter, to add an additional 2–6 tablespoons sugar to offset the bitterness of the rind. However, a distinctive bittersweet taste is desirable in this torte.) Batter will be rather liquid.

Pour batter into the prepared dish and bake in a preheated 400° oven for 60–70 minutes or until a toothpick inserted in the center comes out clean. Cool the cake in the dish and turn out on a platter, or remove the sides of the springform and place the bottom on a platter. Whip the cream and add the confectioners' sugar and Grand Marnier. Slice the torte in wedges and serve topped with the whipped cream.

POPPY SEED TORTE

⅓ cup poppy seeds
¾ cup milk
¾ cup butter, softened
1½ cups granulated sugar
1½ teaspoons vanilla extract
2 cups sifted cake flour
2½ teaspoons baking powder
¼ teaspoon salt
4 egg whites, at room
    temperature
Torte Filling (*below*)
¼ cup confectioners' sugar

TORTE FILLING
½ cup granulated sugar
1 tablespoon cornstarch
1½ cups milk
4 egg yolks, slightly beaten
1 teaspoon vanilla extract
¼ cup chopped walnuts

In a small bowl soak the poppy seeds in ¾ cup milk for 1 hour.

In a large bowl cream the butter until light, slowly add 1½ cups sugar, and continue creaming until mixture is well blended and fluffy. Blend 1½ teaspoons vanilla and milk-seed mixture into the creamed mixture. In another bowl sift together the flour, baking powder, and salt and set aside. In a third bowl beat the egg whites until stiff peaks form. Add the flour mixture to the creamed mixture, stirring until blended. Gently fold the beaten egg whites, ½ at a time, into the batter, folding just enough to distribute evenly. Pour the batter into 2 greased and lightly floured 8-inch round cake pans. Bake in a preheated 375° oven for 20–25 minutes or until cakes spring back when touched and are slightly pulled away from the edges of the pan. Cool in the pans placed on racks for 10 minutes, turn the cakes out on racks, and cool completely. Cut each cake layer in half horizontally. Assemble torte, spreading Torte Filling between each layer. Sift confectioners' sugar over the top and serve. Store the cake in the refrigerator.

To prepare filling, in a 1½–2-quart saucepan mix together ½ cup sugar and the cornstarch. In a mixing bowl combine 1½ cups milk and the egg yolks and gradually stir them into the sugar mixture. Cook and stir over medium-low heat until mixture thickens and boils, about 1 minute. Cool slightly and add 1 teaspoon vanilla and the walnuts. Cool completely before spreading on cake layers.

LEMON GROVE CAKE

SERVES 12 GENEROUSLY

1 cup butter, softened
2 cups granulated sugar
3 eggs, at room temperature
3 cups sifted flour
½ teaspoon baking soda
½ teaspoon salt
1 cup buttermilk
2 tablespoons grated lemon
   rind, packed
2 tablespoons fresh lemon juice

LEMON ICING
¼ cup butter, softened
2 cups confectioners' sugar,
   sifted
1½ tablespoons grated lemon
   rind, packed
¼ cup fresh lemon juice

In a very large bowl cream the 1 cup butter until light, slowly add the granulated sugar, and continue beating until mixture is light and fluffy. Blend in eggs one at a time.

In another bowl sift together the flour, soda, and salt. Add the flour mixture alternately with the buttermilk to the creamed mixture, beginning and ending with the flour and beating after each addition. Mix in the 2 tablespoons rind and 2 tablespoons juice. Pour the batter into a greased and lightly floured 10-inch tube pan or 12-cup (standard) bundt pan. Bake in a preheated 325° oven for 65–75 minutes or until a toothpick inserted in the center comes out clean. Place the pan on a rack to cool for 10 minutes. Turn the cake out on a rack and spread on as much Lemon Icing as the cake can absorb (about ⅓–½ of the icing). Allow cake to cool completely, then frost with remaining icing.

To prepare icing, in a mixing bowl blend together thoroughly the ¼ cup butter and the confectioners' sugar. Mix in the 1½ tablespoons rind and ¼ cup juice, one tablespoon at a time, until the frosting is of desired spreading consistency. If the entire amount of lemon juice is used, the icing will be thin and possibly a little difficult to spread evenly; however, a very tangy frosting greatly enhances the flavor of the cake. The frosting may be chilled for a few minutes to make it easier to spread.

ROLLED ALMOND WAFERS

MAKES 18 COOKIES

½ cup almonds, blanched and
   slivered
½ cup butter
½ cup granulated sugar
¼ cup flour
2 tablespoons milk
⅛ teaspoon salt

Lightly toast the almonds under the broiler and whirl them in the blender a few seconds so that they are partially ground. In a medium saucepan, melt the butter and add the almonds and all remaining ingredients, stirring until completely blended.

Drop by the teaspoon 4–6 cookies, spaced about 4 inches apart, on a greased cookie sheet. Bake in a preheated 350° oven for about 8 minutes or until cookies are evenly browned. Remove the cookies from the oven and cool for about 1 minute. Quickly lift the cookies from the cookie sheet with a spatula and gently roll the undersides around the handle of a wooden spoon. When shaped, cool each cookie on a rack. If unshaped cookies harden while working, return them for a minute to the oven to soften.

NOTE: These crisp cookies are an excellent accompaniment to ice cream, mousse, or custard. They should be stored in an airtight container.

CHERRY CHIP CHRISTMAS CAKE

must be prepared 24 hours in advance

MAKES 1 LOAF (ABOUT 40 SLICES)

2 cups pecans (or slivered almonds), chopped
1½ cups candied cherries, sliced
9 ounces semisweet chocolate chips
1½ cups sifted flour
1½ teaspoons baking powder
¼ teaspoon salt
3 eggs
1 cup granulated sugar

Grease a 9 × 5-inch loaf pan, line it lengthwise with waxed paper, allowing an inch to hang over each end, and grease again. Place the pecans, cherries, and chips into a large mixing bowl. Sift the flour, baking powder, and salt and add to the cherry mixture. Gently mix together with a wooden spoon and set aside. In the mixing bowl beat eggs until lemon-colored and thickened. Add the sugar gradually, continuing to beat. Pour the egg mixture into the flour mixture and blend thoroughly. The dough will be thick and heavy. Pour the batter into the prepared pan and bake in a preheated 325° oven for 1½ hours or until cake is lightly browned and a knife inserted in center comes out clean. Turn loaf out on a rack, paper side up, and cool 15 minutes before removing paper. Continue to cool at least 2 hours (preferably overnight) before slicing.

To serve, slice cake with a sharp bread knife in half lengthwise and ¼-inch slices across the width. Place slices on a serving plate garnished with holly.

NOTE: This cake keeps well, wrapped in foil, in the refrigerator for 2 weeks, but it should not be frozen.

CHINESE ALMOND COOKIES

¾ cup lard
¾ cup plus 2 tablespoons
    granulated sugar
2 eggs
3 cups flour
2 teaspoons baking soda
¼ teaspoon salt
2 tablespoons almond extract
1 cup blanched almonds
    (approximately)

In a large bowl cream the lard until fluffy and add the sugar slowly, continuing to cream until the mixture is smooth. Blend 1 of the eggs into the lard mixture.

In another bowl sift together the flour, soda, and salt and slowly blend it into the lard mixture. Mix in the almond extract. The dough will be very stiff. Pull off small pieces of the dough and roll into 1–1¼-inch diameter balls, continuing until all the dough is used.

On lightly greased cookie sheets flatten each ball to a thickness of ¼–½ inch and press an almond into the center of each cookie. Brush the top of each cookie with the remaining egg, lightly beaten. Bake the cookies in a preheated 375° oven for 13–15 minutes or until golden brown. Remove the cookies to a rack and cool completely. Store them in an airtight container.

BEST OATMEAL COOKIES

1 cup butter, softened
1 cup granulated sugar
½ cup brown sugar, packed
1 egg
1½ cups flour
1 teaspoon baking soda
1 teaspoon ground cinnamon
1½ cups quick rolled oats
¾ cup ground walnuts or pecans
    (may be ground in a blender)
1 teaspoon vanilla extract
Granulated sugar for dipping

In a large bowl cream the butter and add sugars, beating until fluffy. Blend egg into creamed mixture. Sift together into the creamed mixture the flour, soda, and cinnamon. Blend in the oats, nuts, and vanilla. Chill dough for 1 hour or more.

Place small pieces (about 1 teaspoonful) on a greased cookie sheet. Grease the bottom of a small glass, dip in sugar, and press gently on each uncooked cookie, flattening it to a thickness of about ¼ inch, resugaring glass for each cookie. Bake in a preheated 350° oven for 10 minutes. Cool 2–3 minutes on the sheet, remove cookies, and cool completely on racks. Store them in an airtight container.

CHOCOLATE BUTTER CREAM LAYERED COOKIES

1½ cups graham cracker crumbs
1 cup finely chopped walnuts
½ cup butter
¼ cup granulated sugar
⅓ cup unsweetened cocoa
1 egg, beaten
1 teaspoon vanilla extract

½ cup sweet butter, softened
2 tablespoons powdered custard (*see Note*) or pudding mix
3 tablespoons milk
2 cups confectioners' sugar

1½ tablespoons butter
4 ounces semisweet baking chocolate

To prepare the crust, mix together graham crumbs and walnuts in a large bowl and set aside. In a small saucepan mix together ½ cup butter the granulated sugar, cocoa, egg, and vanilla. Cook and stir over low heat until the mixture is well blended and is the consistency of custard, about 3–5 minutes. Pour the cocoa mixture into the crumb mixture and thoroughly blend. Press into an ungreased 7½ × 12 × 2-inch (2-quart) oblong pan and place in the freezer to firm while making the next layer.

To prepare the butter cream custard, cream the sweet butter until fluffy in a large bowl and blend in the custard powder. Blend the milk and slowly add the confectioners' sugar to the creamed mixture. Carefully spread butter mixture evenly over the chilled crumb layer and return the pan to the freezer until quite firm.

To prepare topping, in a small saucepan melt the 1½ tablespoons butter with the chocolate over very low heat, blending together. With a spatula spread a thin layer of chocolate over the chilled butter cream layer. Work quickly and frost a small section at a time, as the chocolate hardens rapidly when it touches the cold butter cream.

Slice the cookies in 1½–1¼-inch squares and store, well wrapped, in the refrigerator for 2–3 weeks or in the freezer for 3 months. These uncooked "cookies" are very rich and are delicious served, in place of dessert, with coffee after a filling meal.

NOTE: Bird's English dessert powder, which may be found in the gourmet section of a supermarket, is preferable.

ORANGE CHOCOLATE CHIP MERINGUE COOKIES

MAKES ABOUT 3 DOZEN

3 egg whites
⅛ teaspoon cream of tartar
⅛ teaspoon salt
1 cup sugar
1 teaspoon vanilla extract
1 tablespoon grated orange rind
1 6-ounce package semisweet
    chocolate chips

In a medium bowl beat together the egg whites, cream of tartar, and salt until soft peaks form (do not overbeat). Gradually add the sugar to whites, beating until blended. With a spoon mix the vanilla and orange rind into whites mixture. Fold in the chocolate chips.

Drop batter by the teaspoon on an ungreased cookie sheet. Bake in a preheated 300° oven for 25 minutes or until cookies are just barely brown and dry.

NOTE: The cookies may be stored in an airtight tin for up to 3 weeks.

CHOCOLATE BUTTER COOKIES

MAKES ABOUT 3½ DOZEN

6 ounces (1½ packages) German
    baking chocolate
1 cup butter
1¼ cups confectioners' sugar
1 teaspoon vanilla extract
1¼ cups sifted flour
⅛ teaspoon salt
1 cup ground walnuts

In a small saucepan melt the chocolate over very low heat and set aside to cool. Cream the butter until light. Add the confectioners' sugar slowly to the butter, continuing to cream until the mixture is fluffy. Blend in the vanilla. Sift the flour and salt into the creamed mixture and stir until smooth. Blend in chocolate and ground walnuts. Drop teaspoons of cookie batter 2 inches apart on an ungreased cookie sheet and bake in a preheated 250° oven for 40 minutes. Cool cookies for 2–3 minutes, remove to a rack, and cool completely. Store in an airtight container.

PECAN BALLS

MAKES ABOUT 2½ DOZEN

½ cup butter, softened
2 tablespoons granulated sugar
1 teaspoon vanilla extract
Pinch salt
1 cup sifted cake flour
1 cup finely chopped pecans
Confectioners' sugar

In a medium large bowl cream butter and add granulated sugar, beating until fluffy. Add the vanilla to creamed mixture. Sift together the salt and flour and add to the creamed mixture, blending until smooth. Stir in the pecans. The dough will be stiff. Pull off sections of the dough and roll into small balls, about 1 inch in diameter.

Bake on lightly greased cookie sheet in a pre-heated 350° oven for 15–20 minutes or until lightly browned. Roll cookies in confectioners' sugar while still hot.

NOTE: The cookies may be stored at room temperature in an airtight tin for 2–3 days or refrigerated for 1 week.

RASPBERRY MERINGUE SQUARES MAKES 6–7 DOZEN

2½ cups flour
6 tablespoons granulated sugar
1 cup butter, at room
　temperature but firm
5 eggs, separated
1 tablespoon vanilla extract
3½ cups raspberry jam
1 cup granulated sugar
1 tablespoon bourbon (or
　vanilla)
2 cups walnuts, finely chopped
3 tablespoons confectioners'
　sugar

In a large bowl mix the flour and 6 tablespoons granulated sugar. With a pastry cutter or 2 knives cut the butter into the flour mixture, tossing and mixing until the mixture resembles fine meal. With a fork or pastry blender, mix in the egg yolks and vanilla extract until blended. Press the mixture into a lightly greased 11 × 16-inch jelly-roll pan. Bake the crust in a preheated 350° oven for 10 minutes or until it barely begins to brown. Remove from the oven and cool on a rack for 15 minutes. Spread the baked crust evenly with raspberry jam.

In a medium-large mixing bowl beat the egg whites until soft peaks form and add the 1 cup sugar and the bourbon or vanilla slowly, continuing to beat until stiff. Fold the nuts into the beaten whites and spread the mixture evenly over the raspberry jam. Return the pan to a 350° oven and continue baking for 30–35 minutes or until the meringue begins to brown. Remove the pan to a rack and cool completely. Dust lightly with confectioners' sugar and cut into 1½-inch squares. These cookies, because they are meringue-topped, are best when served on the day they are made, but may be held in an airtight tin for a few days. They are quite rich and make an excellent tea cookie.

CHOCOLATE CHEESECAKE SQUARES

MAKES ABOUT 2½ DOZEN

1 cup sifted flour
½ cup granulated sugar
3 tablespoons cocoa
1 teaspoon baking powder
¼ teaspoon salt
¼ cup butter
2 eggs
1 teaspoon vanilla extract
½ cup walnuts, chopped

To prepare the crust, into a medium-sized mixing bowl sift 1 cup flour, ½ cup sugar, the cocoa, baking powder, and ¼ teaspoon salt. With a pastry blender, cut the butter into the flour mixture until it is well blended and the mixture resembles fine meal. Add 1 egg yolk (reserve the white) and 1 teaspoon vanilla to the crumb mixture and continue to toss and blend with the pastry blender until the mixture is evenly moistened. Fold in the nuts and press the crumb mixture into a greased 9-inch square or 8 x 12 x 2-inch baking dish or pan. Bake in a preheated 325° oven for 12–15 minutes. Set the crust aside to cool for at least 10 minutes.

8 ounces cream cheese, softened
¼ cup granulated sugar
½ cup sour cream
1 tablespoon flour
¼ teaspoon salt
1 tablespoon grated orange rind
½ teaspoon vanilla extract

1 ounce semisweet chocolate

To prepare the filling, in a medium bowl cream together the cream cheese and ¼ cup sugar until light and well blended. Blend the sour cream into the cream cheese mixture until smooth.

Add the 1 tablespoon flour, ¼ teaspoon salt, the orange rind, and ½ teaspoon vanilla and mix well. In a small bowl beat the reserved egg white and the remaining egg together and blend into the cream cheese filling.

Pour the cream cheese filling over the baked crust and return the pan to the 325° oven for 20–25 minutes or until the top of the batter is well set and slightly puffed. Remove the pan to a rack and cool completely. Garnish the top with shaved curls of the semisweet chocolate. Cut into 1½-inch squares to serve.

CHOCOLATE CREAM CHEESE BROWNIES

MAKES ABOUT 2½ DOZEN

3 tablespoons butter
1 4-ounce bar German
    chocolate or 1 cup semisweet
    chocolate chips

2 tablespoons softened butter
3 ounces cream cheese, softened

To prepare the chocolate mixture, in the top of a double boiler over simmering water melt 3 tablespoons butter and the chocolate. Remove the pan from heat and set aside.

To prepare the cream cheese mixture, in a medium bowl cream 2 tablespoons softened butter

¼ cup granulated sugar
1 egg
1 tablespoon flour
1 teaspoon vanilla extract

2 eggs
¾ cup granulated sugar
½ cup flour
½ teaspoon baking powder
½ teaspoon salt
½ cup chopped walnuts
1 teaspoon vanilla extract
¼ teaspoon almond extract

and 3 ounces cream cheese until fluffy. Blend ¼ cup sugar, 1 egg, 1 tablespoon flour, and the vanilla into the creamed mixture and set aside.

In another mixing bowl beat 2 eggs and add ¾ cup sugar, continuing to beat until blended. Into the sugar-egg mixture sift the ½ cup flour, the baking powder, and salt. Stir melted chocolate mixture, walnuts, vanilla, and almond extract into sugar-egg mixture. Spread ½ the chocolate mixture evenly in a greased 9-inch-square pan. Over the chocolate mixture spread the cream cheese mixture. Drop spoonfuls of all remaining chocolate over the cream cheese. Swirl the top of the batter just slightly with a fork to give a marbled effect. Bake in a preheated 350° oven for 40–50 minutes or until a toothpick inserted in the center comes out clean. Cool slightly. Cut the brownies in squares to serve.

APRICOT BARS

MAKES ABOUT 2½ DOZEN

⅔ cup dried apricots

¼ cup confectioners' sugar
1 cup sifted flour
½ cup butter, softened

2 eggs
1 cup brown sugar
⅓ cup flour
½ teaspoon baking powder
¼ teaspoon salt
½ teaspoon vanilla extract
½ cup chopped walnuts
Confectioners' sugar for dusting

Rinse the apricots, place in a small saucepan, cover with water, and simmer 10 minutes. Drain, cool, chop the fruit, and set aside.

In a medium bowl sift together the confectioners' sugar and 1 cup flour. Cut the butter into flour mixture until well mixed and crumbly. Press mixture into a greased 8 × 8 × 2-inch pan and bake in a preheated 350° oven for 22–25 minutes, until just barely brown. Cool for at least 15 minutes.

Meanwhile, in a medium bowl beat the eggs until well mixed and slowly add the brown sugar, beating until blended. Sift together ⅓ cup flour, the baking powder, and salt and blend into egg mixture. Blend vanilla, chopped apricots, and nuts into egg mixture and pour over the baked layer. Return the pan to the 350° oven for an additional 30 minutes. Remove the pan to a rack and cool completely. Sprinkle with confectioners' sugar and cut in 1½-inch-square bars.

CHOCOLATE CHIP BANANA BARS

MAKES ABOUT 3 DOZEN

¾ cup butter, softened
⅔ cup granulated sugar
⅔ cup brown sugar, packed
1 egg
1 teaspoon vanilla extract
2½ ripe medium bananas,
  mashed
1 cup sifted flour (preferably
  unbleached)
1 cup whole-wheat flour
2 teaspoons baking powder
½ teaspoon salt
1 6-ounce package semisweet
  chocolate chips

In a large bowl cream the butter and add sugars slowly, beating until mixture is fluffy. Add the egg and vanilla and beat until blended. Stir the mashed bananas into creamed mixture.

In another bowl sift together the flours, baking powder, and salt. Add flour mixture to creamed mixture gradually, beating just until blended. Stir chocolate chips into batter. Spread batter into greased and lightly floured 9 × 13 × 2-inch pan. Bake in a preheated 350° oven for 30 minutes or until a toothpick inserted in the center comes out clean. Cool in the pan on a rack. Cut in squares.

NOTE: A slightly less sweet but even more nutritious, chewy bar may be made by substituting 1 cup plus 3 tablespoons "yellow D" sugar (purchased at health-food stores) for both granulated and brown sugars. Either method makes an irresistible cookie bar.

TANGY LEMON BARS

MAKES ABOUT 4 DOZEN

2 cups sifted flour
½ cup confectioners' sugar
¼ teaspoon salt
1 cup butter, chilled
4 eggs
2 cups granulated sugar
⅓ cup fresh lemon juice
1½ teaspoons grated lemon
  rind
¼ cup flour
1 teaspoon baking powder
Confectioners' sugar for dusting

In a medium-large bowl sift together 2 cups flour, ½ cup confectioners' sugar, and the salt. With a pastry blender or 2 knives cut butter into flour mixture until mixture clings together and resembles coarse meal. Press mixture evenly into a 9 × 13 × 2-inch pan and bake in a preheated 350° oven for 20 minutes or until lightly browned. Cool 10–15 minutes.

In a large bowl beat the eggs until blended and slowly add the granulated sugar, beating. Blend the lemon juice and rind into egg mixture. Sift together ¼ cup flour and the baking powder into egg mixture and blend. Spread mixture evenly over baked, slightly cooled crust and return to 350° oven for 25 minutes. Cool in the pan on a rack, sprinkle with confectioners' sugar, and cut in squares.

NOTE: The bars keep in an airtight tin about 4 days or refrigerated about 1½ weeks.

MINCEMEAT BARS

1 9-ounce package dry
  mincemeat
1 15-ounce can sweetened
  condensed milk (1⅓ cups)
1 cup sifted flour
1 teaspoon baking soda
1½ cups corn flakes, crushed
  (⅔ cup)
½ cup butter, softened
1 cup brown sugar, packed
1 tablespoon milk

In a saucepan break mincemeat into small pieces. Add condensed milk and cook over low heat, stirring constantly, until mixture thickens, about 5 minutes. Remove from heat and set aside.

In a medium bowl sift together the flour and soda and mix in the corn flake crumbs. In a large bowl cream the butter, sugar, and milk until fluffy. Add the crumb mixture to the creamed mixture and blend.

Press ½ the crumb mixture in an ungreased 9 × 13 × 2-inch pan. Carefully spread the mincemeat mixture over the batter in the pan and sprinkle with remaining crumb mixture. Bake in a preheated 350° oven for 30 minutes or until bars are golden brown. Cool in pan on a rack. Cut in bars or 1½ × 1½-inch squares.

NOTE: These bars make an excellent Christmas season dessert, served with eggnog ice cream.

ALMOND MACAROONS

16 ounces almond paste
6 egg whites, unbeaten
2 cups granulated sugar
2 cups confectioners' sugar

In a large bowl work the almond paste with 2 of the egg whites until there are no lumps. Gradually add 1 cup of the granulated sugar and 2 more of the egg whites, beating until blended. Blend in the remaining granulated sugar, the confectioners' sugar, and the last 2 egg whites, beating until smooth.

Prepare a cookie sheet by lining it with foil, shiny side up, or greasing and flouring it. Drop cookie dough by the teaspoon on the prepared sheet and bake in a preheated 325° oven for 20–25 minutes or until cookies are golden brown. Remove cookies to a rack and cool completely.

NOTE: The cookies may be stored in an airtight container for at least 1 week.

CHAPTER VIII

THE DESERT VALLEYS

FRUITS, PIES, & DESSERTS

THE California Desert is part of the Great American Desert that stretches from the western edge of the Rockies, all across Utah and Nevada, south to the Mexican border, and over a hundred miles into California. In California there are actually two desert areas. The Mojave Desert is referred to as the high desert. It includes Death Valley to the north, which not only boasts the lowest spot in the United States (280 feet below sea level) but also records the highest temperatures (close to 140°). The lower southern desert, or Salton Sink, extends from below the San Gorgonio Pass to the Mexican Border and includes the Coachella and Imperial valleys.

The desert has a hostile face. Temperatures range from below freezing on winter nights to a scorching 100°-plus on summer days. Blinding sandstorms and burning sun support only the hardiest of wildlife—scorpion, tarantula, coyote, rabbit, rattlesnake, skunk, and predatory birds, to name a few. In spite of this, the desert has always had a special attraction for man. While some men have chosen to cut trails through the desert rather than cross the higher mountains to the north, others have discovered its hidden beauty and stayed to live in harmony with nature as they found it.

The deserts are greatly altered from their primordial state, but man is not wholly responsible. In the beginning of the earth's history, great oceans covered most of the land. Even after mountains had been formed, the California Desert remained underwater. As the earth's crust heaved and buckled, rose and sank, land masses formed, gradually increasing in size. The Gulf of California covered an area extending as far north as the present city of Palm Springs. As the water receded, it left a huge sink or depression in the land. Today the Salton Sink is separated from the gulf by the delta of the Colorado River.

As the mountains rose and formed great peaks, the desert land became drier. On the western side of the California Desert lies the Peninsular Range, and to the east the San Bernardino Mountains, through which runs the famous San Andreas Fault. In these mountains stand the highest peaks in Southern California, San Gorgonio at 11,485 feet and Mt. San Jacinto at 10,805 feet. They serve as a gateway to the present desert and are a barrier to the rainclouds coming from the Pacific.

In ancient times this was a fertile and verdant land. As late as eight thousand years ago—when man first inhabited the desert area—the Colorado River had spilled over and formed a fresh-water lake that extended as far north as Indio. This huge body of water came to be called Lake Cahuilla, and much of the early Indian population lived along its shores and beside its streams. The last natural spill-over from the Colorado River into Lake Cahuilla was approximately six hundred years ago. After that time, it started evaporating as the air became increasingly drier; and a once green and lush valley began its transformation to a dry, arid wasteland.

The early Stone Age inhabitants were hunters and gatherers, sharing the desert with the coyotes, rabbits, and rattlesnakes. As a more arid climate prevailed, the Indians lived on the chuckwalla, lizard, and rat, while the fruits of cactus, including the agave, made palatable additions to their menu. They knew the canyons and hidden springs where water could be obtained. They ground mesquite seed to make a form of flour and used the barrel cactus for the life-saving liquid contained within its thorny exterior.

In the summer when the burning sands became impossible to bear, the Indians retreated to the mountains where larger animals could be hunted and food was more plentiful. It was a harsh land but the Indian survived. This arid wasteland, the hostile California Desert, was their home.

The Spanish first arrived in 1540. Hernando de Alarcón sailed from Acapulco, Mexico, up the Gulf of California to the mouth of the Colorado River. Traveling along the river, he landed near the present site of Yuma, Arizona. Later that year Melchior Díaz, who had left Coronado's expedition to meet with Alarcón, made the same journey. With a group of soldiers he followed the Colorado River for some distance and then pushed to the west. Díaz was supposedly searching for the mythical Seven Cities of Cibola. What he found was a vast desert wilderness that is now known as the Imperial Valley. Diaz named it the Valley of Fortune, but apparently he failed to convince anyone, for it was more than two hundred years before the next known Spanish settlers arrived.

The Spanish had been colonizing present-day Arizona, New Mexico, and Texas as early as the sixteenth and seventeenth centuries, but they had not attempted to explore farther to the west. In 1769 Gaspar de Portolá and Father Junípero Serra, bearing the flag of Spain, threaded their way up the Baja Peninsula to found the first mission and presidio at San Diego. The following year another mission and presidio were established at Monterey and more were

planned. These early settlements had to be supplied and protected in order to survive. The sea was often dangerous or unpredictable, so a land route had to be found. The route from Sonora, Mexico, lay not only through the desert but through country inhabited by the warlike Apache Indians. Beyond was the Colorado River in the territory held by the fearsome Yuman tribes. The vast California Desert, where no trail existed and no water sources were charted, followed.

Undaunted by this grim picture and completely alone, one valiant priest, Father Francis Garcés, set out in 1771 from Tubac, in what is now southeastern Arizona, to find a route west. Arriving safely at the Yuman villages, he established a firm friendship with their chief, Palma, and then headed west after crossing the Colorado River. Going for days at a time without water, this tough little priest pursued a northwesterly course until he saw in the distance the Rocky San Jacinto Mountains and a possible opening in the range. This was the answer he had sought, and he returned to Tubac with his report.

On the strength of this, Juan Bautista de Anza organized an exploratory expedition, which included the indomitable Father Garcés, and set out from Tubac in 1774. After an encounter with the Apaches, Anza finally reached the friendly Yuman villages. Here, he met up with Sebastián Tarabel, an Indian who had escaped from the San Gabriel Mission. This Indian had walked from the mission, crossed the desert, and lived to tell the tale. Anza promptly hired him as a guide and pushed west. Approaching the Salton Sink, they proceeded up the present-day Anza-Borrego Desert, through the Coyote Canyon, and finally reached the San Gabriel Mission. A way had been found. It was hazardous and hard, they had suffered horribly, but they had survived.

Anza returned to Tubac to organize his second expedition, which included 240 colonists. This group reached the San Gabriel Mission on January 4, 1776. From here, they headed north to found a presidio and mission in San Francisco. This successful migration was miraculous for those days, especially since it was accomplished with the loss of only one life. In later years the Anza Trail became an established route for colonists and settlers.

While Anza was leading his expedition of colonists, Father Garcés set off on another trip of his own. Accompanied by guides from the Yuman villages, he once more crossed to the eastern side of the San Bernardino Mountains, pushed north to discover the Mojave River, then through the mountains and down to the San Gabriel Mission. This ancient Indian pathway, called the Mojave Indian Trail, was later followed in part by Jedediah Smith. In 1826 Smith and his party became the first Americans to enter California by land from the east. They traveled at night to avoid the sun and intense heat. Precious water was carried in containers made from animal intestines. The Smith expedition was one of the most important efforts of western trail breaking because it made the great valleys of San Joaquin and Sacramento known. After that year many explorers, trappers, traders, and, eventually, settlers followed this and other trails, variously called the Emigrant Trail, the Colorado Road, and the Old Butterfield Stage Route.

Another main trail into Southern California was the Old Spanish Trail or Santa Fe Trail. It was opened in 1831 by a group of settlers and followed very nearly the same route now indicated on maps as Highway 66, also following the Mojave River and going through the Cajon Pass into San Bernardino.

By 1877, the day of the stagecoach, rolling and rocking its way over the desert, was ending. The Southern Pacific Railroad put down its roadbed and completed its line from Los Angeles to Yuma. It was after this that the cultivation of the area began in earnest.

For some time, agricultural experts had maintained that the sandy areas north and south of the present Salton Sea would be ideal for growing a wide variety of produce. In 1900 George Chaffey, an irrigation engineer from Austria, arrived and changed the name to Imperial Valley. The new name, and also the efforts of the Imperial Land Company, attracted settlers. Chaffey developed a plan to divert water from the Colorado River, and soon irrigation districts began to emerge as political entities.

The first delivery of water from the Colorado came in 1901. With this impetus farmers began arriving at the rate of five a day. The arrival of ample water proved the area to be valuable farm land. In 1905 a canal was cut too deep. Unusually heavy rains that year caused the dam to break, and the Colorado River flowed into the valley. It flowed at a rate of 100,000 feet a day and took months to contain. What remained formed the Salton Sea, a salty body of water 240 feet below sea level that separates the Coachella and Imperial valleys.

The culmination of these massive efforts toward water diversion was the 120-mile-long All American Canal, completed in 1942. The canal brings water to the Coachella Valley, where 900,000 acres are under cultivation, all below sea level.

In the beginning, staple crops—barley, wheat, sorghum, and alfalfa—predominated in the desert valleys; but by 1905 the produce became more varied. Newcomers—undaunted by tests that showed the soil was too high in alkali content for farming—planted grasses, citrus, lettuce, melons, and eventually berries, grapes, and all the garden specialities from back home. And they grew handsomely. Now melons are the most important crop of the Coachella Valley, although the grapefruit is more famous.

Dates are another major crop. The present trees, nearly 200,000 of them, are descendants of a few hundred that had been imported from the Near East. The trees are planted in harems, with one male tree for every fifty female trees. Dates from California find their way all over the country, especially at Christmas time.

The climate in the Coachella and Imperial valleys is ideal. Two complete growing seasons each year produce enough melons, truck crops, and other fruit to make the lower California desert valleys one of the richest agricultural areas in the world.

While the Spanish were under pressure to establish a land approach to California across its lower deserts, there was no such pressure to cross the awesome Mojave Desert somewhat to the north and on the eastern side of the San Bernardino Mountains. The Mojave Desert and Death Valley were left solely to the Indians until a few early trappers struggled through in the 1800s.

In 1841 the first emigrant group into California from the east, the Bidwell-Bartleson Party, managed to cross the Great American Desert, and after much suffering they traversed the Sierras just north of Sonora Pass. They then headed west into Sutter's Fort. A wagon trail had been broken into California. Eight years later, the San Joaquin Company formed the first wagon train to cut a trail through the California Desert. Calling themselves the Jayhawkers, this party was a composite of various smaller groups. One of the smaller groups was the Bennet-Arcane Party, which separated and chose a shorter route west, directly through Death Valley. After traveling on the desert for weeks, they had suffered all the agonies of the waterless wastes. Crossing the Funeral Range, they approached the alkaline sink of Death Valley, where the horrors of the scorching sands nearly overwhelmed them. Completely lost, starving, and suffering from thirst, they would have perished had it not been for the heroic determination of some of the young men in the group. After arriving safely in San Bernardino, they appropriately named the valley "Death Valley." This was the first of many Death Valley sagas that haunted the lives of countless numbers of settlers to come.

The Jayhawkers had gone their separate way, traveled a southward trail through Death Valley, and experienced an equally hazardous crossing of the Mojave Desert. Every member was thankful to come out alive. One man in the party named Towne had an unusual accident while stumbling through the Panamint Range on the western edge of Death Valley. Weakened by starvation, he had fallen and dropped his gun, dislodging the gun sight. While retrieving the gun sight, he noticed a rock beside it clearly showing signs of silver ore. He pocketed the rock, rapidly gathered more specimens, and rejoined his fellow

Jayhawkers. When the specimens were finally tested, the ore assayed out at a spectacularly high grade of silver. Towne appropriately named his mine the Gunsight Mine. However, he could never persuade himself nor his friends to return to Death Valley and claim the mine. As time passed, the name became the Lost Gunsight Mine.

Around 1860, a prospector named Jacob Breyfogle found gold in this same area, but while bringing his specimens out to be tested, he also suffered an accident which left him completely demented. His specimens assayed out at almost pure gold. Once he recovered his health, he led a group back to Death Valley to locate the rich Breyfogle Mine, but he never found it.

The Lost Brefogle and Gunsight mines are still waiting to be found. Desolate as the region is, gold or silver still lures men there. Hundreds, while searching for these famous lost mines, have discovered other mines and millions of dollars in silver, copper, zinc, lead, and even talc. Between 1860 and 1880 numerous mines were opened between the southern base of the Sierras and the Nevada border. The grizzled prospector with his burro will always be the signature of the desert, and today the Panamint Mountains play host to a scattered group of wild burros, descendants of those early prospectors' rugged companions.

In 1873 another ore was discovered in Death Valley: borax. It was one thing to discover a valuable ore and quite another to get it out of this Godforsaken country and to the coast. By 1880 a railroad had been established at Mojave, but it was still another 165 miles to the borax at Furnace Creek. There were only four springs along this route, the last one thirty miles from Furnace Creek. The route crossed miles of sand, salt marshes, and high barren mountains, and yet a road was needed to move the borax. Finally, Chinese laborers were brought in and put to work in the blinding 120° heat. They sledge-hammered out a road for $1.25 a day.

Wagons to haul this valuable borax had to be specially built to withstand the punishment of desert and mountains alike. Standing two stories high and weighing over three tons, they often carried loads of several tons. Two of the wagons were hitched together with a third and smaller wagon carrying water. This dead weight on sand and jagged rocks was drawn by eighteen mules and two horses, the inspiration for the famed 20 Mule Team Borax slogan. The driver, or skinner as he was called, sat 120 feet back from his lead mules with a jerk line in one hand and a 22-foot lash in the other. Beside him on the seat was a pile of rocks to be hurled at any fractious mule too far away to be reached by the lash. The round trip from Furnace Creek to Mojave took twenty long grueling days.

Today this area is somewhat more familiar to us than it was when the borax wagons rolled. Death Valley's Scotty's Castle is a popular hotel and tourist attraction, and both Furnace Creek and Stove Pipe Wells offer comfortable lodging for the wayfarer. Colorful names remain, such as Devil's Cornfield, Bad Water, Bennett Wells, and the Funeral Mountains.

These civilized retreats are recent developments—oases on a dry and untamed land—just as in the southern deserts lavish resorts beckon vacationers to the mild, warm winter weather. Man has finally tamed the desert to his civilized ways—in part. The vastness of this land still defies control, and mysteries continue to prevail.

CARAMELIZED CALIFORNIA ORANGES

SERVES 8

8 oranges, preferably navel and
    not more than 3 inches in
    diameter
2 cups granulated sugar
1 cup water
5 tablespoons curaçao or
    Grand Marnier
1 teaspoon Chinese Fine Spice

Peel the oranges. Scrape the insides of the peel from 3 of the oranges to remove the white pulp. Cut the peels into thin, long strips for garnish. In a 1-quart saucepan place the orange peel strips with enough water to cover and boil slowly for 10 minutes. Drain the peels and set aside.

In a 1-quart saucepan combine the sugar and water and boil for about 10 minutes or until the mixture becomes syrup, about 220° on a candy thermometer. Remove syrup from heat. Roll each whole orange in the syrup and drain them on a small rack. Add the cooked orange rind and the Chinese Fine Spice to the syrup. Add the curaçao or Grand Marnier and heat until the peel becomes transparent. Remove the orange peel from the syrup and reserve. Arrange the oranges on a serving dish. Pour the remaining syrup over the oranges. Arrange the orange peel in a decorative pattern on top of the oranges. Chill in the refrigerator for several hours until ready to serve.

ORANGES BURGUNDY

SERVES 6

¾ cup granulated sugar
1 cup water
1 cup red wine (such as
    burgundy)
2 whole cloves
1 1-inch stick cinnamon
1 1-inch piece vanilla bean
4 lemon slices
6 large seedless oranges
Mint sprigs (optional)

In a medium saucepan combine the sugar and water and cook, stirring, until the sugar dissolves. Add the wine, cloves, cinnamon, vanilla bean, and lemon slices. Bring the mixture to a boil and simmer for 15 minutes. Strain the mixture. Meanwhile, peel the oranges and remove all the white membrane. Slice the oranges thinly. Pour the hot wine syrup over the orange slices and refrigerate for at least 4 hours or until thoroughly chilled. Serve in chilled dessert dishes and garnish with fresh mint leaves if desired.

MINTED GRAPEFRUIT CUPS

SERVES 8

4 grapefruits
⅔ cup grenadine
1 cup strawberries, sliced
2 oranges, sectioned
8 mint sprigs

In a saw-tooth fashion cut the grapefruits in half. Carefully section out the fruit. Cut out and discard the white membrane. In a medium bowl pour the grenadine over the grapefruit sections. Chill for at least 1 hour. Add the berries and the orange sections, mixing gently. Place fruit and grenadine mixture into the grapefruit cups. Garnish with mint sprigs and serve.

AMBROSIA

SERVES 4–6

1 pineapple, sliced and cored
¼ cup chopped walnuts
3 tablespoons brown sugar
¼ cup chartreuse liqueur
   (Cointreau or curaçao may
   be substituted
6 coconut macaroons
1 pint Rich Vanilla Ice Cream
   (*see Index*)

Cut the pineapple into 1-inch cubes. Mix the pineapple, walnuts, sugar, and liqueur together in a large serving bowl. Crush the macaroons with a rolling pin and add to the fruit mixture. Chill the fruit for 1 hour.

Soften the ice cream by taking it out of the freezer and storing it in the refrigerator for about 20 minutes. Shortly before serving, gently fold in the ice cream to the fruit mixture. Serve at once.

STRAWBERRIES ROMANOFF

SERVES 8

2 quarts fresh strawberries,
   washed, stemmed, and
   chilled
2 tablespoons granulated sugar
1 pint Rich Vanilla Ice Cream
   (*see Index*), slightly thawed
1 cup heavy cream
2 tablespoons fresh lemon juice
¼ cup Cointreau
1 ounce brandy
Mint sprigs (optional)

Chill 8 dessert dishes.

In a large bowl combine the berries and sugar. Chill for 2 hours. In a separate large bowl lightly whip the ice cream. In a medium bowl whip the heavy cream until it is stiff and fold it into the ice cream. Add the lemon juice and liquors. Pour this mixture over the berries and stir gently. Serve at once in chilled dishes. Garnish with fresh mint leaves if desired.

STEWED GINGERED FIGS

SERVES 8

1 pound fresh figs
2 strips fresh lemon rind
3 tablespoons fresh lemon juice
1½ tablespoons chopped fresh
   ginger root
1 cup heavy cream or 1 pint
   sour cream
Sugar to taste

Wash the figs and remove the stems. Place the figs in a large saucepan and cover with cold water. Add the lemon rind, 2 tablespoons of the lemon juice, and the ginger root. Stew the figs over moderate heat until puffed and soft, about 20–30 minutes. Remove the fruit to a plate using a slotted spoon. Measure the juice and return ½ of it to the saucepan. Discard the remaining syrup. Simmer the syrup over low heat for 15 minutes until thick. Remove the pan from the heat, add the remaining lemon juice, and return the figs to the saucepan. Stir lightly to blend in the lemon juice. Sugar may be added if necessary, depending on sweetness of fruit. Cool the syrup for 30 minutes and then refrigerate for at least 4 hours before serving.

To serve, place the figs and the syrup in a serving bowl. Pass a pitcher of heavy cream to be poured over the fruit or serve with sour cream to spoon over the figs.

WATERMELON BASKET

SERVES 10

1 whole medium watermelon
2 cups canteloupe balls
2 cups honeydew balls
2 cups fresh hulled strawberries
1 cup blueberries
1 cup seedless grapes
1 cup granulated sugar
¾ cup water
1 cup dry vermouth
¼ cup cognac
2 bananas, sliced
Grape leaves

Make a basket of the watermelon by cutting a 2-inch-wide band across the center of the width of the watermelon, stopping about ⅓ of the way down from the top. (This makes the handle of the basket.) Cut the sides of the melon, about ⅓ of the way down from the top, into scallops. Remove the top sections and hollow out the watermelon in large pieces.

With a melon ball cutter, scoop out balls from the large pieces of watermelon. Place the watermelon balls in a large mixing bowl and add the canteloupe, honeydew, strawberries, blueberries, and grapes.

In a medium-sized saucepan dissolve the sugar in the water over low heat. Increase the heat to moderately high and boil the syrup for 5 minutes. Remove the pan from the heat and let the syrup cool. When cool, add the vermouth and the cognac. Pour the syrup over the fruits and toss the mixture lightly. Place the fruits into the watermelon basket and cover the basket with foil. Chill 2–4 hours. Add bananas just before serving. Place the basket on a platter surrounded by grape leaves.

PEARS WITH FLUFFY BRANDY SAUCE   SERVES 12

must be prepared 24 hours in advance

1 cup granulated sugar
4 cups water
3 tablespoons fresh lemon juice
2 sticks cinnamon
4 whole cloves
6 large firm pears (preferably Anjou or Comice)

FLUFFY BRANDY SAUCE
4 egg yolks
½ cup granulated sugar
¼ cup brandy
⅛ teaspoon salt
1 teaspoon orange flower water (optional)
½–¾ cup heavy cream

In a 4–5-quart saucepan or casserole with a cover, dissolve 1 cup sugar in the water. Add the lemon juice, cinnamon, and cloves, cover tightly, and simmer for 10–15 minutes. Peel and halve the pears. Poach the pears gently in the syrup over low heat for 30–40 minutes or until fork-tender. Remove the pears from the pan with a slotted spoon. Cover and chill overnight on a plate. Save the sugar syrup for another use. To serve, pour chilled Fluffy Brandy Sauce over the pears.

To prepare sauce, about an hour before serving, place the egg yolks in a small mixing bowl and beat well. Gradually add the ½ cup sugar and continue beating about 3 minutes or until the mixture is thick and lemon-colored. Pour the mixture into the top of a double boiler and using low heat, cook over hot water, stirring constantly, for 5–6 minutes or until somewhat thickened. Remove the sauce from the heat and beat it vigorously while adding the brandy and salt. Stir in the orange flower water and let the sauce cool to room temperature. Whip the cream in a mixing bowl until it forms soft peaks. When the sauce has cooled, gently but thoroughly fold in the whipped cream. Cover and chill.

POACHED PEACHES WITH RASPBERRY PUREE SERVES 10

6 cups water
2¼ cups granulated sugar
1 1-inch piece vanilla bean
2 whole cloves
10 fresh peaches, firm and ripe
4 cups fresh raspberries
¾ cup superfine sugar
4 tablespoons kirsch
Mint sprigs

In a very large pan combine the water, granulated sugar, vanilla bean, and cloves. Simmer the mixture over low heat until the sugar is dissolved.

Place the peaches in the syrup and simmer for 8 minutes. Remove the pan from the heat and cool the peaches in the syrup for 20 minutes. Drain the peaches on a rack and peel them while still warm. Reserve the syrup for another use. Arrange the peeled peaches on a serving dish, cover, and chill.

Force the raspberries through a fine sieve or purée in a blender for 10–20 seconds. Add the superfine sugar and kirsch and blend for a few more seconds. Taste for sweetness, adding more sugar if necessary. Place in a bowl, cover, and chill at least 2 hours. To serve, place a peach in a sherbet glass and cover with about 4–6 tablespoons of the raspberry purée. Decorate with fresh mint. Serve at once.

PEARS NOIRS   SERVES 6

1 cup granulated sugar
4 cups water
3 tablespoons fresh lemon juice
2 sticks cinnamon
4 whole cloves
6 firm pears with stems
    (preferably Anjou or Comice)
2 ounces dark sweet chocolate
4 ounces semisweet chocolate
4 tablespoons butter
Mint sprigs

In a saucepan large enough to hold the pears upright, dissolve the sugar in the water over low heat. Add the lemon juice, cinnamon, and cloves. Cover the pan tightly and simmer for 10 or 15 minutes.

Peel the pears keeping the stems intact and cut a thin slice off the bottom of each pear so they stand upright. Poach the pears gently in the syrup for 30–40 minutes. Cool the pears on a rack and chill them overnight.

In the top of a double boiler, melt the chocolates over warm water. Add the butter and stir until smooth. Dip each pear into the chocolate mixture and coat, using a spoon if necessary. This dessert can be held at this point in the refrigerator for 6 hours. Place the pears on a serving plate and garnish with fresh sprigs of mint.

CHOCOLATE FONDUE

6 ounces semisweet chocolate
  chips
¼ cup light cream
2 tablespoons kirsch or Grand
  Marnier
½ teaspoon freshly grated
  orange rind (optional)
2–3 cups fresh fruit for dipping
  such as strawberries,
  pineapple, bananas, pears,
  and cherries, cut into
  bite-sized pieces

In the top of a double boiler over hot water melt the chocolate chips. Add the cream, kirsch or Grand Marnier, and orange rind, stirring to blend well. When heated through, transfer the chocolate mixture to a fondue pot and keep warm.

Arrange the fruit on a serving platter. Using fondue forks, guests help themselves by dipping the fruit into the fondue.

AVOCADO SHERBET

SERVES 4

1⅛ cups granulated sugar
1½ cups water
3 medium avocados
¾ cup fresh lemon juice
1 teaspoon grated lemon rind
Lemon rind curls (optional)

In a medium saucepan boil the sugar and water together for 5 minutes. Peel and pit the avocados. In a large bowl mash the avocado with a potato masher until a pulp is formed (there should be 1½ cups of pulp). Add the lemon juice and lemon rind to the avocado pulp. Slowly add the cooked sugar syrup, blending thoroughly. Pour into a freezer tray and freeze. Stir once during freezing. Serve in dessert dishes or goblets. Garnish with lemon rind curls if desired.

STRAWBERRY ICE

SERVES 8

4 cups fresh strawberries
  (raspberries or apricots may
  be substituted)
2 cups water
1 cup superfine sugar
4 tablespoons fresh lemon juice

Purée the strawberries in a blender and set aside. In a 2-quart saucepan bring the water and sugar to a boil over medium heat, stirring until the sugar dissolves. Let the mixture cook for exactly 5 minutes, timing from the moment the sugar and water begin to boil. Remove the pan from the heat and allow the syrup to cool. Stir the strawberries into the cooled syrup. Add the lemon juice. Pour the mixture into freezer trays. Freeze the ice for 4 hours, removing from the freezer 5 or 6 times to stir the ice well, scraping the sides and the edges of the trays. This stirring will give the ice a smoother texture.

FRESH LIME ICE WITH COINTREAU

3 cups water
1½ cups granulated sugar
½ cup fresh lime juice (2–4
  limes, depending on size)
2 teaspoons finely grated lime
  rind
2 tablespoons fresh lemon juice
¼ cup Cointreau
Pinch salt
1–2 drops green food coloring
  (optional)
1 egg white

In a heavy saucepan combine the water and sugar and bring to a boil, stirring constantly. Boil 5 minutes. Chill. When cold, stir in lime juice and rind, lemon juice, Cointreau, salt, and food coloring. Pour into freezer trays or a 9 × 9-inch pan and freeze until mushy (usually about 45 minutes).

Remove from freezer and pour into a chilled bowl. Beat with a whisk or rotary beater until lime mixture is farily smooth. Beat egg white until it is firm and holds a good peak. Beat egg white into lime mixture. Return to freezer trays and freeze a second time until it is mushy. Remove and beat again in a chilled bowl until smooth. Return to freezer trays and freeze until firm.

RICH CHOCOLATE ICE CREAM

8 egg yolks
1¼ cups granulated sugar
4 ounces semisweet chocolate,
  grated
1 quart milk
1 3-inch piece vanilla bean
4 ounces unsweetened chocolate,
  melted
2 cups heavy cream

In a medium-sized mixing bowl blend the egg yolks with the sugar. Beat the mixture until light and pale yellow. Add the grated chocolate to the egg yolk mixture. In a 3–4-quart saucepan heat the milk but do not boil. Add the milk slowly to the egg yolk mixture, blending and stirring well. Pour this mixture back into the saucepan. Add the vanilla bean, breaking it into 3 pieces, and the melted chocolate. Cook over low heat for 5 minutes, stirring constantly. Take the mixture from the heat and cool for about 15 minutes. Remove the vanilla bean. Add the cream and chill covered for 1 hour. Freeze in an ice-cream freezer according to manufacturer's directions.

NOTE: The ice cream should cure in the freezer for 3–4 hours before serving.

BLUEBERRY ICE

2 pints fresh blueberries
1 cup granulated sugar
1 cup water
8 tablespoons fresh lemon juice

In a large heavy saucepan combine the blueberries, sugar, and water. Bring to a boil, then simmer for 10 minutes. Add the lemon juice and purée the mixture in the blender, a small amount at a time, until smooth, being sure to *hold* the top on the blender tightly.

Pour the mixture into 2 freezer trays and freeze for about 1½–2 hours or until the ice has a solid edge about 1 inch thick. Pour the frozen mixture into a large bowl and beat until mushy. Return to the trays and freeze until firm. Serve in goblets or dessert dishes.

NOTE: Pecan Balls (*see Index*) are a good accompaniment to this ice.

RICH VANILLA ICE CREAM

MAKES 1 QUART

1 vanilla bean, broken into
  pieces
1 cup granulated sugar
2 cups milk
2 cups heavy cream
6 egg yolks

Place the vanilla and the sugar in a blender and pulverize at high speed for about 30–40 seconds. In a heavy 2-quart saucepan add the sugar mixture, milk, and cream. Scald the mixture over medium heat, stirring constantly. Remove from heat.

In a medium-sized bowl beat the egg yolks until thick and lemon-colored. Add the hot cream to the yolks in a slow stream, continuing to beat.

Transfer the custard back to the saucepan and cook over low heat, stirring constantly, until mixture coats the spoon, about 5 minutes. Place the custard in a large bowl and refrigerate for 2 hours, covered with a buttered round of waxed paper. Freeze in an ice-cream freezer according to manufacturer's directions.

NOTE: This ice cream is delicious served with Ginger Pear Ice Cream Sauce, Hot Fudge Sauce, or Butterscotch Sauce (*see Index*).

BISQUE TORTONI

1½ cups crumbled almond
    macaroons
2 tablespoons kirsch
1 cup heavy cream
3 tablespoons framboise or
    other brandy
1 quart vanilla ice cream,
    softened
¾ cup blanched almonds,
    toasted and chopped
½ cup grated semisweet
    chocolate

In a small bowl sprinkle the macaroon crumbs with the kirsch and set aside. In a medium-sized bowl whip the cream until stiff and beat in the framboise. Place in the refrigerator until needed.

In a large chilled bowl beat the ice cream until light and quickly fold in the whipped cream, almonds, chocolate, and saturated macaroon crumbs, blending well. Turn the mixture into 8 individual molds or into a 2-quart ice cream mold. Cover and freeze until firm, about 3–4 hours. To serve, dip the molds very quickly into hot water for a few seconds and invert onto serving dishes or a serving platter.

NOTE: This dessert may be prepared 3–4 days ahead and stored in the freezer.

CHOCOLATE BOMBE

2 quarts vanilla ice cream,
    slightly softened
2 cups Hot Fudge Sauce,
    cooled (*see Index*), plus 1½–2
    cups Hot Fudge Sauce,
    heated (optional)
¾ cup chopped walnuts
1 quart chocolate ice cream,
    slightly softened

Chill until very cold 1 3-quart melon mold or 2 1½-quart molds. Evenly coat the inside of the mold or molds with the slightly softened vanilla ice cream (about 1½ inches thick). Pack firmly and quickly. Place in the freezer for about 1 hour to set. Remove the mold from the freezer and fill the center with 2 cups cooled Hot Fudge Sauce and cover with the chopped nuts. Return to the freezer for 30 minutes to harden. Remove from the freezer and spread the slightly softened chocolate ice cream on top of the nuts, packing down firmly. Cover with waxed paper and press on the lid. Place in the freezer for at least 6 hours or overnight.

When ready to serve, run a wet knife around the edge of the mold. Place a hot towel over the mold for a minute, then turn upside down onto a chilled serving dish. Cut into slices at the table and serve with more warm Hot Fudge Sauce if desired.

ORANGE BOMBE

1½ quarts Rich Vanilla Ice
    Cream (*see Index*)
1 quart orange sherbet
1 cup chopped pecans
¾ cup superfine sugar
½ cup water
8 egg yolks
¾ cup fresh orange juice
⅓ cup orange liqueur
2 tablespoons fresh lemon juice
2 tablespoons grated orange
    rind
2 cups heavy cream
1½–2 cups fresh orange sections

Generously oil a 4-quart mold and set aside. In a large mixing bowl stir the vanilla ice cream to soften to the consistency of stiff whipped cream. Line the inside of the mold, covering the sides and the bottom with a layer of ice cream. It should be about 1 inch thick. Quickly freeze the mold until solid, about 1 hour.

In a mixing bowl stir and soften the orange sherbet to spreading consistency. Cover the vanilla ice cream all over with an even layer of sherbet. Sprinkle the chopped pecans evenly over the sherbet, pressing in well. Return the mold to the freezer until solid, about 1 hour.

In a small saucepan boil the orange juice over high heat until it is reduced by ½ and set aside.

In a heavy 1-quart saucepan bring the sugar and water to a boil over moderate-high heat. Boil until it reaches the soft-ball stage (237° on a candy thermometer).

While the syrup is cooking, beat the egg yolks in a mixing bowl until thick and lemon-colored. Remove the syrup from the heat and add to the yolks in a slow, steady stream while continuously beating. Continue to beat the syrup mixture until thick and cool. Add the orange juice, liqueur, lemon juice, and orange rind and beat in well.

In a mixing bowl beat the cream until it forms stiff peaks. Gently fold the cream into the orange mixture. Remove the mold from the freezer and pour the orange mixture over the pecans. Press down lightly with a spatula to prevent air holes. Return the bombe to the freezer for at least 4 hours.

To unmold, dip quickly in warm water and invert onto a serving platter. Surround by fresh orange slices, reserving some for the top of the mold.

NOTE: This is a refreshing dessert for a warm summer evening. It can be made 1 week ahead and held tightly wrapped in the freezer.

GRAND MARNIER COUPE WITH FRESH FRUIT

SERVES 8

4 cups strawberries, cherries,
and raspberries
1 quart Rich Vanilla Ice
Cream (*see Index*)

Wash, stem, and halve the strawberries and the cherries. In a mixing bowl mix gently with the raspberries. Cover and chill.

In 8 coupe glasses or goblets, place a scoop of ice cream. Top the ice cream with about ½ cup of the prepared fresh fruit and cover with 3–4 tablespoons of Grand Marnier Sauce. Serve at once.

GRAND MARNIER SAUCE
5 egg yolks
½ cup plus 2 tablespoons
granulated sugar
4 tablespoons Grand Marnier
1 cup heavy cream

To prepare sauce, in a 2-quart mixing bowl that will rest snugly on top of a slightly larger saucepan, place the egg yolks and ½ cup sugar. Beat egg yolks vigorously with a wire whisk or portable electric mixer, making sure to scrape around the inside and bottom of the bowl with the beater. Add about 2 inches of water to the saucepan and bring to a boil. Place the mixing bowl on the saucepan, not allowing the bowl to touch the water, and continue beating for approximately 10 minutes or until the yolks are thick and pale yellow. Remove the bowl from the saucepan and stir in 2 tablespoons Grand Marnier. Allow the sauce to cool, then refrigerate until thoroughly cold. In a mixing bowl beat the cream with the 2 tablespoons sugar until almost stiff. Gently fold the whipped cream into the chilled custard sauce. Stir in the remaining 2 tablespoons Grand Marnier. Makes 2 cups.

COLD ORANGE SOUFFLÉ

SERVES 12

2 tablespoons unflavored gelatin
1 cup cold water
8 eggs, separated
¼ teaspoon salt
2 6-ounce cans frozen orange
juice concentrate, thawed and
undiluted

In the top of a double boiler sprinkle the gelatin over the cold water. Set aside to soften. In a medium bowl beat together the egg yolks, salt, 1 can orange juice concentrate, and ¼ cup of the sugar. Stir the orange juice mixture into the gelatin mixture and using low heat, set over boiling water. Stir constantly until the gelatin

1 cup granulated sugar
1 cup heavy cream
1 fresh, thinly sliced orange

is dissolved and the mixture thickens slightly, about 6–8 minutes. Remove the pan from the heat and stir in the other can of orange juice, blending thoroughly. Chill in the refrigerator until the mixture mounds slightly when dropped from a spoon.

In a large bowl beat the egg whites until soft peaks form. Gradually beat in the remaining ¾ cup sugar and continue beating until very stiff. Carefully fold the orange mixture into the egg whites. Whip the cream in a mixing bowl until it forms soft peaks. Gently fold the whipped cream into egg whites mixture. Prepare a 2-quart soufflé dish with a 2-inch collar made by folding a long strip of waxed paper in half lengthwise and tying it around the soufflé dish with a string. It should extend above the top of the soufflé dish about 2 inches. Turn the mixture into the soufflé dish. Chill until firm, at least 4 hours. Serve garnished with fresh orange slices.

COLD CHESTNUT SOUFFLÉ

SERVES 8

4 eggs plus 3 egg yolks
½ cup granulated sugar
2 tablespoons unflavored gelatin
¼ cup dark rum
¼ cup water
2 cups sweetened canned chestnut purée
2 cups heavy cream
½ cup glacéed chestnuts or ½ cup sweetened cocoa and semisweet chocolate for curls

In a large mixing bowl beat the eggs, yolks, and sugar together. In a small saucepan over low heat dissolve the gelatin in the rum and water. Cool. Fold the chestnut purée into the bowl containing the egg mixture. Add the cooled gelatin. In another bowl whip 1 cup of the cream until stiff. Fold gently into the chestnut mixture. Pour into a 1-quart soufflé dish and refrigerate until chilled.

Shortly before serving, whip the other 1 cup cream. Pipe the cream with a pastry bag into rosettes on top of the chilled soufflé. Place the glacéed chestnuts between the rosettes. This can also be served with the cream whipped stiffly and flavored with the cocoa. Frost the top of the soufflé with this cream and decorate with shaved curls of chocolate.

FROZEN MOCHA SOUFFLÉ

SERVES 12

8 eggs, separated
¾ cup granulated sugar
2 envelopes unflavored gelatin
½ cup cold strong coffee
¼ cup coffee liqueur
1½ teaspoons instant coffee
4 ounces sweet cooking
  chocolate, melted
2 ounces unsweetened chocolate,
  melted
2 tablespoons confectioners'
  sugar
2 cups heavy cream
Whipped cream flavored with
  coffee liqueur
Chocolate curls

Cut off a piece of waxed paper long enough to go around a 1½–2-quart soufflé dish 6½–7-inches in diameter. Fold the paper in half lengthwise and brush 1 side with vegetable oil. Wrap the paper around the soufflé dish extending it 2–3 inches above the rim. Tie the paper on with string and set the dish aside.

In a very large mixing bowl beat the egg yolks until they are lemon-colored, about 2–3 minutes. Add the granulated sugar to the yolks and beat until light and fluffy, about 2 minutes. Meanwhile, in a small saucepan soften the gelatin in the coffee and dissolve, stirring, over low heat. Add the coffee gelatin to the egg mixture. Add the coffee liqueur, instant coffee, and melted chocolates and beat until well blended.

In a separate large bowl beat the egg whites until stiff and fold them into the chocolate mixture. In a separate large bowl combine the confectioners' sugar with the heavy cream and beat until it forms soft peaks. Fold the whipped cream mixture into the chocolate mixture. Pour the soufflé mixture into the prepared soufflé dish and freeze for 3–4 hours or until set and thoroughly chilled. When ready to serve, remove the paper collar and decorate the soufflé with whipped cream flavored with coffee liqueur and top with chocolate curls.

FROZEN LEMON-LIME SOUFFLÉ

SERVES 8

Rind of 3 or 4 limes
¾ cup fresh lime juice (3–4
  large limes)
2 tablespoons fresh lemon juice
1 tablespoon unflavored
  gelatin
6 egg yolks
1½ cups granulated sugar
1 cup milk

Grate the rind of the limes and set aside. Strain the lime juice into a small bowl. Add lemon juice and sprinkle gelatin over juice. Stir to soften.

In a large bowl beat the egg yolks with the sugar until the mixture forms a ribbon when the beater is lifted. In a small saucepan scald the milk and add to the egg-sugar mixture in a slow, steady stream, stirring constantly. Transfer this custard mixture to a heavy 2–3-quart saucepan and cook

1–2 drops green food coloring
  (optional)
2 egg whites
Pinch salt
1 cup heavy cream
¼ cup almonds, toasted and
  chopped

over low heat, stirring with a wooden spoon, until the custard thickens and begins to coat the spoon. Do not let the custard boil. Remove from heat and add gelatin mixture and optional food coloring. Stir until gelatin is completely dissolved. Strain the custard mixture into a bowl and add the grated rind of the limes. Put this bowl into a large bowl filled halfway with ice and stir until custard is completely cool and begins to thicken.

In a bowl beat the two egg whites and the salt until they hold soft peaks. In another bowl whip the cream, also until it holds soft peaks. Fold the cream lightly into the egg whites and fold this mixture into the custard.

Fit a 1-quart soufflé dish with a folded and oiled band of waxed paper, forming a collar above the soufflé dish that extends at least 2 inches. Secure with a string. Fill the soufflé dish with the custard mixture. Freeze for at least 6 hours or until firm. Remove collar and decorate with toasted almonds. Serve at once.

FROZEN CHOCOLATE FRANGOS

MAKES 18 TEA OR
8–10 DESSERT SERVINGS

1 cup butter
2 cups confectioners' sugar,
  sifted
4 ounces unsweetened
  chocolate
4 eggs
¾ teaspoon peppermint extract
2 teaspoons vanilla extract
10 vanilla wafers, crumbled

With an electric mixer beat the butter and sugar in a large bowl until light and fluffy. In the top of a double boiler melt the chocolate, add to the butter-sugar mixture, and beat thoroughly. Add the eggs one at a time, beating in well after each addition until well blended. Fold in the peppermint and vanilla.

For luncheon or tea servings, sprinkle ½ the cookie crumbs into the bottom of 18 cupcake papers. Spoon the chocolate mixture into the papers and top with the remaining crumbs. Freeze at least 2 hours before serving. Garnish with mint leaves.

For dinner dessert portions, place ½ the crumbs into 8–10 ramekins and spoon the chocolate on top. Sprinkle the remaining crumbs on top of the chocolate. Freeze at least 4 hours until firm.

FROZEN FUDGE PEPPERMINT ALASKA

SERVES 10

1 9 inch pie shell
2 pints Rich Vanilla Ice Cream,
   softened (*see Index*)
Fudge Sauce (*below*)
3 egg whites
¼ cup granulated sugar
¼ cup crushed peppermint
   stick candy

FUDGE SAUCE
2 tablespoons butter
2 ounces unsweetened chocolate
1 cup granulated sugar
6 ounces evaporated milk
1 teaspoon vanilla extract

Bake the pie shell according to the Basic Pie Crust recipe (*see Index*), using a deep pie plate. Cool the shell. Spread 1 pint of the softened ice cream in the pastry shell. Freeze until firm. Cover with ½ the Fudge Sauce. Freeze until firm. Repeat with additional layers of ice cream and fudge sauce, freezing well between layers. Freeze 6 hours or more.

Prepare meringue by beating the egg whites until frothy. Add the ¼ cup sugar and continue beating until stiff and shiny. When ready to serve, spread the meringue over the ice cream, sealing the edges. Top the meringue with the crushed peppermint candy. Bake in a preheated 475° oven until lightly browned, about 5 minutes. *Watch carefully!* Serve at once.

To prepare sauce, in the top of a double boiler melt the butter and chocolate. Add 1 cup sugar and the milk. Cook, stirring constantly, until thickened. Remove from the heat and cool. When cool, add the vanilla.

NOTE: The secret to this dessert is that the ice-cream pie must be frozen *solid* at the moment it is put in the oven. Make the other preparations while the pie is in the freezer.

SWEDISH CREAM

SERVES 8

2 cups plus 6 tablespoons heavy
   cream
1 cup granulated sugar
1 teaspoon unflavored gelatin
1 pint sour cream
1 teaspoon vanilla extract
2 cups fresh fruit, washed,
   stemmed, and *very* lightly
   mashed (raspberries,
   strawberries, blueberries, etc.)

In a medium saucepan mix together the heavy cream, sugar, and gelatin. Heat the mixture gently over low heat until the gelatin is dissolved, about 5 minutes. Remove from the heat and cool until slightly thickened. Fold in the sour cream and add the vanilla. Pour into goblets, dessert dishes, or a mold and chill in the refrigerator until firm. Top with the fruit and serve.

LEMON MERINGUE TORTE

must be prepared 24 hours in advance

4 eggs, separated
1½ cups granulated sugar
¼ teaspoon salt
¼ teaspoon cream of tartar
1 tablespoon grated lemon rind
3 tablespoons fresh lemon juice
1 cup heavy cream
2 cups fresh strawberries
½ cup confectioners' sugar

In a large mixing bowl beat the egg whites until foamy. Gradually add 1 cup granulated sugar, ¼ teaspoon salt, and the cream of tartar to the whites. This should take about 5 minutes of constant beating. After all the sugar has been added, beat an additional 6 minutes until stiff peaks form.

Cut four 8-inch circles out of brown wrapping paper. Grease the paper well and place on cookie sheets. Spoon the meringue onto the circles and spread very evenly to within ½ inch of the edge. Bake in a preheated 250° oven for 30 minutes or until dry to the touch. Cool completely and lift off of the brown paper.

In a 2-quart saucepan beat the egg yolks and remaining ½ cup granulated sugar together. Add the lemon rind, lemon juice, and remaining ¼ teaspoon salt. Cook over moderate heat, stirring constantly, until thick, approximately 5–8 minutes. Set aside to cool. Whip the cream in a medium-sized bowl until stiff. Fold the cream into the lemon mixture.

To assemble, place 1 of the meringue layers on a serving plate. Frost with ⅓ of the lemon cream filling. Top with another meringue layer and frost with another ⅓ of the filling. Repeat the procedure with the third meringue and the remaining filling. Place the fourth meringue layer on top. Cover the torte tightly and refrigerate for 24 hours. To serve, surround the torte with the fresh strawberries that have been dusted with the confectioners' sugar. Cut in wedges, placing a few berries on each serving.

PEACH TORTE

½ cup butter

¾ cup confectioners' sugar, sifted

4 eggs, separated

1 cup flour

1 teaspoon baking powder

¼ teaspoon salt

3 teaspoons milk

1½ cups granulated sugar

4 tablespoons almonds, sliced

2 cups peaches, peeled and sliced

1 cup heavy cream

Grease and flour 2 9-inch cake pans.

In a large bowl cream the butter and confectioners' sugar. Beat in the egg yolks one at a time. In another bowl sift together the flour, baking powder, and salt. Add to the creamed mixture, alternating with the milk. Divide the batter between the cake pans. In a mixing bowl beat the egg whites to soft peaks. Add 1 cup sugar and continue beating until peaks form. Spread this meringue mixture on top of the batter. Sprinkle each pan with 1 teaspoon sugar and 2 tablespoons almonds. Bake in a preheated 325° oven for 30 minutes. Cool the cakes on racks and then remove from the pans. Sprinkle the peach slices with 2 tablespoons sugar. Place 1 layer of cake on a serving plate, meringue side down.

Whip the cream and add the remaining sugar. Spread the bottom layer with about ⅓ of the whipped cream. Pile the peaches on top of the whipped cream, saving some peaches for garnish. Place the second layer, meringue side up, on the peaches. Mound the remaining whipped cream on the top and around the edges of the torte. Garnish with peach slices. Refrigerate until ready to serve.

CHOCOLATE MOUSSE

4 ounces unsweetened chocolate

½ cup semisweet chocolate bits

1½ teaspoons vanilla extract

3 egg whites

⅓ cup superfine sugar

3 cups heavy cream

1 ounce semisweet chocolate

¼ cup confectioners' sugar

Melt the unsweetened chocolate and the chocolate bits in a double boiler over hot, not boiling, water. Set aside to cool. When cool, add vanilla extract and stir to blend. In a large mixing bowl beat the egg whites until stiff and glossy. Add the superfine sugar to the stiff whites, a small amount at a time.

In another large mixing bowl whip 2 cups cream until stiff. Carefully fold the whipped cream into the egg white mixture. Add the cooled chocolate. Grate the square of semisweet chocolate and fold it into the mousse. Pour into a 1-quart mold and chill in refrigerator for 3–4 hours or until firm.

Whip the remaining 1 cup cream for garnish just before serving. Flavor with the confectioners' sugar. Unmold the mousse on a serving plate. Frost the top with the cream. Instead of molding, this dessert would be lovely served in individual pot de crème cups. The whipped cream should then be passed at the table.

STRAWBERRY CHANTILLY WITH CUSTARD SAUCE

SERVES 8

12 egg whites
1 cup granulated sugar
1 cup confectioners' sugar
2 teaspoons vanilla extract
2 teaspoons cream of tartar
2 teaspoons cider vinegar
1 pint heavy cream
1 pint strawberries

In a large mixing bowl beat egg whites until frothy. Gradually add the granulated sugar, beating continually. Slowly add the confectioners' sugar, beating as before. Add the vanilla, cream of tartar, and vinegar. When the mixture is so stiff that it will no longer drop from a spoon, stop beating.

Dust a 10-inch tube pan or 12-cup (standard) bundt pan with flour. Spoon meringue mixture into the pan. Place in a pan of hot water 2 inches deep and bake for 3½ hours in a preheated 275° oven. Remove from oven, unmold, cool, and then refrigerate for 3–4 hours.

One hour before serving time, whip the 1 pint cream until stiff. Frost the sides and top of the meringue with the cream. Return to refrigerator. Serve garnished with whole strawberries, accompanied by Rum Custard Sauce.

RUM CUSTARD SAUCE
6 egg yolks
1 cup granulated sugar
1 teaspoon fresh lemon juice
½ cup dry sherry
1 cup heavy cream
¼ cup light rum

To prepare sauce, combine in the top of a double boiler over moderate heat the egg yolks, 1 cup granulated sugar, and the lemon juice. Beat well. Add the sherry and continue beating until the sauce thickens. Remove from heat and cool. Whip 1 cup cream until stiff. Fold into the sauce and add the rum. Chill 1 hour before serving.

INDIAN PUDDING

2 cups puréed fresh persimmon
  (*see Note*)

3 eggs, beaten

1¾ cups milk

2 cups flour

½ teaspoon baking soda

1 teaspoon salt

1½ cups granulated sugar

1½ teaspoons ground coriander

3 tablespoons butter, melted

1 cup heavy cream

In a bowl mix together the persimmon, eggs, and milk. In a separate bowl sift together the flour, soda, salt, sugar, and coriander. Pour the liquid mixture into the dry ingredients and add the melted butter. Put the mixture into a shallow buttered pan or casserole. Bake for 1 hour in a preheated 325° oven. Chill before serving. Serve with unsweetened heavy cream poured over the top.

NOTE: A fresh persimmon should feel soft and jellylike when ripe. Cut it in half and scoop the flesh from the skin with a spoon. Then whirl the pulp in the blender until smooth. Use at once or freeze. The purée tends to turn brown if left, and a small amount of lemon juice may be added if desired, to prevent discoloration and enhance the flavor.

DATE CRISP

1½ cups dates, pitted, plus 8
  dates stuffed with nuts

1¼ cups brown sugar, firmly
  packed

¼ cup water

½ cup sherry or orange juice

2 tablespoons fresh lemon juice

¼ cup butter, softened

¼ cup shortening

1 cup flour

¼ teaspoon baking soda

⅛ teaspoon salt

¼ teaspoon ground cinnamon

¼ teaspoon ground nutmeg

1 cup quick-cooking oats

1 cup heavy cream

Chop the 1½ cups dates. In a heavy 2-quart saucepan combine the dates with ½ cup brown sugar, the water, sherry, and lemon juice. Cook over low heat, stirring occasionally. This takes about 10 minutes. Chill.

In a large mixing bowl cream the butter and shortening with the remaining brown sugar until the mixture is fluffy. Sift the flour, soda, salt, and spices into the creamed mixture. Add the oats and blend until crumbly. Set aside 1 cup of this mixture. Press the remaining mixture firmly into the bottom of a well-greased 9-inch-square baking pan. Cover with the cooled date mixture and sprinkle with the reserved crumbs. Bake in a preheated 375° oven for 20–30 minutes. Serve warm with the cream, which has been whipped until stiff. Top with the nut-stuffed dates.

LEMON CHARLOTTE RUSSE

1 envelope unflavored gelatin
½ cup fresh lemon juice
4 eggs, separated
1½ cups granulated sugar
⅛ teaspoon salt
3 tablespoons butter
Rind of 1 lemon, grated
1 teaspoon vanilla extract
1½ 3-ounce packages ladyfingers, split
1 cup heavy cream

In a small bowl soften the gelatin in the lemon juice and set aside. In the top of a double boiler beat the egg yolks, adding 1 cup sugar, a small amount at a time, until thick. Add gelatin-lemon mixture, salt, and butter to the yolk mixture. Cook, stirring constantly, over hot, not boiling, water until thick, about 8–10 minutes. Remove from heat. Stir in lemon rind and vanilla. Cool until mixture begins to stiffen.

Meanwhile line the sides and bottom of a 9-inch springform pan by standing the split ladyfingers around the sides and cutting the ladyfingers to fit the bottom of the pan. In a separate bowl beat the egg whites until very soft peaks form. Add the remaining ½ cup sugar, a small amount at a time, and continue to beat the egg whites until stiff peaks form.

In a separate bowl whip the cream until stiff. Fold the egg whites and whipped cream into the lemon mixture and turn into the ladyfinger-lined pan. Refrigerate at least 4 hours before serving. Remove springform sides, place Russe on serving platter, and garnish with more whipped cream if desired.

MARBLE CHEESECAKE

1¼ cups chocolate wafer crumbs
¼–½ teaspoon ground cinnamon
¼ cup butter, melted
2 ounces cream cheese, softened
½ cup granulated sugar
1 teaspoon grated lemon rind
2 eggs
1½ cups sour cream
8 ounces semisweet chocolate, melted

In a medium bowl thoroughly mix together the chocolate wafer crumbs, cinnamon, and butter. With damp fingers press the mixture onto the bottom and the sides of a 9-inch springform pan and chill.

In a medium bowl combine the cream cheese, sugar, and lemon rind and beat until well blended. Beat in the eggs and stir in the sour cream until smooth. Add the melted chocolate and stir with a fork until the mixture is marbleized. Pour the mixture into the chilled crust and bake in a preheated 350° oven for 35–40 minutes or until set. Chill at least 2 hours, remove the rim, and serve at once.

CHOCOLATE TORTILLAS

SERVES 10

6 ounces semisweet chocolate
2 cups sour cream
3 tablespoons confectioners' sugar
4 8-inch flour tortillas
Shaved chocolate

In the top of a double boiler combine the 6 ounces chocolate, 1 cup of the sour cream, and 1 tablespoon confectioners' sugar. Set the pan over simmering water and stir until the chocolate is melted and ingredients are thoroughly blended. Remove from heat and place pan into a bowl of cold water to cool mixture. On a serving plate place 1 tortilla. Frost top of tortilla with ⅓ of the chocolate mixture, making sure chocolate mixture is spread very evenly. Place second tortilla on top of chocolate mixture and frost evenly with second ⅓ of chocolate mixture. Repeat layering and frosting procedure once more. End with tortilla on top.

In a small bowl blend the remaining 1 cup sour cream and remaining 2 tablespoons confectioners' sugar together well. Frost the top and sides of the tortilla stack with this mixture. Cover the completed tortilla stack with an inverted bowl large enough to cover the stack without touching the top or the sides. Refrigerate for at least 8 hours. Garnish the top of the stack with shaved chocolate and serve.

COFFEE POT DE CRÈME

SERVES 6

2½ cups heavy cream
½ cup superfine sugar
3 tablespoons instant coffee
1½ teaspoons vanilla extract
6 egg yolks
2 tablespoons confectioners' sugar
Cinnamon

Scald 2 cups cream in a small saucepan. Remove from the heat and stir in the superfine sugar and the instant coffee. Blend in the vanilla.

In a separate bowl beat the egg yolks until thick and pale yellow. Add the yolks very gradually to the cream, stirring constantly. Pour into pot de crème cups and place in a pan of hot water. Bake in a preheated 325° oven for 35 minutes.

Remove from oven and cool completely. Chill in the refrigerator for at least 2 hours.

Whip the remaining ½ cup cream in a small bowl until it forms soft peaks. Add the confectioners' sugar and beat in well. Serve the pot de crèmes with a generous spoonful of whipped cream on top. Dust with cinnamon.

ORANGE CHEESECAKE

SERVES 10

1⅔ cups graham cracker crumbs
4 tablespoons butter, melted
¾ cup granulated sugar
¾ cup fresh orange juice
2 tablespoons flour
¼ teaspoon salt
1 pound cream cheese, softened
2 tablespoons fresh lemon juice
2 tablespoons grated orange rind
4 eggs, separated

In a small mixing bowl mix the crumbs and butter together. Add ¼ cup sugar and blend well. Pour crumb mixture into a 9-inch springform pan, pressing the crumbs down well in the bottom of the pan and up the side of the pan approximately 1 inch. Set aside.

In a small saucepan bring the orange juice to a boil over high heat and reduce by ½. Set aside to cool.

In another bowl mix together the remaining ½ cup sugar, the flour, and salt and set aside. In a large mixing bowl beat the cream cheese with an electric mixer, using high speed, until light and fluffy. Add the sugar mixture and beat well. Stir in the lemon juice, orange rind, and orange juice. In a mixing bowl beat the egg yolks until thick and lemon-colored. Add to the orange-cheese mixture and beat at high speed for 2 minutes.

In a mixing bowl beat the egg whites until they form stiff peaks. Gently fold the whites into the orange-cheese mixture. Pour the mixture into the prepared springform pan, spreading evenly. Bake in a preheated 325° oven for 1 hour and 15 minutes. The cheesecake will fall and crack slightly in the center. To minimize this, leave the cheesecake in the oven for 1 hour after it is cooked, with the oven turned off and the door closed. When cooled, remove the sides from the springform pan.

NOTE: This cheesecake may be served at room temperature or slightly chilled. It can be made 6–8 hours ahead.

FRESH STRAWBERRY CREPES

¼ cup cold milk

¾ cup cold water

4 large eggs plus 3 egg yolks

1½ cups flour

½ teaspoon salt

2 tablespoons granulated sugar

4 tablespoons cognac or framboise

4 tablespoons butter, melted

½ teaspoon cooking oil

8 ounces cream cheese, softened

½ pint sour cream

3 tablespoons grated orange rind

½ cup confectioners' sugar

STRAWBERRY SAUCE

3 tablespoons butter

3 tablespoons grated orange rind

¾ cup fresh orange juice

2 tablespoons fresh lemon juice

½ cup granulated sugar

3 drops red food coloring (optional)

3 baskets fresh strawberries, puréed

1 basket strawberries, sliced

3 tablespoons Cointreau or framboise

2 tablespoons cognac

To prepare the crepes, put the first eight ingredients in a blender jar, blend for 2 minutes, cover the jar, and place in refrigerator for 2 hours before making the crepes.

Put the oil in a 6–7-inch skillet or crepe pan and swirl around to coat the pan. Heat the skillet over moderate heat, pour a small amount of batter, a little less than ¼ cup, into the well-heated and oiled skillet and swirl the batter around to coat the pan, pouring off any excess. Cook the crepe for 1 minute or until slightly browned and turn the crepe to lightly brown the other side, about 30 seconds. Remove the crepe to a piece of waxed paper and continue to make as many as needed. The batter will make about 20 crepes. Cover each cooked crepe, as it is made, with a piece of waxed paper until ready to fill.

To prepare the filling, place the cream cheese, sour cream, 3 tablespoons orange rind, and the confectioners' sugar in a medium-sized mixing bowl and beat until fluffy. Put 2 tablespoons of the filling in the center of each crepe and roll up like a cigar. Place the filled crepes seam side down in a 9 × 13-inch ovenproof baking dish. The crepes may be assembled shortly before serving time and covered tightly to prevent their drying out.

To prepare sauce, in a 2–3-quart saucepan combine all the Strawberry Sauce ingredients except the sliced strawberries and the liqueurs. Bring the ingredients to a boil over moderate heat, stirring constantly until the sugar is completely dissolved. Add the sliced strawberries, Cointreau, and cognac to the sauce mixture. Stir over moderate heat just to boiling, about 5–8 minutes.

When ready to serve, place the baking dish in a preheated 350° oven for 10 minutes. Remove from oven and pour hot Strawberry Sauce over the crepes. Return the crepes to the oven for 5 more minutes. Serve at once.

NOTE: The unfilled crepes may be made several days ahead and stored in the refrigerator tightly wrapped, or frozen several weeks. Any remaining batter may be stored covered in the refrigerator.

APRICOT CREPES

SERVES 8   MAKES 16 CREPES

3 eggs
1 teaspoon salt
1½ teaspoons granulated sugar
1 cup flour, unsifted
2 cups milk
3 tablespoons butter, melted
2 teaspoons grated orange rind
3 tablespoons cooking oil
16 ounces apricot jam or
    preserves

In a large bowl beat the eggs with the salt and sugar until light and frothy. Add the flour, milk, and 3 tablespoons butter and mix well. Stir in the 2 teaspoons orange rind. Let the mixture stand at room temperature for at least 30 minutes. Brush a crepe pan lightly with some of the oil and heat it over moderately high heat. Add a scant ¼ cup of the batter and rotate pan to cover the bottom evenly with the batter. Cook for 1 minute, then jerk the pan to loosen the crepe. Turn quickly with hands or 2 spatulas and cook the other side for about 30 seconds. Cover each cooked crepe, as it is made, with a piece of waxed paper until ready to fill. Repeat this process, using all the remaining batter.

Spread each crepe with some of the apricot preserves, dividing evenly. Roll the crepes and place them seam side down in a lightly buttered 9 × 13-inch casserole dish.

Spoon Grand Marnier Apricot Sauce over the crepes. The crepes can be set aside at this point for 2–3 hours. Warm the crepes in a 325° oven for 5–10 minutes just before serving.

GRAND MARNIER APRICOT SAUCE
11 ounces apricot nectar
2 teaspoons grated orange rind
6 tablespoons fresh lemon juice
¼ cup butter, melted
1 1-pound–3-ounce can whole
    unpeeled apricots, drained
    and puréed
⅓ cup Grand Marnier

To prepare sauce, in a heavy 2–3-quart saucepan combine the apricot nectar, 2 teaspoons orange rind, the lemon juice, ¼ cup butter, and the puréed apricots. Cook for about 5 minutes over low heat, stirring frequently. Take off the heat and add the Grand Marnier to the mixture.

NOTE: The unfilled crepes may be made a day or two ahead. Layer them between waxed paper, tightly wrapped, and keep in the refrigerator or freezer.

ORANGE LIQUEUR SOUFFLÉS
IN ORANGE SHELLS

12 very large navel oranges
12 sugar cubes plus granulated
   sugar to make ⅔ cup
¼ cup water
4 egg yolks, beaten
¼ cup orange liqueur (Cointreau,
   curaçao, Bénédictine, or
   Grand Marnier)
1 teaspoon vanilla extract
6 egg whites
⅛ teaspoon salt
⅓ cup confectioners' sugar
Mint sprigs (optional)

Wash and dry the oranges. Rub each orange with a sugar cube until the cube is completely yellow, to absorb the orange essence from the rind. Place these cubes in a measuring cup and add the granulated sugar to measure ⅔ cup. Transfer the sugar to a small saucepan and set aside.

Cut a lid at least ½ inch thick from the top of each orange and peel a very thin slice from the bottom so that each orange sits firmly. Scoop out and discard all the flesh with a small spoon, being careful not to pierce the skin. Place the empty orange shells in a preheated 350° oven to dry for 20 minutes; they will then be warm enough to receive the soufflé mixture. In a small bowl, lightly beat the egg yolks and set aside.

Add the water to the sugar and boil over medium-high heat until the syrup reaches the soft-ball stage: when a little dropped into cold water makes a soft ball (about 237° on a candy thermometer). Immediately pour this boiling syrup in a slow steady stream over the egg yolks, beating vigorously with a whisk until cool. Add the liqueur and vanilla. Return the mixture to the saucepan and heat over medium heat, beating until slightly thickened. Remove from the heat and continue beating until cool.

In a large bowl beat the egg whites with the salt until stiff peaks form. Fold ¼ of the egg whites into the egg yolk mixture and gently fold this mixture into the remaining egg whites.

Increase the oven temperature to 425°.

Fill the orange shells ⅔ full with the soufflé mixture and bake for 8 minutes. Remove from the oven and sprinkle the soufflés with the confectioners' sugar. Return to the oven for 4–7 minutes until the soufflés have risen a good ½ inch above the edges of the oranges and the tops are browned. Garnish with fresh mint sprigs if desired. Serve at once.

NOTE: This is a very pretty, light dessert, excellent for luncheons.

HOT CHOCOLATE SOUFFLÉ
WITH VANILLA VELVET SAUCE

SERVES 6

2 tablespoons butter, softened
3 tablespoons granulated sugar
3 tablespoons sweet butter
4 tablespoons flour
1 cup light cream
2 teaspoons vanilla extract
6 ounces dark sweet chocolate
4 tablespoons brandy
3 tablespoons superfine sugar
4 egg yolks
7 egg whites

Grease the bottom and sides of a 1½-quart soufflé dish with the soft butter. Sprinkle in the granulated sugar, tipping and shaking the dish to spread the sugar evenly. Then turn the dish over and knock out the excess sugar. Set the soufflé dish aside. In a 3–4-quart saucepan melt the sweet butter over low heat. Add the flour to the butter, stirring constantly, and cook for 3–5 minutes.

In a separate small saucepan scald the light cream and add 2 teaspoons vanilla. Add the cream to the butter and flour mixture and cook until it thickens and *almost* comes to a boil. (Do *not* let it boil.) Take the mixture from the heat and cool.

In a separate small saucepan melt the chocolate and add the brandy and superfine sugar. Stir until the mixture is smooth. Add to cream mixture. Add yolks, one at a time, and beat in well. Cover and put aside for 3–4 hours. Do not refrigerate. When ready to bake the souffle, beat the egg whites in a large mixing bowl until stiff. Fold ¼ of the whites into the chocolate mixture and then fold in the rest until just blended. Place the chocolate mixture into the prepared soufflé dish. Place the soufflé dish in the bottom of a small roasting pan. Fill the pan with boiling water that reaches halfway up the side of the soufflé dish. Bake in a preheated 375° oven for 50 minutes. Remove from the oven and serve at once with Vanilla Velvet Sauce, passed separately.

VANILLA VELVET SAUCE
1 cup confectioners' sugar
3 tablespoons butter, melted
1 egg yolk
¼ teaspoon vanilla extract
⅛ teaspoon salt
1 cup heavy cream

To prepare sauce, in a medium bowl beat together the confectioners' sugar, melted butter, 1 egg yolk, ¼ teaspoon vanilla, and the salt.

In a separate bowl whip the heavy cream until it forms soft peaks. Fold the whipped cream into the sugar mixture.

NOTE: The soufflé may be dusted with sifted confectioners' sugar in place of the Vanilla Velvet Sauce.

HOT LEMON SOUFFLÉ   SERVES 6

2 tablespoons butter, softened
3 tablespoons granulated sugar
3 tablespoons sweet butter
3 tablespoons flour
¼ teaspoon salt
1 cup half-and-half
¼ cup fresh lemon juice
3 tablespoons grated lemon rind
3 heaping tablespoons
  granulated sugar
2 tablespoons cognac
4 egg yolks
6 egg whites
Confectioners' sugar

Grease the bottom and sides of a 1½-quart soufflé dish with 2 tablespoons butter. Sprinkle with 3 tablespoons granulated sugar, tipping and shaking the dish to spread the sugar evenly. Turn the dish over and knock out the excess sugar. Set aside. In a medium saucepan melt the sweet butter over medium heat and add the flour to make a roux. Cook, stirring for 2–3 minutes. To the roux add the salt and the half-and-half, stirring over heat until the mixture comes to a boil and thickens. Remove from the heat and mix in the lemon juice, lemon rind, 3 heaping tablespoons granulated sugar, and the cognac. Beat the 4 egg yolks into the mixture.

In a large mixing bowl, preferably of unlined copper, beat the 6 egg whites with a clean wisk or rotary beater until they form stiff, unwavering peaks. Using a rubber spatula, stir a large spoonful of beaten egg whites into the lemon mixture to lighten it. Gently fold the remaining egg whites into the mixture. Spoon the soufflé into the buttered, sugared dish. Place soufflé dish in a pan of hot water about 1 inch deep. Bake in a preheated 375° oven for 1 hour. Sprinkle the finished soufflé with sifted confectioners' sugar and serve at once.

HOT APPLE SOUFFLÉ WITH APRICOT SAUCE   SERVES 6

5 pippin apples (about 2
  pounds)
¼ cup water
¼ cup granulated sugar
5 egg whites
Confectioners' sugar

Core and peel the apples and cut in quarters. In a large skillet cook the apples in ¼ cup water over low heat about 20 minutes or until the apples are soft. Add ¼ cup granulated sugar and mix well. Set aside to cool.

In a medium-sized bowl beat the egg whites until stiff. Stir ⅓ of the whites into the coated apples and fold in the remaining egg whites gradually. Butter the top section and cover of a 1½-quart double boiler. It is best to use a heatproof glass or porcelain double boiler. Sprinkle both with granulated sugar. Add the apple mixture and cover. Place over simmering water, using low heat, for 1¼ hours. Do not remove cover while cooking. Turn out onto a serving dish, sprinkle the soufflé with confectioners' sugar, and serve at once with Apricot Sauce.

APRICOT SAUCE
1 pound dried apricots
¾ cup sugar
½ cup water
4 tablespoons brandy or rum

To prepare sauce, in a medium-sized saucepan place the apricots, ¾ cup sugar, and ½ cup water. Simmer for 15 minutes over low heat or until the apricots are soft. Set aside to cool. When cooled, put the mixture into a blender and puree over high speed. Add the brandy and stir well. Reheat in a double boiler for a few minutes before serving. Makes 2½ cups.

CALIFORNIA WALNUT ROLL
SERVES 8

7 eggs
¾ cup granulated sugar
1½ cups ground walnuts
1 teaspoon baking powder
1½ cups heavy cream
½ cup confectioners' sugar
¼ teaspoon vanilla extract

Brush a 10 × 15-inch jelly-roll pan with oil. Line the pan with waxed paper and oil the paper. Separate the 7 eggs into 2 large mixing bowls. Using a wire whisk, beat the egg yolks with the granulated sugar until thick and pale in color. Beat in the walnuts and the baking powder. In the other bowl beat the egg whites until stiff. Fold the walnut batter into the whites until thoroughly mixed. Spread the mixture in the prepared pan. Bake in a preheated 350° oven for 15–20 minutes. Chill the cake in the pan covered with a damp cloth.

In a medium-sized bowl whip the cream until fairly stiff. Add ¼ cup confectioners' sugar and the vanilla. Cover and chill until needed.

Dust the chilled cake with some of the remaining confectioners' sugar. Turn onto a board covered with 2 overlapping sheets of waxed paper. Strip the paper from the bottom of the cake. Spread with the whipped cream to within 1 inch of edge of cake. Roll up the cake, using the waxed paper as an aid. Slide the roll onto a flat serving plate. Sprinkle with the remaining confectioners' sugar. Chill and serve within 2 hours of assembling.

STEAMED PLUM PUDDING WITH
PLUM BRANDY SAUCE

2½ cups plums with juice
1 cup brown sugar, firmly
   packed
½ cup butter, melted
2 eggs
1 cup flour
½ teaspoon salt
1 teaspoon baking soda
¼–½ cup cognac

PLUM BRANDY SAUCE
1 cup plum juice
⅓ cup granulated sugar
Dash ground nutmeg
Dash ground cinnamon
1½ tablespoons cornstarch
¼ cup cognac
1 tablespoon fresh lemon juice
1 tablespoon butter

In a small saucepan simmer the 2½ cups plums and juice for 6–8 minutes over low-moderate heat. Cool, remove the pits from the plums, and discard the pits. Drain the plums, reserving the juice, and chop into ¼-inch pieces.

In a mixing bowl beat the brown sugar and melted butter together. Add the eggs, beating in well, and blend in the plums. In another bowl sift together the flour, salt, and soda and add to the plum mixture, stirring gently. Generously butter a 1½-quart mold with a cover. Pour the plum batter into the mold. Cover the mold with the top or foil and place on a rack in a large kettle. Fill the kettle with water to reach halfway up the side of the mold. Cover the kettle and bring to a simmer over low heat. Steam for 1 hour.

Remove the steamed mold from the kettle, uncover, and place in a preheated 400° oven for 2–3 minutes to dry the top slightly. Cool the pudding for a few minutes and unmold onto a warm serving plate.

Warm the cognac in a small saucepan. Remove from heat, ignite, and pour over the pudding. Bring the flaming pudding to the table accompanied by Plum Brandy Sauce.

To prepare sauce, in a small saucepan combine the 1 cup plum juice, the granulated sugar, nutmeg, cinnamon, and cornstarch. Mix well and bring to a simmer over low heat, stirring constantly, until slightly thickened. Remove from heat and blend in cognac, lemon juice, and 1 tablespoon butter. Serve warm with plum pudding.

NOTE: This pudding may be prepared 2–3 days in advance, wrapped tightly, and refrigerated. If this is the case, before serving steam again in the mold for about 1 hour. This is a delicious and festive holiday dessert.

STEAMED CARROT PUDDING WITH HOT BRANDY SAUCE

1 cup seedless raisins
1 cup currants
1 cup finely grated potatoes, well drained
1 teaspoon baking soda
1 cup finely grated raw carrots
½ cup granulated sugar
½ cup dark brown sugar, firmly packed
1 cup flour
2 teaspoons baking powder
1 teaspoon salt
1 teaspoon ground cinnamon
½ teaspoon ground cloves
1 teaspoon ground nutmeg
3 tablespoons butter, softened

HOT BRANDY SAUCE
½ cup granulated sugar
2 tablespoons cornstarch
¼ teaspoon salt
2 cups boiling water
4 tablespoons butter or margarine
1 tablespoon brandy
¼ teaspoon ground nutmeg

Put the raisins and currants in a bowl and pour boiling water over them to cover. Set aside.

Place the potatoes in another bowl and stir in the baking soda. Stir the carrots into potato mixture. Set aside.

Sift together the ½ cup granulated sugar, the brown sugar, flour, baking powder, salt, cinnamon, cloves, and 1 teaspoon nutmeg, into a large bowl. Drain currants and raisins well and add to flour mixture with the softened butter and the grated carrots and potatoes. Stir and mix well. Place in a 1½-quart covered steamer that has been well greased with butter or margarine. Place the steamer in a large 6–8-quart covered pot. Add enough water so that it is halfway up the side of the steamer. Cover and steam on low heat for 2 hours. Unmold on a serving platter and serve with Hot Brandy Sauce.

To prepare sauce, combine ½ cup granulated sugar, the cornstarch, and ¼ teaspoon salt in a 1-quart saucepan. Gradually add the boiling water, stirring constantly. Simmer over low heat for 5 minutes until clear and thickened, stirring constantly. Remove from heat and stir in butter, brandy, and ¼ teaspoon nutmeg. Serve warm over carrot pudding. Makes 2 cups.

NOTE: At holiday time, the pudding can be flamed with 2 or 3 jiggers of warm brandy and decorated with holly sprigs. It can be made up to 5 days ahead, unmolded, wrapped in waxed paper and foil, and refrigerated. Return to mold for reheating and steam for 1 hour.

STEAMED CHOCOLATE PUDDING

SERVES 8

4 ounces bitter chocolate
2 tablespoons butter, softened
½ cup granulated sugar
2 eggs, slightly beaten
1 cup milk
2 cups flour
¼ teaspoon salt
2 teaspoons baking powder
1 teaspoon vanilla extract
1 recipe Vanilla Velvet Sauce
  (*see Index*)

In the top of a double boiler melt the chocolate over hot water and set it aside. In a large bowl cream together the butter and sugar. Add the slightly beaten eggs and the milk, blending well. Stir in the flour which has been mixed with the salt and baking powder. Add the melted chocolate and vanilla. Stir to blend thoroughly. Place the mixture into a 1½-quart greased steamer mold. Cover the mold lightly and place it in a covered pan. Fill the pan with water until the water comes up halfway to the sides of the mold. Cover and bring to a simmer. Steam for 1½ hours. Serve the pudding warm with some of the Vanilla Velvet Sauce. Pass the remaining sauce separately.

NOTE: This is a delicious dessert for the holidays.

BAKED PERSIMMON PUDDING WITH HOT LEMON SAUCE

SERVES 8

1 cup granulated sugar
1 tablespoon salad oil
1 egg, well beaten
1 cup flour
1 teaspoon ground cinnamon
½ teaspoon salt
1 teaspoon baking powder
1 teaspoon baking soda
¼ cup milk
1 cup persimmon, sieved
½ teaspoon vanilla extract
½ cup chopped nuts
½ cup chopped dates (optional)

HOT LEMON SAUCE
1 cup granulated sugar
¼ cup butter, softened
Juice and grated rind of 1
  lemon
4 tablespoons water
1 egg, well beaten

In a mixing bowl beat 1 cup sugar and the oil into the well-beaten egg. In a separate bowl sift together the flour, cinnamon, salt, baking powder, and soda. Add this alternately with the milk to the creamed mixture. Mix in the persimmon, vanilla, nuts, and dates. Bake in a covered mold set in a pan of hot water in a preheated 350° oven for 45 minutes. Unmold onto a serving plate and serve with Hot Lemon Sauce.

To prepare sauce, in a heavy 2–3-quart saucepan cream the 1 cup sugar and the butter together. Add the juice, rind, and 3 tablespoons water. Cook all over low heat, stirring, until smooth and creamy. Add the beaten egg and remaining 1 tablespoon water. Stir gently to thicken. Serve the sauce warm over Baked Persimmon Pudding.

NOTE: The pudding can be prepared several days ahead and resteamed in a tent of aluminum foil.

FLAN

1½ cups granulated sugar
1 quart milk
1 1-inch piece vanilla bean or
 . 1 2-inch stick cinnamon
Pinch salt
4 eggs plus 6 egg yolks

In a small heavy saucepan over moderately high heat, cook 1 cup of the sugar, stirring with a wooden spoon, until melted and caramel-colored. Pour the caramel into a 1½-quart mold, rotating the mold until the bottom and sides are covered with the caramel. Work quickly, as the caramel hardens very fast.

In a heavy 2–3-quart saucepan heat the milk and add the remaining sugar, the vanilla bean or cinnamon, and salt and let the mixture simmer briskly for about 15 minutes. The milk should be reduced by about ½ cup. Set the mixture aside to cool.

In a separate bowl beat the eggs and the egg yolks together well. Add the eggs to the cooled milk mixture and stir well. Pour the mixture through a strainer into the caramel-coated mold. (If using a vanilla bean, rinse the bean, dry it, and store it for use again.) Set the mold in a pan of warm water. The water should reach about 1 inch up the sides of the mold. Bake in a preheated 350° oven for 50–60 minutes. Test the center of the custard with a silver knife. It should come out clean. Remove the flan from the oven. Set aside to cool, then refrigerate. To serve, run a sharp knife around the side of the mold and turn out onto a serving dish or platter that has a little depth so that none of the caramel is lost.

NOTE: This is a traditional dessert following a Mexican meal.

LEMON CHOCOLATE CRUMB DESSERT

2 envelopes unflavored gelatin
¼ cup cold water
6 eggs, separated, plus 1 egg
   yolk, at room temperature
⅔ cup fresh lemon juice
¼ teaspoon salt
1½ cups granulated sugar
1 tablespoon grated lemon peel
2 cups heavy cream
2¼ cups chocolate wafer crumbs
2 lemons, sliced paper-thin

In a small bowl sprinkle the gelatin over cold water to soften. In the top of a medium-sized double boiler beat together the 7 egg yolks, lemon juice, salt, and 1 cup sugar; add the softened gelatin. Place the mixture over simmering, not boiling, water and stir until it is thickened and coats a metal spoon. Stir in the lemon peel. Place the top of the double boiler in a large bowl of ice cubes and stir until the mixture is the consistency of unbeaten egg whites.

In a large bowl beat the 6 egg whites with a rotary beater or electric mixer until soft peaks form. Gradually add the remaining ½ cup sugar, beating constantly, until stiff peaks form.

In a mixing bowl whip the cream until it forms soft peaks. Reserve 1 cup of the whipped cream. Fold the remaining whipped cream into the gelatin mixture and then carefully fold the gelatin mixture into the beaten egg whites. Spread ⅓ of the lemon mixture over the bottom of a 9-inch springform pan. Top with 1 cup of the crumbs. Spread another ⅓ of the lemon mixture on top of the crumbs and top with 1 cup of the crumbs. Spread the remaining ⅓ of the lemon mixture. Garnish with the reserved 1 cup whipped cream and the remaining ¼ cup crumbs. Circle the top with the lemon slices. Chill in the refrigerator covered for 4–5 hours or until set. Remove the side of the pan and serve.

PLUM KUCHEN

16 Italian plums
2 cups granulated sugar
2 tablespoons quick-cooking
   tapioca
½ cup butter
1¼ cups flour

Chill the beaters for the electric mixer.

Halve and pit the plums. In a medium bowl mix the plums with 1 cup sugar and the tapioca. Let the mixture stand for 15 minutes. (This is very important to absorb the juices.)

½ teaspoon salt
½ teaspoon ground cinnamon
¼ teaspoon baking powder
1 cup sour cream

To prepare the crust, in a large bowl cream the butter and add the remaining 1 cup sugar, beating until fluffy. In a medium bowl sift together the flour, salt, cinnamon, and baking powder. Add the sifted ingredients to the creamed mixture. The mixture will be crumbly. Set aside ½ cup of the mixture. Press the remaining mixture to cover the bottom and 1 inch up the sides of a 9-inch springform pan. Arrange the plums, cut side down, in the shell. Sprinkle with the remaining sugar-tapioca mixture not absorbed by the plums. Cover the top with the remaining ½ cup of the butter-flour crumbly mixture. Bake in a preheated 400° oven for 45 minutes.

Beat the sour cream with the chilled beaters for 5 minutes at highest speed until doubled in volume. Serve in a separate bowl.

MINIATURE PECAN TARTS

SERVES 24

1 3-ounce package cream
    cheese, softened
½ cup butter, softened
1 cup flour, sifted
5 eggs
1½ cups brown sugar, firmly
    packed
2 tablespoons butter, softened
2 teaspoons vanilla extract
¼ teaspoon salt
1½ cups broken pecans

In a mixing bowl blend the cream cheese and ½ cup butter. Cut in the flour with a fork. Chill the dough 1 hour. When chilled, divide into 24 1-inch balls. Place each ball in an ungreased 2-inch muffin tin. Press the dough against the bottom and sides of the tins gently with your fingers, until it reaches ¾ of the way up. Set aside.

In a mixing bowl beat together the eggs, sugar, 2 tablespoons butter, vanilla, and salt. Divide ½ the pecans evenly among the pastry-lined cups. Pour the egg mixture, dividing evenly, over the nuts and top with the remaining pecans. Bake in a preheated 325° oven for 30 minutes or until set. Cool and then remove from the pans.

NOTE: The tarts can be made ahead and frozen.

BASIC PIE CRUST

1½ cups flour
½ teaspoon salt
6 tablespoons firm butter, cut
  into small pieces
3 tablespoons shortening
5–6 tablespoons ice water
1 egg yolk, lightly beaten

Place the flour and the salt in a large bowl. Add the butter and shortening and work into the flour with a pastry blender or 2 knives until the butter and shortening are about the size of small peas. Add the water and quickly work together with your fingers into a smooth ball. Wrap in waxed paper and chill for at least 15 minutes before rolling.

On a lightly floured pastry cloth or a board, roll out into a circle about ⅛ inch thick, and about 2 inches larger, all around, than a 9-inch pie pan. Roll up on the rolling pin, center over the pan, and unroll. Fit the pastry loosely into the pan, taking care not to stretch it. Then press it lightly into the bottom of the pan. With a sharp paring knife, cut off the surplus overhanging dough, leaving 1 inch extending all around. Fold the extra pastry under and press together to form a high standing rim, then flute. Chill for 30 minutes.

Place a piece of aluminum foil in the pastry shell to form a lining, then fill with dry beans or rice, making certain the beans are well distributed and pushing them up the sides of the shell. This keeps the shell from puffing up while baking.

Place in a preheated 425° oven for 15–20 minutes or until the bottom is set and the edges are lightly browned. Take from the oven and lift out the foil and the beans. With a pastry brush, coat the shell all over with the beaten egg yolk. Return to the oven for 2 minutes to set the yolk. The yolk seals the crust and prevents it from soaking up any liquid and becoming soggy. Cool the shell before filling.

NOTE: For a 2-crust pie, double the recipe, using ½ for the bottom as explained above, only do not bake the bottom shell. Fill the bottom shell with the filling. Roll out the top crust and fit it over the filling. Fold the top crust under the edge of the lower crust and seal all around by fluting. Prick or cut slits in the top crust in several places. Bake as directed in the filling recipe.

STRAWBERRY CHEESE PIE

SERVES 6

1 9-inch pie shell, baked
4 cups fresh strawberries,
    stemmed and hulled
1⅓ cups granulated sugar
3 tablespoons cornstarch
2 tablespoons fresh lemon juice
8 ounces cream cheese, softened
1 teaspoon grated orange rind
2 tablespoons fresh orange juice
2 tablespoons light cream
Whipped cream (optional)

Prepare pie shell according to directions for Basic Pie Crust (*see Index*). Cool the pie crust. Divide the berries into 2 equal portions, the smaller ones in one and the larger ones in the other. Place the smaller berries in a heavy saucepan. Mash them with a potato masher. Add 1 cup of the sugar, the cornstarch, and lemon juice and cook over low heat, blending well, until thick and translucent. Remove from the heat and cool.

In a separate bowl combine the cream cheese, ⅓ cup sugar, the orange rind, orange juice, and light cream. Cream until light and fluffy. Spread the cream cheese mixture smoothly and evenly into the pie crust. Arrange the large berries over the cream cheese mixture and cover all the berries with the cooled strawberry glaze. Refrigerate for at least 2 hours before serving. If desired, serve with dollops of lightly sweetened whipped cream.

CALIFORNIA BRANDY PIE

SERVES 6

2 cups graham cracker crumbs
3 tablespoons brown sugar
⅓ cup butter, melted
1 cup heavy cream
½ cup confectioners' sugar,
    sifted
¼ cup California brandy (dry
    sherry may be substituted)
4 egg yolks

In a medium-sized mixing bowl combine the graham cracker crumbs, brown sugar, and melted butter and mix thoroughly. Reserve about 2 tablespoons of the mixture for topping. Press firmly the remainder of the crumbs into the bottom and about 1½ inches up the side of a 9-inch springform pan. Chill in the refrigerator while preparing filling.

In a large mixing bowl whip the cream until stiff. Blend in the confectioners' sugar and brandy and mix thoroughly. In a separate medium-sized bowl beat the egg yolks until light-colored and thick, about 2–3 minutes. Fold the egg yolks into the cream mixture. Place the filling mixture into the chilled crust. Top the pie with the reserved crumbs and place in the freezer for 3–4 hours. To serve, remove the edge of the pan and serve frozen.

LEMON SOUR CREAM PIE

SERVES 6

1 9-inch pie shell, baked
1 cup granulated sugar
3 tablespoons cornstarch
Dash salt
1 cup milk
3 eggs, separated
4 tablespoons butter
1½ teaspoons grated lemon rind
¼ cup fresh lemon juice
1 cup sour cream
¼ teaspoon cream of tartar
½ teaspoon vanilla extract
6 tablespoons granulated sugar

Prepare pie shell according to directions for Basic Pie Crust (*see Index*). Cool the pie crust. In a medium-sized saucepan combine the 1 cup sugar, the cornstarch, and salt. Slowly stir in the milk. Cook over medium heat, stirring, until the mixture boils and thickens.

In a small bowl slightly beat the egg yolks. Blend a small amount of the hot mixture into the egg yolks. When blended, turn the yolk mixture into the hot mixture. Cook over medium heat, stirring constantly, for 2 minutes. Add the butter, lemon rind, and lemon juice. Cover and cool. Fold the sour cream into the cooled mixture. Spoon the mixture into the baked pie crust.

In a separate bowl beat the egg whites with the cream of tartar and vanilla until soft peaks form. Gradually add the 6 tablespoons of sugar and continue beating until stiff peaks form. Spread the meringue over the pie, sealing to the edge. Bake in a preheated 350° oven for 12–15 minutes or until golden. Cool and serve.

SOUR CREAM APPLE PIE

SERVES 8

1 9-inch pie shell, unbaked
¾ cup granulated sugar
¾ cup brown sugar, firmly
   packed
1 tablespoon flour
½ teaspoon ground cinnamon
¼ teaspoon ground nutmeg
1 teaspoon fresh lemon juice
⅛ teaspoon salt
½ cup sour cream
4 medium apples (4 cups),
   pared, quartered, cored, and
   sliced
½ cup flour
4 tablespoons sweet butter,
   softened

Prepare pie shell according to directions for Basic Pie Crust (*see Index*).

In a large bowl mix the granulated sugar and ¼ cup brown sugar, 1 tablespoon flour, cinnamon, nutmeg, lemon juice, and salt. Add the sour cream and apples. Spoon this mixture into the prepared pie crust and set aside.

In a mixing bowl mix together the ½ cup flour and ½ cup firmly packed brown sugar. Cut in the butter with a fork until mixture is crumbly. Sprinkle this topping on the pie and bake in a preheated 350° oven for 40 minutes. Chill 3–4 hours before serving.

CHOCOLATE PIE

2 cups chocolate wafer crumbs
5 tablespoons butter, melted
½ teaspoon ground cinnamon
¾ cup butter, at room
    temperature
¾ cup superfine sugar
3 ounces unsweetened chocolate
2 teaspoons curaçao or
    Cointreau
3 eggs
1 cup heavy cream
2 tablespoons confectioners'
    sugar
1 teaspoon curaçao
2 ounces semisweet chocolate,
    at room temperature

In a mixing bowl prepare the pie shell. Thoroughly blend together the wafer crumbs, melted butter, and cinnamon. Press into a 9-inch pie pan. Bake for 10 minutes in a preheated 350° oven. Remove from oven, cool, and chill.

In a medium-sized bowl cream the ¾ cup butter with the superfine sugar until fluffy. Set aside. In a double boiler melt the unsweetened chocolate over simmering water and add the 2 teaspoons curaçao or Cointreau. Set aside to cool. When the chocolate has cooled, stir into the sugar-butter mixture, blending well. Gradually add the eggs, beating after each egg is added. Pour the chocolate mixture into the cooled pie shell. Chill in the refrigerator for at least 2 hours.

Whip the cream in a medium-sized bowl until fairly stiff. Add the confectioners' sugar and 1 teaspoon curaçao and beat in well. Spread on top of the chilled pie. Using a vegetable peeler or sharp knife, cut against the edge of the semisweet squares to make curls. Garnish the pie with the chocolate curls. Refrigerate for 1 hour or until serving time.

STRAWBERRY RHUBARB PIE

Pastry for 1 2-crust 9-inch pie
1¼ cups granulated sugar
3 tablespoons quick-cooking
    tapioca
¼ teaspoon salt
¼ teaspoon ground nutmeg
Dash ground cinnamon
3 cups ½-inch pieces fresh
    rhubarb
1 cup fresh strawberries, sliced
1 teaspoon grated orange rind
    (optional)
1 tablespoon butter

Prepare pie shell according to directions for Basic Pie Crust (*see Index*).

In a large bowl mix together the sugar, tapioca, salt, nutmeg, and cinnamon. Add the rhubarb, strawberries, and orange rind and stir until the mixture coats the spoon. Let the mixture stand for 15 minutes. Line the pie pan with the pastry and spoon in the fruit mixture. Dot the top of the fruit mixture with the butter. Cover the pie with pastry or weave a lattice top. Bake in a preheated 400° oven for 35–45 minutes or until crust is brown. Serve warm with French vanilla ice cream.

PUMPKIN PIE

1 9-inch pie shell
1 egg yolk, beaten
1½ cups milk
2 eggs, slightly beaten
1 cup brown sugar, firmly
   packed
1 teaspoon ground cinnamon
1 teaspoon ground ginger
½ teaspoon ground nutmeg
¼ teaspoon salt
1½ cups cooked or canned
   pumpkin
⅓ cup orange marmalade
Whipped cream (optional)
Confectioners' sugar (optional)

Prepare pie shell according to directions for Basic Pie Crust (*see Index*) but bake for only 5–7 minutes. Brush with the beaten egg yolk. Set aside.

Put all the remaining ingredients, except the whipped cream and powdered sugar, in the top of a double boiler and cook over low heat until fairly thick. Pour into the prepared pie crust. Put into a preheated 400° oven, turn down immediately to 350°, and cook until the custard is set, approximately 50 minutes. Cool to room temperature. Serve with sweetened whipped cream dusted with a little confectioners' sugar if desired.

CRANBERRY PIE

Pastry for 1 2-crust 9-inch pie
4 cups cranberries
1¼ cups brown sugar, firmly
   packed
4 tablespoons Golden Syrup
   (*see Note*)
¼ cup water
Granulated sugar

Prepare pie shell according to directions for Basic Pie Crust (*see Index*).

Wash the cranberries, drain well, and cut in half. In a large mixing bowl combine the cranberries and ¾ cup brown sugar, firmly packed, and mix well. Place the cranberry mixture in an unbaked pie shell. Dribble 2 tablespoons Golden Syrup over the berries. Cover with the top crust and seal the edges by pinching the 2 crusts together. With a sharp knife cut a 2-inch cross in the center of the pastry. Fold each triangle back to form an open square.

In a small saucepan combine the remaining ½ cup brown sugar, firmly packed, the remaining 2 tablespoons Golden Syrup, and the water and boil the mixture for 2–3 minutes. At 15-minute intervals, while the pie is baking, pour a bit of this mixture into the open square in the top of the pastry. Bake the pie in a preheated 425° oven for 12 minutes. Then reduce the heat to 325° and bake for 50 minutes or until the crust is golden brown. Remove from the oven and sprinkle generously with granulated sugar. Cool slightly and serve while still warm.

NOTE: Lyle's Golden Syrup, made in England for Tate & Lyle Ltd., can be purchased at most groceries. Light Karo syrup may be substituted.

MOCHA CHIFFON PIE IN PRALINE PIE SHELL

SERVES 8

1 tablespoon unflavored gelatin
¼ cup cold water
⅓ cup cocoa
¾ cup granulated sugar
½ teaspoon salt
4 eggs, separated
1 cup strong black coffee
Praline Pie Shell (*below*)
Whipped cream (optional)
Chocolate shavings (optional)

Soften the gelatin in cold water. In the top of a double boiler, combine the cocoa, ¼ cup sugar, and the salt. Beat the egg yolks well. Stir the yolks and the coffee into the cocoa mixture. Set the pan over hot water and cook the custard, stirring constantly, until it coats the spoon. Add the softened gelatin to the hot custard. Pour the mixture into a cold bowl to cool, stirring from time to time to prevent a crust from forming. In a separate bowl beat the egg whites with the remaining ½ cup sugar until very stiff and glossy. Fold the meringue into the mocha custard. Pour the filling into the cooled pie shell. Chill the pie until ready to serve. Garnish with lightly sweetened whipped cream and shaved chocolate if desired.

PRALINE PIE SHELL
1 9-inch pie shell
⅓ cup butter
⅓ cup brown sugar, packed
½ cup chopped pecans

To prepare shell, follow directions for Basic Pie Crust (*see Index*) but bake for only 5–7 minutes. Combine the butter and brown sugar in a small saucepan. Cook and stir until the sugar melts and the mixture bubbles vigorously. Remove the mixture from the heat, stir in the pecans, and spread the mixture over the bottom of the lightly baked pie shell. Bake in a preheated 425° oven for 5 minutes or until bubbly. Remove from the oven and cool thoroughly before filling.

MARGARITA PIE

1 9-inch pie shell, baked
1 tablespoon (1 envelope) unflavored gelatin
1 cup granulated sugar
1 teaspoon salt
4 eggs, separated
1 cup lime juice
1 teaspoon grated lime peel
⅓ cup tequila
2 tablespoons Cointreau or Triple Sec
½ cup heavy cream
2 tablespoons confectioners' sugar
8 lime peel twists

Prepare pie shell according to directions for Basic Pie Crust (*see Index*).

Mix the gelatin, ½ cup granulated sugar, and salt in a heavy 2–3-quart saucepan. In a separate bowl beat the egg yolks and lime juice together until foamy. Add this to the gelatin mixture. Cook over low heat, stirring, until gelatin is dissolved (takes 3–5 minutes). Remove from heat. Stir in the lime peel, tequila, and Cointreau. Cool and chill until thickened but not firmly set.

In a large mixing bowl beat the egg whites until stiff. Slowly add the remaining ½ cup sugar, beating constantly, until well blended. Gently fold the egg whites into the gelatin mixture. Turn into the pie crust and chill until set.

In a small bowl whip the cream until fairly stiff. Sweeten with confectioners' sugar. Garnish top of pie with sweetened whipped cream and the lime peel twists.

NOTE: For best results serve within 8 hours of preparing.

ORANGE TART SHELLS WITH STRAWBERRIES SERVES 10

¾ cup lard
2 cups flour, sifted
1 teaspoon salt
1 tablespoon grated orange rind
4 or 5 tablespoons orange juice
2 cups milk
4 egg yolks
¾ cup granulated sugar
1 teaspoon vanilla extract
¼ cup flour
½ cup red currant jelly
2 tablespoons granulated sugar
2 pints fresh strawberries, washed and hulled
Confectioners' sugar

To prepare pastry, in a large mixing bowl cut the lard into the 2 cups flour until the consistency is similar to corn meal. (Rub the mixture with your fingers if necessary.) Add the salt and orange rind and mix well. Stir in the orange juice and mix until the pastry holds together. Work the pastry into a smooth ball. Wrap it in waxed paper and chill for at least 2 hours.

On a lightly floured board roll out the pastry to ⅛ inch thick and cut it into 10 3½-inch circles. Fit the circles over the outside of a muffin tin. Prick the bottom of each tart shell *twice* with a fork. Bake in a preheated 425° oven for 10 minutes, until just brown. Watch carefully, as they burn easily. Cool the shells and then remove them from the muffin tins.

Meanwhile, place the milk in a heavy medium-sized saucepan and bring almost to a boil over moderate heat. Set aside until ready to use.

To make the filling, in a medium-sized mixing bowl combine the egg yolks, ¾ cup sugar, and the vanilla. Beat with an electric beater on medium high speed until the mixture makes ribbons, about 3 or 4 minutes. Beat the ¼ cup flour into the mixture. Slowly add the milk, beating constantly. Pour the custard back into the saucepan and place it over moderate heat. Bring it to a boil, stirring constantly with a wooden spatula. Reduce the heat to low and continue to boil, still stirring for 5–6 minutes or until the cream is very thick. Take off the heat and chill at once.

To make the glaze, in a small saucepan place the currant jelly and the 2 tablespoons sugar. Place over moderately high heat for 2–3 minutes, stirring constantly, until the mixture is thick enough to coat the spoon and the last drops are sticky as they fall from the spoon (225–228° on a candy thermometer). Do not boil beyond this point. Pour the glaze while it is still warm.

Fill each tart shell with about 1 tablespoon of the pastry filling. Place the strawberries on top, dividing evenly among the shells. Pour about 1 tablespoon of the warm glaze over the strawberries. Chill until ready to serve. Just before serving, sprinkle the top of each tart with confectioners' sugar.

NOTE: This dessert may be prepared 6–8 hours before serving. Chill until ready to serve.

ORANGE-GLAZED PECANS

1 pound pecans, shelled and
  halved
½ cup grated orange peel
2 cups brown sugar, lightly
  packed
½ cup milk
1 tablespoon white vinegar

Place the pecans and grated orange peel in a large bowl and mix well. Spread the mixture on a buttered jelly-roll pan or low-sided cookie sheet and set aside. Place the brown sugar and milk in a 2½–3-quart enamel saucepan. Bring the mixture to a boil over medium-high heat. Add the vinegar and boil the syrup until it reaches 230° on a candy thermometer or until the syrup forms a soft ball when tested in ice water. Pour the syrup over the nuts, mixing to coat them evenly, and let cool to room temperature. Separate the nuts.

NOTE: Orange-glazed Pecans can be festively packaged to make holiday hostess gifts.

BUTTERSCOTCH HARD SAUCE ROSETTES

⅓ cup butter, softened
1½ cups light brown sugar,
  sifted
½ teaspoon vanilla extract

In a mixing bowl cream together the butter and sugar and beat until light and fluffy. Blend in the vanilla. Place the mixture into a pastry bag and squeeze out the rosettes onto a cookie sheet. Chill 2–4 hours or until firm.

NOTE: These rosettes are good served atop slices of steamed pudding. They can be frozen.

WALNUT BRITTLE

1 cup finely chopped walnuts
2 cups granulated sugar
½ cup white wine vinegar
½ cup butter

Butter an 11 × 16-inch rimmed cookie sheet or jelly-roll pan. Sprinkle the nuts into the pan, shaking the pan to distribute the nuts evenly. Combine the sugar, vinegar, and butter in a 1½-quart enameled saucepan. Bring to a boil over moderately high heat, stirring occasionally. Continue to boil until the mixture reaches the hard-crack stage, or 300–310° on a candy thermometer. Remove from the heat and pour the hot candy onto the cookie sheet over the walnuts and set aside to cool.

Turn the cookie sheet upside down, flexing the pan if necessary to remove the candy. Break the candy into bite-sized pieces with a mallet on a bread board. Store in an air-tight container.

GINGER PEAR ICE CREAM SAUCE

MAKES 4–5 PINTS

6 pounds ripe firm pears, cored and peeled
4 pounds granulated sugar
¼ pound candied ginger, finely chopped
5 tablespoons fresh lemon juice
2 tablespoons grated lemon rind
Red food coloring (optional)

Cut the cored and peeled pears into 1½-inch pieces and place them into a large enameled kettle. Add the sugar, ginger, lemon juice, and lemon rind to the pears in the kettle and stir to blend the ingredients. Bring the mixture to a boil over medium heat, stirring constantly, and boil gently for about 15 minutes until the syrup is thickened to the consistency of honey. If using food coloring, add a drop at a time until a lovely pink color is reached. Pour the hot sauce at once into hot sterilized pint-sized jars to heat-seal.

NOTE: The filled and sealed jars may be stored 6–12 months in a cool dry place. Ginger Pear Ice Cream Sauce is delicious served over vanilla ice cream. This is a marvelously light dessert for an oriental menu.

BUTTERSCOTCH SAUCE

MAKES 1 PINT

⅔ cup light corn syrup
¼ cup butter
1½ cups brown sugar, lightly packed
4 drops white vinegar
⅓ cup light cream

In a heavy 1½–2-quart enameled saucepan combine the corn syrup, butter, and brown sugar. Bring the mixture to a boil over medium-high heat. Reduce the heat to low and continue cooking and stirring for 5–10 minutes until the mixture reaches 238° on a candy thermometer or until the mixture, tested in ice water, forms a soft ball. Remove the saucepan from the heat and blend in the vinegar. Slowly pour in the cream, stirring rapidly.

NOTE: Serve Butterscotch Sauce hot or cold over ice cream or other desserts. The sauce can be stored in the refrigerator in a covered container for up to 3 weeks.

HOT FUDGE SAUCE

MAKES 1½ PINTS

4 ounces unsweetened chocolate
1½ cups granulated sugar
3 tablespoons butter
1 cup heavy cream
1 teaspoon vanilla extract

Melt the chocolate in a 1½–2-quart saucepan over low heat, stirring constantly, until dissolved. Slowly add the sugar, butter, and cream. Bring the sauce to a boil over medium heat. Reduce the heat to low and continue cooking and stirring for 5–10 minutes until the mixture reaches 238° on a candy thermometer or until the mixture, tested in ice water, forms a soft ball. Remove the pan from the heat and blend in the vanilla.

NOTE: Serve the Hot Fudge Sauce warm over vanilla or coffee ice cream. The sauce will harden when it is poured over the cold ice cream. It may be stored for 2 weeks in a covered jar in the refrigerator. Reheat before serving.

HARD SAUCE

SERVES 6

⅓ cup butter or margarine
1 cup confectioners' sugar, sifted
1 teaspoon vanilla extract
Pinch salt
⅛ teaspoon ground nutmeg

In a mixing bowl beat the butter until pale and creamy. Gradually add the sugar and continue to beat until light and fluffy. Add the vanilla, slowly, and the salt while beating. Spoon the sauce into a serving dish. Sprinkle with nutmeg. Cover and chill at least 1 hour.

NOTE: This sauce is traditionally served with steamed or baked puddings.

COFFEE CALIFORNIA

Brown sugar
1 lemon wedge
Tia Maria
California brandy
Hot black coffee
Heavy cream, stiffly beaten

Pour several tablespoons of brown sugar into a saucer. Moisten the rim of Irish coffee glasses or coffee mugs with the lemon wedge and then dip the rims in the brown sugar to coat them evenly.

Pour 1 teaspoon Tia Maria and 1 tablespoon California brandy into the bottom of each glass or mug. Fill to within ½ inch of the top with hot black coffee. Top each serving with whipped cream, making sure that the cream and coffee do not mix. Serve at once.

IRISH COFFEE

Irish whiskey
Sugar
Hot black coffee
Heavy cream, stiffly beaten

Place 1 jigger of Irish whiskey and 1 teaspoon sugar in each Irish coffee glass. Fill the glass to within ½ inch of the top with hot black coffee. Top each glass with whipped cream, making sure that the cream does not mix with the coffee. Serve at once. The coffee should be sipped through the cream.

ACAPULCO MEXICAN COFFEE

Tequila
Kahlúa
Hot black coffee
Whipped cream
Maraschino cherries, with stems

Pour 1 ounce tequila and ½ ounce kahlúa into 5-ounce fizz or frappé glasses. Fill the glasses with hot coffee and garnish each with a dollop of whipped cream and a maraschino cherry. Serve at once.

CHAPTER IX

NAPA, SONOMA, & SANTA CLARA VALLEYS

WINE

In a sunny California meadow, under the shade of a live oak tree, a picnic is in progress. On a snowy linen cloth are spread the contents of a wicker hamper. There are loaves of San Francisco sourdough bread, sausages, Monterey Jack and teleme cheese, peppers, lettuce, and tomatoes—all grown or made in California—olives from the San Joaquin Valley, artichoke hearts from Castroville, and a salad of marinated beans in a tart French dressing. Nearby is a large platter covered with slices of a cold pâté and beside it a delicately flavored ham mousse. For dessert there are baskets of an almost unbelievably wide choice of California-grown fruit: cherries, early grapes, plums, pears, nectarines, strawberries, and oranges. Alongside this movable feast a selection of wines is being offered—a chilled, crisp Chardonnay and a golden, fruity Chenin Blanc. Shimmering in the bright sunlight are glasses of ruby-colored Zinfandel. These are just three of California's famous wines.

Wine has been made in California for over two hundred years, since the padres introduced viticulture to California. The cultivation of grapes and wine making were a basic part of Spanish culture—included in their daily diet, important to their economic life, and a symbolic part of their religion. When Father Serra arrived in San Diego in 1769, he brought with him some vine cuttings from the missions in Baja California. The San Diego Mission was built in the summer of that year, and the first California vineyard was planted. Wild grapes already grew along the riverbanks and hills near the mission, but the grapes from these vines were unsuitable for making wine.

The padres planted a vine of European origin, the *Vitis vinifera*. Today, all the wines of Europe, South America, Africa, Australia, and California originate from the thousands of varieties of vinifera. The vineyards cultivated by the padres contained only one variety of the European grape, known today as the Mission grape. Although inferior in quality to later varieties the Mission grape is still used today in some sweet dessert wines.

San Diego's climate was similar to that in parts of Spain, and in the virgin soil the vines flourished. Cuttings from these first vines were later planted at Mission San Gabriel and resulted in another exceptionally fruitful vineyard. As the missions spread up the coast, so did the vineyards, although some of the northern missions were not very successful. By 1798, grapes grew beside at least ten missions, and of the ten, at least five were making wine. By 1805, there were nineteen missions with cultivated vineyards.

While winegrowing lagged in the northern parts of California, the vineyards of the southern missions expanded and thrived. When the Jedediah Smith expedition arrived at the San Gabriel Mission in 1826, it was greeted with lavish hospitality and an abundance of food and drink. The quality of wines, brandy, and even whiskey was excellent and it was all produced from the vineyards and plantings that surrounded the mission. In Smith's journal entry he described the usual fare at the mission: "In the morning after the sunrise, or at about that time, you have tea, bread and cheese; at dinner fish and fowl, beans, peas, potatoes and other kinds of sauce, grapes, wine, gin and water plenty." At this time, the San Gabriel Mission was producing annually over four hundred barrels of wine and about two hundred barrels of brandy. The sale of these spirits resulted in a yearly income of nearly $12,000. Most of the wines and brandies that were made at the San Gabriel, San Fernando, and San Juan Capistrano missions were sold to the residents of Los Angeles and to the neighboring rancheros. Although prices fluctuated wildly over the years, they would be considered very low today— between three and six dollars a gallon for brandy. Wine was even less.

Santa Clara and San Jose were among the northern missions that experienced success in vitivulture. Their red wine was considered by some to be as good as any made in Europe. The northernmost mission and the last one established, San Francisco Solano in Sonoma, boasted of between one thousand and three thousand vines just one year after its founding in 1823. The vines thrived in the rich soil of the Sonoma Valley and produced excellent wine. This was the beginning of viticulture in one of California's greatest wine-producing districts, the Sonoma Valley.

The church maintained a virtual monopoly on wine making until 1833, when the Mexican Government ordered the secularization of the vast mission lands. Consequently, most of the vineyards were abandoned and died from lack of care. Although a few missions continued to produce wines and brandies, it was laymen from France, Mexico, Germany, Hungary, and other countries who dominated the field.

About 1824, the first commercial winegrowers came from Europe to establish vineyards. Joseph Chapman

and, later, J. J. Warner came to Los Angeles, bought land, and planted vines. Los Angeles was becoming a principal wine center. These commercial growers learned from the priests' experiences that California's climate and soil were ideal for growing the classic *vinifera* wine grapes from the Old World.

In 1831 a new resident arrived in Los Angeles from the famous Bordeaux wine region of France. His name was Louis Vignes. Picking Los Angeles as the location of his enterprise was not surprising, as already there were 100,000 vines growing in and around the town. He developed a vineyard, El Aliso, on the present site of the Los Angeles Union Railway Station. He imported cuttings of different varieties of European grapes. These cuttings traveled by ship from France to Boston, then around Cape Horn to Los Angeles. Until this time, all wines in California had been pressed from various species of the Mission grape, which although good was not versatile. The new cuttings made possible a greater variety of wines. Vignes brought other improvements to California wine making. He introduced the use of oak casks for wine storage, replacing the old clay flasks and wineskins formerly used by the padres and Indians, and enabling him to store and age his wines in quantity. Soon he was selling wine up and down the coast of California, charging, for example, two dollars a gallon for the best white wine. In 1855 he sold his vineyard to a nephew, Jean Louis Sainsevain, for the then fabulous sum of $42,000. Sainsevain was joined by his brother Pierre in founding a pioneer wine firm that had the distinction, a few years later, of making the first California champagne.

Another early pioneer who turned to

viticulture was General Mariano Vallejo, the last military commandant at Sonoma. An early colonizer with vast land holdings, he appropriated the vineyards of the Sonoma Mission in 1836. With characteristic enthusiasm and vigor, he replanted and nurtured the vines. Within a few years, his vineyards were producing a notable wine in great quantity. Using Indian labor, he followed the crude wine-making methods of the early missionaries. Many years later, in 1861, he was able, despite his unsophisticated approach, to win two first prizes for his white wines and three for his reds in state competition.

In 1838 George C. Yount came to establish a homestead in the vicinity of what is now Napa County, on land granted to him by General Vallejo. He planted vines brought from the Sonoma Mission, and the success of his vineyard proved the suitability of the fertile Napa Valley for grape-growing.

The same year, 1838, William Wolfskill planted a vineyard in Los Angeles. Thirty years later his property had grown to include some sixty thousand bearing vines and two thousand orange and lemon trees. The quality of his wines was said to have compared favorably with some of the best French and madeira wines.

The gold rush impelled the expansion of California's wine industry just as it spurred other phases of the California economy. Wolfskill was quick to see the opportunity, and he became the first vintner to ship wine to San Francisco. Grapes were also shipped and brought in high prices. In 1849 Los Angeles grapes were selling for 12½ cents a pound, on the vine, and thousands of boxes were shipped to San Francisco via San Pedro. At the height of the gold rush in San Francisco, grapes were often exchanged for gold nuggets. It was the high prices for grapes, along with the increasing profits from the wine business, that brought a tremendous boom in vine planting during the 1850s.

One of the largest of the early wine companies was formed in 1854 by a pair of unacclaimed musicians, Charles Kohler and John Frohling. Finding that music paid no better in San Francisco than it did in their native Germany, these two entertainers went into the wine business. What they lacked in musical talent, they more than made up in shrewd business sense. They purchased a vineyard of three thousand vines in Los Angeles and opened the first wine shop in San Francisco. Concentrating on quality, they experimented with new grapes, blends and aging processes. Within a few years, they became the largest wine distributors in California, with agents in China, Japan, Russia, and Peru.

The early successful California winegrowers, like Kohler and Frohling, were usually from those European countries where the culture of the vine was most highly developed. Although the pioneer vintners were for the most part inexperienced, it was obvious from the start that California's soil, climate, and vast quantities of unused land were perfect for wine production. Nearly every landowner caught the wine fever. The lack of knowledge by some of the early vintners often took its toll on the wine produced, but still, by the late 1850s, there were millions of healthy vines planted throughout California.

Wine districts had developed throughout the state, and each district was known by the kinds of wine it produced. Port and other sweet wines came mostly from Los Angeles and the warm interior valleys. The coast range, which included Napa and Sonoma counties, produced white and dry red wines. On the foothills of the Sierra Nevadas, including Sonora and El Dorado counties, the fortified wines were prominent—sherry, madeira, and certain German wines.

Although nearly all winegrowers had imported European vines, no real scientific experiments had been made to determine which vines were best adapted to the various soils and climates of California. A Hungarian vintner, Colonel Ágoston Haraszthy, was the first to recognize that superior California wines could be made with systematic experiments. As a consequence he earned the title of the Father of California Viticulture. Haraszthy came to California in 1850, by way of Wisconsin, settling first in San Diego. He planted vines there, but with little success. He then acquired a ranch south of San Francisco, at Crystal Springs, and planted new vines. Again he failed. Determined, he moved his vines to the Sonoma Valley, where he was sure that conditions would be favorable to viticulture. He was right. His first transplantations, Zinfandel grapes from Europe, produced a thriving vineyard. Encouraged by Haraszthy to cultivate the land nearby, Charles Krug established a winery there. And so did Emil Dressel and Jacob Gundlach, bringing German methods of wine making to the Sonoma Valley.

At his Buena Vista Ranch in Sonoma, Haraszthy built a stone winery into the side of a hill, and in the European custom cut tunnels into the granite slopes for the storing and aging of his wines. He wrote a report on grape-growing and wine making in California for the State Agriculture Society, stressing proper vineyard care and the necessity for absolute cleanliness in the wine-making process. Since Chinese labor at the time was paid less than one-third the wage demanded by other workers, he encouraged the employment of the Chinese to cultivate the vineyards. For fifty years this practice continued, enabling California wine to carry a lower price tag than wines from other parts of the world.

Haraszthy believed that California viticulture could best be improved by a firsthand study of the European vineyards and their wine-making methods and the subsequent importation of carefully selected wines. As a result, he was sent, in 1861, by the governor of California to observe vineyard culture and wine making in Europe. During his travels, he collected cuttings from the best wines in various regions of Europe in the hope of finding the most suitable grapes to grow in each of the state's climate zones. Haraszthy purchased over 100,000 vines from various parts of Europe as well as choice cuttings of almonds, oranges, lemons, figs, and Italian chestnuts. Upon his return to the United States, he submitted a bill to the state government for the cuttings, but the state declined to pay. Haraszthy had the misfortune to belong to the wrong political party at the time. He was never paid and personally absorbed the cost of the vines he had so carefully selected. Wine authorities now feel that failure to distribute the vines throughout the state retarded the growth of California viticulture by many years.

The hundreds of wineries that now produce wine in California have diverse origins. Many, like the Christian Brothers, are in their second century. The priests turned to wine making to support their novitiate and school in the Napa Valley. Today, the profits from their wine making support all their schools in the western part of the United States.

An Irishman named Concannon turned to wine making when the Archbishop of San Francisco suggested it to him. Early in the 1880s, there was a shortage of sacramental wine in the area. Concannon was not only an obedient son of the Church but something of a businessman as well. His enterprise was so successful that now the fourth generation of Concannons is being trained in the ways of wine making.

Leland Stanford was a famous railroad builder, later governor, and the founder of Stanford University. He purchased 350 acres near the Mission San Jose, and with his brother planted vines and started a winery. In 1881 he acquired 9,000 acres of the Vina Grant in Tehama County, which with additional land purchases became the largest vineyard in the world. In 1888 it totaled over 2.6 million vines.

The Inglenook Winery, the oldest name in Napa County winegrowing, achieved fame through the efforts of a Finnish seaman, Captain Gustave Niebaum. He imported choice, carefully selected European grape varieties, which accounted for Inglenook's subsequent fame.

In 1876 Jacob Beringer and his brother Frederick built their renowned cellar for Beringer Brothers Winery at St. Helena. In the Santa Clara Valley, Frenchman Charles Le Franc started the Almadén Winery in 1857. Later his son-in-law and successor, Paul Masson, began producing the famous Masson sparkling wines that we enjoy today. In 1884 Charles Wente, a native of Germany, acquired the winery in the Livermore Valley that still bears his name. The Korbel brothers, immigrants from Austria, established a winery at Guerneville in 1865 that still produces their famous champagne.

The Italian Swiss Colony Winery began as a commune, probably the first in California. During the depression of the 1880s, a number of Swiss from the Italian-speaking cantons of Switzerland fell upon hard times in San Francisco. An enterprising philanthropist named Andrea Sbarboro volunteered to help his less fortunate compatriots by establishing the Swiss Colony at Asti, near the Russian River. The commune was an idea whose day had not yet come, but the wine making aspect of the project showed more promise. Sbarboro reorganized the winery, establishing a private company which subsequently evolved into a successful group effort. This co-operative of growers and marketers was called Allied or United Vintners. Today it is a subsidiary of Heublein, Inc.

Acquiring a modicum of wine expertise is relatively easy in California. Many wineries conduct tours and have tasting rooms, giving free and instructive advice on appropriate wines for all occasions. Touring a winery can be a pleasant way to spend a few hours. Some wineries furnish picnic tables for their patrons, and some also sell bread, cheese, and other regional delicacies such as garlic, olives, sausages, and dried fruit.

California wines stem from two main origins and are labeled accordingly. One origin is generic—wines like Burgundy, Chablis, and Rhine. These wines came into being centuries ago through the names of the Old World viticultural districts famous for that particular type of wine. The wines with generic names are similar to other wines from other vineyards bearing similar labels. The other origin is varietal. These are wines whose labels carry the name of the variety of grape from which the wine was made. When a wine contains at least 50 percent of the juice of a single grape variety, it may be labeled with the name of that grape. In general, the choicest grape varieties are the ones used in producing the varietal wines. These wines usually command a higher price than the generic blends. The skill of the vintner, however, is as important as the grapes used in producing an outstanding wine.

Wine is a big business in California. With the coming of Feather River water to the San Joaquin Valley, many previously fallow acres are becoming vineyards. Near King City, grapes are growing for the first time. The demand for wine grows daily and so does production. California has over 500,000 acres of vineyards that annually produce over 275 million gallons of wine. Approximately 85 per cent of all American wine is made in California.

California wines have come a long way from the early Mission grape wines made by the padres. Through a period of tremendous growth and experimentation, despite occasional setbacks, they have achieved a level of specialization and excellence that has proven their fine quality in comparative testings with imported wines. More and more people are learning the pleasures of the wines of which California vintners have been proud for nearly eight generations.

CHAPTER X

CALIFORNIA

SAUCES &
ACCOMPANIMENTS

The name "California" comes from a sixteenth-century romantic novel, *Las Sergas de Esplandían* (The Exploits of Esplandían), written by García Ordóñez de Montalvo. Following the Crusades of the eleventh century, there appeared a number of popular romances of chivalry, including the stories of King Arthur and the Knights of his Round Table. Although these romances had Christian heroes, they often featured bizarre creatures such as griffins, giants, Amazons, and other mythical beings. The craze for this semi-pagan literature became so great that there was talk in Spain of prohibiting "supernatural fiction." The popularity of these romances soon faded after Cervantes completely ridiculed them in *Don Quixote*.

Montalvo wrote *Las Sergas de Esplandían* around 1500 as a sequel to his translation from Portuguese into Spanish of the novel *Amadís de Gaula* (Amadís of Gaul). The hero of this romance, Esplandían, is a perfect knight and the son of Amadís. In this second-rate sequel to *Amadís*, father and son are leading the defense of Constantinople against a siege by pagan forces when Queen Calafía of California appears among the pagans.

Montalvo describes California, the land ruled by this tall Amazon Queen, as being an island "on the right hand of the Indies" and "very near to the terrestrial paradise." The dark Amazons who inhabited this mythical island lived without any men, and made their weapons of pure gold, as there was no other metal available on the island. The island's rugged terrain was inhabited by a great number of griffins, which the women trapped when they were small and fed with their boy babies and the men they took prisoner. The griffins were trained to seize men from the ground and then to drop them from great heights to their death. Queen Calafía ordered her griffins into the battle at Constantinople, but this was unsuccessful, since the griffins attacked the men of both armies indiscriminately. The story ends happily with Queen Calafía becoming converted to Christianity, marrying a relative of the hero, and returning to California with her new husband.

These romances were known to the explorers of the new world where they were received with varying degrees of enthusiasm. Hernando Cortez asked Spain to prohibit romances of chivalry from the American Colonies, an indication that the stories affected the discipline of his men. However, Cortez was apparently familiar with these adventures, including the tale of Esplandían, for in 1524 he wrote to the King of Spain about a rumored "island of Amazons or women only, abounding in pearls and gold, lying ten days' journey from Colima."

Although it is uncertain, probably either Gonzalo Jiménez in 1533 or Francisco Bolaños in 1541 first applied the name "California" to their discoveries in the New World. Initially, the name may have referred only to the tip of Baja California, now known as Cape San Lucas, or to an island in the Gulf of California. However, in time the name came to mean all the land on the western shore from Cape San Lucas northward to the Strait of Anián, as the Spaniards called the nonexistent northwest passage.

The actual history of California has often resembled a romantic novel. It may be entirely fitting that the name came from chivalric fiction.

CROUTONS I

8 slices fresh or stale white
    bread
⅓ cup butter
1½ tablespoons grated Parmesan
    cheese or 1 tablespoon finely
    minced fresh herbs (optional)

Remove the crusts from the bread and cut the slices into ½-inch cubes. Over moderate heat melt the butter in a large skillet, being careful not to let the butter burn. Place the bread cubes into the foaming butter and stir quickly to moisten each cube with the melted butter. Remove the bread cubes from the skillet and scatter them evenly onto a cookie sheet, so that no two croutons are touching. Bake the croutons in a preheated 250° oven 30–40 minutes or until dry, crisp, and golden. Remove the cookie sheet from the oven and let the croutons cool until only slightly warm. If desired, toss croutons in a plastic bag with the cheese or fresh herbs. Use the croutons to garnish soups and salads. Store in an airtight container and use as needed.

CROUTONS II

6 slices stale French bread
¾ cup olive oil
1 clove garlic, split

Cut the bread into ½-inch cubes and soak the cubes in the oil. Thoroughly rub a cookie sheet with the garlic. Place the croutons on the sheet in a preheated 350° oven and toast them until brown, 10–15 minutes, turning occasionally to avoid burning. Allow them to cool before using. Store in an airtight container.

SEASONED BREAD CRUMBS I

1 cup fine dry bread crumbs
½ teaspoon salt
¼ teaspoon pepper
¼ teaspoon paprika
⅛ teaspoon ground ginger or
    nutmeg (optional)

Combine all the ingredients in a small bowl. Store in an airtight container.

SEASONED BREAD CRUMBS II

1 cup fine dry bread crumbs
2 tablespoons grated
   Parmesan cheese
¼ teaspoon dried savory
¼ teaspoon dried basil
¼ teaspoon dried tarragon

Combine all the ingredients in a small bowl. Store in an airtight container.

MAYONNAISE I

1 egg
2 tablespoons fresh lemon juice
¾ teaspoon salt
¼ teaspoon dry mustard
   (optional)
1 cup vegetable oil

Place the egg and the lemon juice into a blender jar. Turn the blender on low speed and slowly add the salt, dry mustard, and ¼ cup of the oil. While still on low speed, add the remaining oil, a few drops at a time, keeping the consistency of the mayonnaise firm and not allowing it to separate. Occasionally turn off the blender and scrape the sides of the blender jar with a rubber spatula to push the mayonnaise down. Pour the mayonnaise into a covered jar and store it in the refrigerator up to 2 weeks.

MAYONNAISE II

½ cup olive oil
½ cup vegetable oil
1 egg
3 tablespoons fresh lemon juice
¾ teaspoon salt
3 dashes cayenne pepper
½ teaspoon dry mustard
   (optional)

Combine the olive and vegetable oils in a small mixing bowl and set aside. Place the egg and lemon juice in a blender jar. Turn the blender on low speed and slowly add the salt, pepper, mustard, and ¼ cup of the oil. While still on low speed, add the remaining oil, a few drops at a time, keeping the consistency of the mayonnaise firm and not allowing it to separate. Occasionally turn off the blender and scrape the sides of the blender jar with a rubber spatula to push the mayonnaise down. Pour the mayonnaise into a covered jar and store it in the refrigerator up to 2 weeks.

NOTE: This recipe makes a more piquant mayonnaise than Mayonnaise I.

BLENDER HOLLANDAISE SAUCE

MAKES 1 CUP

½ cup butter
3 egg yolks, lightly beaten
2 teaspoons fresh lemon juice
¼ teaspoon salt
Pinch cayenne pepper

In a heavy 1½–2-quart saucepan melt the butter until it begins to bubble. Place the egg yolks, lemon juice, salt, and cayenne in a blender jar. Cover the jar and turn the blender on and immediately off. Turn the blender on high, remove the cover, and pour in the hot butter in a slow, steady stream. Turn off the blender. Pour the sauce into a small bowl and keep it warm over a shallow pan of warm water until ready to use.

BLENDER BÉARNAISE SAUCE

MAKES ¾ CUP

2 tablespoons dry white wine
1 tablespoon tarragon vinegar
2 teaspoons minced shallot
1 teaspoon dried tarragon or
   2 teaspoons minced fresh
   tarragon
¼ teaspoon white pepper
¾ cup Blender Hollandaise
   Sauce (*above*)

In a heavy 1½–2-quart saucepan combine the white wine, vinegar, shallot, tarragon, and white pepper. Bring the mixture to a boil over high heat and reduce it until only about 1 tablespoon liquid remains. Add the 1 tablespoon liquid to prepared hollandaise sauce and transfer the mixture to a blender jar. Cover the jar and blend the sauce at high speed for 4 seconds. Pour the sauce into a small bowl and keep it warm over a shallow pan of warm water until ready to use.

WESTERN BARBECUE SAUCE

MAKES 1½ QUARTS

½ pound butter
1 pint catsup
1 pint red wine vinegar
1 tablespoon Tabasco sauce
5 ounces Worcestershire sauce
1 tablespoon brown sugar,
   packed
1 tablespoon onion juice
2 cloves garlic, crushed
1½ tablespoons salt
Dash cayenne pepper
Dash black pepper

Combine all the ingredients in a 3-quart saucepan. Place the saucepan over moderate heat and bring the mixture to a boil, stirring constantly until the butter is melted and all the ingredients are well blended. Brush the sauce generously on poultry, pork, or beef while barbecueing.

NOTE: Store the sauce unrefrigerated up to 2 weeks in a cool dry place.

POULTRY OR LAMB BASTING SAUCE

MAKES 1½ PINTS

⅓ cup wine vinegar
¾ cup vermouth
1 cup chicken broth
1 teaspoon dried rosemary
1 teaspoon dried oregano
1 teaspoon dried dill weed
1 clove garlic, crushed
2 tablespoons grated onion
2 tablespoons tomato paste
2 tablespoons brown sugar or
    honey
1 teaspoon salt
½ teaspoon paprika
½ teaspoon soy sauce
2 teaspoons Worcestershire
    sauce
½ cup oil
Dash Tabasco sauce

Combine the ingredients in the order listed in a 1½–2-quart saucepan. Heat the sauce over moderate heat for about 5 minutes, stirring to blend the ingredients. Brush the warm sauce on chicken or lamb every 30 minutes during the cooking time.

NOTE: The sauce may be stored for 1 week in a covered container in the refrigerator.

CHILI CURRY MARINADE

MAKES 1½ CUPS

½ cup red wine
¼ cup fresh lemon juice
4 tablespoons olive oil
1 onion, chopped
1 clove garlic, crushed
2 teaspoons kosher salt
½ teaspoon pepper
1 teaspoon chili powder
1 teaspoon curry powder
1 teaspoon monosodium
    glutamate

Combine the ingredients in the order listed in a small mixing bowl. Pour the marinade over red meats or sliced tomatoes. Let stand for at least 3 hours, turning occasionally.

NOTE: This marinade is also excellent for lamb shish kebab.

MEXICAN SALSA

MAKES 3 CUPS

8–10 fresh poblano chiles or 7
    ounces whole green chiles
3 large tomatoes, peeled and
    seeded
4 large scallions, including tops
2 tablespoons olive oil

Place the chiles on a baking sheet under the broiler, giving a quarter turn every few minutes until all sides are lightly browned and blistered. Remove the chiles from the oven, wrap in a wet dish towel, and let stand for 20 minutes. Peel the chiles under running water, removing all skin,

1 tablespoon red wine vinegar
1 teaspoon salt
¼ cup chopped coriander leaves (cilantro) (use more or less depending upon your taste)

seeds, and veins. The peeling and roasting is not necessary if canned chiles are used, but be sure to remove the seeds. Finely chop the chiles, tomatoes, and scallions and combine in a medium-sized mixing bowl. Add the olive oil, vinegar, and salt and stir to blend the ingredients. Add the chopped coriander leaves at serving time.

NOTE: This sauce is used as an accompaniment to any Mexican dish. It is a perfect dip for crisp tortilla chips.

BARBECUE SAUCE OR MARINADE FOR MEAT OR POULTRY
MAKES 1½ CUPS

¼ cup catsup
2 tablespoons oil
2 tablespoons white vinegar
2 tablespoons soy sauce
⅛ teaspoon dried thyme
⅛ teaspoon dried marjoram
1 clove garlic, crushed
1½ teaspoons Worcestershire sauce
1 tablespoon fresh lemon juice
¼ cup dry red wine
1 tablespoon prepared steak sauce

Combine the ingredients in the order listed in a medium-sized mixing bowl. For use as a marinade, marinate meats of 1-to-2-inch thickness 1½–2½ hours at room temperature, turning once. For use as a barbecue sauce, brush meats or poultry frequently with this sauce during the cooking time. This sauce may be stored 1 week in a covered jar in the refrigerator.

NOTE: For use with pork add 1 tablespoon brown sugar, 1 tablespoon Dijon mustard, and ⅛ teaspoon sage.

SESAME APPLE RINGS
MAKES 6 APPLE RINGS

3 large red cooking apples
¼ cup butter, melted
¼ cup fine dry bread crumbs
1 tablespoon sugar
2 tablespoons sesame seeds

Core the apples but do not peel them. Cut 2 ½-inch slices from the center of each apple (reserve the rest of the apples for another recipe). Brush the apple slices on both sides with melted butter and coat them with the bread crumbs. Arrange the slices in a greased shallow baking dish and sprinkle evenly with the sugar and sesame seeds. Bake uncovered in a preheated 400° oven for 20 minutes or until golden brown.

NOTE: These make a nice garnish for pork or ham.

CHILI SAUCE

12 large ripe tomatoes, peeled
2 large onions
4 green bell peppers, seeded
2 tablespoons salt
½ cup sugar
1 teaspoon ground cinnamon
1 teaspoon ground cloves
2½ cups cider vinegar

Finely chop the tomatoes, onions, and bell peppers. Place the chopped ingredients in a heavy 3-quart saucepan and add the remaining ingredients. Place the saucepan over low heat and cook the mixture slowly for 45–60 minutes or until thick, stirring frequently. Pour the hot chili sauce at once into hot sterilized pint-sized jars to heat-seal. A layer of waxed paper may be placed over the sauce in the jars to help prevent darkening of the sauce as it stands. Serve the chili sauce with cream cheese and crackers or use it to accompany beef and lamb.

NOTE: For hotter sauce add 2 hot red peppers, seeded and chopped. The sauce may be stored 6–12 months in a cool dry place.

APRICOT SWEET AND SOUR SAUCE

12 cups (6 pounds) apricots,
 pitted and chopped
2 cups yellow raisins
4 cups brown sugar, lightly
 packed
2 teaspoons ground cinnamon
1 teaspoon ground cloves
1 teaspoon ground allspice
4 teaspoons salt
1 teaspoon cayenne pepper
2 large onions, coarsely chopped
8 cloves garlic
5 10-ounce jars preserved
 Japanese ginger
3 cups cider vinegar

Combine the apricots, raisins, sugar, cinnamon, cloves, allspice, salt, and cayenne in a large enamel kettle. Place the onions, garlic, ginger, and vinegar in a blender jar and purée at low speed for 1–2 minutes or until smooth. Add the puréed ingredients to the mixture in the kettle and simmer over low heat, stirring occasionally, 30–40 minutes, until thickened to a catsup consistency. Pour the hot sauce at once into hot sterilized pint-sized jars to heat-seal. The filled and sealed jars may be stored 6–12 months in a cool dry place. This recipe may be halved.

NOTE: Use the Apricot Sweet and Sour Sauce to accompany Chinese food, pork, and lamb or as a basting sauce for barbecued chicken.

TOMATO RELISH

2 pounds firm ripe tomatoes,
    seeded
1 green bell pepper, seeded
1 cucumber
¼ cup vegetable oil
⅓ cup wine vinegar
½ teaspoon Tabasco sauce
3 tablespoons grated onion
1 teaspoon salt
1 teaspoon finely chopped fresh
    mint
½ teaspoon dried basil
½ teaspoon sugar
½ teaspoon dry mustard

Coarsely chop the tomatoes, bell pepper, and cucumber. Place the chopped vegetables in a large mixing bowl and set aside. In a small mixing bowl combine the remaining ingredients. Pour the dressing over the vegetables and toss gently. Cover the relish and chill at least 1 hour before serving.

APPLE BUTTER

5 pounds Newtown pippin
    apples, peeled and cored
7½ cups water
2 cups apple cider vinegar
1 teaspoon ground cloves
1 teaspoon ground allspice
1½ teaspoons ground cinnamon
¼ teaspoon ground nutmeg

Cut the apples into 1½-inch pieces. Combine the apples and water in a large enamel kettle. Bring the mixture to a boil over medium heat and cook for 20 minutes. Pour the apple and water mixture into a blender jar in 3 or 4 batches. Purée at low speed for 1–2 minutes or until fairly smooth. Return each batch of the puréed ingredients to the kettle and set aside. Pour the vinegar into a 1½–2-quart saucepan and bring to a boil over high heat. Boil 3–5 minutes or until reduced to 1 cup liquid. Add the reduced vinegar, cloves, allspice, cinnamon, and nutmeg to the purée in the kettle. Place the kettle over medium heat and boil gently for 30 minutes or until the mixture is thickened. Pour the mixture into a 9 × 13-inch Pyrex baking dish and bake uncovered for 6 hours at 250° or until very thick and dark. Spoon the hot apple butter at once into hot sterilized pint-sized jars to heat-seal.

NOTE: The apple butter may be stored 6 months in a cool dry place.

SWEET PICKLED CHERRY TOMATOES

4 pounds cherry tomatoes
4 pounds sugar
4 cups water
1 lemon, thinly sliced
2 teaspoons grated lemon rind
1 ginger root, peeled and grated
⅛ teaspoon salt

Wash and dry the cherry tomatoes and prick each with a sharp fork. Set the tomatoes aside. Combine the sugar and water in a large enamel kettle. Place the kettle over moderate heat and cook until the mixture forms a clear syrup, about 5–10 minutes, stirring constantly. Add the tomatoes and simmer them in the syrup 10 minutes. Remove the tomatoes and set aside. To the syrup add the lemon slices, lemon rind, ginger root, and salt and continue cooking over moderate heat 15 minutes. Return the tomatoes to the syrup and cook slowly for an additional 30 minutes, stirring frequently. Pour the pickled cherry tomatoes at once into hot sterilized jars to heat-seal. Serve as a garnish for roast turkey, ham, or as part of a cold buffet.

NOTE: Store 3–6 months in a cool dry place.

RED PEPPER JELLY

2½ pounds red bell peppers
2 cups apple cider vinegar
2 teaspoons salt
2½ teaspoons chili powder
9½ cups sugar
⅔ cup fresh lemon juice
9 ounces liquid pectin

Cut the peppers into 1-inch pieces, discarding the membranes and seeds. Place the peppers in a blender jar and whirl at medium speed 1–2 minutes or until puréed. Combine the puréed peppers, vinegar, salt, and chili powder in a large enamel kettle. Bring the mixture to a boil over medium heat and boil gently for 10 minutes. Remove the kettle from heat and add the sugar and lemon juice. Stir the pectin into the mixture in the kettle and return the kettle to medium-high heat. Boil the ingredients for exactly 1 minute. Reduce the heat to low, skim, and pour at once into 7 hot sterilized pint-sized jars to heat-seal. The jelly may be stored 12 months in a cool dry place.

NOTE: Red Pepper Jelly is delicious served as an hors d'oeuvre atop cream cheese and crackers or as a meat accompaniment.

GREEN PEPPER JELLY

2 green bell peppers, seeded
½ cup green chiles, seeded
1 cup white vinegar
½ cup fresh lemon juice
4½ cups sugar
9 ounces liquid pectin
4 drops green food coloring

Cut the bell peppers into about 1-inch pieces. In a blender jar place the cut bell peppers, green chiles, vinegar, and lemon juice. Purée the ingredients at medium speed 3–5 minutes or until well blended. In a 3-quart saucepan combine the puréed ingredients with the sugar. Bring the mixture to a boil over medium heat and boil for 5 minutes. Remove the saucepan from heat and add the liquid pectin and food coloring. Return the saucepan to medium heat and bring the mixture to a boil. Boil for 2 minutes and pour at once into hot sterilized pint-sized jars to heat-seal. The jelly may be stored up to 12 months in a cool dry place.

NOTE: Green Pepper Jelly is delicious as an hors d'oeuvre served atop a mild cheese and crackers.

RHUBARB JAM

5 pounds rhubarb, unpeeled
5 pounds sugar
Red food coloring
¼ pound almonds, sliced and blanched
3 tablespoons fresh lemon juice
1 tablespoon grated lemon rind

Remove and discard the ends of the rhubarb stalks. Cut the rhubarb into 1-inch slices. Place the rhubarb in a large enamel kettle and cover with the sugar. Let the rhubarb and sugar stand 4 hours. Bring the mixture to a boil over medium heat and boil for 30 minutes. Reduce the heat to low and simmer for 30 minutes. Add the red food coloring, a drop at a time, until a lovely red color is reached. Remove the kettle from heat and add the almonds, lemon juice, and lemon rind. Pour the hot jam at once into 10 hot sterilized half-pint jars to heat-seal.

NOTE: The jam may be stored for 1 year in a cool dry place.

NECTARINE CHUTNEY

2½ pounds nectarines
1½ cups brown sugar, lightly
    packed
1 cup cider vinegar
¼ cup diced preserved ginger
1 tablespoon salt
3 tablespoons minced onion
1 teaspoon dry mustard
⅛ teaspoon ground cinnamon
⅛ teaspoon ground cloves
½ cup blanched and slivered
    almonds

Peel, slice, and remove the pits from the nectarines. Place in a heavy 4–5-quart enameled saucepan. Add the brown sugar, vinegar, ginger, salt, onion, mustard, cinnamon, and cloves to the nectarines in the saucepan. Stir to blend the ingredients. Cover the saucepan and cook the mixture over low heat for 30 minutes. Uncover the saucepan, increase heat to medium, and continue cooking for 30 minutes or until the mixture is thickened, stirring frequently. Add the almonds and cook for 2 minutes longer. Pour the hot chutney at once into hot sterilized pint-sized jars to heat-seal.

NOTE: Store the chutney in a cool dry place for at least 3 months before using.

PEACH CHUTNEY

4 pounds peaches, very ripe
⅔ cup preserved ginger
1 onion, coarsely chopped
2 cloves garlic, minced
1 quart cider vinegar
½ pound white raisins
1 teaspoon red chili powder
2 tablespoons mustard seed
1 tablespoon salt
1½ pounds brown sugar
    (3⅜ cups, packed)

Peel, slice, and remove the pits from the peaches. Place in a heavy 5–6-quart enameled saucepan and set aside. Place the ginger, onion, garlic, and vinegar in a blender jar and purée for about 30 seconds or until smooth. Add the puréed ingredients, raisins, chili powder, mustard seed, salt, and brown sugar to the peaches in the saucepan. Stir to blend the ingredients. Bring the mixture to a boil over moderate heat. Reduce the heat to low and simmer the ingredients for 1 hour, stirring frequently. Pour the hot chutney at once into hot sterilized pint-sized jars to heat-seal.

NOTE: Store the chutney in a cool dry place for at least 6 months before using.

CHAPTER XI

CALIFORNIA

MENUS &
HINTS

ROSE BOWL BRUNCH   FOR 12

  Orange Gin Fizzes
*Tahoe Brunch
*Monterey Sour Cream Coffeecake
*Mild Cheese Breakfast Bread
  Fresh Fuit Platter
    Pineapple Wedges, Orange and Grapefruit
    Sections, Avocado Slices, and Papaya Slices
    Garnished with Fresh Mint Leaves
  Hot Coffee

HOLLYWOOD BOWL PICNIC   FOR 6

*Caviar Mold
        or
*Spinach-wrapped Chicken with Oriental Dip

*Chilled Fillet of Beef with Sour Cream Dressing
*Fresh Marinated Vegetable Salad
*Pumpernickel Toast

*Pears Noirs
*Irish Coffee

Serve California Gamay or California Burgundy with the entree —the fillet of beef, salad, and toast.

WINE COUNTRY PICNIC   FOR 16

*Marinated Artichoke Hearts
*Cold Tomato Soup
*California Pâté Maison
*Cold Ham Mousse
*Mediterranean Loaf
  Crudités
*Casserole Rye Bread
  Fresh Fruit Basket
  Assorted California Cheeses
    Teleme, Monterey Jack, and Brie
*Tangy Lemon Bars
*Pecan Balls

Serve Zinfandel, Gamay Beaujolais, California Chablis, Pinot Charbonnay, and Sauvignon Blanc. They are all served at the same time, as are the various dishes, making a wine-tasting picnic.

Dishes marked with an asterisk (*) are included in this volume.

ITALIAN DINNER   FOR 8

Antipasto
  *Marinated Brussels Sprouts, *Basque Pickled
  Beans, Salami, *Pickled Shrimp, *Baclazana,
  *Greek Artichokes, and Italian Ripe Olives

*Osso Buco
*Risotto alla Milanese
  Chicory and Endive Salad with *Vinaigrette
  Dressing

*Bisque Tortoni
  Expresso

Serve Barbera with the antipasto; Malvasia Bianca with the osso buco and risotto.

CHINESE DINNER   FOR 10

*Crab Won Ton
*Chinese Skewered Shrimp
*Chinese Cucumber Soup
*Chicken with Cashews
*Oriental Beef with Vegetables
*Steamed Rice Chinatown Style

*Rich Vanilla Ice Cream with *Ginger Pear Ice
  Cream Sauce
*Chinese Almond Cookies
  Hot Tea

Serve Chenin Blanc, Emerald Riesling, or Grenache Rosé throughout the meal. Any one is a fine accompaniment to a Chinese dinner.

SAN FRANCISCO FISH DINNER   FOR 8

Cold Cracked Crab with *Mayonnaise II
        or
*Oysters Kirkpatrick
*Sourdough French Bread

*Celery Victor
*Fillet of Sole Nob Hill with *Besciamella
*Broccoli in Wine

*Fresh Lime Ice with Cointreau
*Almond Macaroons

Serve Pinot Chardonnay with the first course—the crab or oysters and the bread. Serve Fumé Blanc or Sauvignon Blanc with the entree—the sole and broccoli.

BARBECUE DINNER   FOR 12

*Crudités with Spinach Dip
*Shrimp in Foil
*Jellied Mushroom Soup

*Barbecued Butterfly Leg of Lamb
*Rice Pilaf
*Fresh Corn, Tomato, Zucchini Pot

*Strawberry Cheese Pie

Serve Grey Riesling with the first course—crudités, shrimp, and mushroom soup. Serve Gamay Beaujolais with the entree—the lamb, pilaf, and vegetables.

WINTER BLACK TIE DINNER   FOR 8

*Brie Wafers
*California Consommé

*Crown Roast of Pork with Cranberry Stuffing
  and Mustard Sauce
*Spinach-stuffed Onions
  Endive Salad with *Lemon Dijon Dressing

*Hot Chocolate Soufflé with Vanilla Sauce
  French Roast Coffee

Natural champagne may be served throughout the dinner, including dessert, or only with the first course of wafers and consommé. Cabernet Sauvignon may be served with the pork roast and onions, and California brandy with the coffee.

CINCO DE MAYO FIESTA   FOR 24

*Guacamole
*Mexican Salsa
  Tortilla Chips
*California Quesadillas

*Enchiladas Rancheras
*Enchilada de Pollo Verde
*Refried Beans
  Tossed Mixed Green Salad with *Mexican
    White Dressing
*Corn Tortillas

*Flan
  Fresh Fruit Basket

Serve margaritas with the hors d'œuvres—guacamole, Mexican Salsa, tortilla chips, and quesadillas. Grignolino Rosé or beer may be served with the entree.

SIERRA SKI SUPPER   FOR 8

*Chicken Liver Pâté
  Assorted Cheese and Crackers

*Venison with Chile Verde
  Herb Brown Rice
  Tossed Green Salad with *Parsley Salad Dressing
*Tarragon Potato Bread

*Lemon Grove Cake

Pinot St. George (Red Pinot)
can be served throughout the
entire meal.

CLEANING HINTS

1.   Clean decorative crystal in less time with a solution of ½ rubbing alcohol and ½ water. No rinsing is necessary and the crystal will stay cleaner longer.

2.   To easily clean wine or coffee stains from carpeting, pour soda water directly on the spill and blot with a paper towel.

3.   To remove a wine spill from a tablecloth, immediately rub ordinary table salt directly into the spot. Let the salt stand a few minutes to absorb the wine; brush off the salt.

COOKING HINTS

1.   To prevent eggs from cracking during hard cooking, poke a tiny hole in the large end of each egg with a pin. Start the eggs in cold water. The hole will allow the normal expansion of the eggshell during cooking time without cracking.

2.   To degrease meat juices, pour the juices into a heavy glass jar. The grease will rise to the top of the jar. You may then remove the juices in the bottom of the jar with a baster.

3.   To degrease a large quantity of liquid, such as soup, first spoon as much grease as possible from the top. Open a paper towel and float it across the surface of the liquid to absorb any remaining grease you could not pick up with the spoon.

4.   For improved baking of a custard or soufflé, place the larger pan containing the water in the oven while preheating.

5.   To easily remove a garlic clove from a liquid mixture, insert a wood toothpick into the garlic bud before placing it into the sauce or stew.

6.   To successfully freeze leftover egg yolks, place them in a small freezer container and stir in 1/16 teaspoon salt for each egg yolk. Egg whites may be frozen as is in freezer containers for later use.

7.   Wash and mince fresh parsley easily by soaking it in cold water 5–10 minutes. Drain the parsley and place it in a blender jar until only $\frac{1}{2}$ full. Cover the parsley with water until the jar is $\frac{3}{4}$ full. Turn the blender on high speed 5–6 seconds to mince. Drain the washed and minced parsley and let dry on paper towels.

8.   To freshen celery, cut a washed unpeeled potato into several pieces. Place the potato and celery into a container; cover with water and refrigerate a few hours for crisp celery.

9.   Restore hard, dry lemons by soaking them in lukewarm water overnight.

10.   To extract lemon juice more easily, warm the lemons in a bowl of hot tap water before beginning to squeeze them.

11.   To easily grate Parmesan and other hard cheeses, cut the cheese into about 1-inch cubes and place them in a blender jar. Turn the blender on high speed for 30 seconds or until all the cheese is grated. Grate in small amounts.

12.   Always place the avocado pit in guacamole or cold avocado soup to prevent discoloration. Remove the pit at serving time.

13.   To discourage weevils in flour and other such dry staples, place a bay leaf in the contents of the box or canister. The bay leaf will not impart its own flavor to the staples.

14.   To keep brown sugar light and moist, place $\frac{1}{2}$ a slice of bread in the brown sugar box.

15.   To desalt sauces or soups, add pieces of raw potato to the mixture and cook for 5–10 minutes. The excess salt will be absorbed by the potato. Remove the potato pieces.

16.   Stocks and fresh lemon juice may be conveniently frozen in ice cube trays. Store the frozen cubes in plastic bags in the freezer to be used as needed.

INDEX

salad dressing, 105

See also names of fruit

Fudge

frosting, 302

frozen peppermint Alaska, 350

sauce, 350

hot, 380

Gazpacho, 45

white, 42

German-style oxtail soup, 49

Ginger (gingered)

cream, chicken breasts in, 196

pear ice cream sauce, 379

soy glaze, 17

stewed figs, 338

Glaze (glazed)

currant brandy, 308

ginger soy, 17

ham with brandy, 269

-orange pecans, 378

sour cream orange, 300

white onions, 76

Gnocchi

à la romaine, 135

spinach, 134

Golden Gate halibut, 178–79

Golden Hind crumpets, 298

Gougère, 288

Grand Marnier

apricot sauce, 359

coupe with fresh fruit, 346

Grandmother's chicken and flat dumplings, 211

Grapefruit minted cups, 337

Grapes, Mexican-style chicken with, 201

Gravy, almond, duckling with, 220

Greek-style artichokes, 15

Green bean(s)

bacon and onion, 67

soup, cold, 39

Green chile corn bread, 287

Green goddess salad, 84

Green peppers

jelly, 401

salad, 88

Grits soufflé, 120

Guacamole, 9

Halibut

fillet of, en croute with lemon dill sauce, 180–81

Golden Gate, 178–79

Ham

and asparagus casserole, 270

brandy-glazed, 269

and cheese chowder, 44

and cheese sandwich, 124

cold mousse, 269

sherry sauce, chicken in, 198

split pea soup with, 45

Hangtown fry, 116

Hard sauce, 380

butterscotch rosettes, 378

Herbs (herbed)

French-style salad dressing, 102

rice, 128

toast, 30–31

and walnut quick yeast bread, 287

Hollandaise sauce

blender, 395

cucumber, 186

Hollywood Bowl picnic, 404

Honeydew and Roquefort cheese, 12–13

Hors d'oeuvres, *see* Appetizers

Horseradish, breast of pheasant with cream and, 225

Hot fudge sauce, 380

Huevos

mexicanos con tortillas, 115

rancheros, 115

See also Egg(s)

Ice

blueberry, 343

lime, with Cointreau, 342

strawberry, 341

Ice cream

chocolate, 342

sauce, ginger pear, 379

vanilla, 343

Icing, *see* Frosting

Indian-style

barbecued veal, 251

pudding, 354

Indienne chicken, broiled, 207

Indonesian chicken, 206

Irish coffee, 381

Italian dinner, 405

Italian-style

béchamel sauce, 143

chicken with artichokes, 202

soup

sausage, 50–51

vegetable chowder, 51

tomato sauce, 142

Jalapeño mold, California-style, 8

Jam, rhubarb, 401

Japanese-style salad dressing, 104

Jelly

green pepper, 401

red pepper, 400

Joe's special—San Francisco-style, 250

Josephinas, 36

Kuchen, plum, 368–69

Sausage
  in red wine, 271
  soup, Italian-style, 50–51
Savory sauce, new potatoes in, 80
Scallop(s)
  amandine, 158–59
  and mushroom salad, 94
  terrace, 28
Scampi, 156
Seafood
  filling for molded egg ring, 99
  Louie salad dressing, 105
  salad, 95
    Thousand Island mold with, 98
  See also names of seafood
Senegalese soup, 41
Sesame seed
  apple rings, 397
  cheese puffs, 24
Seventeenth-century haunch of venison, 229
Sherbet, avocado, 341
Sherry
  cream sauce, apple cake with, 307
  ham sauce, chicken in, 198
Shish kebab, lamb, 261
Shrimp
  butter, 13
  fillet of sole stuffed with, 169
  in foil, 155
  au gratin Tiburon, 154–55
  mousse, 29
  Parisienne, 29
  pickled, 9
  with red snapper, 177
  rice salad with, 95
  Russian Hill, 153
  sauce, mousseline of fillet of sole and crab with, 170–71
  scampi, 156
  skewered, Chinese-style, 154
Sierra ski supper, 407
Soubise sauce, abalone with cucumber and, 166
Soufflé
  Camembert, 120
  chestnut, cold, 347
  chocolate, with vanilla velvet sauce, 361
  corn, 74–75
  crab, 119
  frozen
    lemon-lime, 348–49
    mocha, 348
  grits, 120
  hot apple, with apricot sauce, 362–63
  hot chocolate, with vanilla velvet sauce, 361
  hot lemon, 362
  Mexicana, 122
  mushroom, 121
  noodle, 121
  orange, cold, 346–47

orange liqueur in orange shells, 360
  salmon, 118–19
  tomato, 73
  zucchini, 74
Soup, 37–58
  albondigas, 54
  avocado, chilled, 37
  beef broth (or stock), 46
  chablis fish stew, 56–57
  cheese, 43
    and ham chowder, 44
  chicken broth, 37
  cioppino, 55
  consommé, California-style, 40
  crab
    bisque, 41
    Vichyssoise, 44
  cucumber
    Chinese-style, 43
    cold, 38
  eggplant supper, 48
  fish chowder, 57
  Fisherman's Wharf bouillabaisse, 58
  French-style onion, 52–53
  gazpacho, 45
    white, 42
  green bean, cold, 39
  green pea, cold, 39
  ham and cheese chowder, 44
  Italian-style
    sausage, 50–51
    vegetable chowder, 51
  lamb bone with dried bean, 53
  lemon, 42
  minestrone, 47
  mushroom, 48–49
    jellied, 40
  oxtail, German-style, 49
  Senegalese, 41
  spinach, cream of, 54–55
  split pea
    cold, 39
    with ham, 45
  tomato
    cold, 38
    fresh, with dill, 46–47
  winter vegetable beef, 50
  zucchini, cold, 40
Sour cream
  apple pie, 372
  dressing, chilled fillet of beef with, 238–239
  enchiladas, 137
  lemon pie, 372
  Monterey coffeecake, 304–5
  mushroom pie, 125
  orange glaze, 300
  sauce, 163
    dill, 187
  turkey enchiladas with, 224